REINVENTING CHRISTIANITY

Reinventing Christianity
Nineteenth-century contexts

Edited by
LINDA WOODHEAD

LONDON AND NEW YORK

First published 2001 by Ashgate Publishing

Reissued 2019 by Routledge
2 Park Square, Milton Park, Abingdon, Oxon, OX14 4RN
52 Vanderbilt Avenue, New York, NY 10017

Routledge is an imprint of the Taylor & Francis Group, an informa business

Copyright © Linda Woodhead 2001

All rights reserved. No part of this book may be reprinted or reproduced or utilised in any form or by any electronic, mechanical, or other means, now known or hereafter invented, including photocopying and recording, or in any information storage or retrieval system, without permission in writing from the publishers.

Notice:
Product or corporate names may be trademarks or registered trademarks, and are used only for identification and explanation without intent to infringe.

Publisher's Note
The publisher has gone to great lengths to ensure the quality of this reprint but points out that some imperfections in the original copies may be apparent.

Disclaimer
The publisher has made every effort to trace copyright holders and welcomes correspondence from those they have been unable to contact.

A Library of Congress record exists under LC control number:

ISBN 13: 978-1-138-71214-0 (hbk)
ISBN 13: 978-1-138-71212-6 (pbk)
ISBN 13: 978-1-315-19941-2 (ebk)

Contents

List of Figures   vii
List of Contributors   ix

Introduction   1
Linda Woodhead

PART ONE: VARIETIES

I Transcendent Christianity

1. Evangelical Certainties: Charles Spurgeon and the Sermon as Crisis Literature   27
   Andrew Tate
2. Fortress Catholicism: The Art of Ultramontanism at Notre Dame de Fourvière   37
   Nancy Davenport
3. Anglican Controversies: Debating Private Confession   67
   Anne Hartman

II Liberal Christianity and Alternative Spiritualities

4. The World's Parliament of Religions and the Rise of Alternative Spirituality   81
   Linda Woodhead
5. The Swedenborgian Church in England   97
   Ian Sellers
6. Transcendentalists and Catholic Converts in Emerson's America   105
   Shannon Cate

PART TWO: NEGOTIATIONS

III Christianity and Literature

7. Rewriting Genesis: The Nineteenth-Century Roots of D.H. Lawrence's Religion   119
   Terence R. Wright
8. Wordsworth and the Sacralization of Place   127
   Deeanne Westbrook

9. Reactionary and Romantic: Joseph de Maistre and Shelley 139
   Arthur Bradley
10. The Religion of Thomas Carlyle 149
    Trevor Hogan

IV Christianity and Gender

11. The Feminization of Piety in Nineteenth-Century Art 165
    Jane Kristof
12. Women's Theology and the British Periodical Press 191
    Julie Melnyk
13. The Feminist Theology of Florence Nightingale 199
    Hilary Fraser and Victoria Burrows
14. Elizabeth Gaskell, Gender and the Apocalypse 211
    Robert M. Kachur

V Christianity and Science

15. Science and Secularization 229
    John Hedley Brooke
16. Contextualising the 'War' between Science and Religion 239
    Gowan Dawson
17. Philip Gosse and the Varieties of Natural Theology 251
    Jonathan Smith

Conclusion 263
Linda Woodhead

References *269*
Index *287*

List of Figures

2.1	*Serpent eating the Apple of Discord*, Choir Mosaic in the nave, S.M. Perrin, 1886–96, N.D. de Fourvière, Lyon.	38
2.2	*Seven-headed Beast*, Pencil drawing for Chancel Mosaic in the nave, S.M. Perrin, 1886–96, N.D. de Fourvière, Lyon.	39
2.3	*NATURALISM, Vigne et les vers*, Chancel Mosaic in the nave, S.M. Perrin, 1886–96, N.D. de Fourvière, Lyon.	40
2.4	*The Cardinal Sins*, mosaic, program encircling altar in chancel of crypt, 1887–1914, N.D. de Fourvière, Lyon.	41
2.5	*Avant-projet de N.D. de Fourvière*, engraving, Séon, 1856–7.	42
2.6	Cross-section of Fourvière apse with decorative program indicated. E. Hardouin, Fugier, *Miniguide de Fourvière*, p. 57.	46
2.7	*Facade of N.D. de Fourvière*, Lyon, 1872–1964.	48
2.8	*SUPERBIA*, mosaic in front of altar in chancel of crypt, 1887–1914, N.D. de Fourvière, Lyon.	50
2.9	*Das Bild des Ineren eines Menschen der der Sunde dienet und den Teufel in sich herrschen lässt*. J.E. Gossner, Herzbüchlein, Reading, Pa. 1822.	52
2.10	*Gula*, Bavarian woodcut, 15th Century P.A. Lemoisne, *Les Xylographies du XIVe et du XVe siecles au Cabinet des Estampes de la Bibliothèque Nationale*, Paris, 1930, Vol. II, plate 102.	53
2.11	*Ant-lion and ant*, MS. Gg 6.5, 15th Century, University Library, Cambridge.	54
2.12	*Eagle* mosaic in center of ceiling, 12th Century, Salon of Roger, Royal Palace at Palermo, Sicily.	56
2.13	*Stone Medallion*, 14th Century facade of Cathedral of St. Jean, Lyon.	57
2.14	*GEHENNA*, mosaic behind altar in chancel of crypt, N.D. de Fourvière, Lyon.	58
11.1	Francisco Goya, *Capricho 52*, Art Resources.	167
11.2	Hippolyte Bellange, *The Peddler of Plaster Figurines* (Louvre), 1835 Art Resources.	168
11.3	Jean-Francois Millet, *The Angelus* (Musee d'Orsay), 1855–1857 Art Resources.	169
11.4	Alphonse Legros, *The Ex Voto* (Musee des Beaux-Arts, Dijon), 1860 Art Resources.	170
11.5	Wilhelm Leibl, *Three Women in Church* (Kunsthalle, Hamburg), 1878–82 Art Resources.	171
11.6	Istvan Csok, *Do this in Memory of Me* (Magyar Nemzeti Galeria, Budapest), 1890.	172
11.7	Bela Ivanyi Grunwald, *Praying* (Magyar Nemzeti Galeria, Budapest), 1891.	173

11.8	John Everett Millais, *My First Sermon* (Guildhall Gallery), 1862–3 Art Resources.	174
11.9	Adolf Holzel, *Silent Prayer* (Neue Pinakothek, Munich), c. 1885 credit to Bayerische Staatsgemaldesammlungen, Munchen.	175
11.10	Thomas J. Barker, *The Secret of England's Greatness*, 1861, by courtesy of the National Portrait Gallery, London.	176
11.11	Paul Gaugin, *Vision After the Sermon* (National Gallery of Scotland), 1988.	177
11.12	Paul Gaugin, *The Yellow Christ*, 1889, oil on canvas, $36^{1/4}$ x $28^{7/8}$, Albright-Knox Art Gallery, Buffalo, New York, General Purchase Funds, 1946.	178
11.13	V.G. Perov, *Easter Procession* (Tretyakov Gallery, Moscow), 1861.	180
11.14	M.V. Nesterov, *Taking the Veil* (Russian Museum, St. Petersburg), 1898.	181
11.15	Isisdore Pils, *The Prayer in the Hospice* (Musee de l'Assistance Publique, Paris), 1853.	182
11.16	Charles Collins, *Convent Thoughts* (Ashmolean Museum, Oxford), 1851.	183
11.17	Peter Fendi, *The Visit to the Nun* (Collection of the Prince of Liechtenstein, Vuduz Castle), 1834.	184
11.18	Peter Fendi, *Childish Devotion* (Historical Museum of the State of Vienna), 1842.	186
11.19	Charles Cope, *Life Well Spent* (Christopher Wood Gallery, London), 1862.	187
11.20	Winslow Homer, *Sunday Morning in Virginia* (Cincinnati Art Museum, John J. Emery Fund), 1877.	188
13.1	The "Jug" of the Nightingale, *Punch*, 27, 1854, p. 125.	206
13.2	"Immortal Bird", *Punch*, 27, 1854, p. 194.	207
13.3	The Disorderly Housewife, Marshall, 1992, p. 106.	209
17.1	Philip Henry Gosse, Plate V from *The Aquarium*, 2nd edition (London: Van Voorst, 1856). Courtesy of University of Michigan Libraries.	256
17.2	Philip Henry Gosse, Plate II from *A Year at the Shore* (London: Isbister, 1873).	260
17.3	Philip Henry Gosse, *British Sea-Anemones and Corals: Original Sketches and Drawings*, item 69+. Courtesy of the Horniman Museum, London.	261

List of Contributors

Arthur Bradley is Lecturer in English at Chester College of Higher Education. His doctoral research was on Shelley. Recent publications include essays on Romanticism and anti-revolutionary French Catholicism, and the Irish context of Romantic orientalism. He is currently co-editing a collection of essays on *Romantic Biography* and writing a book on deconstruction, negative theology, and atheism.

John Hedley Brooke is Andreas Idreos Professor of Science and Religion at the University of Oxford. Recent publications include *Science and Religion: Some Historical Perspectives; Thinking About Matter*; and, with Geoffrey Cantor, *Reconstructing Nature: The Engagement of Science and Religion*. The latter was based on the 1995 Gifford Lectures.

Victoria Burrows is a postgraduate in the English Department at the University of Western Australia. Her doctoral research is on the interwoven themes of mother/daughter relationships, ambivalence, subjectivity and race.

Shannon Cate is an adjunct Professor of American Literature at The George Washington University, specialising in race in U.S. literature.

Nancy Davenport is Professor at the University of the Arts, Philadelphia. Her most recent work is on the legend of St Antony in visual representation. Published articles include 'Fra Angelico, Matthias Grünewald, and the Revival of Catholic Art in 19th century France'; 'The Cult of St Philomena in 19th century France: Art and Ideology'; and 'Paul Borel, un peintre religieux à Lyon au xixe siècle'.

Gowan Dawson holds a Leverhulme Postdoctoral Research Fellowship on the 'Science in the Nineteenth-Century Periodical' project in the Department of English Literature at the University of Sheffield and the History and Philosophy of Science Division at the University of Leeds. His doctoral research was on 'Walter Pater, Aestheticism, and Victorian Science'.

Hilary Fraser is Professor of English at The University of Western Australia. Publications include *The Victorians and Renaissance Italy* (1992) and *English Prose of the Nineteenth Century* (with Daniel Brown, 1997). She is currently working on Victorian women art historians and a project on women, gender, and the nineteenth-century British periodical press.

Anne Hartman is completing doctoral research on discourses of confession in the late Romantic and Victorian period at Birkbeck College, University of London. She has co-edited a scholarly edition of Dinah Craik, and is working on a bibliography of nineteenth-century women poets for *Annotated Bibliography for English Studies*.

Trevor Hogan is Senior Lecturer in the School of Social Sciences, La Trobe University in Melbourne, Australia. He is a co-ordinating editor of the social and political theory journal, *Thesis Eleven*. Recent publications include: 'Citizenship, Australian and Global'; 'Dead Indians, Flawed Consumers and Snowballs in Hell: On Zygmunt Bauman's New Poor'; 'Sismondi and Carlyle: Reading European Modernity from the Margins'; 'Trafficking in Memory: Newcastle and Fremantle as Post-industrial Ports with Post-modern Urban Imaginaries'. He is currently preparing a book on *Europe and Revolution: Thomas Carlyle and the Origins of Modernity*.

Robert M. Kachur is Assistant Professor of English at Western Maryland College in Westminster, Maryland. Publications include 'Envisioning Equality, Asserting Authority: Women's Devotional Writings on the Apocalypse, 1845–1900' and 'Repositioning the Female Christian Speaker: Christina Rossetti as Biblical Reader in *The Face of the Deep*'. He is currently writing a book entitled *Getting the Last Word: British Women and the Apocalyptic Voice, 1845–1900*.

Jane Kristof is Professor of Art History at Portland State University, Portland, Oregon. Recent publications include, 'Blacksmiths, Weavers, and Artists: Images of Labour in the Nineteenth Century' and 'Rouault and the Catholic Revival in France' in *Through a Glass Darkly: Essays in the Religious Imagination* (ed. John Hawley). She is currently researching Biblical imagery in nineteenth-century art.

Julie Melnyk is Associate Professor of English at Central Methodist College in Fayette, Missouri. Her research focuses on women's religious literature in nineteenth-century Britain, including poetry, fiction, women's hymns, and religious periodicals. She has recently edited a collection of original scholarly articles, *Women's Theology in Nineteenth-Century Britain: Transfiguring the Faith of Their Fathers* and co-edited one entitled *Felicia Hemans: Reimagining Poetry in the Nineteenth Century*. She is completing a book entitled *Christianity, Community, and Subjectivity in Victorian Women's Religious Literature*.

Ian Sellers was Lecturer in History at Manchester University. The chapter written for this book appears by kind permission of his widow.

Jonathan Smith is Associate Professor of English at the University of Michigan-Dearborn. His research focuses on Victorian literature on science. Publications include *Fact and Feeling: Baconian Science and the Nineteenth Century Literary Imagination* (Wisconsin 1994) as well as articles in *Victorian Studies, Nineteenth Century Literature, Victorian Literature and Culture*. He is currently working on a study of Darwin and Victorian literary and visual culture entitled *Seeing Things: Image, Text, and Victorian Culture in the Darwinian Debates*.

Andrew Tate is Lecturer in English at Lancaster University. His doctoral research was on Ruskin and his circle. He has contributed to *Ruskin's Artists: Studies in the Victorian Visual Economy* and to Lancaster University's Leverhulme supported electronic edition of Ruskin's *Modern Painters*.

Deeanne Westbrook is Professor of English at Portland State University. Publications include 'Paradise and Paradox'; 'The Souls of Animals: Evolution of the Combative Ideal'; 'Coleridge and the Crisis of Interrupted Discourse: The Tower of Babel, the *House of Fame*, and the *Biographia Literaria*'; 'Wordsworth's Prodigal Son: "Michael" as Parable and as Metaparable', *Ground Rules: Baseball and Myth*, and *Wordsworth's Biblical Ghosts*.

Linda Woodhead is Senior Lecturer in Christian Studies at Lancaster University. Recent publications include *Diana: The Making of a Media Saint* (edited with Jeffrey Richards and Scott Wilson), and *Religion in Modern Times: An Interpretive Anthology* (with Paul Heelas). She is currently writing an *Introduction to Christianity* for Cambridge University Press.

Terence R. Wright is Professor of English Literature at the University of Newcastle where he co-directs an M.A. in Religion and Literature. He has published books on *John Henry Newman* (ed.) and *The Religion of Humanity*. His most recent publication is *D.H. Lawrence's Bible* (Cambridge University Press).

Introduction

Linda Woodhead

'All Christendom has been decomposed, broken in pieces, and resolved into new combinations and affinities.' (Harrison Grey Otis, 1836)

'All around us I feel the New Reformation preparing, struggling into utterance and being!' (Mrs Humphrey Ward, 1889)

The powerful influence of the secularisation thesis in the academic study of religion and modernity has left its mark on the study of Christianity in the nineteenth century. The question 'An age of faith or an age of doubt?' has become familiar to generations of undergraduates studying the Victorian era, and the debate about the impact of science has assumed a central place in scholarly and popular literature. Whilst this volume does not ignore these important topics, its emphasis falls not so much on questions about the *quantity* of religion in the nineteenth century as on questions of *kind*. It aims to introduce the most important varieties of Christianity in the Victorian era, and to consider their interactions with other aspects of western culture and society.

These twin aims shape the structure of the book. Part One explores the main varieties of Christianity under the headings 'transcendent' and 'liberal' and discusses alternative forms of spirituality like Transcendentalism and Theosophy in their relations to Christianity. The picture which emerges is of a spectrum of different and often antagonistic interpretations of Christianity ranging from the conservative at one end, through the liberal, to alternative spiritualities at the other extreme. Part Two is concerned with the interactions between Christianity and literature, Christianity and gender, and Christianity and science. Together the two parts of the book build up a picture of diversity and change which displaces the more common image of a monolithic 'traditional' Christianity set on a collision course with an equally monolithic scientific and secular 'modern' culture. Instead, Christianity emerges as a tradition in the process of radical reinterpretation.

Contributions to the book come from a number of disciplines: from history, sociology, theology, philosophy, visual arts, literary criticism, cultural studies, gender studies, and religious studies. Its general perspective is cultural insofar as it is primarily concerned with Christian discourses, values and representations and their interactions with other cultural developments of the nineteenth century. Yet culture is interpreted broadly. Different chapters analyse the traces of religion as they appear not only in academic discourse but in art, architecture, fiction, autobiography, poetry, sermons, journals, diaries, and the popular press. The cultural perspective is also broad in its refusal to ignore wider political, social and economic contexts. Christianity is treated throughout not merely as a system of thought, but as an integral component of nineteenth-century society.

The volume is concerned with the reinvention of Christianity in Britain and North America. No attempt is made to cover Christianity in the rest of the world, nor to consider the increasingly vigorous and well-organised missionary activities of the period. In order to at least signal the importance of these wider dimensions of nineteenth-century Christianity, however, chapters have been included which touch on aspects of both colonialism and continental Catholicism. They offer no more than a reminder that this era witnessed not only the reinvention and reconfiguration of western Christianity, but its expansion to become a global religion.

Transcendent Christianity

The book opens with discussion of the invention – or reassertion – of 'transcendent' Christianity. Such Christianity is distinguished from liberal and alternative forms of spirituality by the central emphasis it places on divine transcendence. To think of God as transcendent is to think of Him apart from the world. This is not to deny His status as creator, but to insist on a clear ontological separation of creator from creation. Transcendent Christianity views the created order – human creatures included – as utterly *different* from the God who made them. Whilst He is an eternal and self-subsistent being, they are 'nothing' – purely contingent, and created *ex nihilo*. Human beings are thought to have no natural connection with God, either at the level of being or of knowledge. Indeed, for every quality which can be predicated of God (omniscience, omnipotence, goodness etc.) the opposite must be predicated of human beings (fallibility, weakness, ignorance, and sinfulness).

As the first section of this volume shows, an emphasis on the difference and transcendence of God was given new prominence in the nineteenth century within both Evangelical Protestantism and conservative Catholicism. *Andrew Tate's* chapter on the famous Baptist preacher Charles Spurgeon (1834–92) reveals just how important an emphasis on sinfulness and the torments of hell had become in Victorian Evangelicalism. Unregenerate human life was characterised in terms of captivity, darkness, and dis-ease. The only prospect for those who did not turn to Christ and repent was to suffer the eternal torments of hell. Evangelical preachers like Spurgeon were well known for their terrifying evocation of the terrors which lay in store for those who did not turn to Christ. As he put it in a sermon entitled 'Turn or Burn' delivered at the Music Hall, Royal Surrey Gardens in 1856, for example:

> O sirs! Ye may think that the fire of hell is indeed a fiction, and that the flames of the nethermost pit are but popish dreams; but if you are believers in the Bible ye must believe that it cannot be so. Did not our Maker say, "Where the worm dieth not, and the fire is not quenched". You say it is metaphorical fire. But what meant he by this "He is able to cast both body and soul into hell?"… unless you be renewed all that can be dreadful in the torments of the future world must inevitably be yours. Dear hearer, apply it to thyself, not to thy fellow-men, but to thine own conscience, and may God Almighty make use of it to bring thee to repentence.

Tate shows that Spurgeon's emergence in the 1850s as a significant Evangelical voice coincided with a crisis of authority in the Church of England: after a decade of major controversies this established episcopal church could offer neither the certainties of transcendent Catholicism nor those of a Protestantism based on a Biblical authority now subject to critical scrutiny. In place of these crumbling authorities Evangelicals like Spurgeon offered the authority of the preached word and the inner conviction of the sinner saved from the jaws of hell by an indubitable experience of grace.

It was not only nineteenth-century Evangelicals who placed fresh emphasis on human sinfulness and wretchedness, however. In his classic study of *Catholicism from Luther to Voltaire* (1978) Jean Delumeau noted that 'hyperculpabalization' was a feature of early modern Catholicism in France. The term refers to an increasing stress placed on the reality and severity of sin. In Delumeau's view clergy were the carriers of this new emphasis, though it was absorbed from revivalist monastic pieties. Its target audience was the laity, over whom the church wished to exercise stronger control – particularly in relation to the intimate and private spheres of life.

Nancy Davenport's chapter on the nineteenth-century Catholic basilica of Notre Dame de Fourvière in Lyon indicates that such hyperculpabalization was carried through into the nineteenth century by ultramontane forms of Catholicism (ultramontanism opposed the alliance of Catholicism with national and liberal interests, and looked 'beyond the mountains' – the Alps – to Rome, the Pope, and the Curia for authority). A towering monument to such religiosity, the basilica at Lyon which was conceived in 1846 and begun in 1872, reveals much about the mentality of this dominant form of transcendent Catholicism at that time. As Davenport's discussion of the mosaics inside the basilica reveals, sin and heresy were major preoccupations. In pride of place immediately before the main altar is a large mosaic depicting a writhing snake. Behind it and in the chancel is a second mosaic, depicting the apocalyptic seven-headed beast from the book of Revelation. These two creatures, the Alpha and the Omega, 'represent mankind born into Sin and condemned into eternity'. Directly below them, encircling the altar in the crypt, are ten more mosaics, depicting hell, death, sin, and the seven deadly sins.

Despite the immense emphasis on sin and damnation on the part of both ultramontane Catholicism and Evangelical Protestantism, however, neither was intended simply to engender fear and despair. On the contrary, their insistence on God's transcendence and on human wretchedness served to intensify the need and longing for salvation. Those who contemplated the mosaics at Notre Dame de Fourvière would be left in no doubt about their need for salvation and their inability to escape from their wretched state by their own efforts. Likewise, as Tate shows so well, the Evangelical preacher would paint a similar picture not with stone and tiles but with words: a picture of human corruption and of the hellish torments awaiting the soul that did not repent. The effect was to build up a tension that could be relieved only by laying hold of God's grace. Whilst the Catholic sinner could lay hold of this grace through the church and its offer of sacramental grace, the Evangelical must turn to the Word, written and preached, and to the saving power of Jesus Christ transmitted by this Word. For the Catholic, in other words, the remedy for sin was necessarily communal and sacramental. For the Protestant, by contrast, salvation lay in a powerful personal experience of conversion. In both cases, salvation was made manifest in good works and a life which befitted repentance, but neither Protestant nor Catholic viewed these works as any more than a manifestation of the prior supernatural grace which had snatched them from the jaws of hell.

For transcendent Christianity in the nineteenth century then, the drama of salvation was just that. More than a matter life and death, it imbued the everyday transactions of mundane existence with supernatural significance. Seemingly it was a drama in which the individual 'actor' was denied any real sense of agency. All human beings were born into a state of sin from which they were powerless to escape. Nothing they could do could free them. Salvation came not through active struggle but through passive receptivity to God's grace. For those set free, however, agency was restored – at least in the sense that they became obedient and effective agents of God's will. Not surprisingly, the belief that one acted as a deputy of God could be immensely empowering, just as gratitude to God for rescuing one from the appalling fate of eternal damnation led many men and women to dedicate their whole lives to His service. Here, perhaps, lies one explanation for the immense energy of transcendent forms of Christianity in the nineteenth century – an energy which led so many women and men to dedicate themselves to the new and revived forms of monasticism and mission activity which developed over the course of the century.

There is no doubt then that what we might call the internal logic of transcendent forms of Christianity is a key part of the explanation of their potency. Their energy also derived from the pressing need to resist increasingly dangerous threats to their continued existence and desired hegemony, as well as to the pure deposit of Christianity of which they believed themselves the true guardians. In part the threats came from the modern world. The enemies against which fortress Catholicism and Bible-based Protestantism had to defend themselves were legion. *The Syllabus of Errors* promulgated by Pope Pius IX in 1864, for example, condemned no less than sixty-one errors of the modern world. Some were social and political developments, the majority of them related to the rise of modern liberal states. Such states constituted an enormous threat to Catholicism not only in the obvious sense that the papal states were now in danger, but in the broader and more far-reaching sense that democratic states could not and would not promote Catholicism as a state religion. Where previously the Catholic church had been able to make strategic alliances with various rulers throughout Europe, it now found itself competing for souls in an increasingly open market. Instead of undermining Catholicism, however, these changes stimulated it to establish more effective centralised control, to impose uniformity in belief and practice, and to increase its grip over the faithful through the encouragement of new forms of piety, morality and devotion.

Transcendent forms of Christianity in the nineteenth century were also revitalised by an increased awareness of the existence of different forms of religion. Both transcendent Catholicism and Protestantism were universal faiths in the sense that each believed that it alone possessed the truth and constituted the only path to salvation. Their ultimate goal was therefore sovereignty and the elimination of what was 'different'. Into the latter category fell not only the different religions encountered in the mission field, but different Christian denominations. Nor were the hostilities confined to Protestants and Catholics, for divisions ran within churches and denominations as well as between them.

In his book on *The Reshaping of American Religion* (1988) Robert Wuthnow, following Will Herberg (1955), argues that the religious universe of twentieth-century America prior to the Second World War was divided between Protestants, Catholics, and Jews. In the post-war period, however, these differences gave way to a more fundamental division between religious liberals and conservatives – what Wuthnow calls the 'great fracture' in American religion and society. Whilst it is undoubtedly true that this fracture widened in the late twentieth century, this volume suggests it was already beginning to open in the nineteenth. Thus Protestant Evangelicals, for example, were often implacably opposed to their more liberal brethren, whilst Catholics of a conservative or ultramontane hue were fiercely opposed to liberal tendencies in their own church ('Modernism'). (The 'errors' condemned in the *Syllabus* included Pantheism, Naturalism, Absolute Rationalism, Moderate Rationalism, Modern Liberalism.) What is more, it seems that the liberal and conservative wings of Christianity had already started to become mutually constitutive in the nineteenth century as they began to position and construct themselves over against one another.

In the Roman Catholic church the conflict between liberal and transcendent tendencies was contained, however, by the ruthless suppression of liberalism by an increasingly powerful Pope and magisterium. In the face of such huge changes as the rise of the modern secular state, much nineteenth-century Catholicism developed a fortress mentality, drawing and defending its boundaries against the encroachments of the modern world with a new sense of purpose. As *Anne Hartman* shows, it was therefore the more broadly constituted churches like the Church of England that were more likely to experience internal tensions and divisions. The controversy she examines is that engendered by the introduction of private confession by Anglican clergy of a more Catholic ('Anglo-Catholic') persuasion. Hartman's paper is particularly effective in drawing attention to the 'over-determined' nature of such a controversy – the way in which it quickly accrued meanings and significance that extended beyond its original cause. In this way a relatively small change like the introduction of a voluntary practice of confession could quickly become a mobilizing symbol for all sorts of other divisions, disputes, and boundary skirmishes. In a revealing phrase, for example, Lord Salisbury claimed that 'confession diminished a nation's virility'. His fear seems to have been that the introduction of a Catholic practice would undermine the role of the Church of England in the legitimation of English social and domestic order. The sexual threat derived from the ambiguous sexuality of the celibate priest, as well as from his ability to probe the intimate life of female penitents, thereby subverting the proper authority of fathers and husbands over their womenfolk.

One further feature of transcendent Christianity which Hartman's chapter highlights is its concern to assert its authority in the sphere of private life. Michel Foucault has highlighted the way in which confession not only helped to engender a discourse of the self and privacy; it also enabled the church to extend its control in these spheres. Both developments seem related to the rise of the modern state: as the latter extended its control and pushed the church out of areas of public life like health, education and welfare, the private and domestic realms became the territories in which religion could maintain (or establish) sovereignty. Evangelical Christianity exploited this opportunity through its emphasis on the heart and personal experience as the loci of true religion, as well as by its regulation of a domestic ideal characterised by hierarchical gender relations. Fortress Catholicism similarly exalted the ideal of domesticity, particularly through its encouragement of Marian piety and the ideals of womanhood it supported. Equally, Catholicism consolidated its hold over believers' intimate lives through a tightly regulated process of moral formation and control in which both the confessional and the fear of sin and hell played important roles. Such 'privatization' also involved the 'feminization' of religion – as women, whose sphere of operation was the private and domestic realms, became its most important subjects.

Liberal Christianity and Alternative Spiritualities

Whilst the reassertion of transcendent Christianity was undoubtedly successful in gaining and retaining many believers, it also had the effect of alienating others. Judging by comments made by those who turned their backs on such religion, it was exactly those aspects of religion most emphasised by transcendent Christianity that they found most difficult. Many autobiographies, for example, speak of repulsion at the idea of a God who punishes his creatures for eternity simply for failing to worship him. It is also common to read of a disillusionment with the idea of a God set apart from humanity and the world, as well as with an understanding of human beings as miserable sinners. As a consequence a significant number of nineteenth-century Christians appear to have rejected transcendent forms of Christianity whilst retaining Christian allegiance. As the English Unitarian James Martineau commented in 1840, 'there is a simultaneous increase, in the very same class of minds, of theological doubt and of devotional affection; there is far less *belief*, yet far more *faith*, than there was twenty years ago (quoted by Carpenter, 1905, p. 185, Martineau's italics). In any case, atheism appears to have been extremely rare in the nineteenth century, particularly in the Anglo-Saxon world and particularly amongst the middle classes (Budd, 1977; McLeod, 1981); even Victorian 'agnosticism' presents itself as quasi-religious (Lightman, 1987).

The majority of Victorians who remained or became Christian whilst rejecting transcendent forms of Christianity can be classified as 'liberals'. Confirming a point made earlier – that liberal and transcendent varieties of Christianity were to some extent formed by reaction against one another – the volume suggests that many of the features which define the former are the opposite of those which define the latter. Instead of viewing God as different and wholly other, liberalism affirms continuity and similarity between God and humanity. Christian liberals generally interpreted the doctrine of the incarnation to mean both that there was something of the human in God, and something of the divine in human beings. They were therefore far more optimistic than their transcendent brethren, and their belief in the perfectibility of individuals and society often led to a strongly activist, ethical, and in some cases political stress in liberal Christianity (exemplified by the American Social Gospel movement of the late nineteenth century). Indeed, a stress on the greater importance of deeds (particularly service of one's fellow humans) than doctrines and dogmas became a defining mark of the Christian liberalism which blossomed towards the end of the century.

Whilst the designation 'liberal' was often applied by conservative Christians to those they opposed, many liberals were happy to accept it and the connotations it carried – 'a certain generosity or charitableness toward divergent opinions and a desire for intellectual "liberty"' (Ahlstrom, 1972, p. 779). In this broad sense liberals belonged to a long tradition within Christianity which began at least as early as the late seventeenth and early eighteenth centuries with the advent of Deism and was carried through succeeding generations by reform movements like Unitarianism, Universalism and Transcendentalism. All who belonged to this trajectory saw themselves as Christian *reformers*, and championed the liberty they advocated over the perceived tyrannies and superstitions of 'traditional' Christianity.

Nineteenth-century liberals appear to have felt a renewed sense of reforming purpose. Like Mrs Humphrey Ward, quoted at the start of this Introduction, they believed themselves part of a 'New Reformation'. Ward felt that Christianity must undergo a reformation more profound than any which had preceded, a reformation which would leave the faith not merely purified, but transformed. As she suggested in her influential novel *Robert Elsemere* (1888), it was not so much the corruptions of faith as the unprecedented newness of the modern world that made momentous religious change necessary. Ward, as Owen Chadwick (Vol. II, 1970) observes, 'had a sense of two Christianities struggling for the allegiance of man; the Christianity of the past, with its Calvinism and austerity and relics of past ignorance, and the Christianity of the future, with its freedom and love of creation and consecration of the intellect' (p. 141).

Liberalism's acute sense of the need for a reformation of Christianity was occasioned in part by the many new challenges the nineteenth century brought the churches. At the intellectual level (and liberalism was in many ways an intellectual movement which aimed not to found new churches but to change the mentality of old ones), one of the greatest of these challenges was the rise of a new historical consciousness. The application of historical method to all aspects of Christianity – including Bible and tradition – raised serious difficulties for those who wished to treat these as the unquestionable foundations of belief. The problem was only exacerbated by science, as first geology and then Darwinism cast doubt on the authenticity of the creation narratives in Genesis. Just as important was the application of 'higher criticism' to the Bible, and the ensuing quest for the historical Jesus. As Chadwick (1975) argues, there was no one decisive point at which traditional belief was undermined, but rather a general attrition of old-established certainties. As he puts it:

> In reading the literature of the nineteenth century we keep meeting the difficulties of adjustment, not to recognition that the Bible was fallible as history, but to recognition that picture language was picture language ... now [people] were forced to realise that the pictures were indeed pictures, and to remind themselves of the vast distance between the picture and the reality it shadowed forth. They felt, perhaps, as though they had less clear ideas of what God was like than they thought before. And this was disturbing. (pp. 187–8)

These were not the only challenges Christians had to cope with, however. Even more important were the massive social, economic and political upheavals which characterised the nineteenth century, and which included the rise of urban-industrial society, the nation-state and democracy. These changes occurred at different rates and in different ways across Europe and American, but their impact on Christianity was inescapable. In some parts of Europe, for example, industrialism had the effect of undermining Christianity, as established and monopolistic churches which catered to a largely rural population failed to extend their appeal to the new urban working classes (Chadwick, 1975; McLeod 1974; 1981; 1984). Equally, the Catholic church's continuing support for beleaguered ancien regimes across Europe led to a disillusionment with Christianity on the part of those who fought against these systems in the name of liberty and democracy (Martin, 1978). Here, as in the whole of the western world, the new values of liberal individualism were gradually sweeping aside an older respect for traditional orders and hierarchies in religious and social life. The publication of John Stuart Mill's essay *On Liberty* in 1859 revealed a movement in the ideal of liberty: as Chadwick (1975) puts it, it was increasingly viewed 'as a quality of life; not an instrument, but a good in itself, a quality of man and of society which enabled moral personality, moral development, self-realisation' (p. 29). This shift was bound up with what some sociologists have referred to as a 'turn to the self': a sense of the unique – indeed sacred – value, rights and dignity of each individual. Liberal Christianity was centrally implicated in these broader cultural shifts. Its followers were those who felt their religion could no longer run in the old grooves but must be reshaped and transformed in order to rise to the challenge of the modern age.

The most important carriers of the new values and expectations of the nineteenth century were the new middle classes who, if they are to be defined in terms of their economic status, were white and male (a woman's status tended to be conferred by father and husband). Liberalism rose so successfully to the challenge of accommodating the values of middle class, modernizing culture that some have accused it of capitulation. Not only did liberal Christians meet the challenges of the nineteenth century head on, they often turned them to their advantage. Darwin's theory of evolution, for example, was turned into a theory of general historical progress which was seen to culminate in modern western Protestantism. Equally, the liberty celebrated in post-revolutionary Europe and America was presented as a core value of such Protestantism; the latter was said to be defined by its longstanding opposition to tyranny of all sorts and its natural alliance with the forces of democracy and the free market.

Nowhere was Christian liberalism stronger than in the USA. During its heyday – roughly 1880–1914 – it underwrote the values and institutions of the Republic and helped underwrite a new 'civil religion'. As *Linda Woodhead* shows in her chapter on the World's Parliament of Religions, far from feeling threatened or marginalized by the changes of the nineteenth century, liberal Protestantism viewed itself as an integral part of the process of modernisation. Echoing and reinforcing the optimistic spirit of antebellum America, liberals believed that American society was at the forefront of human progress and that Protestantism played a key role in her 'manifest destiny'. The World's Parliament of Religions and the 1893 Columbian Exposition at Chicago of which it was a part exemplified this triumphalism. Organised by a committee of religious liberals, the Parliament was an unprecedented gathering of representatives of all the world's religions. In many ways it marked the beginning of a new era of religious pluralism in North America (Seager, 1993; 1995), though the intention of the Parliament's liberal organisers had been not to celebrate difference but to cement unity. Like their Deist predecessors, the liberal organisers of the Parliament saw their faith as universal. Its essence, as their President summed it up, was 'the love and worship of God and the love and service of man'. Since they believed this to be 'natural' religion, the organisers of the Parliament hoped its traces could be found in other religions too, and that all might all be able to unite against the forces of secularism, heathenism, faction, and idolatry.

As Woodhead shows, however, in the event the World's Parliament proved subversive of this liberal Christian hope. For the Parliament gave a platform to a number of men, women, and institutions who, whilst retaining some key elements of liberalism, including its universalism and optimism, abandoned others – including its theism and Christian exclusivism. Thus the Hindu monk Vivekananda, for example, affirmed the ideal of a universal religion, but suggested that it was the Hindu sages who had first glimpsed it, and that it consisted not in a 'dualistic' theism like that of Christianity, but in a monistic embrace of the one divine Spirit in which all things participate.

Woodhead goes on to argue that such spiritual monism, premised on belief in the unity of all beings in the one Spirit, represented the beginning of a trajectory of alternative or 'New' spirituality which gained pace in the twentieth century, and eventually issued in such movements as New Age. Despite important variations, the Transcendentalism explored in this volume by Shannon Cate appears as an early manifestation of this trajectory, as do the more popular movements of Spiritualism and Mesmerism which swept American more than a decade later. Though more organised and more influenced by esoteric tradition, the Theosophical Society founded in 1875 also offered an early example of such alternative or 'New' spirituality. Anticipating all these, however, and exercising a considerable influence on a number of them, including Transcendentalism and Theosophy, was Swedenborgianism, whose 'New Church' was founded by the Swedish scientist and mystic Emmanuel Swedenborg (1688–1772) in the eighteenth century.

As *Ian Sellers'* chapter on the New Church in England shows, Swedenborgianism enjoyed a unique period of social and intellectual respectability after the 1840s. His explanation is that it displayed a number of elective affinities with what Houghton (1957) referred to as 'the Victorian frame of mind'. Thus, for example, it helped bridge the gap between transcendent forms of Christianity and a purely inner spirituality; it offered a discourse in which key Victorian obsessions including death and 'conjugal love' could be articulated, and it offered a form of toleration towards other religions much greater than that which even liberal Protestantism could countenance. What is more, Swedenborgianism – like later alternative spiritualities – closed the distance between this world and the next. As Sellers puts it,

> The mind/body dualism of Descartes, the theocentric teaching of Catholic and Protestant orthodoxy, the pessimism of Pascal, the Jansenists and of much contemporary Evangelicalism are here defied in a vision of a modern heaven which extended and perfected the perceived changeless qualities of earthly existence. Love, work, and society, those three major Victorian enthusiasms were the marks of the New Church after-life.

The Transcendentalism which *Shannon Cate* discusses also tried to close the gap between the spiritual and material worlds. Like Woodhead, Cate shows how such alternative spirituality can be understood as a radicalisation of certain Protestant themes, including the ubiquitous presence of God. Yet Cate also shows how such radical spirituality could lead *back* to transcendent Christianity – in this case the Roman Catholic church. Cate argues that prominent converts from Transcendentalism to Catholicism like Orestes Brownson, Isaac Hecker, and Sophia Ripley found in the latter a church which was a) as counter-cultural in relation to an established Protestant elite in New England as was Transcendentalism, b) offered a sacramentalism which echoed the Transcendentalist insistence on the presence of the divine in the world, albeit in a more spatialised, localised form, and c) offered institutional outlets for 'worthy action', an aspiration which Transcendentalism fostered but could not always satisfy. Cate thus confirms a wider conclusion of the first section of this book – that so-called alternative religious movements of the nineteenth century tended to be culturally dissonant in some respects, but culturally conformist in others. In the words of Thomas Tweed (1992), who came to the same conclusion in his study of the American encounter with Buddhism in the nineteenth century,

> There seem to have been limits to dissent ... and few, ... ventured beyond those limits. Both critics' denunciations and apologists' refutations point to similar commitments. They delineate the cultural boundaries. If the public conversation about Buddhism is any indication, optimism and activism were fundamental to Victorian religious culture. And – although this might seem odd – they were often as difficult to denounce as theism and individualism. (p. 154)

Christianity and Literature

The reinvention of Christianity in the nineteenth century took place in response to a range of pressures, some external, some internal. Whilst the second part of this volume concentrates on cultural forces and contexts influencing such change, it also shows how change was bound up with social factors; changing Christian representations of women, for example, were prompted by new social and economic conditions as well as wider cultural shifts. Christianity was far more than a passive partner in this process; it was involved in negotiation with wider cultural and social developments rather than simply in defence, retrenchment or battle. So central was Christianity to Victorian society and 'the Victorian frame of mind' that different varieties of Christianity provided key sites for contemporary social and cultural negotiation, and many of the key debates of the period were articulated and pursued in Christian terms. Very often such debates moved beyond the boundaries of both the churches and academic theology – the chapters in Part Two illustrate how they were played out in literature, the visual arts, and the popular press as well as in academic and political debate.

Literature proved to be one of the key sites for the reinterpretation of Christianity in the nineteenth century. Plays, novels and poetry were consumed by a reading public of unprecedented size. Such literature often had a didactic as well as aesthetic purpose. In some cases, as *Terry Wright's* chapter on the nineteenth-century roots of D. H. Lawrence's religion illustrates, it played an important role in the dissemination and interpretation of debates in theology, philosophy, ethics and Biblical studies. Wright situates Lawrence's work in relation to a Victorian preoccupation with the issue of Biblical authority. He argues that one of the lasting effects of Lawrence's

Protestant upbringing was to make the Bible central to his religiosity. Equally, however, traditional Christian uses of the Bible led Lawrence away from the faith. He objected not only to the fact that the Bible was 'trodden into consciousness', but that 'the interpretation was fixed, so that all interest was lost'. Yet Lawrence 'recovered' the Bible partly through the influence of radical reinterpreters of Christianity like the philosopher Friedrich Nietzsche and the Biblical exegete Ernest Renan, and partly through the influence of representatives of alternative spirituality like Edward Carpenter and Madame Blavatsky (the founder of the Theosophical Society). What he drew from these ostensibly very dissimilar authors was the idea that the Bible must be treated not as monolithically authoritative, but as flawed and fragmentary. As a result Lawrence came to read the Bible, 'like a deconstructionist *avant la lettre*, teasing out the contradictory forces of signification'.

In at least one way, however, the interpreters who inspired Lawrence were very definitely 'modern' rather than 'postmodern', for their readings were inspired by a quest for an authentic 'ur' text behind the Bible. It was their commitment to a 'myth of origins' which enabled them to become masters of suspicion – Nietzsche attempting to recover a Christ before Christianity, Renan digging for the historical Jesus, and Blavatsky recovering an ancient wisdom which she believed to have been 'scattered throughout thousands of volumes embodying the scriptures of the great Asiatic and early European religions, hidden under glyph and symbol, and hitherto left unnoticed because of this veil'. Paradoxically then, a quest originally started by Christian textual scholars concerned to shed light on Christian origins was eventually to help reshape Christian culture and undermine traditional modes of interpretation.

Wright's chapter also shows how challenges to Biblical authority from science and historical investigation did not necessarily lead to a straightforward choice between accepting or rejecting the Biblical text and the faith that rested on it. Renan (1927), for example, proclaimed a 'religion of Jesus' based 'not upon fixed dogmas, but images susceptible of indefinite interpretations' (p. 237). Thus the questioning of the authority of 'scripture' led in some cases not to a disjunction between religion and science, but to a disjunction between materialism, rationalism and literalism on the one hand, and more imaginative, poetic, aesthetic, open and creative modes of religious knowledge and interpretation on the other. For Blavatsky, Renan, Carpenter, and later Lawrence, 'traditional' Christianity fell into the former category and was rejected along with science and materialism, yet without the religious option being closed off altogether. What was needed in the view of such re-shapers of opinion was not the abandonment of sacred texts but their reinterpretation. In other words, not one of these figures conformed to the grand narrative which informs a great deal of secularization theory – the narrative of personal and social progress from religious superstition to rational enlightenment.

Opposition to the heavy literalism and oppressive facticity of a rational-scientific approach in the name of free creativity was, of course, central to the programme of Romanticism which was played out across Europe and America (as well as in some colonies) at the end of the eighteenth and throughout the nineteenth centuries. Despite their rhetoric of opposition to rationalism, however, Romantics actually drew much from the Enlightenment, not least an opposition to institutional religion with its 'external' forms, 'fixed' rituals and dogmas, unnecessary modes of mediation between human and divine, and oppressive and imprisoning regulations and restrictions. Where religious rationalists like the Deists and many Unitarians attempted to bring religion into line with the deliverances of natural reason, however, Romantics found the divine in the exercise of imagination and intuition. And where the former found in nature the evidences of regularity, order and design, the latter found beauty, mystery and infinity.

In her chapter on William Wordsworth's 'Poems on the Naming of Places' *Deeanne Westbrook* shows how Wordsworth's poetry constructs a world in which human, natural, and spiritual are interfused. The 'Poems on the Naming of Places' sacralize sites by 'textualizing' them, inscribing them with human and divine significance. As Westbrook puts it,

> Like a Japanese flower dropped into water, each 'little incident', dropped into the medium of language, expands into an endless allegory. In the process the private, local, and trivial become universal and profound; the ephemeral becomes enduring. Taken as a group, the 'Poems' participate in the mythologizing of the poet's beloved landscape.

As in the case of Lawrence, Westbrook's exegesis leaves no doubt about the extent of Wordsworth's indebtedness to Christian tradition, most importantly the Bible and Cranmer's Prayer Book. She shows that his achievement is unthinkable without these influences. Biblical tropes and images shape his poetry, with certain sites in the Lake District becoming new Bethels, Babels or Bethlehems. No longer is the world seen as fallen, and a man's life like dust or grass; on the contrary, through tying person to place, immortality is assured. The named become part of the eternal cycle of nature, as endlessly self-generating as the wild flowers. In this way 'Poems on the Naming of Places' takes the biblical metaphors for the brevity and oblivion of human life, and makes them serve an opposite purpose – 'to preserve, lengthen, immortalise'. Equally, the divine is called down from the heavens to the earth. Instead of ruling over creation, the spiritual becomes interwoven with it – its innermost significance, recognised and actualised by the poetic imagination and by the poets who become the new priests.

Wordsworth's poetry thus articulates a form of spirituality in which the centre of gravity shifts from transcendence to immanence. As Westbrook points out, there is a strongly autobiographical slant to such religion. For Wordsworth at Grasmere, 'place and life have become one' and the site 'has been transformed into a bit of Wordsworthian autobiography, identifiable now with its author' who has 'achieved a material permanence and ultra-signification through and in this land'. A strongly autobiographical and personalised spirituality is also a feature of some of Shelley's writings. Though often accused of atheism during his own lifetime (a charge which he sometimes encouraged), the God Shelley rejected was the God he regarded as the vengeful tyrant of established religion. Like Wordsworth and many other Romantics, however, Shelley also believed passionately in a God whom he described as 'the interfused and overruling spirit of all the energy and wisdom included within the circle of existing things', and 'the overruling Spirit of all the energy and wisdom included in the circle of living things' (quoted by Webb, 1977, p. 160). In much of Shelley's writing, however, it seems deliberately unclear whether this God is a Power which transcends individual men and women, or is immanent in the individual. In 'Hymn to Intellectual Beauty', for example, the divine is invoked as the poetic imagination and inspiration – but it is also through the exercise of these faculties that humanity becomes divine. The God that Shelley invokes is deeply personal and personalised. Rather than being distant from human beings and the world, He is the inner principle of life, particularly the poet's life. He is 'the ruling spirit' and 'the god of my own heart' (Jones, 1964, Vol. II, pp. 437; 394).

Despite its heavily personalised form, Shelley's spirituality was far from apolitical or quietist. On the contrary, his 'atheism' and rejection of established religion was as much a political as a metaphysical or spiritual protest. Shelley's rebellion against the omnipotent Jehovah of the Bible was part and parcel of his rejection of the established social order of Britain and Europe in his day, for he saw very clearly how a God of Power was used to support the unjust exercise of power by a ruling elite. Politically, Shelley's age was of course dominated by the French Revolution of 1789 and its aftermath. Shelley's great fear was that the abuses which had followed in the wake of the Revolution would extinguish the hope and idealism which had first kindled it. In the epic poem 'Laon and Cythna' or 'The Revolt of Islam' (1817), which forms the focus of *Arthur Bradley's* chapter, Shelley celebrates the cause of liberty against the powers that would crush it. Its narrative of a peaceful Greek revolt against a tyrannical Turkish regime which is violently suppressed by an the Muslim emperor on the advice of a fanatical Christian priest exemplifies Shelley's conviction that the battle for freedom and democracy must be religious as well as political. This was not, of course, a poetic flight of fancy. For many of those who supported the cause of democracy in Europe, the Roman Catholic church was as much the enemy of change as the monarchy. Paradoxically, one effect of the revolution and its harsh measures against the church was to reinforce Catholicism's alliance with the forces of reaction. A clear sign of this was the way in which the fervently Catholic Joseph de Maistre (1753–1821) became the chief French spokesman of conservatism and monarchical power in the years following the Revolution. In *Du Pape* (1819), for example, de Maistre argued that the only true basis of society was authority, and that the authority of kings must be reinforced by the authority of the Pope, who was God's representative on earth. De Maistre also believed that history was under the direction of a divine providence which was manifested through the redemptive power of suffering and blood, most notably the sacrifice of Christ. In every way then, de Maistre would seem to represent all that Shelley most despised. One indication of this, as Bradley shows, was the way in which Shelley took up the theme of bloody sacrifice and used it against de Maistre to explain why the revolutionaries were predisposed towards violence. Like a number of his English contemporaries, Shelley depicted Catholics as cannibals, consuming the bodies of their fellow men in the same way that they consumed Christ on the altar. And yet the relish with which Shelley pursued this theme in 'Laon and Cythna' leads Bradley to conclude that Shelley's revolutionary ideology was in constant danger of being sacrificed on the altar of his anti-revolutionary aesthetics.

Turning to *Trevor Hogan's* chapter on Carlyle (1795–1881), we turn to another revolutionary figure. 'Revolution', indeed, is a key theme of this chapter, for Hogan argues that Carlyle (the author of *The French Revolution*), not only viewed modernity as a set of revolutions, but produced in *Sartor Resartus* (1833–4) a work which is best interpreted as 'revolutionary'. Carlyle, Hogan shows, believed that none of the religions of his day – institutional, traditional, personal, or romantic –

14   *Reinventing Christianity*

were adequate to the revolutionary age which had dawned. Equally, he rejected rationalist secularism. In *Sartor*, Hogan argues, Carlyle therefore set out to create a new Bible – a Book of Books – capable of supplanting the old. Like the old Bible, this was presented not a single work, but as a collection of collections edited, written, and assembled by different hands. Unlike the Bible, however, and unlike its nineteenth-century interpretations, *Sartor* was a book in which the reader had a key role to play. In its radical abolition of human as well as divine author, Hogan suggests that Carlyle anticipated the deconstructive turn of postmodernism. Yet at the same time that he problematized it, Carlyle refused to give up the quest for meaning. No wonder then that this revolutionary text irritated and perplexed Carlyle's contemporaries for, as Hogan puts it, 'it offered no consolation to Protestants, closed off the illusory hopes of the romantic poet as world legislator (Shelley), and yet damned the conceits of the self-proclaimed secularists and materialists. As such, Sartor both anticipates the Victorian debates about 'Culture' as the humanist overcoming of Christianity and contains their destruction *avant la lettre*'.

Christianity and Gender

Section four of the volume turns from the inter-relations between religion and literature to those between religion and gender. In the opening chapter on the depiction of women in nineteenth-century art, *Jane Kristof* shows how the preponderance of women in the pews in Europe and America was reflected in visual representation. She finds not only that depictions of religious devotion concentrate on women worshippers, but that depictions of the religious life are almost exclusively of nuns rather than monks. Likewise, pictures of married couples often differentiate in terms of their respective piety – a nice example is provided by Hippolyte Bellange's painting of *The Peddler of Plaster Figurines* in which the wife admires an image of the Madonna and Child whilst her husband gazes on a statuette of Napoleon.

Of course, as Kristof also points out, the depiction of female piety reveals not only the actual state of religious practice in the nineteenth century, but masculine ideals of religiosity and womanhood. In this context it is particularly significant that visual representations of female piety fall into four main categories: the cloistered nun, the peasant wife, the young mother, and the elderly widow. One explanation offered by Kristof is that these were the categories of woman most isolated from the scientific and philosophical currents of the day, and that they were thus able to represent a pure, untroubled and unsullied faith which men viewed with nostalgic wistfulness. Kristof notes the ambivalence of these images, however, for at the same time that they celebrated such simple piety, men also drew attention to women's mental limitations and their inability to deal with abstract reasoning and conceptual issues – Kristof cites Kant's celebration of his mother as 'a sweet-tempered, affectionate, pious and upright woman', together with his statement that 'the fair sex has just as much understanding as the male, but it is a *beautiful understanding*, whereas ours should be a *deep understanding*'.

According to Kristof, any adequate explanation of the artistic concentration on these four types of female piety must also invoke domestic and sexual ideals of nineteenth-century society. For as well as depicting an ideal of naïve piety, all four also depict a 'safe' form of sexuality which is within the control of men, and which constitutes no threat to men's social and economic dominance. This is obvious in the case of nuns who, as Kristof shows, enjoyed a special favour even amongst artists in Protestant England. Whilst the nun remains safe by virtue of her renunciation of sexual activity and adoption of the ideals of humility, piety, charity, and obedience – including obedience to male clerical control – the peasant wife, young mother, and elderly widow represent a sexuality safely contained within the 'domestic' realm. As scholars like Douglas (1977) and McClintock (1995) have shown, the latter was immensely important to nineteenth-century culture and society. In part it was the product of new social and economic forces which generated new patterns of gendered work and allowed a new middle class to confine their womenfolk to a 'private' realm; in part it was an ideal which helped structure gender relations and justify patterns of social inequality. Religion was deeply implicated in both aspects of domesticity, both actively and passively. Passively it was the victim of privatisation as the social differentiation which gathered pace in the nineteenth century robbed Christianity of its public functions and 'feminised' it (Douglas, 1977). Actively, it was central in the ideological justification of the domestic ideal, with both Catholic and Protestant churches exalting 'the family' as the building block of a Christian society and presenting the feminine virtues of humility, self-sacrifice, and obedience as Christian virtues *par excellence* (McDannell 1986; 1989).

As well as reinforcing the domestic ideal and women's subordination, however, Christianity could also be appropriated in critique. Such a strategy had at least two advantages: first, it was legitimate to the extent that religion in the nineteenth century religion was increasingly seen as the special and proper sphere of women, and second, since Christianity was viewed as uniquely authoritative in relation to norms and values, there was no better tribunal at which to appeal. The potential power which women could harness by using Christianity in this way helps explain why many Victorian men felt the need to proscribe or ridicule women's theological endeavours. In her chapter on women's theology in the British periodical press, for example, *Julie Melnyk* reminds us of Ruskin's identification of theology as the 'one dangerous science for women'. 'Strange and miserably strange', he wrote,

> That while [women] are modest enough to doubt their powers, and pause at the threshold of sciences where every step is demonstrable and sure, they will plunge headlong, and without one thought of incompetency, into that science in which the greatest men have trembled, and the wisest erred.

More effective than all these strictures, however, was the bar to women's participation in theological activity within either the academy or the church, and the practical impossibility of their publishing either theological treatises or sermons. The result, as Melnyk shows, was that whilst some women's theology found an outlet in religious fiction, verse and devotional manuals, much is to be found in the press, and particularly in women's religious periodicals.

Melnyk goes on to consider two of the most important evangelical magazines edited by women, *The Christian Lady's Magazine* and *The Christian World Magazine*. These very different publications – one high brow and the other more popular – served as outlets for some decidedly radical theology. Not surprisingly, given its evangelical pedigree, such theology mainly took the form of Biblical exegesis. Such exegesis, however, was generally disguised, usually within a narrative form. Many women writers, for example, would end narrative accounts of the lives of real or fictional characters with a scriptural text that the preceding story would serve to reinterpret. In addition, Biblical narratives, particularly stories about women, created enormous opportunities for interpretation of texts relevant to women's social position. Thus Lydia, Deborah, Sarah, Miriam and Mary the sister of Martha are all used in order to justify the adoption by women of roles that take them outside the domestic sphere. As one contributor says, such examples 'sanction those occasional instances in which [woman] has emerged from obscurity to act the part of a ruler or a patriot; or to bow the hearts of all by the strains of eloquence and passion...'.

Hilary Fraser and *Victoria Burrows's* chapter on Florence Nightingale's three-volume *Suggestions for Thought* (1850–52) offers another example of the remarkably subversive uses to which theology could be put in the hands of women. Indeed, so forceful is Nightingale's critique of contemporary Christianity (particularly Anglicanism), and so radical her reinterpretations of the gospel, that she can be said to anticipate many of the achievements of feminist theology over a century later. Nightingale's critique focuses squarely on the fact that Christianity has underwritten the confinement of women to the domestic realm and the consequent dissipation of their talents and energies. Again and again she invokes the trope of the body to describe the 'life of starvation' which results, and interplays this image with that of force-feeding, of women gagging on their own enforced passivity and dependency. Her criticism is directed explicitly at the family as a prison-house for many women, and her cry is for an enlarged sphere of activity. This alone, she says, can overcome the self-division that is the fate of so many women – 'there is no longer unity between the woman as inwardly developed, and as outwardly manifested'.

So violent is Florence Nightingale's complaint, and so subversive her uses of scripture, that she not only reconfigures typology in order to make Christ the type of the suffering modern woman, but goes so far as to suggest that Christ's physical suffering on the cross is eclipsed by women's spiritual suffering. As she exclaims, 'How much worse not to strive to save thousands from a crucified *spirit* than to crucify one body'. In a similarly heretical style she speaks of the need for contemporary saviours. For her the Christ is clearly not sufficient as a type of what human nature may become. The continuing process of evolution requires something more, and Nightingale's audacious suggestion is that it may require a *woman*: 'At last there shall arise a woman, who shall resume, in her own soul, all the sufferings of her race, and that woman will be the Saviour of her race'. Or, as she puts it in another passage, 'The next Christ will perhaps be a female Christ'.

It was after she had written *Suggestions for Thought* that Florence Nightingale managed to carve out for herself a public role in the Crimean war. The irony, as Burrows and Fraser remark, is that this role was interpreted by many in domestic terms. It was a small step from the Victorian ideal of the angel in the house to the ministering angel at the front. In this way, Nightingale was herself domesticated – and to some extent appears to have colluded in the process (she maintained that 'we want to extend the family, not annihilate it'). Yet the radicalism of *Suggestions* was not forgotten by all, and it is little surprise to find the Lady with the Lamp's most famous debunker, Lytton Strachey, pouring particular scorn on her theological speculations, and concluding – in tones reminiscent of Kant – that 'her mind was, indeed, better qualified to dissect concrete facts of actual life than to construct a coherent system of abstract philosophy'.

Whilst *Suggestions for Thought* displays an unusual awareness of class issues in Victorian society and some sensitivity to the deprivations suffered by members of a new industrial working class, its more radical proposals are confined to the realm of gender. The same, as *Robert Kachur* shows in his chapter on gender, class, and the apocalypse, is true of Elizabeth Gaskell's social problem novel *North and South* (1855). Just as Melnyk shows that women's theology in nineteenth-century periodicals often took narrative form, so Kachur shows how *North and South* is shaped through its interpretation of the biblical book of Revelation. Kachur sets this in context by showing how the Apocalypse was widely used at the time to interpret social upheaval, particularly labour disputes and calls for the emancipation of women. As he demonstrates, these uses of the Apocalypse were overwhelmingly conservative, many of them associating the antichrist with rebellious trades unions and unruly women. True to her more radical Unitarian heritage, however, Gaskell uses Revelation in a more subversive way by figuring women not in terms of antichrist, but of two common Apocalyptic images of strength: the Woman Clothed with the Sun (Rev. 12) and the heavenly Bride (Rev. 21). Thus Margaret, the Christian heroine of the novel appears as an 'angel in white' who discovers her own agency and challenges the entrenched privileges and conservatism of the new industrial town of Milton in which the novel is set.

Yet Kachur also shows how Gaskell's use of the Apocalypse is much less radical in relation to class than to gender. It is only Gaskell's middle-class heroine Margaret who becomes a public actor, whilst her working-class counterpart Bessy has to be content to project her desire for agency onto this 'angel'. Likewise, Margaret's new role as social actor involves her in defusing a labour dispute in Milton by engendering consensus and an amelioration of present conditions, rather than by advocating more radical social reform. Apocalyptic discourse allows Gaskell to envision a more progressive gender ideology in *North and South*, while still reaffirming prevailing class hierarchies. As Kachur concludes, it registers 'the contradictory impulses inevitably expressed by Victorian women whose advocacy of social reform was qualified by their own investment in class privilege'.

Christianity and Science

Nowhere has the image of a 'war' between Christianity and wider culture been more influential in shaping perceptions of the nineteenth century than in relation to the negotiations between science and Christianity. *John Brooke* opens the fifth and final section of the volume with a wide-ranging attack on this image and the accompanying assumption that new scientific discoveries led directly to a decline in religious belief and practice in the nineteenth century. He shows that the many problems which the familiar trope of a war between science and religion must face include the following:

1. Much talk about the conflict between science and religion assumes that each is a neatly bounded entity distinct from the other. Neither assumption is warranted. The idea of 'religion' is a construct that has been heavily criticised, not least because it has proved impossible to arrive at a definition which covers all the world's religions. Likewise it seems impossible to arrive at a definition of science which does not either include or exclude too much. 'Science' embraces a whole web of varied methods, institutions, cultures, discourses, and bodies of knowledge – some of them contradictory. To say that science is in conflict with religion is thus to beg the question of which science is in conflict with which variety of religion.
2. Not only are science and religion not clearly bounded, but in many cases they shade into one another. Brooke gives a range of examples in which it is very difficult to say where science ends and religion begins, or vice versa. Only the assumption that science and religion are sworn enemies disguises this fact. In reality, however, science and religion have as often worked together as pulled apart.
3. Far from undermining religious belief, science has sometimes reinforced it. As Brooke shows, there are not only many examples of scientists who have been motivated by Christian belief but also of individuals who have been led to faith by their scientific studies. Neither did scientific discoveries always precipitate a crisis of faith outside the ranks of the scientific community. Many believers took them in their stride. Some ignored them. Others adjusted their understanding of God and the world in light of them.
4. Scientists and theologians have *both* contributed to the on-going discipline of 'natural theology' (interpretation of God and the world based on natural reason and observation rather than revelation). Brooke reveals just how important this enterprise was in the nineteenth century, despite its neglect by those who assume science and religion to be incompatible. He also shows how fragmented and internally diverse natural theology was even before Darwin. Far from simply undermining the enterprise, some scientific discoveries were therefore much more damaging to certain versions of natural theology than to others. Indeed, new scientific discoveries in the nineteenth century often lead not to an abandonment of natural theology, but to its proliferation and revision.
5. The belief that the advance of science has led directly to secularization makes what Brooke calls the 'metaphysical mistake' of assuming that religion is primarily a matter of intellectual belief. Not only does this neglect religion's social, economic and political roles and its importance in sustaining local, national and ethnic identity, it also overlooks the material and social aspects of science, and depends upon a naïve picture of the influence and diffusion of intellectual culture.

Much of Brooke's chapter is given over to discussing the varied and complex ways in which science and secularization actually did relate in the nineteenth century. Having cleared away the image of inevitable conflict, a much more complex picture emerges. Brooke uses six categories in order to tease out what he calls the possible 'modes of secularization', and highlights the paradoxes contained in each. Though he attacks the assumption of inevitable conflict between science and religion, it soon becomes clear that it is no part of his intention to support an opposite narrative – that of unbroken harmony between science and religion. As Brooke makes very plain in recent books, his argument is with *any* form of 'master-narrative' that would claim to describe the relation between the two (Brooke, 1991; Brooke and Cantor, 1998). What is more important for our understanding of science and the nineteenth century is not the creation of a more adequate single story, but an investigation of why such stories came about, which contexts supported them, and whose interests they upheld.

It is just such a master-narrative that *Gowan Dawson* explores in his discussion of Victorian scientific materialism as it was exemplified by polemicists like John Tyndall. Whilst the confrontation between T.H. Huxley and Bishop Samuel Wilberforce in Oxford in 1860 has become paradigmatic in many accounts of the 'war' between science and religion in the nineteenth century, Tyndall in fact aroused far more controversy (Turner, 1981). Tyndall's master-narrative, expounded in his notorious Belfast address of 1874, told of the development of science from early and glorious days in Ancient Greece. 'Free-thinking and courageous' pagan philosophers like Democritus and Epicurus invented the scientific mentality, which was then submerged by Christian and other regressive forces, until revived in the Renaissance. Modern science is the heir of these developments, and stands in direct continuity with them.

Not surprisingly, Tyndall's account provoked outrage amongst many Christians, from the Calvinists of Belfast to the leaders of the established Church of England. What Dawson points out, however, is that this was not simply a clash between two metaphysical systems: theism on the one hand and a godless scientific materialism on the other. Dawson illustrates this point by drawing attention (for the first time) to the way in which Walter Pater's *Studies of the History of the Renaissance* (1873) was drawn into the controversy over Tyndall's Belfast Address. The reason, he shows, was that Pater's study also celebrated Ancient Greece, though now in terms of its aesthetic rather its scientific values. There was, however, a link between such aestheticism and scientific materialism since Pater, as Dawson puts it, 'apotheosised aesthetic hedonism as the most astute response to the version of human existence predicated by recent scientific discoveries'. What Tyndall's critics saw in Pater's work, then, were the ethical and social implications of Tyndall's metaphysic writ large. Accept the latter, and the former would necessarily follow: scientific materialism would lead directly to the immoral sensualism which had precipitated the downfall of pagan antiquity and would precipitate the downfall of the contemporary social order in the process.

Dawson's chapter thus contextualizes the so-called war between science and religion in exactly the way that John Brooke advocates. Once it is placed in context – here Britain in the 1870s – it becomes clear is that it is much too simple to picture this 'war' as a simple matter of intellectual disagreement, or a clash between the forces of reaction and enlightenment. At stake was the authority of the established Christian churches and the stable ordering of the 'respectable' society which was seen to be underpinned by Christian values. Likewise, the churches' scientific opponents were not merely disinterested freethinkers, but represented in many cases a new 'knowledge class' vying for power with the established interests of clericalism in the universities (Turner, 1978). As Desmond (1994) has shown, the struggle was further complicated by the way in which some non-conformist dissenters employed science – in particular a competitive, evolutionary understanding of the world – in *their* struggle with monopolistic Anglicanism. The idea of a war between science and religion was a rhetorical strategy from the start; taken out of context it can easily mask the more complicated material and spiritual interests which were at play.

As *Jonathan Smith's* chapter shows, the master-narrative of a war between Christianity and science has also affected the reception of Philip Gosse, an influential and widely-read naturalist and illustrator of the 1850s, 1860s and 1870s. In this case the damage was done by his son, Edmund Gosse, whose autobiographical *Father and Son* (1907) presented the elder Gosse as 'an exemplar of the wrong-headed Victorian Protestant fundamentalism that futiley resisted the advancing tide of scientific naturalism epitomized by Darwin's theory of natural selection'. Smith shows that the reality was once again more complicated. Philip Gosse was neither simply theologian, nor simply scientist. He was a natural theologian, as preoccupied with exploring the natural world as with drawing out its theological significance. Confirming another point made by John Brooke, Smith also shows that the natural theology of Gosse cannot simply be subsumed under some general category of natural theology in general. In fact Gosse was a severe critic of more optimistic forms of natural theology, his transcendent Protestantism leading him to emphasise both the fallenness of the created order and the greater authority of the Bible in matters pertaining to God. This did not, however, prevent Gosse from continually drawing out the moral and religious significance of the marine life he evoked so vividly in words and pictures. Some of his typological readings of nature drew attention to the elements of fallenness in what he observed. But his most famous studies of the teeming life contained within rock pools tended to interpret what he saw as a veritable Eden of contentment and harmony, touched by the fall 'rather corporately than individually, rather nominally, in dignity, than consciously, in pain or want'.

Not only does the example of Gosse confound the idea of natural theology as a unitary enterprise, it also undermines the idea that it was dealt a decisive death-blow by the publication of Darwin's *Origin of Species* in 1859. Whilst Gosse was clearly troubled by this book, and sought to refute Darwin's theory of an evolution which made no reference to God, he did so *through* natural theology. Instead of talking about evolution, Gosse spoke of 'radiations of relation' between different species, and took this as further evidence of the fecundity of the Creator's world and the related but distinct forms that fill every niche of the natural economy. Gosse's primary demonstration of this vision was through his illustrations; Dawson discusses the example of one plate in which Gosse juxtaposes a species of sea-cucumber with a dotted siponocle because of their natural affinity. And yet, as Dawson puts it, 'in its attempt to stand as a silent alternative to Darwinian accounts of species relation, [the illustration] seems almost to invite the Darwinian explanation that these "radiations of relation" are the result of natural selection operating over time on a natural ancestor'. One result was that Gosse became 'vulnerable to appropriations of his work by the very forces he has battling'. This vulnerability, Dawson argues, was the greater because Gosse's visual juxtapositions were artificially constructed. And yet, as all the contributors to this final section of the book point out, every depiction of 'nature' and 'the natural' is inevitably construction. Science itself never yields up a whole world-view; the latter are always underdetermined by science. As John Brooke concludes, 'The sciences have never simply led to secularization. At issue has always been the cultural meaning to be placed on new forms of science'.

Part One
Varieties

I Transcendent Christianity

Chapter One

Evangelical Certainties: Charles Spurgeon and the Sermon as Crisis Literature

Andrew Tate

'Oh! that we might all be converted!' (Spurgeon, 1859, p. 166)

As a successor to the revivalist tradition inaugurated by George Whitefield and John Wesley in the eighteenth-century, Charles Haddon Spurgeon, the English Baptist preacher, was an evangelist *sans pareil*, sermonizing against the evils of the age, and urgently calling for the repentance of his hearers. Beginning his ministry in 1854, Spurgeon preached assurance during a period of radical ambiguity for the English Protestant tradition. In the 1850s the *via media* of the established church was particularly vulnerable, offering the certainties of neither Papal Rome nor those of Calvinist Geneva. Could the Church of England continue to fulfil a prophetic role when so many members of its communion were assailed by scepticism? In 1851 Daniel Wilson, an Anglican clergyman, proclaimed that the impasse was caused principally by the church having lost sight of its evangelistic responsibilities:

> souls are perishing all around. What are we doing for them? Have we a due sense of the value of a soul – of a single soul? What is a lost soul? What efforts ought not to be made to save a soul? A revival of spiritual religion would produce a great change in this respect. There would be a general longing after the conversion of souls, a travailing in birth again till Christ be formed in them. (Wilson, 1851, p. 8)

The Church of England, he maintained, had become apathetic, failing to respond to the challenges posed by the recent re-establishment of the Roman Catholic hierarchy. He observes that 'conversion is not sought for or recognised in the proper sense of the term' (pp. 11, 7). This Anglican clergyman's censure of the Church foreshadows the rise of Spurgeon and a ministry that concentrated on conversion. In a decade of major debates regarding episcopal authority, the individual search for salvation and assurance had, perhaps, not been closely addressed by the Church of England. Wilson's anxieties may have been soothed by the appearance of this Baptist preacher who, from the mid-1850s, marked a 'revival of spiritual religion'.

Speaking at first from the pulpit of New Park Street, subsequently at the Royal Surrey Gardens Music Hall and from 1861, in the Metropolitan Tabernacle, Spurgeon attracted thousands of intrigued listeners to every service. People from all classes came to hear him, and he influenced thinkers whose churchmanship was radically different from his own. He impressed Matthew Arnold, corresponded with Gladstone, and held private discussions with John Ruskin.

This chapter will examine the role of Spurgeon as an emergent Evangelical voice during the 1850s. Spurgeon's personal 'salvation' testimony will be scrutinised in the wider context of 1850s Protestant England. One of his sermons will be read as an important example of crisis literature. His sermons and his personal testimony are at once a reaction against crisis – relying on conservative doctrinal assertions, and biblical authority to refute contemporary ontological uncertainties – and a means of engendering it, exhorting the unregenerate listener to seek the turning point between life and death, where he or she will abandon their sins, acknowledge the atoning sacrifice of Jesus Christ and become 'born anew'.

Learning to tell stories is a foundational exercise for Christians, both Protestant and Roman Catholic alike: in common with all world religions it is a faith of parables and history, of poetry and living myth. Edifying stories are told from the pulpit, written in testimonial pamphlets, and shared in prayer meetings. Roman Catholic and Anglican children are introduced, albeit unconsciously, at an early age into the broad narrative of Christian history through the rite of baptism. The importance of narrative, however, has particular significance in the Evangelical tradition: the personal account of how faith in Christ was found is explicitly regarded as vital proof of regeneration. As one critic has recently claimed, 'to become a Christian ... is to embrace the story of Christ in such a way that we join the story line' (Kallenberg, 1995, p. 348). In his autobiography, Spurgeon prefaces an account of his own conversion with a statement on the importance of Christian testimony. The legitimacy of an individual's claim to conversion can be judged, he notes, by the quality of the story that is told:

> I have heard men tell the story of their conversion, and of their spiritual life, in such a way that my heart hath loathed *them* and their story, too, for they have told of their sins as if they did boast in the greatness of their crime ... Oh! when we tell the story of our own conversion, I would have it done with great sorrow remembering what we used to be, and with great joy and gratitude, remembering how little we deserve these things. (1897, p. 97)

Spiritual autobiography, the preacher reasons, should exist solely to glorify the saviour, and never its 'saved' narrator. Evangelicalism is characterised by an acutely self-conscious form of piety, promoting constant, close scrutiny of the conscience. It also, however, perpetuates a heightened sense of the narrative tradition of which each new convert enters: Spurgeon's emphasis on the way such a story is told is not merely zealous impatience. Nineteenth-century Protestant conversion narratives are foreshadowed not only by the writings of Saint Paul and Augustine but also by those of John Bunyan and John Wesley. For Spurgeon and his co-religionists contemporary narratives had to conform to a specific tradition of conversion: they must be self-abasing, emphasising grace and election, sole gratitude to God, and explicitly acknowledge the necessity of substitutionary atonement.

Spurgeon dates 'that day of days, that best and brightest of hours', when he experienced a 'conversion of the heart', as 6 January, 1850: at the very beginning of the decade when Protestant anxiety would be perpetuated by a number of major challenges. Although the account of the event described by Spurgeon as 'the Great

Change' has its origins in the same tradition as the conversion narratives written by many of his literary contemporaries, it is written from a very different perspective. The preacher's tale is governed by limits from which other narratives are free. Pseudo-autobiography gave Carlyle the liberty to explore scepticism and spiritual re-birth in the influential *Sartor Resartus* (1833–4), without fear of condemnation. In *Christmas-Eve and Easter-Day* (1850) Robert Browning could satirize and celebrate the major interpretative frameworks of European Christianity using the 'mask' of dramatic monologue. Ruskin's writings on his 'unconversion' experience were initially limited to private correspondence with a number of trusted friends, and he produced his first public account eighteen years after the event in Letter 76 of *Fors Clavigera* (1877).

These narratives were all constructed by individuals on the margins of orthodox belief, independent of institutional regulations and without the burden of clerical responsibility. Even Ruskin, who had become an eminent apologist for Protestant thought and was accordingly cautious regarding public proclamation, held no official position that could compromise his narrative. Spurgeon, however, was subject to rigorous doctrinal imperatives. His 'story' had to correspond with the orthodoxy of his professed theological position. As a Baptist minister he was accountable to a powerful leadership, and he also had an obligation to the wider Evangelical community to perpetuate the compelling invitation to repentance and regeneration. Spurgeon's narratives of conversion are, therefore, simultaneously an act of interpretation and persuasion, transforming private experience into public discourse. The accounts he gave had to appear free from artifice, to be pure utterances that communicated the literal truth of a meeting between God and man. Yet, despite the aspiration to purity of representation, his accounts were also informed by the literary tropes invoked by Carlyle and Browning.

Spurgeon's own 'redemption history' is shaped by the paradigm narratives of Puritan tradition, most explicitly those of Bunyan and Wesley. His autobiography acknowledges that particular texts prompted and shaped his conversion: 'I have to bless God for many good books', he states, citing, among others, Doddridge's *Rise and Progress of Religion in the Soul* and Baxter's *Calls to the Unconverted*. He argues, however, that it was another textual encounter that precipitated his decisive Christian commitment: 'but my gratitude most of all is due to God, not for books, but for the preached Word' (Spurgeon, 1897, p. 104). Spurgeon problematizes the traditional Evangelical emphasis on private judgment of scripture by elevating the role of the sermon in his conversion. His experience is auditory rather than literary, one of passive reception rather than of engaged interpretation. The hermeneutic act has already been begun by the preacher. The responsibility of the listening subject becomes radically limited, and he is only granted a choice between total assent or dissent, allowing no ambivalence. The rhetoric of the evangelistic sermon is privileged above private acts of reading:

> The revealed Word awakened me; but it was the preached Word that saved me; and I must ever attach peculiar value to the *hearing of the truth*, for by it I received the joy and peace in which my soul delights. (p. 104)

This affirmation does not, however, indicate that Spurgeon was equivocal regarding the value of regular, solitary reading of scripture. Indeed, in an early sermon focusing on biblical authority, he accused his listeners of abandoning the Bible, counselling them to read it with reverence and expectation:

> This Bible is God's Bible; and when I see it, I seem to hear a voice springing up from it, saying, "I am the book of God: man, read me. I am God's writing: open my leaf, for I was penned by God; read it, for he is my author, and you will see him visible and manifest everywhere". (1856, p. 110)

The emphasis on the 'peculiar value' of the 'preached Word' originates from anxieties of authority: as the Bible became an increasing focus of debate, and its status as the infallible Word of God was openly challenged, so was the possibility of 'innocent' interpretation reduced. Spurgeon suggests that many readers are incapable of reaching the correct interpretation of scripture, and that they need to be guided by orthodox teaching from the pulpit. He censures clergymen who appear to relax the challenges of scripture, arguing that to substitute the word 'damned' with 'condemned' was gross deception: 'Gentlemen! pull the velvet out of your mouths; speak God's word; we want none of your alterations' (p. 112).

Biblical authority was as vital for Spurgeon as autobiographer as it was fundamental to his role as preacher. His generation, both educated and illiterate, was immersed in the language of the Bible; the pietist and the 'infidel' alike would have been familiar with the parables and the ten commandments, and from infancy aware of Old Testament stories of exile and redemption. Victorian popular culture was explicitly rooted in the Bible: from Spurgeon's theatrical preaching before 10,000 strong crowds (significantly most often in a very secular venue, a music hall), to the allusive fiction of Dickens, the language of scripture imbued most forms of public discourse. James Garbett, Keble's successor as Professor of poetry at Oxford, contradicted the emergent *zeitgeist* of biblical criticism by arguing that the Bible was not simply a work of literature but the living, dynamic Word of God:

> When you open the Word, which, like Himself is not dead but living, and shooteth life from it into the dead, do not separate it from Him. Treat it not as words in a book, or as issuing from the lips of man ... The words of the Book are no more mere words, than the promises or the threats of men like ourselves ... They are God speaking, inviting, loving, justifying. (Garbett, 1849, p. 50)

The language of scripture, therefore, was not to be used indifferently, but with reverence. According to this argument the words of the Bible act as the ultimate signifiers of meaning. In a culture pervaded by biblical narrative this 'canonical language' could legitimate private narratives, whether or not they were written by practising Christians, giving implicit credibility to their arguments.

In Spurgeon's narrative, as with all biblical literalists, this use of 'canonical language' becomes more complex. In a recent study Peter Stromberg argues that the individual who, in the Puritan tradition, seeks conversion 'must learn to understand experience and the Word of God in the same terms' (1993, p. 11). Spurgeon, like Garbett, understood the Bible in theological rather than literary terms; scripture was not simply a means of describing personal, religious change but the very source of the conversion. The biblical narrative is reconstructed by its reader as the story of personal redemption, integrating scripture and experience. Spurgeon's narrative of conversion is constructed around a similar trope of integration. Before describing the specifics of 'that day of days', Spurgeon locates his story as part of the unfolding Christian grand-narrative, alluding to scripture and asserting confidence in personal knowledge of salvation:

> Dying, all but dead, diseased, pained, chained, scourged, bound in fetters of iron, in darkness and the shadow of death, Jesus appeared unto me. My eyes looked to Him; the disease was healed, the pains removed, chains were snapped, prison doors were opened, darkness gave place to light. What delight filled my soul! (Spurgeon, 1897, p. 97)

The biblical discourse of condemnation, with its imagery of disease and darkness, is appropriated to represent the initial state of unbelief; redemption is described as a moment of theophany, when 'Jesus appeared' and Spurgeon's 'eyes looked unto Him', and is accompanied by a state of rapture that echoes the experience of Pentecost in the book of Acts. This foregrounding of the narrative is not merely a metaphorical description of the rite of conversion. For Spurgeon these biblical phrases represented the only means of describing his experience; he believed that the moment of repentance, engendered by the vision of Christ, was also the precise instant of his personal salvation. A moment before, he argues, and he was still in the adamite state of ruin. He is also careful to insist on the Evangelical imperative of salvation by grace alone. The narrative of his personal journey begins with reference to his early religious character:

> For years, as a child, I tried to learn the way of salvation; and either I did not hear it set forth, which I think cannot quite have been the case, or else I was spiritually blind and deaf, and could not see it and could not hear it; but the good news that I was, as a sinner, to look away from myself to Christ, as much startled me, and came as fresh to me, as any news I ever heard in my life. (Spurgeon, 1897, 102)

Spurgeon's disclosure that from infancy he had been engaged in seeking 'the way of salvation' is significant. Despite emphasis on his pre-regenerate identity as 'blind and deaf' to the gospel and unequivocally as 'a sinner' he establishes integrity as an individual who has always sought truth and righteousness. This was important for an Evangelical readership. The prior expression of antipathy for those conversion narratives featuring salacious accounts of transgression indicates that his story will not focus on life as 'sinner'. Similarly he makes it clear that at the time of his spiritual rebirth he was actively seeking the 'authentic' faith and the means to gain it for himself. As a fifteen-year-old Spurgeon was living away from home when he became convinced of the necessity of personal faith. He did not, however, discover faith according to the catastrophic Pauline model. Spurgeon was from a Christian background, and had both an earnest belief in God and a sense of conviction for personal sin. His dilemma was one of interpretation, represented by the multiplicity of houses of worship, representing different traditions within one faith. The resolution of his quest transpired in unlikely circumstances:

> I sometimes think I might have been in darkness and despair until now had it not been for the goodness of God in sending a snowstorm, one Sunday morning, while I was going to a certain place of worship. When I could go no further, I turned down a side street, and came to a little Primitive Methodist Chapel. In that chapel there may have been a dozen or fifteen people. (1897, p. 105)

Providence, argues Spurgeon, intervened in the pilgrimage and forced him to enter a place of worship he would otherwise have ignored. This action echoes the beginning of Robert Browning's *Christmas-Eve*, ironically written only months before, and describing a fictional conversion that is actually set less than a fortnight before Spurgeon's moment of crisis. Browning's sceptical traveller stumbles into the Evangelical service at Mount Zion Chapel and joins the underprivileged community of worshippers ostensibly to escape the rain. The Primitive Methodist Chapel of Spurgeon's narrative is similarly humble, representing the margins of mainstream Protestant religion and its preacher is reminiscent of Browning's Evangelical minister, whose lack of learning arouses contempt in the speaker:

> At last, a very thin-looking man, a shoemaker, or tailor, or something of that sort, went up into the pulpit to preach. Now, it is well that preachers should be instructed; but this man was really stupid. He was obliged to stick to his text, for the simple reason that he had little else to say. The text was, "LOOK UNTO ME, AND BE YE SAVED, ALL THE ENDS OF THE EARTH". (p. 105)

Spurgeon casts the preacher as a holy fool, his intellectual limitations superseded by God in order that he can act as a conduit of divine truth: 'He did not even pronounce the words rightly, but that did not matter. There was, I thought, a glimpse of hope for me in that text' (p. 106). In the Puritan tradition conversion is deemed a private transaction between God and the individual without external human influence. The preacher is a figure outside this dyadic union of divinity and sinner but who may be used to engender the final conversion. Indeed, as Lewis Rambo argues, there is often a 'complex interplay between advocate and potential convert' (1993, p. 66). This is true for both Spurgeon and Browning's speaker: 'salvation' is found where it is least expected, either by the earnest seeker or the sceptical inquirer, and the gospel pronounced most convincingly by the most humble lips.

Both poet and preacher were making use of antecedent stories of personal transformation to shape their own narratives. Bunyan's *Pilgrim's Progress* is a distinct presence in both these texts (see Finley, 1987). Spurgeon, we are reminded, was living at a great distance from his family at the time of his conversion. This is resonant of Christian's salvation narrative, as he begins the journey in bidding farewell to his family. Similarly, Browning's speaker is a solitary traveller. Each of these pilgrims is removed from the familiar, domestic sphere and they are each forced to encounter the world with new eyes, as strangers in a strange land. The biblical text pivotal to Spurgeon's conversion focuses on an act of seeing, challenging the listener/reader to look with the eye of faith. The sole emphasis of the sermon, according to Spurgeon, was the charge to 'look' at Christ:

> the text says, 'Look unto Me.' "Ay!" said he, in broad Essex, "many on ye are lookin' to yourselves, but it's no use lookin' there. You'll never find any comfort in yourselves. Some look to God the Father. No, look to Him by-and-by. Jesus Christ says, 'Look unto Me.' Some on ye say, 'We must wait for the Spirit's workin'.' You have no business with that just now. Look to Christ. The text says, 'Look unto Me.'" (Spurgeon, 1897, p. 106)

The sermon is an attempt to generate a decisive moment of theophany in his congregation. Spurgeon suggests that free from intellectual concerns, the preacher personifies authentic faith, based on simple belief in Christ. Whilst Spurgeon is careful to maintain his own intellectual credibility, referring to the preacher as 'really stupid', he also implies that this state of unquestioning belief is necessary to true piety. Spurgeon's narrative has an anti-intellectual agenda: in spite of the references to major theological texts, he indicates that his spiritual regeneration was only secured when he abandoned reason and accepted the arguments of an uneducated preacher. The rhetoric of persuasion is, again, vital to the narrative. Rationalism is implicitly rejected by Spurgeon, who suggests that acquiescence is the only legitimate response to the gospel call to repentance.

Spurgeon recalls that the inexpert evangelist addressed the admonition directly to him. This is an important moment in the account, reinforcing Spurgeon's position as the centre of the drama, separating him from the other members of the congregation. For the Evangelical believer conversion is not a collective experience:

> Just fixing his eyes on me, as if he knew all my heart, he said, "Young man, you look very miserable." ... He continued, " and you always will be miserable – miserable in life, and miserable in death, – if you don't obey my text; but if you obey now, this moment, you will be saved ... he shouted, as only a Primitive Methodist could do, "Young man, look to Jesus Christ. Look! Look! Look! You have nothin' to do but to look and live." I saw at once the way of salvation. (1897, p. 106)

The expected apotheosis of the narrative, when the new convert experiences a surpassing sense of ecstasy is fulfilled. Spurgeon uses a long established vocabulary of imprisonment and release to describe the experience of post-conversion rapture, alluding to Psalm 40:

> I thought I could have sprung from the seat on which I sat, and have called out with the wildest of those Methodist brethren who were present, "I am forgiven ... A sinner saved by blood!" My spirit saw its chains broken to pieces, I felt that I was an emancipated soul, an heir of Heaven, a forgiven one, accepted in Christ Jesus, plucked out of the miry clay and out of the horrible pit, with my feet set upon a rock. (p. 108)

The identification with 'the wildest of those Methodist brethren', and the spontaneous wish to share in their ecstatic mode of worship indicates Spurgeon's joining the 'body of Christ' represented by the Church. His use of phrases integral to the Christian narrative is crucial. The classic locution, 'A sinner saved by blood', is particularly significant as it is not simply an overjoyed utterance but a statement of doctrinal orthodoxy. Conversion, as Brad Kallenberg argues, is at least partly a matter of language acquisition (Kallenberg, 1995, p. 354). Whether or not these precise phrases were used by Spurgeon at his conversion is not very important. It is vital, however, in interpreting a moment of crisis, presumably some years after the event, that Spurgeon could accommodate the 'great change' to his doctrinal framework. Spurgeon confidently asserts that in a poorly attended Primitive Methodist Chapel, on a Sabbath morning in January, 1850 he was saved by acknowledgement of the blood of Jesus Christ. There is a strong impression of retrospective joy:

> I could understand what John Bunyan meant, when he declared he wanted to tell the crows on the ploughed land all about his conversion. He was too full to hold, he felt he must tell somebody. (Spurgeon, 1897, p. 108)

It is important that Spurgeon refers directly to Bunyan, in many ways the father of the Puritan conversion narrative, making him a principal member of the *dramatis personae* of his conversion. This is a means of asserting continuity between past and present faith communities. Nineteenth-century Evangelicalism was extremely suspicious of the concept of 'tradition', connecting it with the apostasy of those who seceded to Rome, and yet it needed a way of connecting the believers of the past with those of the present. Bunyan became a mythical figure for Victorian Evangelicals, and his narrative of pilgrimage viewed as a site of stability and truth. To identify with Bunyan, as Spurgeon does here, was to locate oneself in an enduring lineage of 'pure' gospel ministers, committed to evangelism and free from worldly interests. Spurgeon's account of the 'great change' concludes with an affirmation of his faith in Christ: 'Has Jesus saved *me*? I dare not speak with any hesitation here; *I know* He has. His Word is true, therefore I *am* saved' (Spurgeon, 1897, p.112).

However, Spurgeon was less convinced of the redemption of the vast crowds that attended his meetings in the Music Hall of the Royal Surrey Gardens, many of whom he believed came simply to be entertained. A sermon entitled 'Turn or Burn', delivered at this venue on 7 December 1856, exemplifies his aggressive conversion focused ministry. The apocalyptic locution, 'Turn or Burn', is actually derived from Baxter: 'Earnest Baxter used to say, "Sinner! turn or burn; it is thy only alternative: Turn or Burn!"' (Spurgeon, 1856, p. 421). The sermon, an exposition of Psalm 7.12, reads as a statement of intent for the renewed Puritan community. It attacks the religious lassitude of the age, and contends that an insidious liberalism has undermined the authority of the call to conversion. The future judgment, argues Spurgeon, is no longer at the centre of preaching and is not accorded due solemnity. The message of mercy, preached by the majority of clergymen, is incomplete and, therefore, deceptive:

> of what avail is it to preach mercy unless they preach also the doom of the wicked? And how shall we hope to effect the purpose of preaching unless we warn men that if they "turn not, he will whet his sword?" I fear that in too many places the doctrine of future punishment is rejected. (Spurgeon, 1856, pp. 417–18).

Spurgeon did not interpret the terrors of the future judgment, delineated in the book of Revelation, as metaphor. It was literal truth, a 'reality' that was the fate of fallen humanity, to be experienced both by the damned and the regenerate. The sermon is a stern summons to immediate, and unequivocal conversion. After the initial warning of the imminence and reality of God's judgment, the preacher focuses on the meaning of Psalm 7.12: 'The turning here meant is *actual*, not fictitious – not that which stops with promises and vows, but that which deals with real acts of life' (p. 418). Spurgeon describes conversion as a practical, *literal* act of turning away from sinful deeds. Yet he argues that a sudden sense of conviction for personal sin, and an attendant desire for redemption is not sufficient to indicate genuine conversion: 'There must be a true and actual abandonment of sin, and a turning unto righteousness in real act and deed in every-day life' (p. 418).

Conversion, for Spurgeon, had to be visible. There is a tension here between the insistence on *sola fides* for salvation and the scriptural assertion that faith without works is dead. Evangelicalism may be the 'religion of the heart' but in the Victorian age its major exponents expected converts to provide explicit proof of their regeneration: 'Repentance to be true, to be evangelical, must be a repentance which really affects our outward conduct'(p. 418). For Spurgeon 'Evangelical' repentance seems to be close to the New Testament *metanoia*, the divinely ordained 'change of heart' that results in salvation:

> Do you feel that God has changed your heart and renewed your nature? If not, I beseech you lay hold of this thought, that unless you be renewed all that can be dreadful in the torments of the future world must inevitably be yours. (p. 423)

This is Spurgeon as master of persuasion, appealing not merely to the mass of men, but to the individual. The sermon develops from doctrinal exposition to personal testimony, and Spurgeon tells the story of his conversion. He again describes the 'despised people' of the 'peculiar sect' with whom he found 'God's mercy', recalls the direct address of the preacher, and the immediately perceptible change that accompanied this moment of crisis:

> and in that moment I hope by his grace I looked upon Jesus, and though desponding, downcast and ready to despair, and feeling that I could rather die than live as I had lived, at that very moment it seemed as if a young heaven had its birth within my conscience ... those about me, noticing the change, asked me why I was glad, and I told them that I had believed in Jesus. (1856, p. 424)

In presenting his own story of salvation to the congregation, Spurgeon enacts an important ritual of reinforcement: he locates himself as a living part of the Christian grand-narrative, in the same story-line as St Paul and Bunyan. The listener could dispute doctrine, but not the 'evidence' of his own experience, resonating clearly with the Puritan narrative, and standing before the congregation as proof of the regenerative power of belief. Potential converts were presented with a new frame of reference in which to view their own anxieties and hopes. As Lewis Rambo has argued, public testimony has a twin function within religious communities: the act of 'biographical re-shaping' strengthens the commitment of the narrator, and the body of believers is similarly galvanised by the affirmation of its interpretative scheme: 'Audience and speaker form a powerful matrix of support and reinforcement' (Eliade, 1987, p. 77).

Spurgeon's emphasis on individual conversion as a vital part of the divine plan was, arguably, a reason for his popularity. In an age of anxiety regarding 'change', particularly after Darwin's *Origin of Species* (1859), Spurgeon negotiated the tension between the permanence of God and the necessity of personal transformation. Victorians who feared that the major sign-posts of belief were threatened by the new intellectual discourses may have found reassurance in the literalist hermeneutic defended by this Baptist preacher. His calls to conversion offered escape from the *zeitgeist* of doubt and a sense of integration with the sacred narrative of the Christian faith. Whatever the challenges of the age, Spurgeon maintained that there was only one legitimate question, What must I do to be saved? And how can I escape from the great damnation that awaiteth me? (Spurgeon, 1857, p. 192).

Acknowledgements

I would like to thank my doctoral supervisor Professor Michael Wheeler for many important discussions that helped shape my thinking in writing this chapter. I am also grateful to the staff of St Deiniol's residential library, where much of the research for the chapter was undertaken.

Chapter Two

Fortress Catholicism: The Art of Ultramontanism at Notre Dame de Fourvière

Nancy Davenport

Sin, Heresy, and Notre Dame de Fourvière

In A.D. 180 Irenaeus, archbishop in Lyon of France's first diocese,[1] wrote grimly and passionately about heretics. 'Slippery as snakes, they seek to break out in all directions' (Irénée de Lyon). In the same city over seventeen hundred years later, Pierre Bossan (1814–1888) and Marie-Louis-Jean Perrin (Sainte-Marie Perrin 1835–1917), ecclesiastical architects and themselves rigorous defenders of orthodoxy, designed a large mosaic roundel depicting a writhing snake with its jaws clamped on a branch bearing the 'apple of discord' (Figure 2.1). They placed it on the floor of the choir directly in front of the main altar dedicated to the Virgin Immaculate in the great new Ultramontane basilica of Notre Dame de Fourvière in Lyon. Behind this roundel and in the chancel, they placed a second mosaic, like the first in its design, depicting the apocalyptic Seven-Headed Beast crowned with seven crowns from the Book of Revelation (XII.3) (Figure 2.2). These two creatures, the Alpha and the Omega, represent mankind born into Sin and condemned into eternity. To the left of the latter roundel, a third, one of the series of ten that encircles the altar, has on it three worms gnawing on the Eucharistic vine (Figure 2.3). The worms represent those who secretly and relentlessly destroy the very foundation mystery of the Church itself, the grapes of the Sacramental wine. This mosaic is labeled *NATURALISM* and bears the date 1884, the year of the Papal Bull *Humanum Generis*, a manifesto of conservative Catholic orthodoxy that attacked the 'Naturalists' and other proponents of secular Modernist society. The title and date on the eight other mosaics in this series links each to an historical heresy illustrated by one or more vicious creatures. In the apse of the dark and low crypt that stretches the entire length of the nave and directly below the nave altar and its heresy mosaics, ten other mosaic roundels encircle the altar dedicated to St. Joseph. The subjects of this series, each represented by means of an animal and an inscription, are Hell, Death, Sin, and the Seven Deadly Sins (Figure 2.4).

The placement of these threatening images seems not fortuitous. The officiating clergy trample them daily as they offer Mass for the living and the dead, smudging the pale stone tesserae but never obliterating or even diminishing the threat they embody: that sin, corruption, and false prophets are an ever-present danger to the

38 *Reinventing Christianity*

Figure 2.1 *Serpent eating the Apple of Discord*, Choir Mosaic in the nave, S.M. Perrin, 1886–96, N.D. de Fourvière, Lyon.

Fortress Catholicism 39

Figure 2.2 *Seven-headed Beast*, **Pencil drawing for Chancel Mosaic in the nave, S.M. Perrin, 1886–96, N.D. de Fourvière, Lyon.**

Church. It is remarkable how resoundingly these two series of mosaics express the ideology of their makers. It is, therefore, to these mosaics installed between 1896 and 1914 to encircle the two altars, and to their form, their iconographic sources, their meaning, and their powerful message, that this research has been directed.

Briefly, the history of the conception and the construction of Notre Dame de Fourvière is as follows. The lyonnais architect Pierre Bossan sketched his first plans for a *fortress church* (*église fortresse*) at Fourvière in honor of the Immaculate Virgin while on a visit in 1846 to the great Norman Byzantine basilicas in Montreale and Palermo (Thiollier, 1891). At that time, there was little or no interest in his project in Lyon. Ten years later, an engraver named Séon made a print which was widely circulated from Bossan's plans. It was entitled: Early Project for Notre Dame de Fourvière approved by his Eminence the Cardinal de Bonald (*Avant-*

Figure 2.3 *NATURALISM, Vigne et les vers*, **Chancel Mosaic in the nave, S.M. Perrin, 1886–96, N.D. de Fourvière, Lyon.**

Projet de N.D. de Fourvière apprové par son Em. le Cardinal de Bonald), who was the then archbishop of Lyon (Figure 2.5). By 1856, apparently, his project had gained the attention of the Church hierarchy. On October 8, 1870, when German armies were threatening to overrun Lyon, Ultramontane Catholic leaders made a solemn vow to transform a 12th-century chapel dedicated to Mary into the great basilica dedicated to the Immaculate Conception (received dogma after Pope Leo III's Bull of 1854 *Ineffabilis Deus*) that Bossan had imagined, if their city escaped invasion. When, in fact, it did, church leaders moved quickly. The first stone for the basilica was blessed by the Archbishop of Lyon, Monseigneur Ginoulhiac, on December 7, 1872. Money to construct the basilica was raised by private solicitation in Lyon, by Joannès Blanchon's (1819–97) indefatigable efforts as editor of the journal *l'Echo de Fourvière* to rally the widespread international devotion to the

Figure 2.4 *The Cardinal Sins*, mosaic, program encircling altar in chancel of crypt, 1887–1914, N.D. de Fourvière, Lyon.

Figure 2.5 *Avant-projet de N.D. de Fourvière*, engraving, Séon, 1856–7.

doctrine of the Immaculate Conception, and by the astute statecraft of the lyonnais church hierarchy in the Vatican and among the regular clergy worldwide.

Pierre Bossan and Sainte-Marie Perrin, Architects of Fourvière

Pierre Bossan, who had been appointed chief architect of the project, moved from Lyon to La Ciotat in Provence almost as soon as the work began in the 1870s. His reasons for doing so are not clear, although both his poor health and his inclination to a life of monastic solitude seemed to have weighed heavily in his decision. He relinquished all daily operations at the site to a young lyonnais architect of his own choosing, Marie-Louis-Jean Perrin [Sainte-Marie Perrin] (1835–1917), 'imbued with his ardor and his faith' (Thiollier, 1891, p. 4) and employed at the time in the architectural office of Tony Desjardins in Lyon. Sainte-Marie Perrin, conscientious and self-effacing, calling himself in a letter to Bossan 'only an echo',[2] in another asked '... for pardon for the inconveniences which I have caused you from the beginning because of my spirit of independence ... against which I must often struggle and which has often conquered me'.[3] He dutifully executed all of Bossan's directives transmitted to him by mail, by mutual friends, or by personal directives during his regular visits to La Ciotat. Often, Sainte-Marie Perrin had either to cajole or to maneuver a path around both the Church hierarchy, the generous but opinionated donors who paid all the bills, and Bossan. When too heavily pressed to compromise on issues that were important to him, Bossan simply refused either to answer urgent letters or to make any decisions at all. When Bossan died in 1888, Perrin took over the entire project and remained in charge of it until his death thirty years later. In a letter from a Jesuit dated 9 November 1891, it was he, rather than Bossan, who was given the credit for Fourvière. 'Allow me to tell you of my profound admiration for the wondrous work to which you have consecrated your life. The Holy Virgin has prepared a beautiful place for you and your loved ones in heaven in return for the home which you have built for her on earth'.[4] In truth, Fourvière belongs to both Bossan and Sainte-Marie Perrin, the first the visionary, the second the devoted disciple. In the Cemetery of Louasse behind Fourvière, Bossan's rough white stone burial marker, crowned by a Byzantine palmette and bearing the crudely incised letters of his name painted in rusty red like some early Christian burial *titulus*, is a stark reminder of his spectral and visionary role in the creation of Lyon's most visible and controversial monument.

The extravagant basilica project generated ideological passion from both sides of the aisle throughout its construction: vitriol from the left (Liberals, Gallican Catholics, secularists) encomia from the right (monarchists and conservative Catholics). The favorite liberal metaphor for it was that of an upside down elephant, That is, a kind of enormous and unwieldy exotic, its four enormous towers like the animal's legs pointing futilely toward the heavens (Hardouin-Fugier, 1982). From the contrary persuasion, inflated support for it in the conservative Catholic press prophesied that the basilica would become a wellspring of spiritual regeneration, eliciting '... in their unanimous outpouring of praise, the fervor of the city, of France, and of all Christianity' (Thiollier, 1891, p. 4). Irrespective of these wordy enemies and friends in the press, the builders and fund raisers of Fourvière never stopped working, and in 1896, a mere twenty-four years after construction had begun, Notre Dame de Fourvière, nearly built if only partially decorated, was inaugurated by the Archbishop of Lyon, Monseigneur Coullié.

Motivation and Meaning at Fourvière

Today, the basilica stands tall, like a giant citadel, above the city between the rivers Saône and Rhône far below. It can be seen from every section of the city. Tourists and pilgrims still climb up to visit it. The citizens of Lyon still take sides about it, many preferring their 4th-century Gothic Cathedral of St. Jean in the old city directly below to the *église fortresse* on the hill.

But while it is difficult to ignore the building itself, its extensive program of decoration seems largely to have been overlooked, the one recent exception being a chapter by Hardouin-Fugier in *Voir, Revoir Fourvière* entitled 'Le poème mariale' [Poem in honor of the Virgin Mary] (Hardouin-Fugier, 1988, p. 176). Such neglect is surprising in the face of Fourvière's decorative grandiloquence. Massive red and white granite piers support its vaults. Appealing nesting and preening stone doves and glittering gold and aquamarine mosaic peacocks and palmettes turn up unexpectedly in corners and on capitals and on its soaring twenty-seven meter high vertical surfaces. Enormous rectangular narrative mosaics cover its nave walls, some of them illustrating many separate episodes by means of smaller inserts and overlays. (An example of these is the mosaic illustrating the life and martyrdom of the saint par excellence for Ultramontane monarchists, St. Joan of Arc entitled *Epopée de la libération de la Patrie à travers la vie de Jeanne d'Arc, inspirée et guidée par Dieu* [Epic celebrating the Liberation of the homeland through the life of Joan of Arc, inspired and directed by God], on the south side of the nave, designed by Charles Décôte, and completed between 1908 and 1917.) The scale and narrative breadth of these mosaics suggest the Norman Byzantine churches of Palermo that inspired Bossan's first drawings, although their compositions are vast High Renaissance perspective grids. Behind the altar are six tripartite Gothic stained glass lancet windows. One might conclude from these interwoven Gothic, Byzantine, and Renaissance motives that Fourvière was either (1) a product of high Victorian materialistic splendor or (2) an exotic unorthodox extravaganza embodying the visions of someone like the Symbolist painter Gustave Moreau (1826–98).

In some respects, it was both of these, but its creators also had political goals. For throughout the long process of construction and decoration, its builders and supporters were both constrained and motivated by their initial vow in 1870 to rededicate France to the Catholic Church and, as a corollary, to a revived Catholic Monarchy through devotion to the Immaculate Virgin. As Ultramontanists, a term literally meaning those whose allegiance was to leaders from across the mountains (i.e. the Vatican), they campaigned for a universal Roman Catholic Church that was more strongly centralized both in governance and in doctrine, and correspondingly, for a decrease in power of the Gallican church and the secular liberal state in all matters of the faith.

A quotation from Ultramontanist Joseph Marie de Maistre's *Les Soirées de Saint-Petersbourg*, written just after the French Revolution when the author was in Russia and quoted, in part, by Sainte-Marie Perrin in his text on the symbolism of Fourvière published in 1896,[5] suggests the longevity and continuity of rage and despair that fired the men and women who banked their lives and much of their fortunes on Fourvière.

> So deep is the sorrow of these men that they no longer can even wish for their own regeneration, not only because, as is well known, one cannot desire what one does not know, but also because they find themselves frighteningly caught up their own moral decrepitude ... such is the man who no longer prays; and if the official church (there is no greater proof of its indispensable necessity) does not do something to oppose this universal degradation, I believe, on my honor, that we will in the end all become veritable beasts. (de Maistre, 1993, p. 567)

Sainte-Marie Perrin himself wrote in 1897, 'Religious architecture is going through a terrible time. Who is now interested in it? The flow of ideas lies elsewhere. Christian faith seems ancient and more than a bit out of date to our contemporaries'.[6] Mourning the world *sans Dieu* [without God] was a popular pastime in Ultramontane Catholic publications in the 19th-century. The basilica at Fourvière, not unlike its counterpart, l'Eglise du Sacré-Coeur on the hill of the martyrs (Montmartre) for Ultramontane Catholics in Paris, embodied the hopes and prayers of believers in Lyon, among whom were the architects, mosaicists, sculptors, glaziers, and muralists who had been longtime associates in the architecture and decoration of churches and monasteries, 39 of them, according to Bossan's biographer, Félix Thiollier, in the dioceses of Lyon and Belley. The complexity and breadth of Fourvière's iconographic programs, the richness and diversity of its building materials, its dynamic control over its hilltop site, were all persuasive weapons meant to awe, to inspire, and finally to recover for the faith the fractured Catholic population of France.

The interdependent and polemical energy of the Fourvière design is particularly evident in the plan and decoration of the tall semicircular apse structure which houses both the altar in the crypt, the one in the nave, and their respective encircling mosaic roundels. It is the one section of the basilica that was largely complete before the death of Bossan in 1888. Hardouin-Fugier has characterized this apse as '... a gigantic battle of Good against Evil ... the iconographic axis of Fourvière, which is the universal theme of this monument as it is of the history of the world' (Hardouin-Fugier, 1988, p. 175). Her diagram from *Miniguide de Fourvière* reveals the powerful axis created by the spear of St. Michael thrusting vertically downward into the dragon, which then acts metaphorically as a lynch pin connecting the bronze archangel warrior to the white marble *Immaculata* in the nave and to Joseph on the altar in the crypt around which the heresies and cardinal sins, respectively, revolve (Figure 2.6). Standing on the north side of the apse below the plaza that acts as a lookout site to the city below, one can most fully experience the physical synergy of this design concept, which integrates architecture, sculpture, and mosaic to order to evoke the tensions of an eternal *psychomachia*. In a similar fashion, Bossan intended that believers who climbed from the dark crypt excavated out of the steep slope of the hill and dedicated to the earthly life of the Virgin (Hardouin-Fugier 1988, 1983) into the brightly lit nave above it dedicated to the Virgin's miracles and mysteries would understand their ascent as a pilgrimage leading to revelation. His design was, in other words, intended to be experiential, providing emotional as well as spiritual transformations for the pious visitor who would unlock its mysteries. As a church built on the scale of the Gothic cathedrals but, unlike the latter, built within the lifetimes and under the tight control of one generation of architects and designers dedicated to their God and to their task, no iconographic or structural detail capable of embodying liturgical meaning seems to have been ignored.

Animal Imagery at Fourvière

The meanings one expects to find are not, however, equally accessible. For instance, while the mosaic narratives in the nave clearly illustrate events in Church and Marian history that celebrate tradition and hierarchy,[7] the purpose of some of the veritable honor guard, or perhaps carnival, of sculpted and mosaic animals at Fourvière is more elusive. Thus, when Sainte-Marie Perrin asked Emile Mâle's opinion about the bestiary he had designed to illustrate his heresy mosaics, this scholar of medieval iconography who had recently published his seminal studies on the subject for the 12th and 13th centuries both praised the architect-designer in a spirit of generosity for his creativity but also gently pointed out its non-canonical nature. 'Your symbolism is extremely ingenious', Mâle wrote. 'The relationships

46 Reinventing Christianity

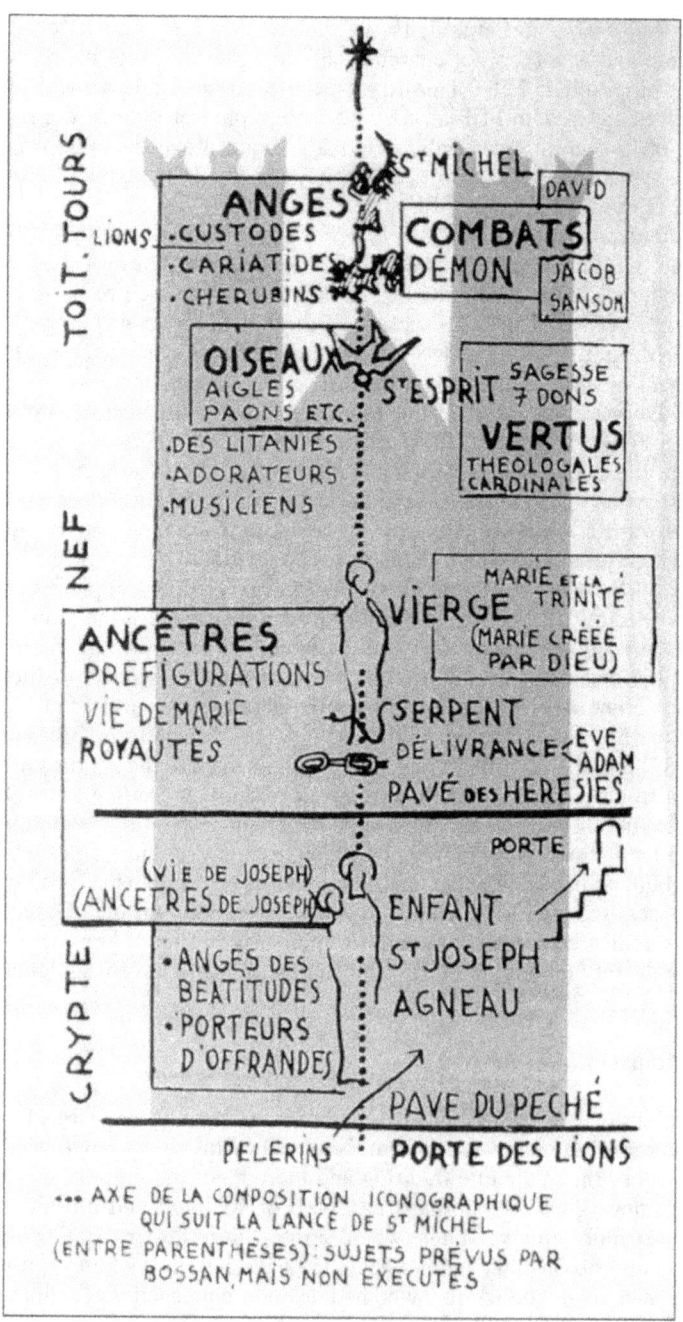

Figure 2.6 Cross-section of Fourvière apse with decorative program indicated. E. Hardouin, Fugier, *Miniguide de Fourvière*, p. 57.

that you have established between the heresies, the animals and the Biblical texts are very felicitous. I believe that the early symbol makers of the 12th century would have approved of these combinations. It would have been hard for them to have done any better; for in these cases, there is no tradition; one must invent it all' (Sainte-Marie Perrin, 1896, p. 26).

Hardouin-Fugier has provided the names of some of Bossan's and Sainte-Marie Perrin's tutors in matters of symbolism. In addition to Emile Mâle, she identified Chanoine Didelot, Curé of the Cathedral at Valence who Bossan met in 1858; A. de Boissieu of Lyon 'whose interventions in this case are recognized'; and a book from Bossan's library, *Le Cité Mystique*, the visions of the sixteenth century Spanish mystic Marie-Jesus de Agréda, which proves to be generally in agreement with all of the Marian imagery at Fourvière (Hardouin-Fugier, 1988, pp. 178–9). With the exception of the latter Spanish text, however, little has been attributed specifically to the writings or thought of any of the above-mentioned ecclesiastical and scholarly mentors. Since it is unlikely that the traditionalist Sainte-Marie Perrin would have worked without benefit of an historical precedent, tracking the multitude of Fourvière animals at least to the vicinity of their original literary and pictorial lairs is, therefore, essential in any serious investigation of the iconographic program at Fourvière.

Some of the choices of animals can be easily explained. On the outside of the basilica, for instance, they borrow their character and form from the ancient pre-Christian concept of guardian deities. Charles Dufraine's monumental winged lion, an embodiment both of the city of Lyon and of the Lion of Judah guarding Solomon's Temple, reclines in front of the bronze doors of the basilica on the projecting stone platform that overhangs the entrance to the crypt. Without his arcing wings, this lion would have nearly replicated the reclining felines that guard the ceremonial passageway at Karnak. In the spandrels above the three arches on the facade, the four Evangelist symbols, cow, lion, eagle, and angel, with their giant wings outstretched as if to echo the prophecy about them in *Ezekiel*, also closely resemble ancient guardian dieties (Figure 2.7). The column capitals at the entrance to the basilica from the crypt replicate the horned animal capitals at Persepolis. These ferocious creatures, all outside the light-filled nave of the Virgin Immaculate, characterize the stern Old Testament world *sub lege*.

The nave itself resembles an aviary. Along the walls and around the altar rail are both sculpted and mosaic pelicans, peacocks, soaring eagles, and tufted doves, representing respectively, Christ's sacrifice, his Resurrection, Christian souls yearning for the Eucharist, and the Holy Spirit. The doves, in particular, are everywhere, nestling around the bases of columns, in the grape vines on reliefs, in unexpected places on marble railings and church furniture; '... birds of passage resting on the capitals, symbols of pilgrims' (Thiollier, 1891, p. 7).

The striking utilization of animal imagery to represent the Heresies of the church, the Cardinal Sins, and Death is, on the contrary, hidden away, visible only to the clergy serving at the altar and to those persons kneeling to receive the Eucharist at the altar rail, in other words only to persons in a state of grace. Sainte-Marie Perrin illustrates the Cardinal Sins in his text on the symbolism of the basilica, but does not discuss them (Sainte-Marie Perrin, 1896, pp. 24–5). In a general sense, little explanation is needed. Like the marble snakes that writhe around the column base

Figure 2.7 *Facade of N.D. de Fourvière*, Lyon, 1872–1964.

on which the Virgin Immaculate stands and like the inscriptions on three roundels below St. Joseph in the crypt (*Stipendia Peccati Mors* [The wages of sin are death], *Habeo Claves Inferni* [I hold the key to Hell], and *Vade Retro Satanas* [Get thee behind me, Satan]), they represent, as do the heresies, the ominous and ever-present threat of evil in this otherwise triumphal holy place. Yet, while they were and are sequestered behind the altar rail and although they were not completed until 1914 long after Bossan's death in 1888, the magnetic pole of Bossan's original grand design for the apse lies in them.

The Mosaics of the Cardinal Sins in the Crypt

The history of the codification of the Cardinal Sins is an ancient one. The Egyptian cenobite, Evagrius of Pontus, (d. A.D. 400) seems to have been the first to have given them form. John Cassian (d. A.D. 435), a student of Evagrius' who settled in Marseille, disseminated his teacher's ideas in the west through his own writings (Bloomfield, 1952, p. 57). Each of the Cardinal Sins, which Cassian identified as *Gula, Luxuria, Avaritia, Ira, Tristitia, Acedia, Vana Gloria,* and *Superbia,* is the subject of a book in his *Institutes*. Pope Gregory the Great (d. A.D. 604) also wrote a lengthy discourse on the Cardinal Sins in his *Moralia,* a commentary on Christian ethics based on the *Book of Job*. Gregory singled out *Superbia* as the root of all sin. Gregory's text, written in Constantinople, was disseminated throughout the Eastern Church while Cassian's, written in France and copied largely by Irish monks, was the model for the West. A third commentator on the Cardinal Sins, Henry of Susa, in the 13th century, in his *Summa super titulis decretalium*, also privileged *Superbia* as the first of the Cardinal Sins. And first it remained. 'Pride meant rebellion, dangerous independent thinking, setting up one's own interest as supreme, meant disobedience, upsetting the divinely appointed order, and – above all – ultimately heresy' (Grundmann, 1927, p. 94). It is first as well in the crypt at Fourvière, where *Superbia* represented by a peacock proudly displaying his plumage is to be found directly in front of the statue of St. Joseph on the altar (Figure 2.8).[8]

Traditional illustrations of the Cardinal Sins in illuminated manuscripts utilized a number of formats – the ladder, the wheel, the tree, and particular allegorical, historical or contemporary personages standing, seated, or riding on appropriate animals. The one of most interest to this study is, of course, the one used at Fourvière, the representation of each sin by a different animal (Bloomfield, 1952, p. 103). This formulation, well-established by the High Middle Ages, had been initiated 'within the cultural orbit of Alexandria, and in the Roman province of Egypt or Syria' (Theobaldus Episcopus) with the work of an anonymous Greek Christian who wrote the original *Physiologus* in the second century A.D. This early bestiary related particular behaviors of animals as recorded in classical natural history texts with the purposes of God and the nature of man. The immediate popularity of the *Physiologus* is evident from the fact that it was widely referred to by learned early Christians such as Tertullian, Origen, and Clement of Alexandria. In the early 12th century, relying on versions of the *Physiologus* as well as on other sources available to him, Honorius of Autun produced his learned study *Speculum ecclesiae*. It is to this great encyclopedist that Sainte-Marie Perrin's correspondent

Figure 2.8 *SUPERBIA*, **mosaic in front of altar in chancel of crypt, 1887–1914, N.D. de Fourvière, Lyon.**

Emile Mâle gives credit for most of the symbolic imagery on the cathedrals of France (Mâle, 1972, p. 45).

What might the iconographers at Fourvière have learned from Honorius' text? Strangely enough, not a lot. They might have learned about the horned billy goat that charges across their mosaic to represent *Luxuria*. But then they might have learned that almost anywhere. Wrote E. Topsell in *The History of Four-Footed Beasts and Serpents and Insects*, 'There is no beast that is more prone and given to lust than is a Goat, for he joyneth in copulation before all other beasts' (Topsell, 1658, p. 181). Not surprisingly, the bestial habits of the goat, often seen in medieval manuscripts and on portals, were not engaged in the conservative Ultramontane mosaic at Fourvière. The goat's horns, his springing posture, and charging gait have been subsumed into the circular format of the mosaic, making him look more like the astrological sign of Capricorn than like his lascivious medieval forebears.

The other animals selected for the crypt mosaics had been less often singled out as Cardinal Sinners than the almost universally recognized peacock and goat. Precedents can be found for them, but these may not always have been the particular sources used by the mosaic designers at Fourvière. *Acedia* at Fourvière is, for instance, a lumbering tortoise. This creature, although by nature well suited for the role, had been rarely called on to fill it (Wenzel, 1967, p. 107). One instance when it was, however, was in a book first published in France, then in Wurzburg in 1732, and then in twelve editions in the United States in the mid 19th-century entitled *The Heart of Man, either a Temple of God or a habitation of Satan* (Johannes Evangelist Gossner, 1822. The British Museum Catalogue lists a German edition, printed at Augsburg, 1824, with the title *Das Herz des menschen, ein tempel Gottes, oder eine Werkstatte des Satans* as edited by Johann Gossner (1773–1858) and Philipp Friedrich Poeschl. Deutsches anon.-lex. 1501–1850 lists a German edition, with this same title, printed at Augsburg, 1815, as written by Johann Gossner and Phil. Friedrich Poeschl. Reports the British Museum entry, 'This little work was translated from the French and at the earnest request of some pious persons, was published in the year 1732 at Wurtzburg, by the engraver of the University, with the following title: Spiritual mirror of morality'). All the illustrations in this book are of the same large human heart, into and out of the center of which animals representing the Cardinal Sins move, in response to the ever-changing spiritual health of the soul (Figure 2.9). The author of this text wrote, 'The slow paced *tortoise* is an emblem of indolence and (indifference) lukewarmness, which deprives man of all disposition and will to do good'.

In and out of this same heart move other animals used at Fourvière: *Ira* (Anger) as a snarling striped tiger, *Invidia* (Treachery) as a dragon/snake, *Superbia* (Pride) as a peacock, *Luxuria* (Lasciviousness) as a lascivious goat. That as many of the same animals appear on the roundels as in the book strongly suggests that it may have been in the possession of the pious builders of Fourvière, ever mindful themselves that hearts are temples both of God and Satan (Gossner, 1822, pp. 9–10).

With respect to the other animals illustrating the Cardinal Sins, the use of a mastiff or wolf with one bone in his mouth and one under his left front paw to represent *Gula* (Gluttony), while not unknown, is as uncommon as the use of the tortoise for *Acedia*. The sin was commonly represented, as in the above text illustrating 'the heart of man', by a pig. There is, however, a 16th-century woodcut from Bavaria, which illustrates *Gula* by an image of two dogs snarling over a bone. While Sainte-Marie Perrin could hardly have seen this tiny woodcut on the border of a manuscript housed in the Bibliothèque Nationale, one may imagine some common model from which both drew their inspiration (Figure 2.10).

The most unusual, seemingly almost inappropriate, animal used to illustrate a Cardinal Sin at Fourvière is the long ant-like creature with wings folded along its back surrounded by twelve smaller ants representing *Avarita* (Greed). One scholar's list of the most commonly represented symbols of *Avarita* includes the ape, the elephant, the wolf, the squirrel, the mole, the badger, the hedgehog, the toad, the tortoise, the ass, and the crocodile (Chew, 1954, p. 49). Ants, on the other hand, were generally considered to be generous, provident, and prudent creatures (Cahier, 1874, p. 126). As early as the 6th-century, St. Gregory's *Moralia* described an insect called a mymicoleon or ant-lion (*Patrologia latina*, t. 75, caput XX.11.40, 43). The name and species have persisted. Entomologists still call the largest of the five families of myrmeleontoidea, ant-lions. They report that:

> The larvae of this species are terrestrial and many live at the bottom of tunnel-shaped pits in sand. When a potential prey insect or other small arthropod passes close to the pit, the antlion creates a miniature landslide, bringing the prey down within reach of its prehensile, sucking mandibles, and subsequently dines. (Rosomer and Stoffolano, 1994, p. 365)

Figure 2.9 *Das Bild des Ineren eines Menschen der der Sunde dienet und den Teufel in sich herrschen lässt*. J.E. Gossner, Herzbüchlein, Reading, Pa. 1822.

Figure 2.10 *Gula*, **Bavarian woodcut, 15th Century P.A. Lemoisne,** *Les Xylographies du XIVe et du XVe siecles au Cabinet des Estampes de la Bibliothèque Nationale*, **Paris, 1930, Vol. II, plate 102.**

St. Gregory was only slightly less perceptive and, of course, more moralistic about this insect. 'For the ant-lion is a very little creature', he wrote, 'a foe to ants, which hides itself under the dust and kills the ants laden with corn and devours them when killed' (*Patrologia Latina*, t. 75, caput XX.11.40). Gregory equates Satan with the lion, the tiger, and the ant-lion. Of the last of these, he wrote:

This same creature, the ant-lion, which hides in the dust and kills the ants carrying their corn, signifies the Apostate Angel, who being cast out of heaven upon the earth, besets the minds of the righteous in the very pathway of their practice, this is, providing for themselves the provender of good works; and whilst he overcomes them by his snares, he as it were kills them by surprise as the ants are carrying their corn. (Patrologia latina, t. 75, caput XX.11.43)

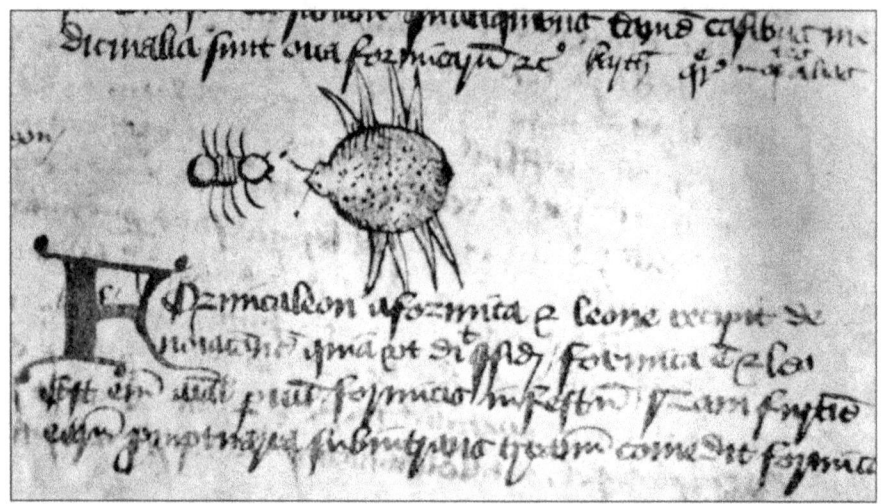

Figure 2.11 *Ant-lion and ant*, MS. Gg 6.5, 15th Century, University Library, Cambridge.

G.C. Druce, in 1923, published a tiny and crude illustration of this creature from a 15th century Latin manuscript (ms. Gg–6–5; University Library, Cambridge), and some link between Sainte-Marie Perrin's far more sophisticated and decorative illustration of the ant-lion bringing twelve tiny ants 'within reach of its prehensile sucking mandibles' and this one can be imagined (Figure 2.11) (Druce, 1923). From what source Sainte-Marie Perrin might have learned about the strange creature is unclear. Nonetheless, his decision to use the ant-lion was inspired. How better to depict *avaritia* than with a greedy 'ant-eater' preying on twelve tiny, patient, provident (apostolic?) ants.

In conclusion, reference to these earlier prototypes does not provide one single iconographic source for Sainte-Marie Perrin's sin-filled bestiary in the crypt. It does, however, reveal the traditions he followed and indicate deviations from the standard norms that he embraced. Sainte-Marie Perrin seems to have been eclectic in his tastes, turning, perhaps, to animals that permitted the creation of pleasing patterns in his mosaics – the ants, the tortoise shell, the stripes on the tiger, the peacock's tail feathers – or curvilinear forms and graceful contours that echoed the circular format – the serpent, the dragon, the charging goat – rather than to the animals that were more commonly used in earlier representations of the Cardinal Sins. While pious values prevailed, the value of sumptuous decoration was certainly not denied at Fourvière.

With respect to the above-noted decorative impetus, further stylistic sources can be postulated for the basilica. E. Mâle noted the close connection between medieval floor mosaics and the carpets brought into Europe from the Middle East in the 12th century. 'The oriental carpet on the floor often served as a model for the mosaic which was laid as the pavement in the sanctuary. Nothing could have been more natural than these imitations: the mosaic serving, itself, as a carpet...' (Mâle, 1924,

p. 346). One can imagine that the designers of Fourvière may have thought as well of exotic carpets, mosaics, and embroidery. As a young man and first conceiving Fourvière, Bossan himself would have seen the decorative Italo-Byzantine floor and vault mosaics and marble reliefs in Norman palaces and churches in Sicily and South Italy (Figure 2.12). The style of the mosaics are, in fact, combinations of realism and heraldic imagery. The animals are volumetric, suspended in empty space, appropriately covered with colorful feathers, scales, fur, or skin, and yet constrained by the frontal or profile requirements of heraldic reliefs. Some, like the animals in Medieval animal art, seem to have been drawn from experience, some are pure fantasy, others a combination of both, redesigned to fit a circular format.

There was, as well, a visual source closer to home in Lyon: the sculpted quattrofoil medallions influenced by many of the same exotic Byzantine sources on the facade of the cathedral of St. Jean. One of last roundels to be completed is labeled *Gehenna* on an Islamic horseshoe arch surrounding the heavily barred gate of Hell engulfed in flames. On top of this image is a second inscription noted above, *Habeo Claves Inferni* [I hold the Key to Hell]. This mosaic closely resembles, the only one to do so, one of these small quattrofoil medallions, that are stretched, a patchwork quilt of biblical narratives, fantastic creatures and fables, heraldic devices, and ribald marginalia, across the door jambs of the cathedral portals through which pious lyonnais had been passing since the 14th century (Figures 2.13 and 2.14).

By recognizing the appropriation of this one fantastic quattrofoil from among many on the cathedral portal as well as the wide-ranging use of obscure texts, one can measure the seriousness of the Fourvière iconographers' search to find appropriately heinous creatures and images to serve the pious purposes of their grand design.

The Heresy Mosaics in the Nave

Directly above the crypt in the apse, the sequence of heresy mosaics begins with the one directly below the Virgin on the altar noted on page 1, 'the medallion that the priest tramples on when he ascends to the altar' (Sainte-Marie Perrin, 1896, p. 24), representing the 'great red dragon, having seven heads and ten horns, and seven crowns upon his heads' from the Book of Revelation (XII.3). Rotating counter-clockwise and according to a chronological sequence, the nine heresy mosaics represented by animals would seem to have presented a difficult problem for any iconographer. For, unlike the Cardinal Sins, no pictorial tradition exists for the heresies. Therefore, searching for them in Emile Mâle's texts which relied so heavily on Vincent of Beauvais, would seem to be as bootless as searching for them in the illustrated bestiaries themselves. In the latter, the most vicious of carnivores or craven of carrion eaters, since they had all been created by God, often seemed to have been able to teach some lesson to the willing believer. And even if they embodied some evil tendencies as occurred in the crypt at Fourvière, they generally, in the bestiaries themselves, embodied some human virtue as well.[9]

Sainte-Marie Perrin, fully responsible for the execution of the heresy mosaics, seems to have labored mightily with this program, one perhaps envisioned for his

56 *Reinventing Christianity*

Figure 2.12 *Eagle* mosaic in center of ceiling, 12th Century, Salon of Roger, Royal Palace at Palermo, Sicily.

Figure 2.13 *Stone Medallion*, 14th Century facade of Cathedral of St. Jean, Lyon.

apse by Bossan before he died in 1888. In a folder at the Archives de Fourvière is an exchange of letters between the Vicar General in Lyon and Sainte-Marie Perrin, a number of pencil sketches, lists on scraps of paper, and pencil drawings of the heresies in Sainte-Marie Perrin's hand, and some printed and hand-colored sketches for the heresies. One proposed title was that of the 13th century heresy connected to Peter Waldo: *Valdeus 1215*. This one was, in the end, not included in the series. Another list suggests other possible titles: *Luthesus Calvinus + 1520* and *Jansenius Quesnelleus Innocentius X, Clemens XI 1713*, the latter suggesting that the founder of the Jansenists be linked with the Popes who condemned him. The decision about whether to combine in one image the Nestorian and Pelagian heresies, condemned in 431 at the Council of Ephesus, seems to have come up. A text exists for this mosaic, *Leo rugiens et ursus esuriens* [roaring lion and ravenous bear], as does a small pencil sketch of a large growling bear resting its front paws on the back of a lion. In the end, the idea was deleted. The letters between the Vicar General, M. Dechelette and Sainte-Marie Perrin were both written on 10 July 1891, five years before the completion of the project. Apparently, the architect had delivered his entire program of the heresies to the archbishopric for review. He seemed particularly interested in getting feedback on proper abbreviations for his heresies. And of even greater importance in that period of delicate political maneuvering in French religious circles, he also asked about whether to title the heresy which he

Figure 2.14 *GEHENNA*, mosaic behind altar in chancel of crypt, N.D. de Fourvière, Lyon.

planned to devote to the Reformation as Lutheran or Protestant. He received an answer, one might even suggest an order, from Dechelette. The cleric warned the architect not to modify the scriptural texts on the mosaics. 'It would be preferable, as much as is possible, to cite Holy Scripture precisely; you do it in all other cases; I would not wish for any exceptions'. He stated that he preferred the term Lutheranism to that of Protestantism. '*Lutheran*, in designating the founder of the heresy, offers a closer analogy to that of the other denominations'. Most of the heresies in the series are, in fact, named after their actual or putative founders. Archly, he added that 'our brothers the Protestants' might be more dismayed at seeing the latter than the former: that is, what would amount to an attack on the entirety of Protestantism rather than simply on one denomination of Protestants. While Sainte-Marie Perrin had simply indicated *oiseau de proie* [bird of prey] on one of this own lists, Dechelette states his preference for the symbol of the eagle, 'a more expressive and energetic demon' to represent Lutheranism. The Vicar General was a stickler for specificity, but remembering the nature of the ideology being proclaimed, this attention to dogmatic authority should come as no surprise.

An invaluable record in the Archives de Fourvière is a chart sketched in pencil in Sainte-Marie Perrin's hand dated 1890–1896, which specifically identifies each of the animals used on the mosaics. The chart is an essential tool in the identification of the heretical animals, many of which are generalized in form. Following the boar characterizing Arianism on the right of the altar on the chart, the creatures are listed as *requin* (shark), *serpent et petit oiseau* (snake and little bird), *épervier* (sparrow hawk), *renards* (foxes), *vampire* (bat), *aigle et l'agneau* (eagle and lamb), *vipère et le colombe* (viper and the dove), and *vigne et les vers* (vine and worms). Armed with this evidence, one may follow Sainte-Marie Perrin's tracks in his hunt for appropriate animals to symbolize the nine heresies.

Since it was to Emile Mâle's commendation about the iconographic program of his heresy series that Sainte-Marie Perrin himself turned, the scholar returns perforce to Mâle for clues. In *The Gothic Image*, there is a brief discussion of an ancient text entitled the *Clavis* of Melito. Mâle said of it, 'The so-called *Clavis* of Melito was published by Dom Pitra in the *Spicil. Solesm.* Paris, 1855, II and III. He made an unsuccessful attempt to prove that the work belonged to the second century'. He continued, 'Whatever its date, however, the book is of great interest. It is in the form of an encyclopaedia of nature, in which man, metals, flowers and animals are studied in turn' (Mâle, 1972, p. 32, n. 3). J.B. Pitra, a Benedictine working out of Solesme, the command post of the conservative interest in the revival of the use of the medieval Gregorian chant, was, in fact, a passionate advocate of what he called *Clavis Meltonius*. In a text of 659 pages, Pitra published the recensions of the Clavis manuscript in Latin, Greek, and Armenian that he had discovered in a long life devoted to research in the manuscript collections of Europe. At the end of the second volume, he provided a synopsis of his efforts, entitled *La Clef du symbolisme par Saint Meliton, Eveque de Sardes (vers 160)* (Pitra, 1884, p. 605). In it, he offered his evidence for the early date and the authorship of Saint Meliton of Sardis. Emile Mâle some forty years later and on the basis of his own scholarship argued for a date of the 9th or 10th century for the manuscript. Irrespective of this scholarly disagreement between Mâle and Pitra on chronology and authorship, however, there is strong internal evidence that Sainte-Marie Perrin made extensive use of this lengthy ancient/early medieval moralized glossary of natural history in developing the iconographic program for the heresies at Fourvière.

In the first place, unlike the authors of the standard bestiaries who devotedly followed each others' benevolent formulae and generally provided brief moralized fables of single behavioral patterns for each animal, the encyclopedic author of the *Clavis* listed a number of separate moralized behaviors for each animal, some benevolent, some malevolent. Each is related to an appropriate biblical reference. All nine of the malevolent animals on the heresy mosaics and on the chart in Sainte-Marie Perrin's writing can be found in the *Clavis* text: *aper* (*sanglier* [boar] on the chart), *piscis* (*requin* [shark] on the chart), *serpens* (*serpent* [snake] on the chart), accipiter (*épervier* [sparrow-hawk] on the chart and *vautour* [vulture] in Sainte-Marie Perrin's text on Fourvière's iconography),[10] *vulpes* (*renards* [foxes] on the chart), *vespertilio* (*vampire* [vampire] on the chart and *chauve-souris* [bat] in Sainte-Marie Perrin's text on Fourvière's iconography), *aquila* (*aigle* [eagle] on the chart and *un oiseau de proie* [a bird of prey] in Sainte-Marie Perrin's text on Fourvière's iconography), *vipera* (*vipère* [viper] on the chart), *vermis* (*vers* [worm] on the chart).

Secondly, of the biblical texts identified by book and verse in Dom Pitra's notes that the *Clavis* author used to legitimize the evil natures of these nine animals, five were used by Sainte-Marie Perrin himself in his text on the symbolism at Fourvière. The text for Arianism illustrated by the boar is in the *Clavis* manuscript: *Psalm*

80:13: 'The boar out of the wood doth waste it, and the wild beast of the field doth devour it'. The text for Nestorianism illustrated by a serpent is as well: *Genesis* 3:1: 'Now the serpent was more subtil than any beast of the field which the lord God had made. And he said unto the woman, Yea, hath God said, Ye shall not eat of every tree of the garden'. So is that for Iconoclasm illustrated by foxes consuming the Eucharistic vine: *Song of Solomon* 2:45: 'Take us the foxes, the little foxes, that spoil the vines', and that for Manichaeanism illustrated by a bat: Isaiah 2:20: 'In that day a man shall cast his idols of silver, and his idols of gold, which they made each one for himself to worship, to the moles and to the bats'. Sainte-Marie Perrin's Jansenist text illustrated by a viper is there as well: *Job* 20:16 'He shall suck the poison of asps: the viper's tongue shall slay him'.

Thirdly, evidence for the use of the *Clavis* manuscript is apparent in other texts Sainte-Marie Perrin used. For instance, *Habeo Claves Inferni* [I have the key of Hell] (*Revelation* 1.18: *Habeo claves mortis et inferorum* [I have the key of death of the lower regions) beneath the shrouded skeleton on the mosaic behind the altar in the crypt is used in the manuscript *Clavis* as part of the author's definition of the word *Clavis* itself. So is the quotation (*Revelation* V.5) he used in his text to describe his guardian lion 'Behold, the lion of the tribe of Judah'. And again, his quotation from *Psalm* XXXIV.3, 'Yea, the sparrow hath found an house, and the swallow a nest for herself, where she may lay her young' when he describes garlands of flowers and fruits as the shelter for small birds, is also in the *Clavis* manuscript. With so many animals and texts in common, one may conclude beyond a reasonable doubt that the iconographers at Fourvière discovered many of the demonic animals, moralized behaviors, and biblical texts they needed to legitimate their heresy *bestiary* within the pages of this devoutly and conscientiously produced 19th century publication. Perhaps Emile Mâle introduced the book to them; perhaps, since they seemed to take it more seriously than he, the Fourvière architects introduced it to Mâle.

And finally the Benedictine, Dom Pitra, like the artists of Fourvière, laid out in his text a challenge to his age and its religious artists to make authentic, traditional, and non-heretical Christian art following the text he had rediscovered. One can imagine Sainte-Marie Perrin taking up this challenge in his mosaics on the heresies. Pitra wrote,

> Ever since ancient Gnosticism, all heresies have overthrown recognized symbols, even those made of sculpture. It is curious to consider Jansenism as convulsionism. Is it not to the dryness of Gallicanism and to the rigidity of its compromise with the liberal and modern spirit, that we owe the feebleness of contemporary Christian art, the inept affectations of current imagery, the fastidious mediocrity of holy texts? Who now can produce another Raphael, whose powerful brush shook off secular shadows from the old symbols, who revived the proud faces of our Holy Fathers and painted in immortal colors, in a new gallery in the Vatican, an entire series of symbols from Melitus? (Pitra, 1884, p. 616).

If, historically, the Church's war against heresy may be said to have started in Lyon in the 2nd-century at the time of Iraeneus' *Contra Haeretica*, it is clear that the battle was still engaged in the 19th-century at Fourvière when Sainte-Marie Perrin himself wrote about his heresy mosaics: 'The Virgin Mary sees at her feet the trophies of her victories throughout the ages: the vanquished heresies' (Sainte-Marie Perrin, 1896, p. 24). He inscribed the Antiphon to the Third Nocturne of the Little Office of the Blessed Virgin Mary: 'Cunctas haereses sola intermisti in universo mundo' [Rejoice, O Virgin Mary, thou alone hast destroyed all heresies in the whole world] along the border of the sanctuary in the nave. He characterized the heresies identified by his *animaux malfaisants* [malevolent animals] as '... the principal theological errors which have unsettled the world' (Sainte-Marie Perrin, 1896, p. 24).

A brief history of the heresies selected by the Fourvière artists to represent the policies of the traditional Church with respect to orthodoxy offers a window into late 19th-century Ultramontane ideology in a shrinking Catholic world. Significantly, the date on each roundel marks the year in which the heresy identified on it was officially condemned by the established authority of the Church. The late 2nd century Arian Heresy, ravaging the early church as, the mosaic tells us, a boar might damage a vineyard, revolved around differences in belief about the nature of Christ before he become Man. The date on the roundel of 325 indicates the year of the Council of Nicaea where both the concepts of the followers of Bishop Arius were anathematized and the Nicene Creed, codification of orthodox belief, was created. The Macedonian heresy was concerned with a different aspect of doctrine, the nature of the Trinity. Its adherents questioned the *Consubstantiality* of the Holy Spirit with that of God the Father and God the Son. Since the Nicene Creed had already declared the unity of the Triune God, it remained for the Council of Constantinople in 381, the date given on this second roundel, to reconfirm the tenets of Nicaea. The Nestorian heresy argued that there were two natures in Jesus Christ, Human Nature and Divine Nature. Parties in the controversy, waged between Antiochene and Alexandrian Christians, differed as to how and when the union between Christ's divine and human Natures had been effected. The date of 431 on the Nestorian roundel refers to the Council of Ephesus, when the hypostatic or absolute union between the Godly and Human Natures of Christ, existent at the moment of His Incarnation and not at the moment of His Birth, was made orthodox doctrine. The Council's position was that the Human Nature of Jesus was inseparable from his Divine Nature. 'Thus', wrote Cyril of Alexandria, 'every act that the Gospels say Christ did, whether ordinary or miraculous, was the act of a single being, God-in-Christ' (*Oeucumenical Documents of the Faith*, 1950, pp. 87–137). As a consequence of this doctrine, the Council of Ephesus also declared the status of the Virgin Mary to be that of *Theotokos*, Mother of God, not merely *Christokos*, Mother of Christ, as the Nestorians had believed; i.e., she was declared to have been both the Bearer and Mother of the Man Jesus Christ, and of God. (This official recognition of the Virgin Mary, who had always been venerated by the Christian community in Ephesus because she was believed to have died there, is illustrated in one of the mosaics on the north wall of the basilica.) The Eutychian heresy was named after its leader, Eutyches of Constantinople, who was an extreme Monophysite. His position was that Christ had two complete and separate Natures, a Human and a Divine one before his Incarnation, but that after it He only had one; i.e. that his Human Nature had been entirely dissolved into his Divine Nature. Eutyches' position was condemned because he and his followers refused to acknowledge belief in the *hypostatic* union of the two Natures of Christ. The roundel date, 451, refers to the Council of Chalcedon, when the Council of

Ephesus' declarations on the Nature of Christ and on the Virgin as *Theotokos* were reconfirmed.

The next roundel, characterizing Iconoclasm, the heretical political, religious, and artistic revolution in Byzantium in the 8th century, with the three foxes ravaging the Eucharistic vine, is dated 787, the year of the Second Ecumenical Council of Nicaea. The Iconoclasts, predominantly drawn from the ascetic monastic orders, were opposed to the creation of images of Jesus Christ/*Logos*, because these images reduced the limitless nature of Christ/*Logos* into mere personhood. Narrowly interpreting the doctrine declared at the Council of Ephesus on the *hypostatic* union between the two Natures of Christ, they stated that Christ/*Logos* could not be depicted at all because 'his humanity cannot be separated for the purpose of delineation and his divine nature cannot be circumscribed or depicted' (Gero, 1977, p. 45). Even more central to the later concerns of the Catholics at Fourvière was the Iconoclasts' assertion, particularly during the reign of Emperor Constantine V (741–775), that prayers offered to images of both the Virgin Mary and the saints were not efficacious, but only those offered to Christ/*Logos*. The Iconoclasts acquiesced in the belief that the Virgin was *Theotokos* and that She and the Saints had Divine gifts during their lives, but they contended that this divinity had not been transferred to them after death, thus reducing all worship of imagery of them by Christians to idolatry. The Second Ecumenical Council of Nicaea nullified some of the more radical decisions about the worship of imagery made at the Iconoclastic Council of Hiereia in 754, which had led to the mass destruction of icons and mosaics. The Council redefined both the legitimacy and the limitations of the veneration of images.

The gun metal gray bat, *idolorum monstra tenebris dedita* [monstrous idol of the night] according to *Clavis*, deftly symbolizes the Manichaean god of darkness and evil who wars eternally with the Christian God of light and truth. Manichaean dualism originated in the preaching of a 3rd century Persian priest, Mani. The Manichaeans believed that God was wholly transcendent and good, unknowable and unfathomable, and that man and matter were evil, opposed to God and independent of Him. Further they postulated that since the human body was evil, it could not have been the creation of a just and loving God but of some fallen emanation of God; that in order for man to partake in divine grace, his body and mind had to be rigorously chastised and restrained. The term Manichaean has been used to stigmatize the beliefs of a number of Christian sects, in particular the 10th century Bulgarian Bogomils, the 12th century Waldenses from Lyon, the Cathari in Italy, and the Albigensians in southwestern France, all of which sects were puritanical, ascetic, and evangelistic in nature. The date on the roundel, 1139, is that of the Second Lateran Council, held in Rome under Pope Innocent II. This Council, one of three presided over by powerful 12th century pope-jurists, codified papal principles of government as distinct and independent from secular powers and laid the groundwork for the attacks on the Manichaean or semi-Manichaean sects waged in that century and the next by the newly established Dominican and Franciscan mendicant orders, by Louis VIII's Crusade, and by the Inquisition Court. Ultramontane 19th century Catholics would have defended, without question, the judicial rigor, unquestioning sense of authority, and carefully composed doctrinal explications of the medieval Lateran Councils. Moreover, since the role and transcendent importance of the Virgin Mary was greatly reduced in Manichaean doctrines, its threatening heretical presence was particularly appropriate beneath the main altar dedicated to the Virgin of the Immaculate Conception at Fourvière.

Lutheranism, which according to Sainte-Marie Perrin 'had seized kingdoms from the Church', is represented in the form of what seems to be a Habsburg eagle, carrying off a limp sacrificial lamb resembling a sheared version of the symbol of the great Germanic award of merit, the Order of the Golden Fleece. Its close similarity to the mosaic of an eagle with a hare in its talons in the center of the vault of the 12th century audience chamber of the Norman King Roger II in Palermo, Sicily, which Pierre Bossan had seen in his youth, may also be more than coincidental (Figure 2.12). The quotation from *John* X.1, abbreviated on the roundel, which calls that man a robber or thief who 'cometh in some other way' than by the door, was a not-so-veiled attack on Martin Luther, whose followers included two thirds of the German population and much of Scandinavia and Poland by the end of the 16th century. The date on it, 1561, refers to one of the many reconvenings of the Council of Trent late in that year, following a nine year hiatus caused by a Protestant uprising in Saxony against Emperor Charles V. In that the Council of Trent spearheaded the Counter-Reformation and strengthened the power of the Papacy against the secular monarchs of Europe by its rigorous attention to both codification of doctrine and internal reform, the Fourvière Catholics celebrated it on the roundel at the same time as they attacked Lutheran heresy.

Although the Jansenists never repudiated the Roman Catholic Church as did the Lutherans, Jansenism, the eighth of the heresy roundels, complements the one preceding it in its attack on post-medieval schismatic and reform movements. Jansenism is identified with the name of the Flemish theologian Cornelius Otto Jansen (1585–1638), but the Jansenists did not come into prominence in France and the Low Countries until the 17th century. In France, they drew their strength from the pious nuns at Port-Royal, from the writings of Blaise Pascal, Antoine Arnauld, and Pasquier Quesnel, and from devout French aristocrats. Their interests were both in spiritual matters – the efficacy of grace and the nature of predestination – and in political matters – the excessive power of the Jesuit order in determining secular policy. The particular dislike that the Catholics at Fourvière would have felt for the Jansenists, other than the by now familiar one that they had contested official orthodoxy, was the Jansenists' contention that the Virgin Mary should not be worshipped as a mediatrix between man and God, because only God could hear the prayers of men. The words quoted by the Jansenist Adam Widenfeldt as being those of the Virgin herself seem to echo those of the 8th century Iconoclasts, if for different reasons: 'Do not honour me as if God were not enough for you. If you love God you have no need of anything ... Blessed is he who, like the apostles, wants to know nothing but Christ and his crucified' (Miegge, 1955, p.145). The papacy rallied against this radical rejection of Marian devotion as did influential priests such as Alphonsus Liguori (1696–1787), founder of the Congregation of the Most Holy Redeemer in Italy, whose charismatic preaching and writing contributed to the development of the dogmas of the Immaculate Conception, Papal Infallibility and the growth in devotion to the Eucharist and to the Virgin Mary. The date on the roundel, 1713, is that of the bull *Unigenitus Dei Filius*, in which Pope Clement XI condemned one hundred and one Jansenist principles. Clement had been strongly pressured to issue this bull by Louis XIV, who one year before he died and as a final effort, was seeking the papacy's assistance in finally closing the religious house at Port-Royal. Such a unified effort by 'throne and altar' to preserve orthodoxy which is the glorious vision of the Fourvière wall mosaics and was the hope of Fourvière Catholics, had been sadly disappointed by the demise of the Bourbon heir, the Duke of Chambord, some years before these mosaics had even been started. In 1883, the still mourning Bossan wrote of this loss to Sainte-Marie Perrin, 'There is no ... tomb large enough to contain all the broken hopes which go down with him into the tomb'. That the mild revolt of the Jansenists from within the Church is represented in the mosaic by a viper *à la langue perfide* [with perfidious tongue] attacking a small white dove is evidence of the weight the Fourvière Catholics placed on loyal orthodoxy in the face of 20th century secularism.

Naturalism, a category which does not refer to a particular or recognized group of heretical believers but rather to the general tendancy toward secular thinking in late 19th-century, is the last named mosaic on the left of the altar (Figure 2.3), opposite Arianism, the first named. The use of the word Naturalism to castigate the modern secular world came directly from Leo XIII's bull of 1884, *Humanum Genus*.

> For the primary principle of the Naturalists is that nature and human reason are mistress and sovereign. Having determined this, with respect to one's duties towards God, either they make little of them or they deny that God might be the author of any revelation. For them, outside of that which human reason can comprehend, there is no religious dogma, no truth, no master whose word, because of its official mandate as doctrine, which escapes their attack. ... The Naturalists go even further. Boldly engaged in the path of error on the most important of questions, they are carried along and, as it were, driven by the logic of human nature itself toward the justly deserved punishment with which God will inflict their pride. It follows from this that they cannot even protect the truths accessible in their integrity and certitude to the pure light of natural reason, which are, surely, the existence of God and the spirituality and immortality of the soul.[11]

The papal Bull continues in an anguished tone. It imagines society and culture literally being eaten away at its very roots by secular rationalists. Sainte-Marie Perrin, in this one instance, took his image directly out of the bestiary tradition, as it pertains to the *Salamander*, which 'slowly twines itself about a tree, all the fruits get infected with venom, and thus it kills the people who eat them',[12] except, as Sainte-Marie Perrin has so richly imagined, the *Salamanders* have become barely noticeable, relentless, omnivorous, and slimy worms.

This cautionary tale might best be concluded with more wisdom from the distant past, which the Fourvière Catholics so passionately mourned and sought passionately to revive. The Roman philosopher Boethius (470?–525 A.D.), in *De Consolatione Philosophiae* (Book VI, ch. 41), wrote too about men and animals and how they are both alike and different.

> Thou mayest perceive that many an animal moves variously upon the earth, and they are of very dissimilar form, and go differently. Some lie with the whole body on the earth, and so go creeping, because neither feet nor wings support them; and some are two-

footed; some four-footed; some flying; and all, nevertheless, are inclined downward towards the earth, and then seeing either what they list, or what is needful for them. But man alone goes upright. This betokens that he ought more to direct his thoughts upwards.

And thus it is revealed that only by casting one's thoughts upward and one's eyes downward can one fully comprehend Pierre Bossan's and Sainte-Marie Perrin's vision and their impassioned Ultramontane orthodoxy.

Notes

1 Lyon, called Lugudunum during the Roman Empire, was the first officially recognized Christian diocese in France. Irenaeus was its first bishop, serving from 177–195 A.D. The Catholic Church in Lyon has always cherished its premier role in French Catholicism, celebrated in l'Institut Catholique in the city and in the numerous ancient and modern religious houses, many of which are located on the steep slope leading up to the hilltop basilica at Fourvière. One of the large rectangular mosaics in the nave of the basilica illustrates, in the serene, static, and timeless monumental style of the lyonnais – turned Parisian – muralist, Pierre Puvis de Chavannes, *L'arrivée de Saint Pothin à Lyon* [The Arrival of St. Pothin in Lyons], designed by Charles Lameire. According to tradition, St. Pothin introduced Christianity to ancient Lugudunum.
2 Sainte-Marie Perrin to Pierre Bossan, letter of 3 November 1882.
3 Sainte-Marie Perrin to Pierre Bossan, letter of 1 January 1884.
4 Lyonnais Jesuit to Sainte-Marie Perrin, letter of 19 November 1891.
5 This text, Sainte-Marie Perrin 1896, *La Basilique de Fourvière, son origine, son esthétique, son symbolisme*. Lyon: Vitte, is the creed of an insider and a believer, published well before much of the decoration was complete. It is an essential document for understanding the decorative program at Fourvière, but one that must be interpreted carefully.
6 Sainte-Marie Perrin, 'Une Promenade à Fourvière', Discours de reception prononcé à l'Academie des Sciences, Belles-lettres et Arts de Lyon, scéance publique du 6 Avril 1897, p. 6.
7 The subjects of the mosaics on the north side of the nave are the Council of Ephesus (431) at which the Virgin was heralded as Theotokos (Mother of God), the Battle of Lepanto (1588) during which the Virgin protected the Catholic armies from Islam, and the proclamation of the Doctrine of the Immaculate Conception (1854) in Rome by Pius IX. On the south wall, mosaics illustrate Saint Pothin bringing Christianity and the cult of the Virgin to ancient Lyon (Lugdunum) (2nd C.), the life and martyrdom of Joan of Arc (14th C.) and the Vow of Louis XIII (16th C.). There is an emphasis here on monarchy: the Virgin as queen of heaven and of humanity as well, the Virgin aiding Emperor Charles V at Lepanto, the Virgin accepting the crown and sceptre of Louis XIII, the celebration of Joan of Arc's vow to crown the king at Reims and the correspondingly minimal attention given to her martyrdom, the great ecclesiastical courts at Ephesus and in Rome celebrating the doctrines which elevated the status of the Virgin. Also noticeable is a strong emphasis on legitimization and on authority: imposition of the true church on the heathen Gauls, defense of Europe against heathen Moslem inroads, sanctification of concepts of kingship and sanctity through grandiose ritual. Here, the Church Militant has been celebrated rather than the otherworldly mystical Virgin. But it should be emphasized that this part of the decoration was done, like most of the exterior sculpture, well after Bossan's death, and that it embodies motives that were, without question, more prosaic, more factual, and more historically and politically driven than his own.

8   Another commonly used animal used to represent Superbia was the lion, but this animal had, of course, already been used on the facade as a guardian figure of the city and the basilica. Thus the peacock, used elsewhere in the basilica in another of its traditional roles as a symbol of Resurrection, is, in the crypt '... the proud sun-brauing peacock, (who) with its feathers walks all along, thinking himselfe a king, prognosticates all weathers ...'. Robert Chester, *Loves martyr or Rosalins complaint*, late16th c. England.
9   Victor Henry Debidour 1961, *Le Bestiaire sculpté du Moyen Age en France*. Paris: Arthaud, pp. 290–191. 'The other kingly animal, the eagle, is itself, justifiably a double symbol. Its rapacity and its cruelty make of it a figure of evil-doing' (Lamentations, IV.19). In the large majority of cases, the eagle is on the side of God. The eagle is Christ, reported *La Clef* de pseudo-Méliton (Jeremiah XLIX.22) ... when it ascends at break of dawn toward the sun without being dazzled, it represents the Ascension; when it forces its eaglets to look directly at the stars and rejects that one whose glance weakens, it represents Judgment. But it represents Christians as well on the basis of a verse from Saint Luke (XVII,37) which says: 'Wheresoever the body, is, thither will the eagles be gathered together'.
10 This bird flies downward and holds a dove in its beak. The particular image relies on a tradition in bestiary lore about 'The Eyes of a Dove'. *The Medieval Book of Birds, Hugh of Fouilloy's Aviarium* 1992,Willene B. Clark ed., trans., Binghamton, NY: SUNY Press, p. 133. 'The Dove is accustomed to sit most often above water, in order that when it sees the shadow of a hawk flying above it might avoid it by escape. Surely the church defends itself with scripture, so that it can avoid the Deceits of the devil lying in ambush'. See also *Song of Solomon* 5:12; 'His eyes are as the eyes of doves by the rivers of waters, washed with milk, and fitly set'. At Fourvière, the unwary Christian dove had not seen the heretical hawk's shadow.
11 *Lettres apostoliques, encycliques, brefs de S.S. Léon XIII*, Lettre encyclique de S.S. Léon XIII aux Cardinaux français, 20 Avril, 1884, *Humanum Genus*, p. 253.
12 *The Book of Beasts, being a translation from a Latin Bestiary of the twelfth century* 1984. Theodore H. White ed. NY., p. 182. "The SALAMANDRA has its name because it prevails against fire. Of all poisonous creatures its strength is the greatest. For although others may kill one at a time, the salamander kills most at one blow. If it slowly twines itself about a tree, all the fruits get infected with venom, and thus it kills the people who eat them. Even if it falls into a well the power of its toxin slays those who drink the water. This animal is the only one which puts the flames out fire fighting. Indeed it lives in the midst of the blaze without being hurt and without being burnt – and not only because the fire does not consume it, but because it actually puts out the fire itself."

Chapter Three

Anglican Controversies: Debating Private Confession

Anne Hartman

> Confession is the life of the Parochial charge – without it all is hollow – and yet I do not see my way to say that I should not do more harm than good by more than the most distant mention of it. (John Henry Newman, 1842)

Newman would cite the barriers against practising confession in the Anglican church as a major cause for his conversion to Catholicism in 1845. The significance confession held for him is indicated in the quote above, but it is also suggested that the public unease confession caused meant that it could not be discussed openly (Newsome, 1993, p. 151). Nineteenth-century scholars are often surprised to learn that private confession – a ritual normally associated with Roman Catholicism – was practised in the Church of England throughout the nineteenth century. From the late 1830s when a group of Anglican clergymen began hearing confessions, the practice became a contentious issue of public concern, which was debated in letters and pamphlets, the national press, and eventually in Parliament. Private confession was so controversial because it provided a location for the articulation of a web of interconnecting issues: it was associated with Catholicism (and therefore encouraged nationalistic fervour); it allowed the Church to reassert its authority against the privacy of the individual and the encroaching claims of a reformed Parliament; and it created an arena for the production of a discourse on domesticity, sexuality and shifting definitions of gender. While discussions condemning the practice are easily in evidence, those in favour tend to follow a pattern of textual inversion most commonly noted in representations of homosexuality. What may appear to be scant reference to the issue may turn out to represent *reticence* to discuss a subject which was so contentious and problematic. Here I construct a history which draws on post-Victorian scholarship of the period (none of which provides a single comprehensive narrative), and a selection of the contemporary letters and treatises which comprised the discursive contexts for the debates. My aim is to draw out the issues which foreground the conflict.

Existing historical treatments of the issue divide into those which address confession within the context of the Oxford Movement or within the later Ritualist movement in the 1870s – neither offers a continuous history. Peter Nockles (1994) acknowledges the significance of the debates, saying that they were responsible for creating a division among churchmen as great as that division which arose over the issue of church versus state (p. 251). Owen Chadwick (1970) briefly addresses the issue of confession but does not suggest what I argue to be the far more widespread nature of the debates. The pivotal figure in the debates was E.B. Pusey, and useful accounts are available through treatments of his life and work by David Forrester (1989) and Henry Liddon (1894). Other useful accounts of confession in the Oxford Movement are provided in G.C.B. Davies (1954), Geoffrey Faber (1933) and S.L. Ollard (1915). Representing the later chronological period is Nigel Yates (1983 and 1988), who has written a comprehensive account of ritualism and the most thorough assessment of the debates around confession in the 1870s. He claims that the issue was 'one of the most explosive religious issues ... of the late nineteenth and early twentieth centuries' (Yates, 1988, p. 202). Additional accounts of confession during the ritualist period are available in James Bentley (1978) and John Kent (1978).

The Oxford Movement and the Age of Reform

For nearly three hundred years the Church of England had quietly complied with the teaching of the Reformers regarding the superfluity of habitual private confession. This changed in the late 1830s, when private confession was reintroduced by the Oxford Movement (or 'Tractarians') – namely Edward Bouverie Pusey, John Keble, and John Henry Newman – and subsequently adopted by Ritualist and Anglo-Catholic clergymen from the 1850s until the end of the century. Although private confession was a logical outgrowth of the spiritual, devotional, and theological innovations of the Tractarians, it also represented an attempt by the Church to reassert its authority, which was increasingly under threat during a period of radical reform of the State and with repeated calls for disestablishment. The institution of confession is commonly regarded as an efficient method of social control (Hepworth and Turner, 1982, p. 14). The Tractarian emphasis upon the importance of spirituality and faith was part of an anti-rationalism characteristic of Romantic anti-Enlightenment ideology, and can be partly interpreted as a backlash against the widespread influence of Benthamite utilitarianism and its embodiment in the liberalising politics of the era (Nockles, 1994, pp. 200–6). The Oxford Movement revolutionized the theological and devotional traditions of the Church of England, responding both to a charged religious temperament created by Evangelicalism, and to the perception that the teachings of the Church had become staid in the hands of the orthodox 'High and Dry' Anglicans.

A reactionary movement at heart, the Tractarians advocated the return of ritual practices (such as turning eastward during prayer, fasting, the wearing of vestments and surplices, and private confession) perceived to be in line with ancient church practice. Supporting these spiritual and ritual beliefs was a reinterpretation of the sacraments (baptism, the Eucharist, and confession) now seen not only as symbols of grace, but as necessary vehicles through which grace might be received.[1] The Tractarians held dear the rite of baptism, and Pusey was particularly known for his emphasis upon the possibility of post-baptismal sin – meaning that after the cleansing process of baptism, subsequent sinful acts could despoil the individual's purity. Pusey's emphasis upon the seriousness of post-baptismal sin became part and parcel of his recipe for advocating the necessity of private confession and priestly absolution. In general, the Oxford Movement created a heightened awareness of sin through their emphasis upon asceticism and self-examination, both of which are central to the doctrine and practice of confession (Nockles, 1994, p. 184).

Of all the Tractarian innovations, private confession was the most controversial because of the nature of the doctrinal and political issues at stake. In order to understand the impact of the reintroduction of confession in the English Church during the nineteenth century one needs to understand the aversion English Protestants felt towards the ritual – an aversion centred on the perception that confession embodied the characteristics of the Medieval church which the Reformers had succeeded in overcoming. The Roman Church had elevated private confession to the status of a sacrament in 1215, when the Lateran Council decreed that all Church members should confess to a priest at least once a year. The Church of England drew a sharp distinction between itself and the Roman Church by strongly denying any scriptural evidence for such an *obligatory* practice. According to Richard Hooker, the sixteenth-century divine, 'the minister's power to absolve is admitted and private confession is allowed, but not commanded' (Hooker, 1901 [1600], p. 71). Protestantism sought to promote the individual's relationship to God, freed from authoritarian ecclesiastical structures. Auricular confession was indelibly linked in peoples' minds with Roman Catholicism, and in the early decades of the century there was already strong opposition to confession as it was practised in Roman Catholic churches in England. It was believed that confession gave priests untold powers over the private thoughts of individuals, and that it consequently provided a means whereby the entire fabric of society could be contaminated. (See, for example, Frederick Edwards (1829), *Inez, A Spanish Story Founded on Facts, Illustrating One of the Many Evils of Auricular Confession,* for an instance of the many literary representations of the perceived effects of confession.)

The Church of England had traditionally drawn a distinction between the sacrament of General Confession and Absolution in the church service, and private (or 'auricular') confession to a priest, with the conviction that the former was sufficient in all but very few select cases, that there was no biblical evidence to support the elevation of the latter to a sacrament, and that the cases in which auricular confession could be practised were few and discrete. There were two situations in which auricular confession was held to be appropriate: 1) in the event of exceptionally sinful acts or to relieve an intolerably overburdened conscience; and 2) to relieve the conscience of the individual approaching death. These are the two instances in which the Book of Common Prayer recommends confession, and from Richard Hooker to as recently as the Canons of 1969, the Church's formal doctrine on confession has remained steadfast to this principle. However it is easy to see how the first of these two provisions was susceptible to varied interpretation since the definitions of 'exceptionally sinful acts' and 'an intolerably overburdened conscience' are subjective and historically contingent, and that since auricular confession had been practised (albeit on a limited scale) in the Church of England, it was available to be revived and become the centre of controversy in the way it did (Ollard, 1915, p. 122).

During the nineteenth-century private confession played a unique role in the Church of England, inherently connected with the Church's occupation of a 'middle' position in between the extremes of Roman Catholicism and Protestant Dissent. The Tractarians looked to the sacrament of absolution and confession both to draw a distinction between the Church of England and Dissent, and to provide an appealing service to meet the needs of a heightened religious temperament shaped by Evangelicalism (Chadwick, I: 1970, pp. 4–21; Nockles, 1994, p. 255). However, since confession attracted such controversy, clergymen who favoured the practice stressed the difference between the Romish practice of *obligatory, habitual* private confession, and the Church of England's interpretation of confession as a *voluntary* practice limited to *exceptional* circumstances. On the other hand, the Church's doctrine on confession and absolution needed to remain sufficiently distinct from the attitude of Dissenters, who asserted that the clergy had no scriptural authority to practice any form of the absolution of sins whatsoever.[2]

As I have suggested, private confession appeared to be compatible with the major doctrinal and practical teachings of the Oxford Movement; that is, the emphasis upon the apostolicity and the authority of the clergy; the return to the teachings of the ancients (although it was argued that some selective misreading took place here); the emphasis upon spirituality, asceticism, and the gravity of post-baptismal sin; and the importance placed upon the sacraments. Pusey and Keble are both known to have acted as confessors extensively from the late 1830s and early 1840s, with Keble hearing Pusey's confession in 1846. In a letter of 1843, Keble expressed his discomfort with the prohibition against confession: 'How blindly I go about the Parish, not knowing what men are really doing ... our one great grievance is the neglect of Confession. Until we can begin to revive that, we shall not have the due severity in our religion; and without a severe religion, I fear our Church will practically fail' (Coleridge, 1869, pp. 299–300). Of all the elements which produced encouragement for private confession, the most powerful was the renewed fear of sin and need for discipline the Tractarians emphasised in their battle against what they perceived to be a complacency plaguing their parishioners.

Pusey deserves the most credit for this accomplishment; although in the early thirties he shared anti-Roman Catholic views held by the other Tractarians, his obsessive emphasis upon sinfulness and the need for asceticism and self-mortification eventually led him closer to Roman Catholic practices. Orthodox High Churchmen criticised Pusey's maverick views on baptism and sinfulness, and in 1839 Pusey responded to accusations of Romanism in a letter to the Bishop of Oxford. In this letter he stresses that the difference between the Romish and Anglican attitudes is that the former 'practically frees a man from his past sins; our church bids him confess that he is "tied and bound with the chain" of them' (Pusey, 1839, p. 89). It is this view of being tied to one's past sins which underwent change, probably as a result of the arduous and therefore unappealing path it presented for the penitent. By 1846, Pusey had been entirely won over by the notion of priestly absolution and penance, as one can see in the sermon *Entire Absolution of the Penitent* where he puts forth his present views on the subject, saying that 'by His absolving sentence, God does efface the past' (Pusey, 1846).

Once private confession began to be practised on a wide scale in the 1840s, criticisms came from a number of directions. As well as its affiliation with Roman Catholicism and the unorthodox power which it gave to the priest, it was claimed that the system necessitated educating the confessant about sin in a way which actually encouraged the proliferation of sin. In his attention to the most minute of sins, Pusey was accused of asking probing, invasive questions, and it was along these lines that Bishop Samuel Wilberforce informed him in 1850 that 'You seem to me to be habitually assuming the place and doing the work of a Roman confessor, and not that of an English clergyman'. Wilberforce accordingly withdrew his right to practice in the diocese of Oxford (Wilberforce, 1881, p. 17). Although there is evidence that Pusey had a particular interest in young men and their predilection for masturbation (Pusey, 1878, p. xxi), it would appear that among the general population it was more likely to be the female parishioner rather than the male who approached the priest with a burdened conscience. Geoffrey Faber (1933) presents an amusing portrait of Pusey's female penitents: 'To confess to Dr. Pusey became something very like a fashion. For the most part his penitents were women. "Flys came to the door ... from which descended ladies, Una-like in wimple and black stole ... obtained their interview and went away"' (p. 402). For most opponents of confession, the interface between the male priest (who might be young, inexperienced, and even celibate) and the female penitent was extremely troubling, enacting a subversion of the authority of fathers and husbands over their womenfolk.

One of the original points of contention over the legitimacy of private confession in the Anglican Church had fixed on the distinction between 'habitual' practice (which had been traditionally associated with Roman Catholicism), and the more limited and isolated practice of the rite as endorsed by orthodox Church doctrine. Although Pusey went to great lengths to insist that he did not 'enjoin' confession – that he was merely responding to the entreaties of his parishioners – under Tractarian encouragement the practice tended to become habitual. Pusey insisted that 'I have been simply passive in this matter. I have not preached upon the subject, except before the University, eight years after persons had first come to me to open their griefs' (Pusey, 1851, p. 3). As Denison (1983) claims, 'after they had made a first confession, penitents found that they needed to return to their confessor' (p. 215). The practice of policing one's private thoughts and dwelling upon transgressions has a tendency to inculcate obsessive and addictive behaviour. The clergyman W.J. Butler describes in a letter to Keble that 'though many are desirous to make a confession and to continue it as a habit through life, the thing is all but impossible' (Quoted in Kent, 1978, p. 265). Having initiated the practice, confessors were aware of how quickly penitents came to rely on it, and this increased their sense of frustration at the prohibition against it. In 1839 Newman used the language of addiction to describe the dilemma they faced in trying to institute ritual practices such as confession in the Church: 'Our blanket is too small for our bed ... We are raising longings and tastes which we are not allowed to supply' (letter reprinted in Newsome, 1993, p. 151). This sense of frustration at being prevented from providing a remedy for discomfort is a sentiment which echoes throughout the writing of the proponents of confession. They successfully convinced their parishioners to accept the premise of human susceptibility to sin, and engage in perpetual self-examination toward the identification and censoring of sinful behaviour, thus creating the compulsive need for a penitential spirit and the confessional.

Mid-century Debates on Confession and Ritualism

After Newman's secession to Rome in 1845, followed by a number of his disciples, the Oxford Movement proper lost momentum, and the remaining Tractarians became absorbed into the growing Ritualist movement, which attracted even greater public and political approbation. Ritualism originated with a group of Cambridge clergymen, under the leadership of John Mason Neale, who were influenced by the Victorian Gothic revival and displayed antiquarian interest in church ornaments and devotional rituals (Chadwick, I: 1970, p. 213). The traditional practice of the Church of England had been determined as much by tradition as by interpretation of the Articles and Prayer Book. As ritualist clergymen began assuming individual responsibility for deciding which rituals were supported by the ambiguous formularies of Anglican rubric, Bishops responded by issuing statements regarding what standard practice should entail. In 1842, Bishop Blomfield condemned a number of practices, including 'the placing of flowers upon the holy table; the mixing of water with wine in the chalice; the beginning of service with a psalm or hymn; private confession' (Chadwick, I: 1970, p. 215).

By 1850, confession had been assimilated into the practice of a large number of Tractarian and Ritualist followers, although it remains unclear whether it reached a corresponding level of popularity amongst the laity. Yates (1983) believes it did not, saying confession 'remained unpopular with the laity, and even in Tractarian parishes only a small proportion of the congregation were penitent' (p. 27). Of all the practices which were condemned by opponents of Ritualism, confession drew the most attention and occupied the most print – particularly when prevalent anti-Catholicism was reignited in the mid-1840s with the numerous conversions to Catholicism, and then later in 1850 with the 'Papal Aggression' represented by the reinstitution of a Catholic hierarchy in England. The controversy over confession would peak in the 1870s; during the 1850s and 1860s disturbances remained local, and debates were largely confined to theological exchanges between churchmen.

Nockles states that in 1848–50 'a new source of division within High Churchmanship, which transcended that between old High churchmen and Tractarians, opened up on the doctrine of confession, no less than on the issue of church and state' (Nockles, 1994, p. 251). The source of division which Nockles identifies was centred around Bishop Phillpotts of Exeter, a noteworthy character during the early and mid-Victorian period, renowned for his pugilism – his biographer claims that 'the ring was the only element in which he seemed to enjoy himself; and while other boys were happy in the number of their friends, he rejoiced in the multitude of his foes' (Davies, 1954, p. 29). Phillpotts entered into endless pamphlet wars with a number of clergymen and politicians. He had long opposed Roman Catholic Emancipation, and had expressed an early anti-confession stance in his 1825 exchange of letters with Charles Butler (a Roman Catholic priest whose writings appeared to suggest that there was less difference between the Roman and Anglican churches than people supposed), which he republished in 1848 in light of the controversy which had arisen around confession (Phillpotts, 1825, p. 210). The next year, William Maskell, a friend and follower of Phillpotts, published his own tract on confession and absolution, in which he states a pro-confession view very similar to that of Pusey: the Church of England allows private confession, and the distinction from Roman Catholicism is that it is voluntary rather than obligatory. The point of contention seemed to circle around the issue of what it meant for a priest to allow confession, and what behaviour might be interpreted as encouraging rather than simply allowing. The alliance between the two men broke over this issue. The Gorham crisis of 1850 was the final straw for Maskell, and he subsequently converted to Roman Catholicism.[3]

The most publicised confessional incident during this period occurred in Plymouth in the late 1840s, and the repercussions continued well into the 1850s. Phillpotts had appointed to the new district of St. Peters a young Puseyite named George Prynne, who attracted considerable attention due to his zealous practice of auricular confession with girls as young as twelve from a neighbouring sisterhood. Pusey had assisted in the setting-up of the sisterhood (run by a Miss Sellon) and Phillpotts initially gave his approval even though such religious communities incited anti-Catholic sentiment. Prynne acted as confessor for the girls in the sisterhood, and it was reported that upon hearing the confession of a girl named Augusta Wale, Prynne assigned her the penance of drawing a cross on the ground with her tongue. When questioned, Prynne stated that he could not remember whether or not he had assigned this penance. A second allegation concerned a 14 year-old girl who had confessed to Prynne an act of incest committed with her brother; opponents claimed that in order to elicit such a confession Prynne must certainly have asked her indelicate and probing questions. An enquiry into these allegations by Bishop Phillpotts was held on 22 September 1852, at the Royal Hotel in Plymouth. Most interesting in this case was that the girl prepared a statement – claiming that Prynne had asked her indelicate questions – which was read aloud at the inquiry.[4] Prynne was acquitted on all charges, but many considered his behaviour to have been, at best, somewhat dubious. The incident received enormous publicity, igniting the numerous fears people had about male priests and female penitents.

The event was debated in countless treatises and letters, including an exchange between Pusey and the Rev R.H. Fortescue in 1854, when Fortescue responded to the enquiry at Plymouth as well as another inquiry regarding similar issues held in Leeds (Pusey, 1854).[5] Fortescue emphasises the heinousness of Prynne's alleged transgressions, and gives a full transcript of the girl's statement from the Royal Hotel enquiry. In the statement (the kernel of which is transcribed in Latin) the girl recounts the circumstances of the sinful act and her subsequent confession. Fortescue believed that the priest must surely have been responsible for an indiscretion, and in his exchange with Pusey his tone grows increasingly vitriolic in the face of the latter's staunch support of the errant confessor. Pusey acknowledges that it is bad practice for a priest to asks probing questions; but he comes to Prynne's support by pointing out that 'one witness retracted; a second most shocking witness invented out of the defilements of her own wretched mind questions which only the most polluted mind could have invented, which related to sins which I never heard of, and which, if they exist at all, minds only the most brutalised could be guilty of' (p. 11). The exchange between the two men becomes increasingly hostile; Fortescue insists on the extreme indelicacy of the entire operation of confession, whilst Pusey denies the most excessive accusations, and attempts to justify the rest. Fortescue expresses indignation at the fact that confessionals nearly always turn on the 7th Commandment, and accuses the priest of voyeuristic enjoyment: 'the private intercourse of men with females on this subject must ever by attended with the greatest temptation, the greatest risk of sin ... I hold the opinion that it is the power of questioning females on this commandment, which gives to confession much of its real interest in their eyes' (p. 24). Yates (1983) confirms that 'there is no doubt that Anglican confessors were particularly concerned with sins of a sexual nature'; however, in good faith he continues to explain that 'what some critics regarded as obsessive interest of a voyeuristic type was probably no more than a response to established need' (p. 212). It is most likely that the priest and the penitent colluded in a mutual interest in, and joint construction of, a discourse around sexuality. Fortescue cites another case of a woman who was asked indelicate questions about adultery; the letters and sermons produced by male clergy who opposed confession proliferate with these case studies detailing the interaction between priests and female sinners, expressing covert interest in both the women's character, intentions, and actions, and the priest's probing inquiry. The tone and style of these accounts resemble Freud's descriptions of his female hysterics, indicating, perhaps, a similar impulse to understand and regulate female desire and behaviour.[6]

Another profusion of tracts on confession appears in 1858, when at least two distinct controversies occurred: 'in the summer of 1858 profligate women in two parishes – one St. Barnabas in Pimlico, the other Boyne Hill at Maidenhead – were persuaded to complain that their curates asked them improper questions' (Chadwick I: 1970, p. 505). In the case of Boyne Hill, the guilty curate was Mr. Richard West, who was accused of asking a woman indelicate questions after insisting that she make her confession, and furthermore advising her not to reveal her confession to her husband (Ollard, 1915, p. 124). Likewise, the curate of St. Barnabas, Alfred Poole, was accused of participating in the coercion of a woman to make her confession (Chadwick, I: 1970, p. 503; Rowell, 1983, p. 135). Archbishop Tait withdrew Poole's licence over the affair, and both incidents attracted widespread publicity (Ollard, 1915, reports that *The Times* in particular gave coverage to the Boyne Hill affair). The spate of tracts which appeared as a result of this publicity merely reiterated, for the most part, the standard objections to the practice. An issue which emerged from the Poole incident was that of the setting of confession, a typical focus for prurient anxieties. When an enclosed vestry (or 'confessional box') was used, it increased the association with Roman Catholicism and also exacerbated people's distrust of priests. In the seventies, Ritualist clergymen would show their awareness of this widely-held public fear by having priests hear confessions in well-lighted open settings in the church, with only a curtain separating the penitent and confessor (Rowell, 1983, p. 135).

While the sixties was a relatively calm decade in the debates, in 1869 confession reclaimed a prominent position due to the enthusiasm of Anglo-Catholic revivalists who as well as advocating missionary work abroad initiated domestic 'missions'. Critics agree that in the famous 'Missions to London' in 1869 and 1874 confession played a key role (Kent, 1978, pp. 266–271; Rowell, p. 134). One reason was that in their missionary zeal, the Ritualists were vying for attention with Evangelicals. Confession was again perceived as a 'catch': it could offer an comparable experience to the Evangelical conversion. Kent (who has produced a valuable study on Victorian revivalism) explains that the perception was that 'where the Evangelicals offered them a subjective kind of self-forgiveness for their sins, Anglo-Catholics should offer them the objectivised forgiveness of priestly absolution in the Confessional' (Kent, 1978, p. 266). In the post-Darwin era of secularisation and unsettlement in faith, one might speculate that an 'objective', inter-personal form of forgiveness might bear up under the weight of doubt more successfully than the entirely subjective nature of Evangelical faith. Kent stresses the degree to which 'revivalism and confession had become intertwined'; Ritualists had clearly come to believe that it offered the most appealing element of their devotional repertoire (Kent, 1978, p. 273). The evidence Kent uses to support this claim is that in the preparations made for the second Anglo-Catholic revival in 1873, 483 priests signed a petition urging changes in the Prayer Book, which would 'provide for the education, selection and licensing of duly qualified confessors'. The petition was presented to the Upper House of Convocation, where it was overwhelmingly rejected but nevertheless caused a flurry of outrage. It is clearly not merely coincidental that it was during this year that Queen Victoria would write 'the archbishop should have the *power* given him, by *Parliament*, to *stop all* these ritualistic practices, dressings, bowings, etc., and everything of that kind, and *above all*, *all* attempts at *confession*'.[7]

That same year Lord Salisbury claimed that 'confession diminished a nation's virility', a statement which conflates the discourses of gender and nation and shows how confession threatened the boundaries of both (Kent, 1978, p. 268).[8] An anti-confession clergyman, Joseph Harris (1852), articulates the precise anxieties provoked by the confessing priest: 'it is a question of the invasion of your homes – or the desecration of the sanctities of individual consciences and of most blessed domestic unity' (p. 11). In the sensational style typical of texts in the debates, Harris (1852) amusingly describes the typical progress of the female confessant:

> The first result, on the part of a penitent, is a deadness of heart to all but the Confessor's or Director's influence. Then succeeds a sneering morbid religionism, coincident with a too consistent disregard and scorn of household duties and domestic obligations .... Meanwhile, the confessing Priest is assiduous in probing every thought of his luckless confessees ... until the hour arrives when confessor and confessee should apostatise to Rome (p. 13).

Giving priests the power to act as intermediaries between God and the lay population was considered audacious by Protestants: aside from allowing the Church too much power, it was deemed unscriptural, a usurpation of the authority which rightfully belonged to God. One Reverend Magee expresses the nature of these concerns: 'The priest will not only be your director...but the director of your wives, and of your daughters, and your servants. Your households will also be absolutely in his possession; and he who attempts to resist the director will soon find himself surrounded by a network of domestic influences, the potency of which you all know. There will be an estrangement of the affection of your wives, disobedience on the part of your children, insults from those who are bound to honour and serve you, until you again submit to the man who sets himself up as a spiritual tyrant' (quoted in Brown, 1877, p. iv). Anglican clergymen who practiced confession became associated with Roman Catholic priests, who were additionally distrusted for taking the vow of celibacy. In *The Ring and the Book*, Robert Browning (1971 [1868]) reflects the disconcerting sexuality of the priest in his description of the lover/priest Caponsacchi: 'man and priest – could you comprehend the coil!' (I.1016). Within a society where sexuality was carefully monitored and contained according to strict notions of domesticity, gender roles, and class divisions, the priest's autonomy made his sexuality seem perverse and uncontrollable. According to the opponents of confession, by contaminating the power dynamics of the domestic sphere the practice provided an arena for the celibate male priest, with his surreptitious links to Rome, to emasculate Englishmen.

During this period, public concern over Ritualist practices reached such a pitch that politicians began to legislate to regulate their activities, resulting in the passage of the Public Worship Regulation Act in 1874 by the Conservative government. Along with the support of Shaftesbury and Archbishop Tait, 'it was finally the Queen who gave the initial impetus to a bill which got through Parliament' (Machin, 1987, pp. 73–74). The Act was uncompromising in its transfer of power from church to state. Although the public may have initially supported the Act, when Ritualists opposed the regulations, five were imprisoned – something for which the public was not prepared. In the end, the Public Worship Regulation Act did not achieve much more than to sever the few remaining bonds between High Churchmen and the Conservative Party. Many people believed that it also had the effect of increasing the likelihood of a disestablished church.

The concluding event in this history of confession is the publication, circulation, and prohibition enacted upon the 1877 manual for confessors, *The Priest in Absolution*. Countless manuals to direct both confessors and confessants had been produced throughout the century. Some of these were clearly Roman Catholic texts, produced to guide Catholics in the practice, or perhaps revised to suit the needs of Anglo-Catholics. A number were circulated by extreme Protestants in an effort to advertise the worst excesses of their arch enemies. Manuals written by Ritualists were produced anonymously and circulated secretly. The manual in question had its origins in 1862, when the Society of the Holy Cross initiated the project of compiling a manual which drew on the experience of a number of prominent confessors, one of whom was Pusey. The manual was prepared by J.C. Chambers, the first part published in 1866, and the second in 1870 (Yates, 1983, p. 211). According to Bentley, whereas the first part was published openly, the second was circulated secretly; it was this second part which dealt with a more detailed description of sins and the kind of questioning the priest should conduct (Yates, 1988, p. 211). With the anti-ritualist frenzy of 1874 still in full swing, the manual was displayed in the House of Lords by the Earl of Redesdale in 1877. Machin reports that Redesdale's opposition to parts of the book was supported by Tait, and for a time the issue attracted attention in both Convocation and in the Commons. The result was that the press became involved; 'a Times leader said that Ritualism as represented by the society of the Holy Cross was a conspiracy against public morals' (Machin, 1987, p. 83). By 1880, interest in the confessional manual had largely died down, but the debates over confession continued on a small scale into the early 20th century.

We have seen that public opposition to confession usually centred on moral issues. A noteworthy opponent of confession was Frances Power Cobbe, a highly-respected philanthropist and writer on religious and social issues. She produced a number of tracts on confession, including a pamphlet *The Practice of Confession in the Church of England* (1898 [1850]), which went through several editions. She argues with an impressive Foucauldian prescience that while the self-examination promoted by confession is tolerable, the practice serves as a place where a discourse on sin and sexuality can take place, therefore promoting interest in these issues and actually encouraging transgressions. Her primary objection, however, is the power which the confessional gives to the priest: 'the enormous influence given thereby to the priesthood over the minds of their flocks' (p. 103). Nor did it escape the notice of many 19th century clergy and concerned lay people that private confession functions as a highly effective means of social control, bridging private thought and public behaviour (Hepworth et al, 1982, p. 14). This may well have been an element of confession's appeal to those clergymen who wished to practice it. For those opposed to it, however, there was something highly problematic in the way confession could invade the sanctity of the private thoughts of the individual. Walter F. Hook, Vicar of Leeds, published a sermon on confession where he criticized the way in private confession, sinners are 'required to submit, not only to general questions as to a state of sin and repentance, but to the most minute and searching questions as to their inmost thoughts' (Hook, 1848, p. 23).

Whilst confession can thus be regarded as a ritual which helps maintain institutional power, it can also be interpreted as providing a method of resistance to dominance. Paradoxical as this may seem, one need only observe the vulnerable position in which the Church found itself in the nineteenth century as a result of the secularising tendencies of the age and the increasing spread and democratisation of the state. In this analysis, those who practised confession were 'resisting the dominant culture and asserting that the Church could make absolute demands for submission on the individual, in his private as well as in his public life' (Kent, 1978, p. 290–91). Equally, it is possible to see that confession might have fulfilled a counselling role necessitated by the shift from rural to urban living and the attendant changes in the structure of communities (Rowell, 1983, 137).

As I hope I have shown, the debates surrounding confession provide particular insight into the religious and political culture of the period. Opposition to the practice could spring out of a familiar anti-Catholic nationalism, to then stray into discourses exploring issues of sexuality and gender. While the debates take their impetus from socio-political changes – changing relations between the individual and society, the Church and State, and the public and private – they were equally adept at registering correspondent shifts in notions of subjectivity. This indicates the degree to which the ritual of private confession is implicated with the broader epistemological issues surrounding the notion of confession. As a category of thought, confession does not remain stable but shifts to accommodate historically-situated problems of subjectivity and sociability. My analysis of these debates might be seen to support the thesis that around 1830 there was a 'crisis' of the subject, as traditional power relations became reconfigured and dividing lines between private and public redrawn. In the 16th century, private confession in the Protestant church disappeared partly because it was believed that subjects could internalise rules of conduct, with the proviso that any transgression of societal norms could be regulated through secular judicial institutions. Confession, through its various means of creating discourses of the self, reconstructs and reconfirms the subject, so perhaps it re-emerged as a religious practice as a response to concerns about shifting boundaries between the private and public. With the age of reform, public discourse gained a dominance which created anxiety around the location of the private, introducing the tendency to *fetishize* privacy, a tendency which I believe we can see fuelling the arguments over the propriety of the confessional. Although private confession in the Church of England transgressed the norms of a Protestant, democratic society, it was welcomed by some confessants because it provided a cathartic realm for, as Foucault has argued, a discourse on the self and privacy. It also gave the Church of England a way to reassert authority during a period when the issue of disestablishment was increasingly on the agenda. What had been an institution with power beyond question suddenly became the object of public debate, and in fact one of the most striking characteristics of the confessional debates is how they bring the private experience of confession into the arena of public debate.

Notes

1 See McGrath, 1994, p. 427–47, for an explanation of the doctrine of the sacraments.
2 The scriptural evidence for the absolution of sins is located in Christ's indication to his Apostles that 'whosoever sins ye remit, they are remitted; whosoever sins ye retain, they are retained', which from the Roman and High Anglican point of view also provides justification for apostolical succession and authority (Nockles, 1994, p. 248). Theological interpretations of the doctrine vary tremendously, and the issue of authority at stake suggests that High Church interpretations during a period of institutional insecurity could hardly remain untainted by political interests.
3 The Gorham crisis occurred over differing interpretations of the sacrament of baptismal regeneration. The Evangelical Reverend Gorham was derided as heretical for his views and nearly defrocked by Bishop Phillpotts in 1850, but for the (unwelcome) intervention of the largely secular Judicial Committee of the Privy Council. This incident was highly significant because it set a precedent for secular intervention into ecclesiastical matters.
4 See Davies (1954, p. 287); Phillpotts (1852); Hatchard (1852); Harris (1852); Lowe (1852); Fortescue (1854).
5 Ollard (1915) reports that in 1848 the charge was brought against the clergy at St. Saviour's, Leeds, that 'a regular system of Confession was taught and practised there' (p. 123).
6 As a site for the production of a discourse on sexuality, discussions around confession at times merge with subcultural genres of the Gothic and pornography. For an example, see William Hogan (1846). Hogan, a former Roman Catholic priest, converted and emigrated to Georgia with the mission of educating vulnerable American southerners to the dangers of Catholicism. His work enjoyed widespread popularity; *Auricular Confession and Popish Nunneries* went through at least four editions, and a reading suggests that this popularity may have partly derived from erotic titillation. Freed as they are from the conventions of the Victorian family, religious communities are presented as alternative arenas for sexual activity; in a style eerily reminiscent of de Sade, Hogan describes how nuns have sexual relations with their confessors who also enjoy concubines on the side. Hogan's theory is that the hospitals commonly attached to nunneries are in fact dedicated to aborting the fruits of illicit sexual activity (p. 39).
7 Queen Victoria to Dean Stanley, 13 November 1873; *Letters of Queen Victoria*, II, ii, 290–1. Quoted in Chadwick, II: 1970, p. 321.
8 In his 1990 essay 'The Anglican Tradition: from the Reformation to the Oxford Movement', Geoffrey Powell confirms that 'the confessional like the convent could all too easily be portrayed as part of a conspiratorial undermining of the virtues of Victorian Christian manliness' (Powell, 1990, pp. 109–10).

II Liberal Christianity and Alternative Spiritualities

Chapter Four

The World's Parliament of Religions and the Rise of Alternative Spirituality

Linda Woodhead

'Unity in variety is the plan of nature, and the Hindu has recognized it.'
(Vivekandanda's speech to the World's Parliament, 1893)

The twentieth century has both confirmed and confounded the ideas of scholars who predicted widespread secularization. Whilst it is true that some forms of traditional religion have declined, it is also true that the late modern west has witnessed the spread of a 'luxuriant undergrowth' of religiosity (Martin, 1967). There is as yet no theoretical consensus about the way in which this upsurge of post-traditional religion should be understood. Whilst categories of investigation and analysis such as 'NRMs' (New Religious Movements), 'New Age', and 'unofficial religion' are most commonly employed to make sense of the field, they conflict with one another. What is more, such categories are often conceived and deployed in a very short historical perspective: NRMs, for example, are usually *defined* as those forms of religion which have come into existence since 1945 (see, for example Barker, 1985; Clarke, 1992; 1997).

In order to address some of these problems, this chapter suggests the broad category of the 'New Spirituality' as a tool which can help map and make sense of the modern religious scene. This designation draws attention to a broad religious current or trajectory which has undergone periodic revivals throughout the course of the twentieth century and which, as this chapter will show, was active at the end of the nineteenth century (investigation of its earlier antecedents and manifestations falls outside the scope of this chapter, but see the studies by Ellwood, 1979, Godwin, 1994, and Hanegraff, 1997). A number of scholars have already drawn attention to the significant unity of this current of modern religiosity, and have characterized it in somewhat similar terms to those proposed here. Of these Ernst Troeltsch (1931) was perhaps the earliest (see his comments on 'Mystical' religion, pp. 793–5), whilst more recently Steven Tipton (1984) and Robert Bellah and his collaborators (1985) have spoken in related terms of an 'expressive' style in modern religious culture.

Despite considerable internal diversity it is possible to classify the New Spirituality as a single current because of the significant number of characteristics shared by its variants. For a start, the New Spirituality in all its forms is *detraditionalized* in the sense that it rejects any form of religion which locates authority in a source which transcends the individual – whether that be God, scriptures, a particular community, its rituals, sacraments or priesthood. Instead, authority is characteristically located in the heart, feelings, intuition or experience of each individual. In more metaphysical terms, the New Spirituality is therefore *radically immanent*. It views everyday or phenomenal reality as a manifestation of a deep and unifying spirit or life-force, a stance may also be described as *this-worldly monism*, for it maintains both that 'All is One', and that it is through the phenomenal world (natural and human) that we gain access to 'the One'. It is therefore characteristic of the New Spirituality to *divinize the human and the natural*. Furthermore, the New Spirituality's continual stress on unity gives rise to a *universalist stance* in relation to other religions and cultures, all of which are viewed as potentially one by virtue of their common ability to bear witness to 'the One'. Finally, the New Spirituality tends to be strongly *optimistic, evolutionary* and *progressivist*, maintaining that a new age of unity, peace and spiritual enlightenment is currently dawning.

To stress the importance of the unifying features of the New Spirituality is not to deny the diversity of its manifestations, particularly at the social and institutional levels. This diversity takes many forms. On the one hand, for example, there are more 'esoteric' forms of such spirituality (like some forms of Theosophy) which are usually characterised by tightly bounded communities with shared – and often secret – knowledge and ritual practices. On the other hand, there are manifestations of the New Spirituality which reject all such 'externals' of religious belief and practice and maintain that the only locus of true religion is the heart and inner experience of each individual. Another important distinction concerns the extent to which some forms of the New Spirituality are world-rejecting and counter-cultural, whilst others are more world-affirming. Different manifestations of the New Spirituality also fall along a spectrum ranging from those which actively involve themselves in politics and the public realm on the one hand, and those which are more privatized on the other. Equally, some forms of the New Spirituality adopt a cosmic stance, whilst others are concerned only with the self and self-realisation. Furthermore, and particularly in the late twentieth century, more 'instrumentalized' forms of New Spirituality have developed which may be distinguished by the different techniques they offer for the attainment of various ends including healing, self-realisation and the attainment of a unified consciousness – techniques which range from chanting and dousing to massage and meditation (Heelas, 1996). More work is needed to develop a typology of the New Spirituality which can help make sense of these different forms and their inter-relations. Equally, more work is needed to map their historical manifestations and evolutions.

This chapter is intended as a small contribution to the latter task. Whilst much has been written about the New Spirituality as it is manifest in the late twentieth century (as 'NRMs' and 'New Age'), my aim here is to take a sounding in its nineteenth-century history. I do this by examining the presence and influence of the New Spirituality at one of the more significant events in the history of modern religion, the World's Parliament of Religions, held in Chicago in 1893. By so doing I hope to offer a portrait of some of the New Spirituality's most important characteristics at this time, as well as some reflections on its relation to wider socio-cultural contexts of the late nineteenth century. My purpose is thus to offer a broader historical perspective in which more recent manifestations of the New Spirituality may be better understood.

The World's Parliament of Religions and the Columbian Exposition of 1893

The World's Parliament was part of one of the great world fairs which littered the end of the nineteenth century. Styled the Columbian Exposition, this American spectacular was held to celebrate the 400th anniversary of Columbus's discovery of the New World. Including those who attended the Exposition more that once, it attracted over 27 million visitors (Rydell, 1984, p. 40). Like the numerous other world fairs held between 1851 and 1939, the Columbian Exposition was intended as a device 'for the enhancement of trade, for the promotion of new technology, for the education of the ignorant middle classes and for the elaboration of a political stance' (Greenhalgh, 1988, p. 3). Like many other world fairs too, Chicago's horizons were both national and international. One of its stated aims was to promote brotherhood amongst mankind, and to this end nations from around the world were asked to exhibit and participate in the fair. In practice, however, the rhetoric of unity was undermined by a strong drive to prove the supremacy of the American nation and people not only in arts and sciences, but in 'civilization' more generally.

The discourses of 'civilization' and the 'brotherhood of man' which were so dominant at the Columbian Exposition took their place within a wider evolutionary framework. The fact that the word 'Progress' appeared in more world exposition mottos and subtitles than any other (Greenhalgh, 1988, p. 23) is hardly surprising, for the very raison d'etre of the fairs was to celebrate and exhibit modern progress and to indicate that civilization was advancing in a known direction. In most cases the achievements of the host nation were presented as at the cutting edge of such evolutionary progress. In Chicago this idea shaped the very space of the Exposition, at the heart of which lay the neo-classical buildings of the 'White City' in which were displayed the commodified cultural and technological achievements of western – particularly American – civilisation (Findling, 1994). Away from this core site, other tribes and nations were exhibited along a mile-long street named the 'Midway Plaisance'. Whilst more 'advanced' nations were represented on the Midway by buildings and artefacts, the most 'primitive' were represented by living villages of men, women and children. Dahomeyan Africans and North American Indians, for example, took up their alloted places at the end of the Midway furthest away from the White City. In the words of one of the Expositions's anthropological advisors from the Smithsonian Institute, the Columbian Exposition was intended to 'illustrate the steps of progress of civilization and its arts in successive centuries, and in all lands up to the present time'. It was to be 'an illustrated encyclopedia of civilization' (G. Browne Goode, quoted in Rydell, 1984, p. 45).

By the latter part of the nineteenth century the idea of technological and national progress which guided the world fairs had 'became laced with scientific racism' (Rydell, 1983, p. 5), an outcome which was in turn related to the growing power of western imperialism. The grand expositions offered western nations the chance both to display and to justify their imperial conquests, and belief in cultural and biological evolution was often used to justify these enterprises and the subjection of 'inferior' races. The imperial theme was first sounded at the Great Exhibition of 1851 where displays of commodities from around the empire were used to 'sell' the idea of Greater Britain to the British public; by 1924 when the British Empire Exhibition was held at Wembley the imperial theme had become dominant, with every colony and dominion of the British empire represented by an elaborate display (MacKenzie, 1985). Even the Columbian Exposition was not immune from imperial display, for what America lacked in imperial possessions it made up for with representations of its power relations with 'lesser' nations and peoples. By such means the American public was left in no doubt about the position the Republic occupied in relation to its geographical neighbours, as well as in relation to coloured peoples in its own land. The organisers of the Chicago exposition conveniently forgot about their treatment of women, negroes and American Indians when they presented America as superior even to Europe by virtue of the more advanced state of its democracy and republicanism.[1]

Religion was far from incidental to the key themes, interests and representations of the Columbian Exposition, for American civilization was presented as superior to all others not only in terms of trade and manufacture, but also in terms of religion and culture. In particular, the traditions of liberal Protestantism were seen to occupy the same place at the apex of mankind's moral religious progress as did America's traditions of democracy and republicanism in relation to political development, and her achievements in trade and manufacture in relation to material development. In recognition of this, a formal space place was given to religion at the Columbian Exposition by the 'World's Congress Auxiliary' which was formed in order to balance the visual displays of the Fair with intellectual gatherings or 'congresses'. Chaired by Charles Carroll Bonney, the Auxiliary was formed as the 'Intellectual and Moral Exposition of the Progress of Mankind' which would bring 'all the departments of human progress into harmonious relations with each other' (Rydell, 1984, p. 68). A centrepiece of the Congress Auxiliary's offerings was 'The Congress on Evolution', specifically intended to advance ethics, politics and religion by diffusing evolutionary ideas; the 'Columbus of the new epoch', Herbert Spencer, was a principal speaker. Equally if not more important was the 'World's Parliament of Religions', the capstone of a series of denominational congresses held throughout the course of the Exposition.[2]

At a time when even the different Christian denominations had not come together in once place, the idea of gathering together representatives of all the world's religions was unique. According to the chronicler of the Parliament, John Henry Barrows, over a million invitations were sent to representatives of religions around the world to gather in Chicago to pool their accumulated spiritual wisdom. Whilst rather fewer accepted the invitation, the results were nevertheless impressive. In the event, the majority (almost 80 percent) of the speakers at the Parliament were Christian, and of them roughly 65 percent were Protestant – though most churches and denominations were represented. Also present at the Parliament, however, were representatives of all the world's major religions, including Judaism, Hinduism, Buddhism, Taoism, Confuicianism, Shintoism, Jainism, Islam, Zoroastrianism and Sufism. Smaller, and in some cases newer, traditions were also represented, including Quakerism, Theosophy and Brahmoism (notable exclusions included Mormonism and native American and African religions).

The Parliament, held over seventeen days, was declared by many visitors the highlight of the whole Columbian Exposition (Burg, 1976). Whilst it consisted of a series of 'keynote' addresses by delegates, and parallel gatherings of smaller religious congresses, the Parliament's appeal was immediate and visual as well as intellectual and spiritual, as this account of the Parliament's opening by one whom Barrows describes as 'an eye-witness who was affected by no small personal concern in the doings of the day' makes plain:

> Long before the appointed hour the building swarmed with delegates and visitors, and the Hall of Columbus was crowded with four thousand eager listeners from all parts of the country and foreign lands. At 10 o'clock there marched down the aisle arm in arm, the representatives of a dozen world faiths, beneath the waving flags of many nations, and amid the enthusiastic cheering of the vast audience. The platform at this juncture presented a most picturesque and impressive spectacle. In the center, clad in scarlet robes and seated in a high chair of state, was Cardinal Gibbons, the highest prelate of his Church in the United States, who, as was fitting in this Columbia year, was to open the meeting with prayer.
>
> On either side of him were grouped the Oriental delegates, whose many-colored raiment vied with his own in brilliancy. Conspicuous among these followers of Brahma and Buddha and Mohammed was the eloquent monk Vivekananda of Bombay, clad in gorgeous red apparel, his bronzed face surmounted with a huge turban of yellow. Beside him, attired in orange and white, sat B.B. Nagarkar of the Brahmo-Somaj, or the association of Hindu theists, and Dharmapala, the learned Buddhist scholar from Ceylon, who brought the greetings of four hundred and seventy-five millions of Buddhists, and whose slight, lithe person was swathed in pure white, while his black hair fell in curls upon his shoulders.
>
> There were present also, Mohammedan and Parsee and Jain ecclesiastics, each a picturesque study in color and movement, and all eager to explain or defend their forms of faith.
>
> The most gorgeous group was composed of the Chinese and Japanese delegates, great dignitaries in their own country, arrayed in costly silk vestments of all the colors of the rainbow, and officially representing the Buddhist, Taoist, Confucian and Shinto forms of worship ...
>
> The ebon-hued but bright faces of Bishop Arnett, of the African Methodist Church, and of a young African prince, were relieved by the handsome costumes of the ladies of the company, while forming a sombre background to all was the dark raiment of the Protestant delegates and invited guests ... (Barrows, 1894, pp. 62–4)

Understood thus, the Parliament was in perfect harmony with the evolutionary perspective embodied by the living displays of the Midway Plaisance; indeed, it took its place with them as an 'entertaining' legitimation of Anglo-Saxon power. This was exactly as the Parliament's organizers had hoped. Their interpretation would, however, be challenged from the floor of the Parliament itself – first and foremost by representatives of the New Spirituality. But in order to understand their subversion, it is first necessary to understand the liberal Protestantism in relation to which it operated.

'Have we not all one Father?': The Liberal Protestant Agenda at the Parliament

The ideals which inspired the World's Parliament of Religions were not those of religious pluralism as most people would understand that today. Whilst difference and diversity might be appreciated at the level of visual spectacle, the Parliament's organisers certainly did not mean to celebrate them at the level of religious and moral truth. Rather, their goal was to display and celebrate *unity*, an aim clearly laid out in the opening address which Charles Bonney delivered at the start of the Parliament. 'WORSHIPPERS OF GOD AND LOVERS OF MAN', Bonney began:

> Let us rejoice that we have lived to see this glorious day; let us give thanks to the Eternal God, whose mercy endureth forever, that we are permitted to take part in the solemn and majestic event of a World's Congress of Religions. The importance of this event, its influence on the future relations of the various races of man, cannot be too highly esteemed.
>
> If this Congress shall faithfully exectute the duties with which it has been charged, it will become like a new Mount Zion, crowned with glory and marking the actual beginning of a new epoch of brotherhood and peace.
>
> For when the religious faiths of the world recognize each other as brothers, children of one Father, whom all profess to love and serve, then, and not till then, will the nations of the earth yield to the spirit of concord and learn war no more ...
>
> In this Congress the word "Religion" means the love and worship of God and the love and service of man ...
>
> As the finite can never comprehend the infinite, nor perfectly express its own view of the divine, it necessarily follows that individual opinions of the divine nature and attributes will differ. But, properly understood, these varieties of view are not causes of discord or strife, but rather incentives to deeper interest and examination. Necessarily God reveals himself differently to a child than to a man; to a philosopher than to one who cannot read. Each must see God with the eyes of his own soul. each must behold him through the colored glasses of his own nature [...]
>
> We seek in this Congress "to unite all Religion against irreligion; to make the golden rule the basis of this union; and to present to the world the susbtantial unity of many religions in the good deeds of the religious life." [...]
>
> ... I welcome the first Parliament of the Religions of the World. (Barrows, 1894, pp. 67–72)

Bonney was a Swedenborgian. The Parliament's other organisers included a Roman Catholic and a Reform rabbi, plus fourteen local Protestant ministers from as many denominations. The secretary was a Unitarian and the chairman, Barrows, a Presbyterian. To some extent then we may already begin to glimpse in the constitution of this committee the beginning of the process whereby a gradual weakening of Protestant hegemony in north America would take place as the religious mainstream began to be divided between what Herberg (1955) later described as the 'equilegitimate subdivisions' of 'Protestant-Catholic-Jew'. At this early stage, however, the hegemony of Protestant liberalism in America was little challenged, since the Catholic and Jewish voices at the Parliament largely echoed the liberal views of its Protestant organisers.

Bonney's speech not only exemplifies the dominance of the liberal agenda at the Parliament, it also reminds us of the distinctive features of this agenda in its late nineteenth-century American guise. These themes derived from an Enlightenment thought shaped and formed by the distinctive features of American republicanism and by the particular interests of the emancipated white male middle classes whose interests it served and regulated.

At the heart of Bonney's speech lies the unifying Enlightenment category of 'Man' (the exclusion of women is, of course, significant). Like the Enlightenment thinkers of the seventeenth century, Bonney assumes that this common humanity lies beyond the differences which divide man from man. For Bonney, the guarantor of this common humanity is the Father God (of Protestantism) in relation to whom all men are brothers. The Parliament is premised on this common humanity, and it is this which makes Bonney confident that the speakers at the Parliament will, despite their differences, be able to communicate and learn from one another. Far from being a static or merely biological category, humanity here becomes an ideal and a *telos* towards which the whole of religious and human history is seen to move. Whilst Bonney admits that 'individual opinions of the divine nature and attributes will differ', he is confident that the Parliament will inaugurate a new era of agreement and a 'new epoch of brotherhood and peace'. Why? because ultimately all must unite in the one true religion towards which human history moves – 'the religion of the love and worship of God and the love and service of man'.

The 'golden rule' religion which Bonney commends as the true universal religion is, of course, nothing other than liberal Protestantism. Its similarities with the 'natural religion' depicted by the latter's forebears, the sixteenth and seventeenth century Deists, are unmistakable. Like them, and like their later American spokesmen (Jefferson and Franklin, for example), Bonney and his fellow organisers viewed those features of a religious tradition which distinguish it from others as merely 'historic' – incidental accretions which pollute a pure religion of service to God and man. In championing a universal natural religion the Deists hoped to bring to an end the sort of religious wars which had ravaged Europe (Toulmin, 1992). Bonney also hopes for an end to 'sectarian strife'. He may have had in mind any number of possible disruptions to the fragile social and political order of the late nineteenth century: gathering pressures for the emancipation of women; racial strife in America; class unrest; rebellions against colonial rule. Whatever his fears, it seems clear that Bonney commends the present world order and a religion which legitimates it. Of greater scope than the 'civil religion' identified by de Tocqueville (1965), Herberg (1955) and Bellah (1967) as such an important part of American life, the universal religion of Bonney and his fellow liberals at the Parliament thus had a scope which, like the Exposition itself, was both global and national. Its promotion went hand in hand with the promotion of a world order in which American supremacy would be guaranteed and the interests of the new propertied middle classes secured.

To assume, as do many commentators on religion and modernity, that Christianity found itself profoundly threatened by the rise of modernity in general and the modern democratic state in particular is thus to ignore both the importance and the confidence of what Sydney Ahlstrom (1972) has called 'crusading Protestantism'. 'Mankind is drifting towards religion and not away from it', proclaimed Barrows (1984, pp. 1569). Allied with social and political power, and as yet unthreatened by the rise of conservative, charismatic and fundamentalist forms of Christianity, the liberals' belief that Protestantism would conquer the world is understandable. Not even the so-called acids of religion like science and rationalism could dent liberal confidence, for far from being threatened by theories like evolution, religious liberals claimed them as their own. It is thus no coincidence that the religious themes which Bonney rehearsed in his opening speech at the Parliament meshed perfectly with the themes of the Exposition as a whole. Rather, it is an indication of the way in which such Protestantism help formed the core values of the society of which it was such a central part.

Of course Bonney was not representative of *all* Protestants at the Parliament. As a Swedenborgian he took his place alongside other more radical Protestant groups like the Unitarians, Universalists, and Transcendentalists who were generally less exclusive in outlook than the mainline denominations. Other Protestants at the Parliament – like Barrows, for instance – could be a little more defensive of Christianity. In his summation, for example, the latter felt the need to assert that 'no religion excepting Christianity put forth any strong and serious claims to universality' (1894, p. 1572). Others took a more extreme position: Francis Edward Clark, for example, told the Parliament that, 'The greasy bull of Madura and Tanjore has little in common with the Lamb of God who takes away the sins of the world' (Seager, 1993, p 318). Yet this sort of exclusivism was remarkably rare at the Parliament. On the whole, the Protestants there united seamlessly behind their banner of belief in the fatherhood of God, the brotherhood of man, and the superiority of liberalism. Yet despite their unity and their confidence, forces subversive of their established belief were already at work. And ironically, it was liberal Christianity which had in part inspired them, and the Parliament which gave them a platform.

'The Pure and Formless One': Colonial Voices and the Subversions of the New Spirituality

Judging by the reaction of the press and those who attended the Parliament, the man who stole the show was the Hindu 'monk' Vivekananda. Even today it is Vivekananda's name which is most often associated with the Parliament – as a web search for 'World's Parliament of Religions' will quickly confirm. Accounts like that of the 'eye-witness' quoted above suggest that it is in terms of Vivekananda's difference and exoticism that his success at the Parliament should be explained. This appeal was clearly sensual as well as intellectual, for it is in terms of his 'gorgeous red apparel' and 'bronzed face surmounted with a huge turban of yellow' that Vivekananda is celebrated. As has already been suggested, however, the Columbian Exposition offered a framework in which such difference could be easily contained through classification in terms of a hierarchy of progress and civilization. As Said (1978) and other post-colonial theorists have shown, this framework often inhibited serious engagement with non-western cultures and helped foster a range of stereotypes in terms of which other cultures – here 'the Orient' and 'Orientals' – could be understood with a minimum of effort. Not surprisingly, those Orientals who conformed most closely to western expectations tended to be the most favourably received, and it is in these terms that Vivekananda's impact must be understood. Even in his adoption of robes and turban we see an acute reflexivity at work – for this was the sort of attire which a western audience would expect of an eastern holy man, and certainly not the natural attire of a middle class Bengali.

It was not only in his appearance that Vivekananda both satisfied and exceeded the expectations of his audience, however. His triumph was equally complete in relation to his message, for Vivekananda managed to restate the liberal universalism of the Parliament in fresh, compelling and radical terms (as well as in fluent English). What many of Vivekananda's audience conveniently overlooked was that he was a highly educated and westernised member of the new middle class or *bhadralok* created in Bengal by the arrival of the British; as such he understood very well the nature of the liberal creed and was able to affirm many of its central tenets.[3] But his 'exotic' credentials as a Hindu holy man also gave him the liberty to push this creed beyond its contemporary Christian limits, and in so doing to develop an influential new version of the New Spirituality.

Vivekananda's speech at the Parliament was entitled simply: 'Hinduism'. His task was to interpret Hinduism to his audience, but unlike some other members of the Asian delegation, his interpretation was far more than a dryly 'scientific' account (on the importance of the World's Parliament in the development of the scientific study of religion see Ziolkowski, 1993). Rather, Vivekananda's 'Hinduism' was a work of creative reconstruction and reinterpretation. At its heart lay a stress on the unity and universalism of Hinduism. Vivekananda was willing to admit the seeming multiplicity of Indian religion, a multiplicity which embraced Buddhism, Jainism and even polytheism, but there was, he claimed, a still centre to this multiplicity, a centre in which variety became unity. This centre was, he explained, the 'One through whose command the wind blows, the fire burns, the clouds rain, and death stalks upon earth ... He is everywhere the pure and formless one' (Barrows, p. 972). Vivekananda, in other words, identified Hinduism with an absolutist monism – the belief that the universe and all its inhabitants are ultimately one, united within a Spirit which flows through all things. For Vivekananda, it is not Christianity but Hinduism which has most perfectly realized this truth. 'To the Hindu', he told his audience,

> the whole world of religions is only a travelling, a coming up, of different men and women, through various conditions and circumstances, to the same goal. Every religion is only an evolving a God out of the material man; and the same God is the inspirer of all of them. Why, then, are there so many contradictions? They are only apparent, says the Hindu. The contradictions come from the same truth adapting itself to the different circumstances of different natures.

And then, using the same image used by Bonney, Vivekananda concluded:

> It is the same light coming through different colors ... But in the heart of everything the same truth reigns ... The Hindu might have failed to carry out his plans, but if there is ever to be a universal religion, it must be one which would have no location in place or time, which would be infinite like the God it would preach ... which would recognize a divinity in every man or woman, and whose whole scope, whole force would be centered in aiding humanity to realise its divine nature. (Barrows, p. 977)

Adopting without demure the liberals' assumptions about religious unity as the ideal towards which all human history moves, Vivekananda thus presented Hinduism rather than Christianity as the end of such striving. At a stroke, this trumped Christian suprecessionism with a Hindu version, and answered western criticisms of Hindu disunity and polytheism. Polytheism, he argued, was but the worship of God under different forms suited to different times and conditions and was not worse – and probably a good deal better – than the images found in the churches of the Catholics and the minds of the Protestants. At the same time, Vivekananda's Hindu universalism suggested not only the superiority of Hinduism in relation to Christianity, but in relation to other Asian religions as well. As such it helped to foster a growing pan-Asian sentiment, whilst at the same time safeguarding the position of Hinduism (on the rise and fall of pan-Asianism in the later colonial period see Hay, 1970).

In turning Christian liberalism against its own supporters, Vivekananda was, of course, exploiting the radical potential of liberalism itself. In the religion of the Parliament's organisers this potential had been neglected as liberalism became the legitimating religion of a social and political order organised around the interests of a propertied middle class. In Vivekananda's hands, however, the critical cutting edge of the liberal critique was sharpened once again. Like the Deists two centuries before, Vivekananda launched an attack on the 'externals' of religion and on their potential for superstition, exclusivism, and division. God, Vivekananda insisted, lay behind all images and symbols, and behind the divisions of historic religion. The Almighty must be discovered by individuals for themselves, and not imposed by religious authorities. 'External, material worship is the lowest stage' insisted Vivekananda, 'the Hindu does not want to live upon words and theories – if there is an all-merciful universal soul, he will go to him direct' (Barrows, p. 974). Likewise, Vivekananda recovered the radical potential of a liberal stress on human perfectibility. The human soul, he insisted again and again, 'is eternal and immortal, perfect and infinite', and in conscious opposition to a Christian emphasis on human sinfulness, he made the following heady appeal to his audience:

> Allow me to call you, brethren, by that sweet name, heirs of immortal bliss – yea, the Hindu refuses to call you sinners. Ye are the children of God, the sharers of immortal bliss, holy and perfect beings, ye are divinities on earth. Sinners? It is a sin to call man so; it is a standing libel on human nature. Come up, Oh, live and shake off the delusion that you are sheep; you are souls immortal, spirits free and blest and eternal ...' (Barrows, p. 971).

Not surprisingly, Vivekananda's message made some Christians at the Parliament a little restive. In his history of the Parliament, for example, Barrows (1894) goes out of his way to insist that the Conference promoters had no intention of supporting a cosmic or universal faith separate from Christianity and that 'their objects were more reasonable and important'. Furthermore, Barrows notes that 'while the men of India ... were at no intellectual disadvantage with the men of Christian America and Europe, it must be said that the training which they brought to the Parliament was largely from Christian sources' (p. 1572). Whilst it is hard to determine how widely Barrows' views were shared, the scraps of evidence available suggest that it was those who shared the values of the liberal establishment, yet who felt partially excluded from it, who were likely to be most positive. Of these, women almost certainly formed the largest group. We know, for example, that women figured prominently in the Vedanta Society which Vivekananda founded in 1895, and that they were amongst his most active and loyal supporters in the USA from that time on (see, for example, Burke, 1983–87). No doubt Vivekananda's message of individual empowerment through unmediated communion appealed to women unhappy with their position of spiritual dependence on male clergy and unable to enjoy the economic, political and social advantages reserved for middle class men. What is more, Vivekananda appears to have taken pains to accentuate this appeal, commenting in his speech to the Parliament, for example, that the authors of the Vedas were the true founders of Hinduism and that he is 'glad to tell this audience that some of the very best of them were women' (Barrows, p. 969). A poem written in dialect by Minnie Andrews Snell, and presented as 'Aunt Hannah's' impressions of the Parliament, offers another interesting fragment of evidence.[4] Speaking of Vivekananda 'Aunt Hannah' comments:

> Then I heered th' han'some Hindu monk, drest up in orange dress,
> Who sed that all humanity was part of God – no less,
> An' he sed we was not sinners, so I comfort took once more,
> While the Parliament of Religions roared with approving roar.

Then, after an unflattering comparison with the sectarianism of the Christians, she concludes:

> Must I leave all this sarchin' 'tel I reach th' other side?
> I'll treat all men as brothers while on this airth I bide,
> An' let "Love" be my motto, 'tel I enter in th' door.
> Of that great Religious Parl'ment, where creeds don't count no more.

In many important respects then, the spirituality which Vivekananda articulated at the World's Parliament – and which was reproduced by some of his admirers – conforms closely to the ideal type of the New Spirituality outlined at the start of this chapter. It would be misleading, however, to suggest that Vivekananda was a lonely pioneer of the New Spirituality in his day – or even at the Parliament. In fact Vivekananda had many predecessors both in India and the west. In the former liberal Christianity, particularly in its Unitarian guise, had long exercised an influence on Hindu reformers, and had helped shape the universalist spirituality of the culturally important Hindu reform sect the Brahmo Samaj (Kopf, 1979). A fellow Bengali and spokesman of the Brahmo sect, Protap Chandra Majumdar ('P. C. Mozoomdar') (1840–1905), was also present at the Parliament, and articulated a spirituality which, though more Christocentric and acceptable to many of the Parliament's organisers than Vivekananda's, shared the latter's monistic universalism. Tracing the common channels of influence even further back, both Majumdar and Vivekananda had been influenced by a Brahmo teacher of the previous generation, Keshub Chandra Sen (1838–84), who eventually broke from the offical Brahmo Samaj and attempted to pioneer a new fully synthetic universalist religion which again displays many similarities to Vivekananda's.[5] Keshub and Majumdar had both undertaken successful lecture preaching tours to the west earlier in the nineteenth century, and had established the pattern of the Indian holy man bringing his wisdom to the west which undoubtedly aided and influenced Vivekananda.

Nor was it only Hindus at the Parliament who articulated the New Spirituality. Amongst the Asian delegates a synthesis of Asian religion, liberal Protestantism, and evolutionary idealism with interesting parallels to Vivekananda's was also offered by a young Ceylonese Buddhist monk, Anagarika Dharmapala. Dharmapala also spoke directly to his audience in English, addressing them on the subject of 'The World's Debt to Buddha'. Like Vivekananda, he embraced the idea that the world was moving towards a new universal religion, and like Vivekananda he presented Christianity as part of the old rather than the new dispensation. Instead of presenting Hinduism as the religion of a new humanity, however, Dharmapala reserved this honour for Buddhism. As he explained,

> the tendency of enlightened thought of the day all the world over is not towards theology, but philosophy and psychology. The bark of theological dualism is drifting into danger. The fundamental principles of evolution and monism are being accepted by the thoughtful. History is repeating itself. Twenty-five centuries ago India witnessed an intellectual and religious revolution which culminated in the overthrow of monthesim, priestly selfishness, and the establishment of a synthetic religion, a system of life and thought which was appropriately called Dhamma – Philosophical Religion. (Seager, 1993, p. 412)

Dharmapala also stressed the nondogmatic and experiential nature of Buddhism – a philosophy which every man and woman must test for him or herself. Lacking Vivekananda's strong idealist and monistic stress, however, Dharmapala presented Buddhism as primarily an ethical religion – a religion of love, peace and self-purification, virtues which were – just like those which Vivekananda associated with Hinduism – fully compatible with a liberal Protestant ethos. (In other speeches and essays, particularly those addressed to an Indian audience, Vivekananda often developed a Hindu version of a work ethic, and placed great stress on the 'manly' virtues which were also celebrated by nineteenth century muscular Protestantism.)

Like Vivekananda, Dharmapala's ability to appeal to a western audience was due to his extensive knowledge not only of his own tradition, but of western thought. Like Vivekananda too, his knowledge of western thought and Christian liberalism was closely related to his status as a subject of a country under British colonial rule, with all the educational and cultural opportunities and frustrations that implied.[6] Unlike Vivekananda, however, Dharmapala's religious mission was later decisively influenced by his contact with the Theosophical Society, which had been established in Sri Lanka (then Ceylon) by Madame Blavatsky and Colonel Olcott after their arrival on the island in 1880. It was Olcott who did most to defend and revivify Buddhism on the island, and the version of the Dharma which he propagated anticipated Dharmapala's address at the World's Parliament in its stress on Buddhism as an ethical religion which is highly 'scientific', 'eminently practical' and 'not a creed but a philosophy' (Bartholomeusz, 1993, pp. 237–8; Murphet, 1972, pp. 106–7).[7] In later life Dharmapala would break from Olcott and develop a more militantly nationalist form of Sinhalese Buddhism (Obeyeskere, 1995). In 1893, however, as in the lecture tours in Britain and America which followed his success in Chicago, Dharmapala would continue to present a version of Buddhism which – as Tweed (1992) has argued – provided an avenue for dissent, without necessitating a wholesale break from the ethical consensus of mainstream Victorian culture.

Dharmapala was not the only member of the Theosophical Society present at the Parliament. An entire denominational congress was held by the Theosophists, presided over by key representatives like Annie Besant and William Q. Judge. What is interesting about the Theosophists is the way in which they offered a version of the New Spirituality identical in essentials with Vivekananda's, though they came not from the east but from the west. As Judge explained in his 'Presentation' at the Parliament, 'three objects' of the Theosophical Society were:

> First, to establish the nucleus of a universal brotherhood, without distinctions of race, creed, sex, caste, or color; Second, to promote the study of Aryan and other religions, literatures and sciences, and the demonstrate the importance of that study; Third, to investigate unexplained laws of nature and the psychical powers latent in man. (Barrows, 1894, p. 1517)

Thus we find in Theosophy yet again an illustration of the way in which the New Spirituality adopted key elements of a universalist liberal humanism (such as the hope for a universal brotherhood of humanity), whilst opening these up to include women and other races, and moving beyond Christianity (though western, the Theosophists claimed to be supernaturally inspired by Oriental masters). Thus for the Theosophists God was no Almighty Father but, in Olcott's words, 'an Eternal and Omnipresent Principle which, under many different names, was the same in all religions' (quoted by Fields, 1992, p. 93). As Judge explained at the Parliament,

> Theosophy postulates an eternal principle called the unknown, which can never be cognized except through its manifestations. This eternal principle is in and is every thing and being. It periodically and eternally manifests itself and recedes again from manifestation. In this ebb and flow evolution proceeds and is itself the progress of that manifestation. (Barrows, 1894, p. 1518)

The message was the same as that delivered by Vivekananda. The explanation for the greater impact of the latter must relate therefore not only to his message, but to his provenance and person. What, after all, could be more convincing to those who already believed in a universal religion, and who were willing to push the hope of a new dawn of fraternal co-operation between different nations and races to its more radical conclusions, than the sight of a man from distant and exotic parts of the Orient confirming that these very same hopes and beliefs had been echoed many centuries before by the ancient seers of Vedic India?

Conclusion

Attention to the most celebrated examples of alternative spirituality at the Parliament – alternative, that is, to the mainline liberal Protestantism of its organisers – helps confirm the hypothesis that the end of the nineteenth century witnessed the rise of a form of religiosity sufficiently unified to be described as a single current. It is this current which is referred to here as the New Spirituality. As the Parliament shows, spokesmen for this form of modern spirituality came from both west and east, and from a variety of religious traditions, though it was the message of the Hindu Vivekananda which won the greatest attention.

Study of the Parliament and its context also helps shed light on the factors which encouraged the growth of the New Spirituality at this time. Above all, it reveals the constitutive relation between such spirituality and the Victorian liberal Protestant consensus. The New Spirituality came into being through the simultaneous retention, radicalization, and rejection of key themes in such Protestantism. It retained the ethics of liberalism, including a characteristic stress on the importance of work, activism, service to humankind, individualism, temperance and moral (especially sexual) purity. It radicalised and subverted liberalism's belief in evolutionary progress towards a new universal religion and culture by broadening the category of those who would be able to participate in this new religion to include women and other races, and by denying that this new universal religion would be Protestant. And it rejected what it referred to as liberal Protestantism's 'dualism', its belief in a theistic God and a sinful creation wholly separate from this God; in its place it offered a more 'scientific' monism which exalted each individual and gave moral and metaphysical underpinning to the idea that all was truly part of the 'One'.

The World's Parliament also reveals some of the wider socio-cultural dimensions of the New Spirituality. In terms of culture, the Parliament reveals the impact of Asian religions on the west – an impact which had begun as early as the eighteenth century (see, for example, Schwab (1984) and Halbfass (1988)). To explain the rise of the New Spirituality merely in terms of what is sometimes called the 'easternisation' of the west is not sufficient, however, since the categories of 'Asian' or 'eastern' religion embrace such a multitude of religious forms and beliefs. In more specific cultural terms then, the World's Parliament reveals the process by which a central stream in eastern religion – metaphysical monism – was isolated as the essence of true religion, and set over against the 'dualism' of western religions, particularly Christianity.

In broader social, economic and political terms, the World's Parliament helps us see clearly the way in which the New Spirituality – despite the mask of the 'merely spiritual' – staged a subversion not only of the dominant Protestant ideology, but of the material interests it served. As we have seen, the ideology of mainline Protestantism was fully compatible with the interests of adult males of the new urban middle classes. As we have also seen, the embrace of a truly universal religion which acknowledged neither man nor God as master, but affirmed the divinity and common humanity of all men and women, subverted these interests in a number of ways. Not only did it undermine the interests of Christian clergy (just as in India it undermined the interests of the hereditary brahmanical elites), it also undermined the ideology of domesticity and the unacknowledged and economically under-rewarded domestic labour of women on which Victorian society rested. What is more, such radical universalism subverted belief in white Euro-American supremacy (and so in western colonialism) both within America and throughout the world. In this sense, speakers like Vivekananda helped undermine the sacred geography of the World's Fair with its 'White City', hall of women, and 'evolutionary' arrangement of different races and nations along the Midway Plaisance.

To speak in these terms of the possible socio-political implications of the New Spirituality is not, of course, to imply that all those who represented or received it exploited them. The variety internal to the New Spirituality noted at the start of this chapter was evident to some degree at the Parliament where the Brahmos and Dharmapala, for example, offered a less politically radical version of the New Spirituality than Vivekananda (a difference which may be related to the reluctance of both the former to go as far in the direction of monism as Vivekananda). Despite this variety, however, the Parliament makes it very clear that the charges of individualism and political quietism often levelled against more recent manifestations of the New Spirituality are wide of the mark in relation to its nineteenth century forms. Indeed, it would appear that in its day such religiosity provided one of the few possible forums in which those outside a white, male, middle class establishment could give voice to their concerns and further their interests. For many women and colonized peoples, the New Spirituality offered a sense of identity and purpose – and even of superiority – which might otherwise have been unattainable.

The necessary price for a public voice and public influence at the end of the nineteenth century, however, was assent to some of the fundamental values of mainline Protestant culture. As we have seen, even the most radical proponents of the New Spirituality echoed belief in progress and the ideal of religious unity, as well as in the values of industry, indvidualism, and service. The gradual dissolution of this cultural world throughout the first half of the twentieth century inevitably led to changes in the New Spirituality in the twentieth. When it re-emerged with new force as part of the counter-cultural revolution of the 1960s, it did so minus the baggage of a muscular Protestant ethic, with less emphasis on metaphysics and cosmology, and with less concern to prove its 'scientific' credentials. By the end of the century it had also spawned many varieties (often grouped under the heading of 'New Age') which were at least as concerned with self-development as with political change. Yet the central affirmations of the New Spirituality outlined at the start of this chapter remained significantly the same.

Notes

1. On the unsuccessful struggle of blacks for representation in the organisation of the Columbian Exposition see Rydell (1984) and Greenhalgh (1988). The latter comments, 'the American Negro and Indian posed grave problems to the organisers, who pushed freedom and democracy as the ideals of the Fair, yet who had no wish to give either race a position of equality at any level' (p. 98).
2. Our basic knowledge of the Parliament comes from John Henry Barrows's *The World's Parliament of Religions: An Illustrated and Popular Story* (2 vols) and *Neely's History of the Parliament of Religions*, edited by Walter Houghton (edited extracts from both can be found in Seager, 1983).
3. For more on Vivekananda's intellectual and spiritual development see Raychaudhuri (1988) and *Life of Swami Vivekananda* (1979).
4. The poem appeared in the Chicago *Open Court* in 1893, a few weeks after the Parliament's close. It is quoted by Ziolkowski (1993, pp. 16–18).
5. One reason why Vivekananda distanced himself from Brahmoism in Bengal appears to have been that he wished to immerse himself more fully in an 'authentic' Hinduism of the people (Brahmoism being largely the religion of a westernised elite in India). Vivekananda realised this aim through his contact with the Bengali *sanyasi* Ramakrishna, whose disciple he became.

6 Dharmapala, previously David Hewivitarne, came from a Buddhist household, but was educated at Christian mission schools in Sri Lanka. For more on Dharmapala's life and teaching see Fields (1992); Tweed (1992) and Prothero (1996).
7 Prothero (1996) argues that Olcott's Buddhism was a 'creole' faith whose 'grammar' remained Protestant even though his 'lexicon' was Buddhist and his 'accent' Theosophical (see, for example, p. 96).

Chapter Five

The Swedenborgian Church in England

Ian Sellers

Swedenborgianism enjoyed a period of social and intellectual respectability in England in the 1840s which it had not experienced before. Emerson's lecture tours in the New World and the Old in which he poured scorn on the Swedish seer served only to highlight how deeply indebted he was to his subject's insights. (The same had been true at an earlier time of Emmanuel Kant.)[1] A remarkable story in *Frazer's Magazine* in 1849 by J.A. Froude ('The Swedenborgian') highlighted the established status and attractiveness of the movement, while J.J. Tayler in the *Prospective Review* for 1850 analysed its spiritual content with serious purposiveness and without the usual gibes about Swedenborg's believing in men on the moon.

Yet by 1876 the Liverpool satirical magazine *Porcupine* dealt with the New Church as an exotic, half-forgotten and transitory phenomenon in its series 'Sundays in Strange Churches'. In the judgement of men of letters the Swedenborgian movement had come and apparently gone. Indeed from about this time onwards the many individuals who found inspiration in the 'Buddha of the North' did not really bother to link up with or even enquire about the organised New Church.

By this date the movement was fragmented into two separate denominations in the USA (one Episcopal, the other not so), and two in England, though here the 'Bible Christians' were an ephemeral minority sect. More seriously, the Swedenborgian Society, a study centre for attached and unattached Swedenborg scholars, existed in uneasy and occasionally hostile relationship to the mainstream New Church societies. The movement had been weakened seriously.

In the 1840s, however, this remarkable Church was everywhere spoken about (and often spoken against). In England it cut through the whole gamut of social classes, except the extremes at both ends, embracing captains of industry such as the Haworths of Accrington, 'cottentots' who made this town the Swedenborgian centre par excellence, down to mill workers in other Lancashire towns (Lancashire was its heartland), silk weavers in Failsworth near Manchester, and fisherfolk in Brightlingsea, Essex. It also attracted an unusual number of educators, scientists and students of the human mind, as well as a number of highly innovative entrepreneurs whose faith seemed to inspire them into a kind of 'lateral thinking' as to what might be the next phase of technical innovation now that the old patterns of industrialisation were well established. The latter included Sir Isaac Pitman of shorthand fame, William Harbutt who delighted generations of children with his plasticene, and Mr. E. W. Banks with his Ewbank carpet sweeper. The New Church in England is today very much an affair of interrelated families: but one hundred and fifty years ago its doors were wide open to potential converts on the lookout not merely for novelty, but for a deeper apprehension of spiritual truths to which the established churches were in Swedenborg's own sight largely impervious. In six different ways, I suggest, the New Church resonated with the spiritual longings of Victorian people.

1. The first and most obvious strength of the Swedenborgians was their ability to integrate those two most powerful thrusts of the period, popular evangelism and a search for a stately, aesthetic and emotionally satisfying mode of worship. Not that they were alone in trying to fill this gap. In their different ways Irving's Catholic Apostolic Church and Robert Aitken's Catholic Evangelicalism and the late Victorian Anglo-Catholic parochial missions were symptomatic of the same quest. Nevertheless the New Church was unusual in that in its origins it was both methodistical and 'high church'.

It was methodistical in that some of its earliest preachers like James and Robert Hindmarsh, Joseph Salmon and Ralph Mather were former Wesleyan evangelists, and that William Clowes, the Manchester Anglican minister who pioneered the new creed in Lancashire had a large Methodist following and preached from Methodist pulpits, while his movement drew heavily on converts from the various branches of Methodism and shared a building with several nonconformist groups, constituting what Ward (1972) has called a type of 'cross-bench' ecumenism. All these evangelists moreover seem to have tapped into a current of working class religious sensibility which embraced lingering folk religion, the mystical neo-platonism of Jakob Boehme (1575–1624) and William Law (1686–1761), a smattering of popular Enlightenment insights, a dash of High Tory loyalism and nostalgia – with the added excitement of a new revelation, that the Lord had indeed returned and in 1757 the New Jerusalem had descended to earth, Swedenborg being its witness. A map of 'mystical Britain' and one of Swedenborgian evangelistic success would show a remarkable overlap (see Garnett, 1984 and Lineham, 1988).

At the same time there is the use (a parallel here with Lindsey, Disney and the first Unitarian congregations) of a 'reformed' Anglican prayer book, authorised by the first New Church Conference of 1789. Soon New Church ordinands could have hands laid on them by an inner core of 'ordaining ministers' and a kind of apostolic succession could be guaranteed. Worship was staid, reverent and liturgically correct. The ministers wore white robes and coloured stoles on which the Alpha/Omega symbols and the Sun (a vital ingredient in the Master's teaching) were prominent. There were stained glass windows, altars and candles. The baptismal rite and the Holy Supper were observed. The 'gorgeous temples' of the New Church evoked some mirth and resentment among plain Dissenters. Bogue and Bennett in 1812 prophesied that this craze would soon decline: in effect the movement was then on the verge of a period of great expansion in Britain and the United States.

How may this phenomenon be satisfactorily defined? It has been called a cult, a sociological term which may be applicable to assorted twentieth century fanaticisms, but is most inappropriately used of a movement as broad and open-minded as the New Church. Was it therefore a sect, as Jones (1974) has argued? (Jones sees the sect's main role as fertilising later Spiritualism, the New Thought movement, Christian Science and Theosophy). If so, its sectarian and denominational stages overlap so markedly and at such an early stage that it is hard to tell where one ends and the other begins. Was it a movement? The Swedenborg Society may certainly be thus designated, though hardly the organised New Church itself. Perhaps it is best to allow the Swedenborgians' own description of themselves as a, or rather the, New Church to stand in default of any more satisfactory definition.

2. A second way of exploring the attractiveness of Swedenborgianism for the Victorians is to study it as a revival both of the neo-platonist and gnostic strands of earlier Christian history. Both had a peculiar fascination for the Victorians in revolt against orthodox dogmatisms. Neo-platonism (reflected particularly in the Liberal Anglican experience from Coleridge through Maurice to Dean Inge) exerted a certain allure. That this is a tradition to which Swedenborg belonged is without question. The parallels between his thinking and that of Renaissance Platonists such as Nicholas of Cusa and Ficino are marked, notably (once we can penetrate to the heart of what they were thinking) in their preference for an idealised 'Christian religion' (Ficino) or 'True Religion' (Swedenborg) without the definite article. (Both of course wrote in Latin which lacks this participle. Nonetheless the purport of their reasoning is plain.)

Swedenborg was at pains to distinguish the Church Universal (secret, hidden, known only to God) from the Church Specific, its 'many' institutional forms. As for the gnostic undertones 'mystery religion' was of great interest to the Victorians, as their popular fiction showed. 'Mystery' was encapsulated in the esoteric and private vocabulary (Swedenborgese) which the New Church taught its members to master, terms such as the Grand Man, the Divine Human, influxes, the proprium, ruling love etc. Once excited by these concepts humble Swedenborgians would club together to purchase translations of the Master's most significant work, the *Arcana Coelestia* (Secrets of the Heavens). Here were revealed the Correspondences, the very core of Swedenborg's teaching, one's understanding progressing from the literal to the spiritual to the celestial sense both of Scripture and of created things. Thus the New Church teaches that the walls of the New Jerusalem in revelation represent truths keeping out undesirable thoughts; the gates represent means of entry to the Church for earnest seekers; the foundations stand for fundamental doctrines; and the streets for lesser ones linking the major teachings together. To probe these intricate mysteries and find answers in the Master's writings (or, more correctly, Writings) was clearly a thrilling exercise for dedicated enquirers.

There are three other related questions. Religious sociologists have pointed out à propos the Irvingites, for example, or the early Salvation Army, that outré and exotic creeds and forms of worship have a special appeal in an age of rapid mobility, upwards or downwards, to families feeling themselves especially threatened by the pace of change. The New Church, embracing such a wide range of occupational groups, would well repay investigation on this score.

On a broader front still, did Swedenborg answer another religious dilemma which was by now becoming acute, the growing gulf between the propositional religion of Catholic and Protestant scholasticism and innate religious principles ('natural religion')? By the simple expedient of introducing a fresh revelation, the Writings, in the light of which the Word should be read and interpreted but which at the same time illuminates the status, psychology and perfectibility of human kind, was Swedenborg trying to bridge the great divide? Those who glimpsed that he was, and were convinced that his quest was successful, were naturally drawn to the New Church (Harrison, 1990).

Finally, the spirit world, of angels, dreams and visitations, as their literature again underscores, was a very real concern for the Victorians. Here New Churchmen had to steer a very careful course, between the Scylla of interest in these matters (Swedenborg like Blake was after all the seer who explored the spiritual world and to whom these experiences were commonplace) and the Charybdis of popular Spiritualism, particularly as this developed in working class circles after about 1850. The latter could be dangerous, reacting uncomfortably on established Swedenborgian work. (The strong Keighley society was nearly wrecked by a 'Spiritualist' secession.) Spiritualists were thus held at arm's length. Yet paranormal experience could not be outlawed altogether, especially when it was associated with persons of intellectual calibre who had read Swedenborg: hence the Church's interest in the Society for Psychical Research, and in Conan Doyle, Oliver Lodge, Vale Owen and W.H. Myers.

3. Certain themes intrigued the Victorians, but the mores of their culture rendered them curiously reticent and confused in their handling of them. They favoured oblique and embarrassed approaches to children, to sex and to the status of animals. Only brave spirits, including the New Church people, were courageous enough to bring them out into the open.

How dependent on Milton is Swedenborg's teaching on sex and married love must remain a moot point. Sufficient to note that *Conjugial Love* (1765) explores male/female relationships on earth and treats of 'scortatory' i.e. unnatural love also, as well as depicting the close companionship of male and female angels in heaven. Here love is freed from all lust, guilt, and, as Swedenborg put it, 'sadness'. Reunited souls are married in heaven and sexual enjoyment continues: Swedenborg on one of his heavenly visits beheld angels coming towards him locked together. He also (as a bachelor) claimed to know the identity of his heavenly bride. Thus the heavens for the Swedish seer are places of heightened sensual experience where angels perceive truth, 'with far more charity, crispness and vividness' than on earth. Hence heavenly love he describes as conjugial to distinguish it from its earthly, conjugal, variety.

Childhood fascinated the Victorians: were the young wild beasts needing to be tamed angelic beings or, maybe, (a hangover from the eighteenth century) miniature adults? Or were they a strange hybrid mixture with a special, almost indefinable status, like that which Charles Dickens' child-mothers possessed? The New Church gave a clear answer to these problems. On the whole Swedenborg prized adult virtues more than childish ones, which is why education was so important to him, for by this process children learn to distinguish the good and the true and to exercise free will creatively. The implications of this belief are two-fold: on earth Swedenborgian Sunday, Day and private schools offered a particularly child-centred form of education, based on a mental/moral/spiritual trichotomy. This merged in the thought of many New Church educators with the teachings of Pestalozzi. The result was that in persons like Goyder, Buchanan and the controversial Samuel Winderspin the Swedenborgian body made a contribution to educational theory and practice quite disproportionate to its size. In heaven, meanwhile, children who die in infancy were said to receive special care in nursery-type surroundings, so special that their heavenly nurture is entrusted to women of an advanced psycho-spiritual state who alone can guarantee that their charges take their proper place in the 'heavens of angels'. In this way the child is at the heart of New Church concerns. (For Swedenborg's influence on Oberlin and the development of the kindergarten see Woofenden 1981, chapter 1.)

Swedenborgian interest in animals is a controversial topic, for the reason that the strong-willed men who embraced the cause of animal rights in the 1810s and 1820s – Cowherd, Schofield, Brotherton and the outstanding Rowland Detroisier, a name to conjure with in Radical history – felt constrained to disown the New Church and set up their own Bible Christian societies, including the famous Round House in Manchester, of such significance in history of local Chartism. Nonetheless, vegetarianism was put by these pioneers firmly on the map. Manchester and Salford were especially affected, which is why the Vegetarian Society's head office is still located in nearby Altrincham, a tribute (and a largely forgotten one) to these Swedenborgian crusaders. Before long their movement had begun to infiltrate the mainstream New Church also.

4. A fourth point of contact and interaction between Victorian seekers and the faith of the New Church hinges on the latter's remarkable openness to other religions and religious experiences. Swedenborg was writing at the end of the Enlightenment period with its concept of the Great Chain of Being and of those principles which Arthur Lovejoy has defined as underlying it: plenitude, continuity, gradation. He also stands on the threshold of the nineteenth century discovery or rediscovery of other faiths, an intellectual quest taken up in Britain by individuals such as Max Müller and later on by Unitarian thinkers, Estlin Carpenter in particular. (In much the same way Swedenborg may be regarded as a scientist or psychologist as likewise straddling two worlds.)

We should recall his teaching that the Churches where the Word is gladly received become, by correspondence, like the heart and lungs of the human body, providing a vital force for the whole race. Though increasingly this supportive function devolves on the New Church, other religious bodies can share in the work. The 'Universal Church' embraces not only the Christian Churches but those who seem to stand apart from them. In the end all religions comprise the Homo Maximus, for separate individuals and groups fuse in Swedenborg's mind into the similitude of a single being composed of innumerable organs, members and tissues.

This teaching has surprising implications. According to Swedenborg, in regard to the heavens and the hells, it is the Ruling Love (i.e. character and disposition) of a Hindu, Jew or Muslim that makes a person an angel or a devil – and the angelic host recruits from all over the world. This echoes the seventeenth century 'eternal gospel' and is certainly the philosophy of William Blake. On one of his heavenly journeys Swedenborg encountered Moslem communities in one of the remoter heavens, taking the form of angels.

There are likewise fascinating Swedenborgian insights based on his teaching on colours, especially on the rainbow, where the spectrum corresponds to our perception of the virtues, or in his own words our attainment of spiritual regeneration, from red, the good life, through mercy, peace, liveliness, truth, wisdom and mutual care to outflowing peace, innocence and love. (In Swedenborg's teaching mortals tend to reverse this order and see the rainbow ladder upside down.) There is a marked similarity here to the Chakra system of ascending spiritual natures of the eastern mystical tradition (Curry, 1988). The 'Correspondences' were a source not just of private intellectual speculation but of emotionally satisfying cosmic enlightenment for earnest seekers. With reference to Linda Woodhead's chapter which precedes this, it is not really surprising therefore that in 1893 it was not a Unitarian but a Swedenborgian layman, Charles Carroll Bonney, who chaired the Chicago World's Parliament of Religions.

5. Swedenborgianism seemed to answer another deep-felt nineteenth century need: for a more domesticated and anthropomorphic, less etherialised, ascetic and theocentric picture of heaven. This is a theme of McDannell and Lang's important study, *Heaven, A History* (1988). They underscore the New Church's 'vigorous alternative' to what had gone before. The Swedenborgians stressed the thin veil which separates earthly existence from the spiritual world, a teaching which coheres perhaps more closely with African rather than European traditional beliefs – hence the rapid spread of the New Church in Black Africa in recent decades. The Victorians desired a heaven of quasi-material, not to say sensual, quality, a place of endless enjoyment rather than of 'eternal rest', an intensification of familial loves and social relationships, a progression to ever more exciting experience of angelic/human encounter. Angels thus continue to serve the heavenly community: without such service they do not belong in heaven. 'Charity' must prevail here as on earth. And once again the hyper-active Victorians would have responded to such a vision.

In Swedenborgianism, Purgatory, Judgement and soul-sleeping all disappear, and the immediacy of heavenly bliss is taken for granted. 'Man after death' the Seer wrote, 'is as much a man as he was before, so much so as to be unaware that he is not still in the former world'. Physical and sense experience, like gender differences, persist in this heavenly sphere. Sleeping and waking, eating and drinking are the stuff of angelic activity. Flowers, blue skies, light and shade are all to be experienced, while living arrangements are remarkably like those of the New Jerusalem depicted in Revelation – though there is some suggestion that the evolving aesthetics of the modern city life-style may have inspired Swedenborg also (Curry, 1988).

There is another aspect of the Swedenborgian heaven worth commenting on. The Seer was an engineer but his heaven is no mechanistic construct. Here is dynamism prevailing over inertia, organic growth over permanence, motion over stasis, progressivist optimism over judgement from the eternal throne. Swedenborg in one striking passage depicts a group of new arrivals in heaven expecting to find an 'eternal Sabbath' and having to be re-educated in the truth that the spiritual world is at the opposite from the idleness of perpetual rest.

Needless to say there are varieties of otherworldly existence, 'heavens' as well as 'hells'. The spirit world is simply the door to heaven: thereafter lie the natural heaven (an existence very like our earthly one), a spiritual heaven corresponding to our highest ideals, and a celestial heaven, the ultimate stage of paradise restored, where the angel's outward appearance achieves total harmony with his/her innermost feelings. So the New Church heaven answered not only the Victorians' longing for 'a heaven of angels' but their ethical progressivism also. 'People in heaven develop steadily towards the springtime of life', Swedenborg wrote. Many a Victorian meliorist would have applauded that, while perhaps substituting 'earth' for 'heaven'. Yet it is a mark of the strength of the Swedenborgian position that this gloss would have had the Master's approval also. After all, if the Divine had designed an earth with people, not Himself, in mind, would He not logically have framed the heavens with similar intent?

The revolutionary character of the New Church heaven would surely have appealed to an age longing to be free from the old shibboleths. The mind/body dualism of Descartes, the theocentric teaching of Catholic and Protestant orthodoxy, the pessimism of Pascal, the Jansenists and of much contemporary Evangelicalism are here defied in a vision of a modern heaven which extended and perfected the perceived changeless qualities of earthly existence (McDannell and Lang, 1988). Love, work and society, those three major Victorian enthusiasms, were the marks of the New Church after-life.

In short, the Swedenborgian heaven was a joyful prospect (here perhaps the Wesleyan taproot of the movement continued to provide vital sustenance). So complete and reassuring was their vision that in 1866 a group, mainly New Church people, founded the Anti-Mourning Association to abolish mourning clothes and solemnities and introduce a buoyant, even cheery, note into the proceedings. Here the ritual became a sort of party to celebrate a natural rite of passage to a new but engagingly similar 'spiritual world' to the one being left behind.

6. 'Till we have built Jerusalem in England's green and pleasant land', as Blake put it in his triumphant Swedenborgian prophetic poem or, as the Seer declared, 'all religion has relation to life and the life of religion is to do good'. (Blake had a curious relationship to the Swedenborgians: with the movement till it began to assume institutional forms, then against it, and finally veering towards it again.)

Salvation for the New Church is not by faith alone – hence Swedenborg's particular dislike of Luther – but by 'Uses' i.e. usefulness or good deeds, themselves the fruits of Charity, a right disposition, which is in turn rooted in faith, but faith redefined as a perception of that which is true and good. Human relationships exhibit the divine purpose for humankind, or, as Swedenborg scholars put it, the Lord in his Divine Human works within us as individuals, leading on to transformed inter-personal relationships, of which marriage is the type. The word 'regeneration' is frequently encountered in Swedenborg: regeneration of the individual and of society in its train. In some ways he seems to be reaching out to the idea of Personalism, a vital concept in twentieth century American thinking, but for the Victorians here was a practical alternative to fruitless theological wrangling of which they, particularly in the 1830s and 1840s, were growing weary (we think of George Eliot and her circle). The New Church in these decades embarked on a whole series of good works quite disproportionate to its size, especially in relation to children, schools and orphanages. (The idea of the orphanage, save as a temporary expedient, offended these enlightened people: 'family placement' of parentless or abandoned children is what they were about.)

Meanwhile, Swedenborgians were active in both English political parties. Radical Liberalism had a special attraction: all the three nineteenth century

Swedenborgian MPs, C.A. Tulk, Joseph Brotherton, and Sir William Agnew, were of this persuasion. There was a particular contribution to the radical politics of Manchester and Salford (see Lineham, 1978). In 1896 there was founded a new Church Socialist Society whose magazine was called intriguingly 'Uses' (Smith, 1994).

Thus, whilst it is certainly an exaggeration to say, with Lineham (1978), the most thorough recent researcher into English Swedenborgianism, that the New Church 'replaced theory with anthropology' (p. 445), it certainly contributed greatly to the humanisation of Victorian religious thought and practice, giving humankind an exaggerated (to its critics) or a proper (to its adherents) role in the divinely ordained scheme of things.

Note

In assessing which particular qualities in the Victorian psyche would particularly respond to Swedenborgian thought I have been greatly indebted to W.E. Houghton's classic *Victorian Frame of Mind* (1957), especially his chapters on Progress and Love.

1   The most generous of Emerson's published comments on Swedenborg is probably this: 'he is lustrous with points and shooting spirals of thought and reminds me of one of those frosty winter mornings when the air is sparking with crystals' (1975, XI, p. 181). Emerson derived from Swedenborg his emphasis on correspondences, much of his scientific insight and a number of moral principles (Allen, 1981; Albanese, 1977). On Kant and Swedenborg see Woofenden (1981, pp. 65–80).

Chapter Six

Transcendentalists and Catholic Converts in Emerson's America

Shannon Cate

Orestes Brownson, Isaac Hecker, Sophia Ripley. These people all have two things in common. First, they were noted Transcendentalists, associated with Ralph Waldo Emerson (1803–82), the journal *The Dial*, and the communal experiments at Brook Farm. Second, they all converted to Roman Catholicism following their participation in the Transcendentalist movement. What seems at first glance to be a strange but isolated incident of a radical religious shift among a handful of prominent Transcendentalists turns out to be something of a trend. Many second generation Transcendentalists also became Catholic, as did people not necessarily associated with Transcendentalism, but closely related to those who were. Thus in Katherine Burton and Georgianna Pell Curtis's books of late nineteenth and early twentieth century American Catholic conversions family names like Dana, Peabody, Channing, and Hawthorne appear in testimonials and descriptions of people on the road to Rome. But what would lead people deeply involved in a movement noted for its infidelity to traditional Christian doctrines and its anti-authoritarian radicalism to embrace 'popery'? The phenomenon becomes even more curious when the Calvinist, even virulently anti-Catholic, backgrounds of most of the converts are taken into consideration.

I propose that the Transcendentalist movement *itself* was in a large part responsible for this shift in faith on the part of some Boston Brahmins and their friends and relations. While the momentum of Transcendentalism involved breaking free of certain kinds of tradition and forms of authority for some of its adherents, for others it actually functioned to open a way for the acceptance of new traditions and forms of authority. And by shaking up long-held Protestant religious doctrines and old New England social habits, the Transcendentalist movement actually served to break down some old prejudices and to inspire a craving for something radically different, though still devout and thoughtful. For some, the Catholic Church seems to have satisfied this craving. When viewed from this perspective, it appears that perhaps Transcendentalism did not exactly die out as its progenitors aged. For some of its adherents, it simply evolved into something different – though legitimately related.

On the other hand, the primary figure associated with Transcendentalism did not become a Roman Catholic, nor did he sympathize much with those who did. Ralph Waldo Emerson, who defined Transcendentalism for most of America in the nineteenth (and to a great extent, the twentieth) century, absolutely refused to consider the idea of church association once he left his own Unitarian pulpit. Rather, Emerson made it clear that association with or work for social or religious organizations of any kind was entirely inconsistent with his philosophy.

A close look at Emerson's essay, 'The Transcendentalist' will help to identify some of the main ideas, attitudes and emotions associated by a Transcendentalist with Transcendentalism, while a look at Katherine Burton's accounts of Transcendentalist conversions will help identify the reasons given by a Catholic for Catholic conversions. Both of these sources are problematic, in that they speak for others, and from a prejudiced point of view. Emerson lectures on what the Transcendentalists believe and how they behave, though he refers to no-one but himself as the authority on these matters. Burton writes expressly for the purpose of inspiring the already devout among her readers, of proselytizing the seekers, and of offering an apology for the Catholic church in America. She too speaks for others, though she draws on some outside biographical and autobiographical materials. While neither of these voices can be trusted entirely to express the experiences of the third parties for whom they give voice, I think it is possible to respect their intentions to do so, and to read their accounts as revealing and representative, if not accurate in every personal detail. Between the two voices, it should be possible both to discern something of the appeal of the Catholic church for Transcendentalists, as well as to identify why Emerson rejected all churches in the pursuit of authentic Transcendentalism.

In 'The Transcendentalist', Emerson explains to his listeners that Transcendentalism, or the 'new views', are not new, but the very oldest thoughts cast into the mold of new times (Emerson 1983, p. 193). He asserts that Transcendentalism is in fact a new mode of idealism, and contrasts idealism, or the perception that 'the senses are not final' with materialism, or a Lockean understanding that all that is known comes to be known through the senses. Emerson claims for the idealist a 'way of thinking [that] is in higher nature' than that of the materialist, and maintains that the idealist 'insists on ... the power of Thought and Will, on inspiration and miracle, on individual culture' (Emerson p. 193).

Beyond this, Emerson goes on to describe the Transcendentalist as someone who is able to discern the spiritual dimensions of physical events and objects (pp. 193–94); as someone who believes in and appreciates 'miracle, in the perpetual openness of the human brain to a new influx of light and power; [who] believes in inspiration, and in ecstasy' (p. 196). He decries a capitalist mentality in America that does not provide great and sensitive people with worthy work for their ambitions and heart (pp. 199, 203), and expresses the Transcendentalist desire for withdrawal from the banality of the bourgeois social world in favor of sympathetic, if less fashionable, society among like-minded friends (pp. 200, 202). And above all, claims Emerson, Transcendentalists 'are true lovers and worshippers of Beauty' (p. 206).

Many of these ideals and sentiments of Emerson's exemplary Transcendentalist can also be identified in the conversion stories of actual Transcendentalists, as their motivations for joining the Catholic Church. In her short article about becoming a Catholic, Henrietta Channing Dana Skinner describes her fascination as a child with the ritual and mystery of Catholicism. When confronted repeatedly by Catholic worship at her European boarding school, she grew to appreciate the idea of transubstantiation during the consecration of bread and wine at the mass. She reports: 'I gradually came to feel a certain solemnity and awe at the moment of the Elevation [of the sacrament]' (Curtis, 1909, p. 385). 'Transubstantiation', as explained in the *Handbook of Theological Terms*, is a sacramental understanding that the substance of the elements of bread and wine is transformed by God's power into the substance of the body and blood of Jesus Christ directly upon the words of the priestly consecration in the Mass. However, also according to the *Handbook*, it is not that the 'qualities of bread and wine are changed ... but that the inner substantial reality underlying its appearances has been transformed' (Harvey, 1964, pp. 244–5).

This understanding sounds remarkably similar to Emerson's claim that the Transcendentalist,

> in speaking of events, sees them as spirits. He does not deny sensuous fact: by no means; but he will not see that alone. He does not deny the presence of this table, this chair, and the walls of this room, but he looks at these things as the reverse side of the tapestry, as the other end, each being a sequel or completion of a spiritual fact which nearly concerns him. (pp. 193–4)

The similarity in the ideas is striking. Neither deny physical appearances, but both affirm a more substantial, spiritual validity in the physical world. The notable difference, of course, is that whereas the Catholic theology allows for such a sacramental reality in respect of very specific kinds of physical objects (bread and wine) at a very specific moment (the consecration), Emerson's philosophy extends this sacramental perspective to the entire world. It seems clear, however, that with respect to Catholic sacramental theology, Transcendental philosophy could serve as preparation for the convert.

It is thus possible to see how in relation to sacramental theology Transcendentalism opened a way for Catholic conversions where the Calvinist and Unitarian traditions had not. The Calvinist churches denied transubstantiation as mere superstition, insisting instead that God was no more present in the sacrament than in the rest of the physical world, and that the presence of God anywhere was based on the faith of the individual (Walker, 1985, p. 474). Churches in Boston of Puritan or Anabaptist origins (Mennonites, Baptists) had an even lower understanding of the sacrament, believing it was only a memorial act by which to remember the death of Christ (Walker, 1985, p. 475). Emerson's idealist acknowledgement of the spiritual essence of the physical world may, of course, have been influenced by the Calvinist idea – to the extent that Calvinism maintained that God was present throughout the world. Yet Emerson clearly felt that in practice Calvinism had failed to sacralize the everyday world, and had led to a sense of day to day banality in religion rather than a growth of religious fervor. However hard some Transcendentalists may have found it to maintain such a strong sense of the sacramental in daily life, it seems that a number were quite satisfied with the experience of mystery and miracle at the altar of a Catholic church, during the Mass.

Another of the features of Transcendentalism which seems to have been a factor in conversions of Catholicism was its contempt for trivialized charitable works and a desire for truly noble and worthy activity. In an age almost obsessively preoccupied with social and personal improvement, this emphasis seemed almost counter-cultural. Yet Emerson did not shrink from it. In 'The Transcendentalist' Emerson defends Transcendentalists against charges of apathy in the area of social reform movements, claiming that the Transcendentalists,

> feel the disproportion between their faculties and the work offered them, and they prefer to ramble in the country and perish of ennui, to the degradation of such charities and such ambitions as the city can propose to them. They are striking work, and crying out for something worthy to do! (p. 199).

While Emerson doubtless considered Catholic church work to be no worthier than the other charity and social reform work he mentions in the essay: 'public charities, public religious rites ... the enterprises of education ... missions foreign or domestic ... the abolition of the slave trade ... the temperance society ...' (p. 203), some Transcendentalists seem to have found in the latter the truly worthy work they sought.

According to Katherine Burton, for example, Sophia Ripley was able to begin in earnest an ambitious career after her conversion, whereas during her period of deep involvement in Transcendentalism she had been allowed merely to support her husband's work. As a talented woman in the nineteenth century, Sophia Ripley doubtless understood what it was to 'feel a disproportion between [her] faculties and the work offered [her]' beyond what Emerson could have imagined. At the time of Ripley's conversion, her husband, George, was suffering from the recent loss of his hopes in the Brook Farm experiment where he and Sophia had labored to bring about a Transcendentalist utopian community. The couple were in serious debt and Sophia had to work to help make ends meet (Crowe, 1967, p. 216). In spite of this situation, however, she also threw herself into her own work, first visiting women in prisons and hospitals, and gradually organizing a new approach to aid street prostitutes in New York. She found an order of nuns who were willing to take up this cause, in spite of its unpopularity both with lay people in the area and the bishop himself. After locating a house for the Sisters of the Good Shepherd, Ripley collected money for the rent until the convent could be bought outright (Burton, 1942, pp. 38–9).

Ripley had always been an ambitious intellectual, starting a women's post-secondary school before her marriage (which later became Radcliffe College), teaching modern languages at Brook Farm, and reading widely in Italian, classics and early church fathers. After her conversion, she translated Christian writings from Italian and classical languages, especially the writings of Catherine of Genoa, Ripley's patron saint, with whom she believed she had many life experiences in common – including a mysticism and a calling to charity work and writing (Burton, 1942, p. 39). Sophia Ripley, like many Transcendentalists, never shared Emerson's staunch cynicism about social works. In fact, she worked very hard at 'causes' all her life, first as her husband's wife and supporter of his projects, and finally finding her own professional fulfillment in church work.

Sophia Ripley's conversion and subsequent accomplishments were not unique among Transcendentalists. Her friend and neighbor at Brook Farm, Isaac Hecker, was a young man when the Transcendentalist movement was at its height, and eventually became not only a priest, but founded his own order, the Fathers of Paul the Apostle (Paulist Fathers) whose primary work was the conversion of Americans to the Catholic Church (Burton pp. 77–108; Ahlstrom, 1972, pp. 552–3). Doubtless, this was not the kind of work Emerson was waiting for the Universe to call him to (Emerson p. 204), but for the Catholic convert it became the highest sort of work.

Emerson's complaints about causes and charities stemmed from his belief that they had become trivialized, consumerized and commodified:

> Each 'Cause' as it is called, – say Abolition, Temperance, say Calvinism, or Unitarianism, – becomes speedily a little shop, where the article, let it have been at first never so subtle and ethereal, is now made into portable and convenient cakes, and retailed in small quantities to suit purchasers. You make very free use of these words 'great' and 'holy', but few things appear to [Transcendentalists] as such. (1983, p. 203)

The kind of philanthropy Emerson complains of is a sort of part-time, middle-class diversion. It does not originate in a heartfelt calling to the cause, but in a desire to consume a position in the most convenient and socially correct way possible. Though Emerson may not have found them so, some Transcendentalists who possibly shared his dissatisfaction with consumption-oriented philanthropy found that the Catholic works they performed as converts were of a truly 'great' and 'holy' magnitude. Ripley and Hecker made their church work their life work, not merely their bourgeois leisure activity. In this way, the Catholic Church provided real satisfaction for the Transcendentalist-inspired contempt for trivialized work and longing for worthy work.

Another feature of the Transcendentalism which may have helped smooth the path to conversion was a dissatisfaction with the society of unsympathetic people. In 'The Transcendentalist', Emerson explains:

> [Transcendentalists] are lonely; the spirit of their writing and their conversations is lonely; they repel influences; they shun general society; they incline to shut themselves in their chamber in the house, to live in the country rather than in the town, and to find their tasks and amusements in solitude. (p. 200)

Emerson's justification for this solitary lifestyle is a lack of understanding and fellow-feeling between Transcendentalists and 'general society'. Though he asserts that 'they have even more than others a great wish to be loved' (p. 200), he insists that the Transcendentalists 'wish a just and even fellowship or none'. Therefore they must withdraw from society which values 'who is my cousin and my uncle' more than true friendship between compatible people (p. 201).

Such impulses led some Transcendentalists to withdraw (Emerson, somewhat, Thoreau, radically) from 'general society'. But a related impulse led others to form small groups of the like-minded and create social alternatives like Fruitlands (Bronson Alcott) and Brook Farm (the Ripleys). The desire for 'just and even fellowship' inspired these communities and their governance and practical support systems. At Brook Farm, for example, every member had to participate in both the intellectual and the physical labors necessary to run the farm (Sams, 1958).

While Brook Farm members did not take vows of poverty, chastity and obedience, they did commit themselves to a simple lifestyle, and displayed personal submission of a sort to the running of the farm and the general good of all its members. Some of those who chose to participate in Transcendentalist communitarian experiments would later find that other types of related counter-cultural alternatives were possible in the Roman Catholic Church. Thus it may not be so surprising that Ripley, Hecker and Brownson, who were involved to varying degrees in the Brook Farm experiment, later found themselves drawn to Catholic religious communities. Hecker especially, after experimenting with communities at Brook Farm, Fruitlands, and a Shaker settlement, became deeply involved in the organized religious life as a priest and later as the founder of his own order. Brownson was involved in apologetics and publishing with other Catholic theologians, while Sophia Ripley worked closely with the Sisters of the Good Shepherd in New York City. For all of them, the Catholic church provided a social alternative that drew like-minded people together and considered itself to be in a critical relationship to the larger social world within which it was embedded.

Those who were willing to give up 'general society' for communitarian experiments were only the most committed. Transcendentalism provided the impetus and something of an excuse to onlookers for their radical behavior. Emerson's lecture is an exercise of just such an excuse. It attempts to answer a baffled upper-class society's questions as to why educated, people of 'good' families were willing to give up some of their privileges and voluntarily take on not only unaccustomed labor (such as was required at Brook Farm), but also social ridicule.

Transcendentalist philosophy of inclusion and judgement of individuals based on their own merit led many in the movement to accept new relations to the old New England society. Sophia Ripley from a 'Boston Brahmin' family, left the Boston social circle to join her husband George in the Brook Farm endeavor, which included not just the educated and elite, but opened itself to the farm community around it, offering that elite education to farmers' children in exchange for labor. It was not so radical a shift then, when after her conversion, she devoted herself to work among the most socially outcast group in her culture, New York street prostitutes. Once again, this was probably not the kind of companionship Emerson had in mind when he explained that Transcendentalists,

> are repelled by vulgarity and frivolity in people. They say to themselves, It is better to be alone than in bad company. And it is really a wish to be met, – the wish to find society for their hope and religion, – which prompts them to shun what is called society. (1983, p. 202)

Emerson was not of the communitarian mind as some of those whom he inspired were. Rather, he was personally more interested in retreat from society, and was skeptical, if supportive, of the communities his philosophy launched. He visited Brook Farm, but did not live there. But whatever Emerson's personal preferences, his description of a new kind of relationship to society made room for others following his ideas, to change their own social lives.

Where Transcendentalism opened the minds and hearts of the socially privileged, fervent Catholicism could step in and provide ever more opportunities for work, reform and like-minded companions beyond the mere philanthropic, if socially acceptable role chosen by the less earnest. As Brook Farm, Fruitlands and other attempts at Transcendentalist social projects failed, some must have found that the Church provided a stable, time-tested social alternative (especially among religious orders) for the individual who had, through the Transcendentalist movement, become discontented with social norms.

Though the Protestant denominations of New England had rejected the Catholic church and its doctrines, Transcendentalism thus opened the minds of some of Protestant church leaders to new ideas, and encouraged them to reject older orientations and representations after careful scrutiny. In the process some were led to reject their anti-Catholicism and to give new consideration to the Catholic church. So while there are certainly features of the Catholic Church that seem inconsistent with Transcendentalist philosophy and its distant, but influential Calvinist origins, it makes sense that some would find themselves able and even eager to convert, once they had begun to look through Transcendentalism, beyond their former expectations. (It is interesting to compare the turning towards Rome in the Anglo-Catholic movement of the Church of England at the same time; at least one point of similarity appears in the latter's strongly counter-cultural stance, a stance highlighted in the study by Reed (1996).)

In spite of the fact that several found it possible to convert, however, it remains true that Roman Catholicism was rejected by the majority of Transcendentalists. Emerson remained entirely opposed to affiliation with any organized church throughout his life, and whilst 'The Transcendentalist' provides some ideas about how some may have found Catholicism consistent with Transcendentalism, or why Transcendentalists may have found the Catholic church appealing, its overt message is just the opposite. Ultimately, the lecture communicates Emerson's radical individualism and dissatisfaction with any institution or social arrangement of his time. Emerson would probably have accused anyone who said his ideas led to the Catholic Church as grossly misunderstanding him. As the Transcendentalist he:

> does not respect government, except as far as it reiterates the law of his mind; nor the church; nor charities; nor arts, for themselves; but hears, as at a vast distance, what they say ... His thought, – that is the Universe. His experience inclines him to behold the procession of facts you call the world, as flowing perpetually outward from an invisible, unsounded centre in himself, centre alike of him and of them, and necessitating him to regard all things as having a subjective or relative existence, relative to that aforesaid Unknown Centre of him. (Emerson, p. 195)

Obviously there is no room in this philosophy for deference to the pope! The strong antinomian, anti-authoritarian sentiments of Emerson's lecture make it clear that his understanding of Transcendentalism is incompatible with the institutional and creedal arrangements of any church. The only sympathy Emerson ever did express for the Catholic church was aesthetic. This interest in the art, architecture, music and ritual of Catholic worship was in keeping with Emerson's strong emphasis on the importance of beauty to the Transcendentalist. His admiration for the beauty of Catholic churches and his disappointment at the lack of aesthetic pleasure in his own tradition found expression in letters to his wife and to Margaret Fuller written during a stay in Baltimore, during which he attended services at the Catholic cathedral. To his wife he wrote: 'It is well for my Protestantism that we have no cathedral in Concord ... I should be confirmed in a fortnight' (Rusk, 1939, p. 117). To Fuller, he explained in more detailed (and Transcendentalist) terms what he liked about the Catholic tradition:

> It is so dignified to come where the priest is nothing and the people nothing, and an idea for once excludes these impertinences. The chanting priest, the pictured walls, the lighted altar, the surpliced boys, the swinging censer every whiff of which I inhaled, brought all Rome again to mind ... It is a dear old church, the Roman I mean, and today I detest the Unitarians and Martin Luther and all the parliament of Barebones. (Rusk, 1939, p. 116)

Emerson's temporary rejection of Martin Luther was based merely on an appreciation of beauty, however. As for what lay behind the ritual and ornamentation of the Roman church, Emerson had no interest. Years after writing 'The Transcendentalist', he would meet with Isaac Hecker and record some of their conversation; in the exchange, Emerson is bitingly contemptuous of what he sees as Hecker's attempt to persuade him to reconsider the Catholic church. In his commentary on Emerson's unfinished manuscript, 'Hecker, & Catholic Church', Johnson (1993) argues that Emerson associated Catholicism with a pre-rational historical past, as well as with Europe. He was baffled, according to Johnson, by a young, native-born American choosing to '[march] about face into the past and the foreign' (p. 60). Youth, according to Johnson, had always been Emerson's trope for the 'newness' which was his term for what others called Transcendentalism. Johnson (1993) speculates that in his later years Emerson developed a growing animosity towards the Catholic Church and Hecker personally – due at least in part to conflicts within the families of Emerson's friends over conversion to Roman Catholicism (pp. 59–61).

In the end then, Emerson had plenty of reasons, both Transcendental and personal, to reject Catholicism. But while it can hardly be viewed as the culmination of the Transcendentalist movement, conversion to the Roman Catholic church was the end of many individual Transcendentalist searches for a more meaningful way to interpret life and the universe. As Katherine Burton quotes Sophia Ripley saying to her husband George,

> they have never found anything but arguments and no contentments at all. Yet they are looking for something even if they deny it ... we must find an enduring peace ... and a content that will make ... earthly life worthwhile.

For Hecker, like Ripley and Brownson, the Catholic Church provided an 'unreachable quietness' and a 'deep repose' (Johnson, 1993, p. 56) at the end of the Transcendental search. Hecker interpreted Transcendentalism and other religious and social movements of the times as a manifestation of spiritual hunger that could ultimately be fulfilled only by the Catholicism. To the extent that his Paulist Fathers eventually met with great success in their efforts to convert Americans to Catholicism, he may have been right.

Transcendentalism was a radical movement that presented all who followed it with an opportunity to challenge settled ways of thinking. While it may seem inconsistent for this radical movement of 'newness' to lead people to a very old tradition, that is exactly what it did for some. By making a space for questioning the established, middle class New England social customs and religious traditions, Transcendentalism opened a space for the 'respectable' intellectual classes to consider seriously a church that heretofore had been made up largely of often disrespected, uneducated recent immigrants. And as Katherine Burton strives to make clear in her introduction to *In No Strange Land*, the conversions of many of these prominent New Englanders gave the Catholic church new status and authority as a truly American institution. In turn, those immigrants from Ireland and Italy and other 'Catholic' countries became a little more accepted as Americans, too. Today, the church Emerson saw as inherently 'foreign' is the single largest denomination in the USA; it is an ironic thought that in some small measure this can be viewed as part of Emerson's continuing legacy to contemporary America.

Part Two
Negotiations

III Christianity and Literature

Chapter Seven

Rewriting Genesis: The Nineteenth-Century Roots of D.H. Lawrence's Religion

Terence R. Wright

Lawrence was in many respects a late Victorian, struggling to reconcile his passionate need for belief and his love of the Bible with a recognition of the inadequacy of traditional Christian doctrine, and the flawed and fragmentary nature of its key documents. A number of recent studies have explored these struggles in some detail. Daniel Schneider (1986) has written of his 'passionate effort over a lifetime to develop a religious alternative to contemporary scepticism or outworn belief' (p. ix), Virginia Hyde (1992) of his 'revisionist typology', his remoulding of traditional biblical material in unconventional and sometimes esoteric ways. Robert Montgomery's study of *The Visionary D.H. Lawrence* (1994) depicts a writer whose imaginative reading and rewriting of the Bible reflects his encounters with a range of nineteenth-century thinkers, notably Nietzsche, while a book entitled *D.H. Lawrence and Tradition* (Meyers, 1985) explores his relationship with such obvious precursors as Blake, Carlyle, Ruskin, George Eliot, Hardy, Nietzsche and Whitman, all of whom are shown to have contributed to his intellectual development.

Lawrence himself, of course, is generally labelled a modernist since he produced novels which broke with the nineteenth century realist tradition (Pinkney, 1990). He was most definitely not a disciple of modernity, however, in Lyotard's sense of a believer in the grand narrative of enlightenment, of rational emancipation from religious superstition. He is more like T.S. Eliot in this respect, mixing literary modernism with religious anti-modernity. Eliot himself, whose critique of Lawrence in *After Strange Gods* was subtitled *A Primer of Modern Heresy*, recognised this, emphasising his belief that tradition, whether literary or religious, was not static or fixed, not a matter of 'the maintenance of certain dogmatic beliefs' but rather a developing and shared way of life. It should not be seen as 'immovable' or even 'hostile to all change' (1934, p. 18). Even heresy, Eliot argues, has a contribution to make to the ongoing religious tradition: 'It is characteristic of the more interesting heretics [which, for him, included Lawrence] ... that they have an exceptionally acute perception, or profound insight, of some part of the truth' (p. 24). So, although he writes dismissively of the 'vague hymn-singing pietism' of Lawrence's mother (p. 39), Eliot praises Lawrence himself for his 'extraordinarily keen sensibility and capacity for profound intuition' and his powerful campaign against 'the living death of modern material civilization' even though though this have led him to 'wrong conclusions' (pp. 58–60).

Lawrence himself is not altogether to be trusted when he writes about the religious tradition in which he was brought up, tending often to play down the extent to which it moulded his view of life. In an account of the place of 'Hymns in a Man's Life', written in 1928, after recalling fondly the cadences of some of his childhood hymns, he claims to have 'criticised and got over the Christian dogma' by the age of sixteen. John Worthen (1991) has shown that the break with Christianity came much later, when Lawrence was in his early twenties, and was never complete (pp. 64–8). The same essay, in fact, acknowledges how glad Lawrence was to have been 'brought up a Protestant', and a Congregationalist in particular, because of 'the direct knowledge of the Bible' that it gave him (Lawrence, 1968, pp. 597–600). In *Apocalypse*, written between 1929 and his death the following year, he explores further his feelings of ambivalence, grateful to have been imbued with a profound knowledge of the Bible, but angry about the narrowness with which he was instructed to read it:

> From earliest years, right into manhood, like any other nonconformist child, I had the Bible poured every day into my helpless consciousness, till there came almost a saturation point. Long before one could think or even vaguely understand, this Bible language, these 'portions' of the Bible were douched over the mind and consciousness till they became soaked in, they became an influence which affected all the processes of emotion and thought. So that today, although I have 'forgotten' my Bible, I need only begin to read a chapter to realise that I 'know' it with an almost nauseating fixity. And I must confess, my first reaction is one of dislike, repulsion, and even resentment. My very instincts resent the Bible (1980, p. 59).

It is not only the insistence with which the Bible was 'trodden into consciousness' to which Lawrence objects but the fact that 'the interpretation was fixed, so that all interest was lost'. A book lives, he insists only 'as long as it is unfathomed. Once it is fathomed, it dies at once ... A book lives only while it has power to move us, and move us *differently*; so long as we find it *different* every time we read it', discovering new levels of meaning on each occasion. 'The Bible', he concludes, anticipating the language of later literary theory, 'is a book that has been temporarily killed for us, or for some of us, by having its meaning temporarily fixed' (pp. 59–60).

An earlier draft of *Apocalypse*, published as an Appendix to the new Cambridge edition (itself a most fragmentary text), develops this point, that it is not the Bible that is dead, but we who have failed to recognise its vitality, 'years of narrow monotheism' having contributed to a 'widespread misreading' (1980, p. 158). Lawrence celebrates his own escape from generations of second-rate interpreters in order fully to appreciate the 'strangeness' and variety of the Bible and to 'rescue it from parsons and Sunday School teachers' (pp. 153–4). His 'Introduction' to Frederick Carter's theosophical *Dragon of the Apocalypse* (another fragment incorporated in the new Cambridge edition of Apocalypse) dismisses 'the final intentional meaning of the work' as 'a bore', an attempt by orthodox Christian writers to cover over the pagan traces of earlier strands of the text: 'Gradually we realize the book has no one meaning. It has meanings. Not meaning within meaning;

but rather meaning against meanings' (1980, pp. 47–8). Lawrence reads The Book of Revelation like a deconstructionist *avant la lettre*, teasing out the contradictory forces of signification of which it is composed. He also employs Foucauldian archaeological metaphors for the embedding of different ideological layers within the text, claiming to detect,

> the ruins of an old temple incorporated in a Christian chapel. Is it any more fantastic to try to reconstruct the embedded temple, than to insist that the embedded images and columns are mere rubble in the Christian building, and have no meaning? (1980, p. 56)

The same metaphor recurs in Apocalypse itself, which claims to detect several different 'layers' in the text, like the 'layers of civilisation as you dig deeper and deeper to excavate an old city' (1980, p. 81).

How Lawrence learnt to read the Bible differently is a long story, far too long to tell in full. It involved voracious reading both of respectable thinkers such as Renan and Nietzsche and of some less reputable writers such as Edward Carpenter and Madame Blavatsky. From Renan, whom he read in 1906, Lawrence would have gathered the inappropriateness of that literal mode of reading the Bible characteristic of orthodox Christianity. Renan is now accused (by Said and others) of orientalism, a patronising attitude to the east, and there certainly are passages in the *Life of Jesus* which play up the contrast between 'the deeply earnest races of the West', with their commitment to honesty, and 'the Oriental', for whom 'literal truth has little value' and who thinks nothing of embellishing a sacred text with what 'we should term a fraud' (Renan, 1927, p. 147). The primary target of Renan's criticism, however, is the inappropriate mode of reading the Bible characteristic of literalism, which brings modern western assumptions to ancient eastern texts. In the west, he explains, 'a rigorous distinction between the actual and the metaphorical must always be observed' (p. 172), but this was not the case with the composers of biblical or apocryphal texts. Renan goes on to discuss Aggadah and Midrash in some detail in later volumes of the *History of the Origins of Christianity* (of which the *Life of Jesus* was the first of seven). We do not know if Lawrence read these later volumes of the *History of the Origins of Christianity*, but the *Life of Jesus* itself makes it clear how Renan believed biblical texts should be read. Its final chapter proclaims a 'religion of Jesus' based not upon 'fixed dogmas, but images susceptible of indefinite interpretations' (p. 237). If Lawrence had needed any encouragement to read the Bible creatively, he would certainly have found it in Renan.

From Nietzsche, whom he began to read in the winter of 1908–9, Lawrence learnt to be even bolder in his criticism of conventional Christianity (Milton, 1987). Nietzsche, who had himself escaped from a Lutheran background as constricting as Lawrence's own (his father and both grandfathers had been ministers), was at the height of his influence in Britain between the turn of the century and the outbreak of the First World War. Lawrence goes out of his way in a 1913 review of 'Georgian Poetry' to mention Nietzsche's 'demolishing…the Christian religion as it stood' (1936, p. 304), but the last three words of this quotation are of great importance: Nietzsche provided a model for the rejection of conventional Christianity, with its fear of the body and slave morality, but his whole opus, as Hollingdale demonstrates in the introduction to *Thus Spoke Zarathustra* (1961), can be read as a reformulation of Christianity in non-metaphysical terms (pp. 28–9). In Harold Bloom's terms it is certainly a 'strong' reading, a violent misprision or swerving away from the original, but a consistent and powerful one whose appeal to the young Lawrence it is easy to imagine.

The culmination of Nietzsche's critique of Christianity, of course, comes in *The Anti-Christ*, the German title (*Der Antichrist*) being perhaps better translated as 'The Anti-Christian', given the distinction Nietszche makes between the admirable if misguidedly otherworldly figure who died on the cross and the mischievous followers who invented the religion that bears his name. Christianity is held responsible for the 'anti-natural castration of a God into a God of the merely good'. Nietzsche, like Lawrence, displays a preference for the Old Testament over the New, which represented 'a reduction of the divine' (Nietzsche, 1990, p. 139). Even within the Hebrew Bible Nietzsche detects a 'denaturalizing' process by which the Yahweh of Genesis, 'the expression of their consciousness of power, of their delight in themselves' became abstract, the antithesis of life'. The Bible thus documents this 'falsification' of the concept of God (pp. 147–9).

The Anti-Christ, which goes on to explore the falsification of Christ by his followers, contains an entertaining reading of the opening chapters of Genesis which may well have provided Lawrence with a model for his many retellings of the myth of Eden. In Nietzsche's version, 'The old God, all "spirit", all high priest, all perfection, promenades in his garden: but he is bored'. So he invents man to entertain him: 'But behold, man too is bored'. So God, whose 'sympathy with the only kind of distress found in every Paradise knows no bounds', creates the animals, only to discover that this is his 'first blunder'. Man doesn't find the animals entertaining (and certainly doesn't want to be one) so he dominates them. Whereupon God makes woman, his 'second blunder'. She, like a true serpent, hankers after knowledge, allowing science into the world. And since 'science makes equal to God', this makes man a rival. So man has to be expelled from Paradise and prevented from thinking, to which end God 'invents distress, death, the danger to life in pregnancy, every kind of misery, age, toil, above all sickness', with which Nietzsche, at this stage of his life, was all too familiar. Thus the 'beginning of the Bible', according to Nietzsche, 'contains the entire psychology of the priest', the hatred of independent thought, the inducement of guilt and the consequent need for punishment and forgiveness (pp. 176–7). It is a powerful vision of the origins of religion as recounted, albeit unwittingly, in the opening book of the Bible.

That Lawrence saw himself in some ways continuing the Nietzschean tradition of irreverent and critical but nevertheless prophetic writing is evidenced by the titles he played with for material he worked on in 1915 which eventually became his *Study of Thomas Hardy*. He told Bertrand Russell, 'I used to call it *Le Gai Savaire*', a title clearly owing affinities to Nietzsche's *The Gay Science* (*Die Fröhliche Wissenschaft*). *Le Gai Savaire*, in fact, appears on the typescript as the title (Lawrence, 1985, p. 3). Another potential title was 'Morgenrot', presumably modelled on Nietzsche's *Daybreak* (*Morgenröte*) (Lawrence, 1979–93, Vol II, p. 295; Ref, pp. xx–xxi). Not that Lawrence or his characters are uncritical of Nietzsche, but the German philosopher provided him with a model for a radical revision of traditional ways of reading the Bible.

Other contributors to the way Lawrence re-interpreted the Book of Genesis, widely read in their own time but now less intellectually respectable, include Edward

Carpenter and Madame Blavatsky. The point is not so much to establish 'influence' as to recognise that broader intertextuality comprising the ideas which were common among the circles in which Lawrence moved, a matter of what Delavenay (1971) calls the shared late-Victorian 'mental atmosphere' associated with early Fabianism, the Fellowship of the New Life and journals such as *The New Age*, to which Carpenter regularly contributed and which Lawrence frequently read (p. 11). Of particular relevance to a reading of the Book of Genesis is the twist Carpenter gives to the doctrine of the fall. A section of *Civilization, Its Cause and Cure* (1889) entitled 'The Fall and the Return to Paradise' argues that the purpose of the fall is the development of human self-consciousness. Civilization, as in other romantic accounts of human history, is the villain of the piece, accounting for 'the abandonment of the primitive life and the growth of the sense of shame (as in the myth of Adam and Eve). From this follows *the disownment of the sacredness of sex*', which ceases to be 'a part of religious worship' (Delavenay, p. 63). The recovery of paradise, the return to Eden, involves escaping the sense of guilt about sex, casting off clothing altogether, and returning to a state of unity with nature. *Love's Coming of Age* (1896), Carpenter's best-known casting off of Victorian sexual inhibitions, celebrates the joys of outdoor sex in a way that clearly left its mark on Lawrence's fiction, continuing the motif of a return to Eden, a paradise characterised by 'free woman' and 'free love', with a chapter devoted to 'Woman in Freedom' (p. 105). Carpenter, according to Delavenay, anticipates and provides a model for Lawrence's own attempt 'to rejuvenate and interpret anew Christian and Jewish religious concepts' even if Lawrence goes further than Carpenter in the way in which 'he tears at the law, and deifies the Flesh at the expense of the Word' (pp. 116–7), most violently in the 'Foreword to Sons and Lovers', which sets Genesis (with its emphasis on the flesh) against John (whose gospel gives priority to the Word).

Lawrence's voracious appetite for alternative ways of thinking took him into some strange areas of the occult. His first encounters with theosophy and Blavatsky, through *The Occult Review* and in studies of the Book of Revelation such as James Pryse's *The Apocalypse Unsealed*, appear to have taken place between 1912 and 1915 (Tindall, 1972, p. 134). But Lawrence was soon reading Blavatsky's main works, *Isis Unveiled* (1877) and *The Secret Doctrine* (1888), reporting to David Eder in 1917 that the latter was 'in many ways a bore and not quite real. Yet one can glean a marvellous lot from it' (1979–93, Vol. III, p. 150). He was to tell Waldo Frank in July 1917 that he was 'not a theosophist' but found 'the esoteric doctrines...marvellously illuminating' (p. 143). Kinkead-Weekes (1996) dates from this time Lawrence's enthusiasm for the ancient civilisations of Egypt and Mexico along with 'a new hostility to science in all its modern forms' (p. 388).

Most people have heard of *Madame Blavatsky's Baboon*, the title of Peter Washington's recent book (1993), one of a collection of stuffed animals which used to decorate her apartments, bespectacled and respectably dressed in wing-collar, morning-coat and tie, 'carrying under its arm the manuscript of a lecture on *The Origin of Species*'. This creature, as Washington explains, symbolises the pretensions of modernity or 'materialist science' to explain away the mysteries of religion, however inadequately these are represent by conventional creeds (p. 45). Less well known perhaps, although more vital to her argument, is her Bible, the sacred ancient text on which the Hebrew and Christian Bibles are said to draw, fragments of which she published as 'The Book of Dzyan', complete with ancient commentaries, in *The Secret Doctrine*. The point, as the preface to that book explains, is that this ancient wisdom can still be discerned in our extant sacred texts, 'scattered throughout thousands of volumes embodying the scriptures of the great Asiatic and early European religions, hidden under glyph and symbol, and hitherto left unnoticed because of this veil' (p. vii).

This belief, of course, embodies its own myth of origins, that search so characteristic of modernity in its nineteenth century phase for 'a single key that would solve the mysteries of the universe' (Washington, 1993, p. 9). Washington compares Blavatsky to George Eliot's Casaubon and his search for the 'Key to All Mythologies'. What he does not notice is the extent to which Blavatsky's enterprise could be said to be founded upon the failure of that fictitious cleric and his real counterparts: Christian scholars responsible for the reawakening of interest in ancient eastern religious texts, including the apocrypha, pseudepigrapha and the Kabbala, along with Buddhist and Hindu sacred texts such as the Vedas, many of which were properly edited for the first time in the nineteenth century (p. 36) even if, in the case of rabbinic texts, the main motive of this predominantly Christian scholarship was to shed light on early Christianity (Charlesworth, 1983, p. xii).

The subtitle of *Isis Unveiled*, 'A Master-Key to the Ancient and Modern Science and Theology', reveals even in Blavatsky that belief both in origins and in master-narratives characteristic of modernity. She insists that the 'real Hebrew Bible was a secret volume, unknown to the masses', not to be confused with the exoteric volume carefully constructed by a later priestly caste in Israel (1970a, Vol. II, p. 471). She finds traces of that ancient text in the Kabbala, printed portions of which contained 'ruins and fragments, much distorted remnants still of that primitive system which is the key to all religious systems' (1970b, Vol. II, p. 461), just as extant texts of such pseudepigrapha as the Book of Enoch were merely copies of 'some scripture of a prehistoric religion'. The Book of Revelation, she argues, had adapted some of this material to Christianity and it was in this way that the 'off-shoots of the never dying tree of wisdom have scattered their dead leaves even on Judaeo-Christianity' (1970b, p. 483).

Reading the 'exoteric' or 'translated' Bible, as Blavatsky labels the Bible as we have it, is a matter of reading between the lines, detecting the traces of an older strand of sacred wisdom now lost. She attacks the naivety of 'accepting the narratives literally, and as a whole', insisting with the pioneering biblical critics of her own time, Wellhausen and Gunkel, that 'the Hebrew Scripture wears on its face the mark of its double origin', a surface level produced by redaction at the time of the Babylonian captivity and a deeper level containing much older material, some of which could be traced back to the Chaldeans (1970a, Vol. I , p. 575–6). Genesis is the book for Blavatsky which contains the most ancient material: 'Alone among all the books of the Bible, Genesis belongs to an immense antiquity' (1970a, Vol. II, p. 457). She finds difficulty, however, in accepting its anthropomorphic deity, sneering at the idea of Jacob 'boxing with the Creator' (p. 429).

The Secret Doctrine continues to insist that the Hebrew Bible requires deconstructive double reading:

> Read by the light of the Zohar, the initial four chapters of Genesis are the fragment of a highly philosophical page in the World's Cosmogony...Left in their symbolical disguise,

they are a nursery tale, an ugly thorn in the side of science and logic, an evident effect of Karma. To have let them serve as a prologue to Christianity was a cruel revenge on the part of the Rabbis, who knew better what their Pentateuch meant. It was a silent protest against their spoliation... (1970a, Vol. I, pp. 10–11)

A section on 'The Evolution of Symbolism', with an epigraph from Carlyle, insists yet again that 'no Hebrew scroll should be read and accepted literally': 'to accept the dead-letter of the Bible' is to be guilty of superstition (1970a, Vol I, p. 303–5). The core truth, the secret inner meaning of scripture, has to be uncovered through layers of distortion and misinterpretation, whether Patristic impositions of Platonic metaphysics upon Jesus and his initiates or rabbinic misreadings of Moses and his teaching, itself derived from Egypt. Only occultists and kabbalists, according to Blavatsky, have penetrated the 'real meaning' of the Bible: orthodox Jews and Christians 'cling to the husk and dead letter thereof' (1970a, Vol. I, p. 316). Nevertheless,

> there is as much esoteric wisdom in some portions of the exoteric ...Pentateuch, as there is of nonsense and of designed childish fancy in it, when read only in the dead-letter murderous interpretations of great dogmatic religions... (p. 336)

A chapter on 'Tree and Serpent and Crocodile Worship' discusses the esoteric symbolism of the Book of Genesis in terms of phallic symbolism and mysterious sources of energy. After quoting a Kabalistic manuscript which discusses the womb as 'the MOST HOLY PLACE, the SANCTUM SANCTORUM, and the veritable TEMPLE OF THE LIVING GOD', Blavatsky deplores the way 'the Hebrew Bible, and its servile copyist, Christian theology' made this merely metaphorical. The Genesis account of the Fall can be read in two ways, however. On the surface level it may appear to describe 'a temptation of flesh in a garden of Eden' with God 'CURSING for ever an act, which was in the logical programme of that nature' as He had created it:

> All this exoterically, as in the cloak and dead letter of Genesis and the rest; and at the same time esoterically he regarded the supposed sin and FALL as an act so sacred, as to choose the organ, the perpetrator of the original sin, as the fittest and most sacred symbol to represent that God, who is shown as branding its entering into function as disobedience and everlasting SIN. (1970a, Vol. I, pp. 382–3)

Elsewhere Blavatsky writes rather dismissively of the 'phallicism' of the rabbis, preferring Hegel's notion of 'God (the Universal Spirit)' who 'objectivises himself as Nature, and again rises out of it' (1970a, Vol I, p. 257n) to the rabbis dragging the divine into the animal: 'Nothing so gross exists in Eastern Occultism' (1970a, Vol. II, p. 85). At one point she labels Judaism 'this sexual religion' (p. 274), while at another she complains of the 'gross... realism of the Jews, explaining David's uncovering himself before the ark in sexual terms, the ark being an 'emblem of female generative power' (p. 459). Her perpetual praise of Aryan over Semitic theology was to have sinister implications in the development of Nazi ideology (Goodrick-Clarke, 1985). Blavatsky's main concern, however, was to undermine literal readings of the Bible, whether Jewish or Christian, to reiterate Renan's point that Christian theology had failed to understand 'the paradoxical language of the

East and its Symbolism' (Blavatsky, 1970a, Vol. I, p. 95). Lawrence, while accepting her view of the Bible, was excited by David's dance, which reappears both in *The Rainbow* and in the *Study of Thomas Hardy*.

Other passages in *The Secret Doctrine* which appealed to Lawrence were Blavatsky's esoteric readings of the story of the Sons of God going into the daughters of men in Genesis chapter 6 (the passage so dear to Ursula in *The Rainbow*). These Sons of God, demonised by orthodoxy, are celebrated by Blavatsky as initiates, representing the angels in the Book of Enoch who teach the daughters of men the secrets of heaven. For Blavatsky, this represents a 'fall' into sexuality, part of a five-stage process by which the human race as we know it had evolved through a series of 'root-races', a process esoterically encoded in the early chapters of Genesis. The serpent, of course, is phallic, while the ark as a symbol of the female principle explains the esoteric meaning of the Flood. The secrets into which Blavatsky's Sons of God initiate the daughters of men are, again, more heavenly than they become in Lawrence (both *The Rainbow* and *Lady Chatterley's Lover* dwell on this episode of Genesis in more sensual terms than would have appealed to Blavatsky). But there can be little doubt that Blavatsky's double reading of Genesis contributed to his rewriting of these scenes.

Blavatsky's reconstruction of the supposed 'originals' of biblical texts is itself often plainly fictitious. In discussing the Chaldean tablets containing the Babylonian account of creation, she blithely introduces her view with the phrase, 'were the tablets less mutilated, they would be found to contain ...' (1970a, Vol. II, p. 3n). Not content with references in Jerome to an original secret Gospel of St. Matthew (1970b, Vol. II, p. 182), she refers at various points to 'the ORIGINAL Acts of the Apostles' (1970a, Vol. II, p. 481), 'the real original text of I Corinthians ' (p. 153) and a whole host of speculative pseudepigrapha and midrashim. The biggest fiction of all, of course, is her supposed Book of Dzyan, on which *The Secret Doctrine* is an extended commentary. This text 'utterly unknown to philologists', whose doctrines were scattered through 'thousands of Sanskrit MSS' (1970a, Vol. I, pp. xxii–iii), was, of course, as imaginative a construct as any of Lawrence's novels.

Blavatsky's myth of origins, her fictitious sacred fragments, differ from the more acceptably scientific versions of this myth in being so outrageously fraudulent. Lawrence was clearly aware of this, but in incorporating esoteric elements into his writing, most notably in *The Symbolic Meaning*, the first version of what was to become his *Studies in Classic American Literature*, but also in *The Plumed Serpent*, *Apocalypse*, and *The Man Who Died* (in which the risen Christ is initiated into sexual pleasure by a priestess of Isis), Lawrence could be seen to be developing the imaginative freedom Blavatsky herself had shown in her approach to the Bible. These sketchy examples provide some indication of the complicated intertextual web informing Lawrence's own work, which should not be presented as the isolated products of a lone genius but as part of a wider cultural wrestling with (and recognition of the fragmentary nature of) the Judaeo-Christian tradition. It may also illustrate the fact that fictions, in many cases, speak louder than scholarship; they certainly have a wider readership.

Chapter Eight

Wordsworth and the Sacralization of Place

Deeanne Westbrook

[Some minds] find tales and endless allegories
By river margins, and green woods among. (Wordsworth, 1952, Vol. 2, p. 486)

In the five 'Poems on the Naming of Places' (1799–1800) (hereinafter the 'Poems'), Wordsworth adapts the biblical etymological tale, whose effect, as in the story of Jacob's dream, is not only to textualize a place, but to spiritualize it, or to acknowledge a spirituality which was always already there, but unknown because unnamed. Just as Jacob, his remarkable dream and dialogue hover through the millenia about an uncanny place named Bethel, 'house of God', so in the 'Poems' persons called Emma, Joanna, Mary, and William are inscribed in the permanent and mysterious text of land. The enterprise has specifically poetic goals, permitting Wordsworth to explore and develop for himself the effects of allusion to and revision of powerful biblical pre-texts, and to produce works wherein language may be made to rescue humans from silence and oblivion and provide through the association of person, act, land, and text what one might call a more dense significance.

While evident throughout his works, Wordsworth's intense and quite idiosyncratic interest in the relationship of person, language, and land is focused in the 'Poems' written in his first year of residence at Grasmere. In what follows, I shall consider three of the five poems composed in the ten-month period between December, 1799, and October, 1800. The epigraph is found in MS. M as *Motto for Poems on the Naming of Places*. It appears to issue a caution against reading these poems as personal history and even invites close attention to their poetic devices. The phrase 'endless allegories' is particularly suggestive, for, as in Robert Lowth's *Lectures on the Sacred Poetry of the Hebrews*, the term allegory at this time suggested a master trope of resemblance – often a created rather than an intrinsic resemblance, and especially evocative of biblical models, encompassing metaphor, continued metaphor, parable, and mystical allegory.[1] Yet Wordsworth in the 'Advertisement' to the poems, seems to claim the status of personal history for the poems, and even to trivialize their subject matter – 'little incidents'. This apparent discrepancy in authorial claims provides one dimension of the poems' difficulties. Are the poems found tales and endless allegories, or are they an exercise in recording the '*private and peculiar* interest' attendant on certain unnamed sites near Grasmere? Here is Wordsworth's 'Advertisement':

> By persons resident in the country, and attached to rural objects, many places will be found unnamed or of unknown names, where little Incidents must have occurred, or feelings been experienced, which will have given to such places a private and peculiar interest. From a wish to give some sort of record to such Incidents, and renew the gratification of such feelings, Names have been given to Places by the Author and some of his Friends, and the following Poems written in consequence. (1952, Vol. 2, p. 111)

Perhaps one reason the poems have not received much critical attention is just this curious understatement (or misstatement) of their nature and the author's purpose. That the motto and advertisement offer very different perspectives on the poems is perhaps appropriate, for I believe that this discrepancy is only one of many indications that the 'Poems' are not exactly what they seem, and why they tend to produce conflicting responses. 'It was an April morning', to which I shall return below, illustrates the conflict. At first reading, the poet/speaker may seem ingenuous, artless, 'natural'. His language is simple; his images are concrete, apparently descriptive of no more than the natural scene in which the poem is set; and the poem's meaning is, so it seems, transparent: The poet discovers a pleasant, 'wild nook', dedicates it to his sister, and names it 'Emma's Dell'. In a brief discussion of these poems, Stephen Gill (1989), in his fine biography of Wordsworth, remarks, in line with the claims of the advertisement, that 'Most of [the 'Poems'] relate some new pleasure found locally ...' (p. 181). Further consideration, however, undermines one's sense of an artless narrator who tells a simple tale. Indeed he begins to sound not ingenuous, but ingenious, or, more intriguingly, actually disingenuous.

A certain disingenuousness may be seen even in the language of the advertisement. Its difficulties are several, but chief among them is the ambiguity of the phrase, 'some sort of record'. If Wordsworth had said, 'From a wish to record such incidents', the names and the poems would seem more clearly to have an objective, historical relationship to incidents of 'private and peculiar interest'. The actual wording, however, makes it reasonable to assume that 'some sort of record' might be quite different from a history: it might be a fiction, for example, a found tale, an allegory, or a figurative rendering (such as a mythological etymology), whose relationship to the incident, real or imagined, need be neither objective nor historical. I want to accept the challenge of the motto and argue that the 'Poems' are imaginative, complex works ('tales and endless allegories') which reward careful study and, indeed, express concerns and develop theories central to Wordsworth's poetry and poetics. I will argue further that in these poems, as so often elsewhere, Wordsworth mines sacred poetry, finding in the biblical etymological tale his narrative model and in biblical language, his own language, tropes and images. In appropriating and adapting these to his purposes, Wordsworth establishes powerful intertextual echoes and effects radical revisions of the precursor texts.

Background: Naming Places

Certainly human beings have always named places important to them and told stories about the naming, but the great textual precedent for Wordsworth's poems is to be found in the etymological tales of the Old Testament. There the tale and its effects, as in the story of Jacob's dream (Gen. 28:10–19), are powerful and enduring. No matter how barren, isolated, or undistinguished, if a place has a name like Bethel, 'house of God', and a story to explain the name, it gains 'significance'. Or a story about the naming of a ruined tower (Gen. 11) may haunt Western humanity in perpetuity. Bethel, Babel – both sites are textualized by being inscribed, as it were, with human signs. More than that, they are spiritualized, taking on the character of sanctuary, and named so as to acknowledge a hovering, atemporal uncanniness. In the process, the human actors and acts take on a form of permanence or immortality. In Jacob's naming of Bethel, he remarks, 'How awesome is this place! This is none other than the house of God, and this is the gate of heaven' (Gen. 28:17). Not only does the name single out for attention an apparently unremarkable space by bestowing an extraordinary name, but the act of naming itself appropriates the permanence of land to the human awareness of the uncanny, to a mystery of spiritual space, to human deeds and human feelings. Hence through the millennia, Jacob, his uncanny dream vision, and his dialogue and covenant with God hover about a place named Bethel, 'house of God', preserved in the narrative, the place name, and the permanence of land.

The biblical etymological tale requires three elements: an event or deed, perhaps fictional, occurs or is said to have occurred at a particular place; the place is named to suggest the nature of the event, deed, outcome, or its participants; and, finally, the story of the event or deed is told and recorded so as to assign a meaning to the place name which then encapsulates, calls up, or verifies (by its objective being in the world) the narrative of events. In the process, a merging of the human actor or actors, the name of the place, and the language of the narrative occurs, often producing a curious blend of empirical and imaginative 'facts'. Without the place name, which can be shown on a map, the narrative and its characters have the status not of history, but of fiction; without the narrative, the name of the place is essentially meaningless; without both the named place and narrative, the human actors pass away like most things human without a trace. Only in the coincidence of place name and narrative are the person or persons and human acts protected from oblivion. Only in the coincidence of both are the significance and spirituality of place established and preserved.

Each element must endure for the etymological tale to perform its functions, but those are achieved only through language, ephemeral in its oral form and even in its written form subject to change and decay. As we have seen, in his advertisement, recognizing the fate which most human acts and feelings suffer, Wordsworth announces the linguistic defense he has erected against oblivion – naming places and writing poems about those acts of naming.

As I mentioned above, although focused in the 'Poems', the philosophical and artistic concerns of these 'Poems' are evident throughout Wordsworth's works. Therefore, before turning my attention to individual poems in the group, I want to draw into this discussion some suggestive passages from 'The Ruined Cottage' and *The Prelude* (1799, 1805) which prove helpful in understanding the 'Poems'.[2] In 'The Ruined Cottage', Wordsworth's old peddlar, Armytage, who narrates Margaret's tale, says, speaking of the effects of a drought, 'And of the poor did many cease to be,/And their place knew them not' (1987, p. 34, ll. 143–4). Psalm 103, to which these lines allude, offers two metaphors for human life – grass and wild flowers: 'As for man, *his days are like grass;*/he *flourishes like a flower of the field;*/for the wind passes over it, and it is gone,/and its place knows it no more' (my emphasis). Without the permanence of the relationship with land forged through language – name and narrative – a man flourishes and dies like grass, without significance, without effect, without memory, especially without the memory of land: 'its place knows it no more'. In the 1805 *Prelude*, as the poet is looking about for 'time, place, and manners', a theme for his work, images of wild flowers and place recur. The poet suggests that he might select 'some old/Romantic tale' neglected by Milton, for example a tale of Wallace, who

> ... left the name
> Of Wallace to be found like a wild flower,
> All over his dear Country, left the deeds
> Of Wallace, like a family of Ghosts,
> To people the steep rocks and river banks,
> Her natural sanctuaries, with a local soul
> Of independence and stern liberty. ([1805], p. 40, Bk I, ll. 177–219; my emphasis)

These passages reveal a cluster of associations among ideas of mortality, names, places, and vegetal images of grass and wild flowers. A human being as grass or flower is fragile, short-lived, and doomed to oblivion. By contrast, Wallace's name, planted like a wild flower 'All over his dear Country', endures, suggesting a kind of self-perpetuating power *as name*, to be endlessly repeatable, self-reiterative, self-regenerating like the wild flowers. Moreover, the suggestion in the Wallace passage is that the naming of place substitutes a 'clonable' name for the person, permitting the place to 'know' the human, ephemeral flower of the field, after it is gone, because person and place have become one in the name. With the name or the naming, a kind of numinosity adheres to place, through which the human being achieves a place-bound immortality, becomes a sort of local spirit, or uncanniness: like Jacob's acts in Canaan, 'the deeds/Of Wallace, like a family of Ghosts,/[are left] to people the steep rocks and river banks,/[his country's] natural sanctuaries', that is, her sacred places. The name of Wallace as a place name is thus a metonymy not only for the man, but for his 'deeds' and the accounts of deeds, all of which are rendered sacred and immortal in and through the permanence of place.

This same cluster of associations may be found in the 'spots of time' passage, which recurs in all versions of *The Prelude*. The lines in question immediately precede a description of a murderer's 'grave', a passage which undergoes intriguing revision between the 1799 version and the 1805 and 1850 versions. In its earliest form, the passage reads as follows:

> ... I led my horse, and stumbling on, at length
> Came to a bottom where in former times
> A man, the murderer of his wife, was hung
> In irons. Mouldered was the gibbet-mast;
> The bones were gone, the iron and the wood;
> Only a long green ridge of turf remained
> Whose shape was like a grave. ([1799], p. 9, First Part, ll. 307–315)

The sight of the hanging place, with its grave-shaped 'ridge of turf', triggers in the narrator, then a child, a preternatural awareness of spirituality in this place, casting a 'visionary dreariness' on ordinary sights – a pool, a beacon, a woman walking against the wind (ll. 315-27). Here human mortality and grass are virtually one. Nothing survives of the long-dead man, his crime, his execution, or even his body ('the bones were gone'), and certainly not his name; grass only remains, a sign of the brevity of human life: 'his days are like grass... for the wind passes over it, and it is gone, and its place knows it no more'. Indeed it is difficult to see how the child 'knows' about the murder and execution, unless he is sensitive to some ghostly investment. In the 1805 revision, however, the source of the child's knowledge is explicit, as emphasis shifts from that which passes to that which remains. Now the turf in the shape of a grave is gone, and in its place is monumental writing, text, epitaph – a name carved in the turf:

... I led my horse, and stumbling on, at length
Came to a bottom where in former times
A murderer had been hung in iron chains... .
Some unknown hand had carved the murderer's name.
The monumental writing was engraven
In times long past, ... and to this hour
The letters are all fresh and visible.
Faltering, and ignorant where I was, at length
I chanced to espy those characters inscribed
On the green sod ... . ([1805], pp. 430-32, Bk XI, ll. 287-301; my emphasis)

Through such repeated images Wordsworth smudges the boundaries between death and immortality, between oblivion and fame. When a person is like a wild flower or grass, he or she perishes quickly and is unremembered; when that person's name is planted like a wild flower in a particular place – rendered as text, written on a map, or engraved in grass – it endures. Wallace and the murderer perish like flowers of the field or like bible grass; yet they are rescued from oblivion through language – names – planted like a wild flower, in the case of Wallace, and carved in turf, in the case of the murderer. In this way, Wordsworth has made the biblical metaphors for the brevity and oblivion of human life become names, and then to serve an opposite purpose – to preserve, lengthen, immortalize. Both men have become names; their places know them because place and man have become textualized and, bearing a common name, are essentially one.

If the place name, actors and events are coincident with an oral narrative, they can 'live' and retain their significance and spirit only so long as they survive in the memories of the living. When memory fails, as Wordsworth suggests, it is necessary to create a text, to give 'some sort of record', to such names and incidents. Certainly the incidents recounted in the biblical etymological tales survive because they have been recorded, and it therefore appears that implicit in the cluster of ideas surrounding the etymological narrative is the notion of text. To endure, the narrative must be written; the name of the place must be inscribed on a map, perhaps mental. Wordsworth's faith in the saving powers of language is thematic in 'Home at Grasmere,' which he composed during the same period as the 'Poems'. In 'Home at Grasmere,' the poet says that he has been given an 'internal Brightness .../That must not die, that must not pass away'. This gift, he says, he would impart, 'Immortal in the world which is to come':

> I would not wholly perish even in this,
> Lie down, and be forgotten in the dust,
> I and the modest partners of my days
> Making a silent company in death.
> It must not be, if I divinely taught
> Am privileged to speak as I have felt
> Of what in man is human or divine. (1987, p. 196, ll. 886–909)

To 'speak' clearly implies to write. A recurring idea of this period (one might even say an obsession of this period), evident in both the 'Poems' and 'Home at Grasmere', is of the powers of language to rescue from oblivion, to avert an unthinkable fate – membership in a 'silent company' – so as to prolong, to save or to render 'immortal'. Such linguistic powers reside in the processes of speaking, naming, and composing. Wordsworth asserts that he will not 'wholly perish' if he is 'privileged to speak'.

'It was an April morning'

This capacity of language to rescue from death and oblivion is thematic in the 'Poems'. At the end of 'It was an April morning', Wordsworth speculates that some of the local shepherds, years after he and his sister 'are gone and in [their] graves', will call the place by the name he has given it, 'Emma's Dell'. This briefer, oral mode of endurance is dependent on human memory and inclination. But Wordsworth hedges his bets. While purporting to depend on the humble remembrance of local folk, he nevertheless writes the poem, merging name, place and person in the more permanent mode of text. A deeper mystery inheres in the fact that the poet permits Dorothy (if, in fact, Emma is Dorothy) to 'live' through the record of his own observations, experiences, and dedication, but paradoxically under a pseudonym, Emma, which may be only a metrical equivalent for 'Dolly', a childhood nickname for Dorothy (de Selincourt, 1952, Vol. 2, p. 486), making hers a twice-deferred sort of immortality: The place is 'Emma's Dell', not 'Dorothy's Dell' or even 'Dolly's Dell'. The name on the poem is, however, William Wordsworth, the one privileged to speak.

Another example of the sort of language that leads to a perception of artful complexity and misdirection in this poem may be found in the phrase, 'The voice/Of waters'. The phrase has a familiar sound, and when traced to its source is found in the book of Ezekiel: 'And behold, the glory of the God of Israel came from the way of the east: and his voice was like a noise of many waters: and the earth shined with his glory' (43:2). (Revelation 1:15 presents a similar image: 'And his feet like unto fine brass, as if they burned in a furnace; and his voice as the sound of many waters'.) For Ezekiel, God's voice sounds like 'many waters'. At the opening of his book, Ezekiel says that he saw 'visions of God', the visions occurring 'in the thirtieth year, in the fourth month, in the fifth day of the month, as [he] was among the captives by the river of Chebar' (Ez. 1:1). Ezekiel's vision includes a detailed description of the cherubim surrounding the divine throne, and the observation that when they moved he 'heard the noise of their wings, like the noise of great waters, as the voice of the Almighty, the voice of speech, as the noise of an host' (Ez. 1:24). (The association of the wheels with voice has resulted in a tendency to understand that the wheels are words, as Stephen Prickett points out, 'even, specifically, a manifestation of *the* "Word" or *logos*' [1986, p. 172].) As the water in the Chebar canals flows by him, Ezekiel hears in its sound the voice of God, which, taking visual form, appears before him as the remarkable vision of cherubim, wheels, throne, and God. Both the wings of the cherubim and the voice of God sound like waters.

The opening of Wordsworth's poem reveals intriguing parallels: Wordsworth is writing also of a time in the fourth month – April, in 1800, his thirtieth year (perhaps even on his birthday; he would have been thirty on April 7) – beside a rivulet, whose 'voice' he hears. (Because the numbering of months was different for Ezekiel than for Wordsworth, Ezekiel's fourth month and fifth day refer to what would be July 31 by a modern Western calendar; his mysterious 'thirtieth year' apparently does not refer to his own age, but perhaps to the last year of Israel's final Jubilee cycle [Rosenberg, 1987, pp. 195; 204].) Like Ezekiel's vision, Wordsworth's is full of sounds suggested by the waters; like Ezekiel's vision of wheels within wheels associated with the living creatures, whose movement is also like the sound of waters, Wordsworth's narrator hears a 'circling', as 'The spirit of enjoyment and desire,/And hopes and wishes, from all living things/Went circling, like a multitude of sounds'. Ezekiel remarks twice within successive verses that 'the spirit of the living creatures was in the wheels' (Ez. 1:20–21); Wordsworth's 'spirit' goes 'circling', like wheels. By contrast to Ezekiel, Wordsworth's experience remains auditory, rather than visual. Ezekiel transposes the experience of the voice of waters into a visual image of the divine; Wordsworth's perception of the numinous remains that of audition – indeed that of language, or almost language, as he hears the voice of waters, the 'circling' of spirit, like the wheels of the divine chariot 'seen' by Ezekiel, the voice of uncommon pleasure, and the remarkable antiphonal chant between the voice of waters and the 'song' of nature that appears not only natural, but eternal. It is a song which 'seemed like the wild growth,/Or like some natural produce of the air,/That could not cease to be'. In tone, Wordsworth's account is altogether different from Ezekiel's. In Ezekiel, the dark passions prevail. The watery voice of God is angry, threatening destruction; in Wordsworth's poem, the voice of waters has been 'softened down into a vernal tone'. The song of the 'living things' (Wordsworth's counterpart of Ezekiel's 'living creatures')[3] is characterized by 'the spirit of enjoyment and desire,/And hopes and wishes'. In effect, Wordsworth calls Ezekiel into his text to transform the perception of the divine, the relationships between natural and supernatural, and the character of the visionary experience.

Despite the strong revisionary impulse, the oblique invocation of the theophany in Ezekiel and the common prophetic experience of hearing the voice of waters have the effect of 'raising the stakes' in the poetic transaction, for they alter the status of the narrator, whose voice is authorized by the prophetic experience and amplified to that of bard; it creates a numinous dimension for the scene and the perception of the scene; it discloses a divine accent and cadence in the sound of the rivulet; and, all in all, it implies a deep significance in the place and in each word of the poem. This place, this 'wild nook', like Jacob's desert, is awesome. Like Jacob's desert and like Ezekiel's riverbank, Wordsworth's place has been textualized and intertextualized; the experience of the poet-prophet has been given, to say the least, 'some sort of record', and rescued from oblivion.

The poet's dedication of this remarkable, spirit-filled place to 'Emma' is difficult. It succeeds the ecstatic experience just described and seems to call the ownership, if not the reality, of the poet's experience into question. The poet actually quotes himself and the formal performative language uttered on that occasion, commenting, 'to myself I said,/Our thoughts at least are ours; and this wild nook,/My EMMA, I will dedicate to thee'. How is one to understand 'Our thoughts at least are ours'? Does 'thoughts' simply mean something like, I own the right to think of this place as Emma's, although it really is not hers? Or does 'thoughts' encompass the entire visionary experience just recounted? If so, does this imply that though the poet may not own the site personally, the visionary experience of the place and his record of it constitute a kind of quitclaim deed, transferring textual ownership of the site? Or have they transformed it, in the process creating an internalized mind place, an imaginative mirror of the place over which the poet has all rights? These are possibilities, since the next lines continue the narrative, after a typographical hiatus in the form of a dash, to assert a kind of ownership: 'Soon did the spot become my other home,/My dwelling, and my out-of-doors abode'. 'Owning' the place – the place itself or the imaginative replication – clearly bestows a kind of immortality, for the poet, his experience, and his thoughts, and for the sister (whose name does not appear), because they abide while place abides:

> And of the Shepherds who have seen me there,
> To whom I sometimes in our idle talk
> Have told this fancy, two or three, perhaps,
> Years after we are gone and in our graves,
> When they have cause to speak of this wild place,
> May call it by the name of EMMA'S DELL.

Voicing this modest hope for a paradoxical and brief immortality contradicts the more ambitious motives implicit in the making of the 'record' – the poem which encompasses by allusion and 're-vision' all of time from Ezekiel to Wordsworth and inscribes itself on the place, this bit of earth, which, as the author of Ecclesiastes says, 'abideth forever'.

'A Narrow Girdle of rough stones and crags'

The fourth poem in the series is one that breaks a pattern established in the first three. In each of these, a place is named by a single person and given a personal name – Emma in the first, Joanna in the second, William (appearing as author) in the third. Moreover through each of the first three runs a theme, overt or muted, of uncanny exuberance, gradually toned down from the 'glad sound' of the stream and the echoing laughter of the rocks, to the jovial serenity and isolation prevailing on the eminence. By contrast, the fourth poem, 'A Narrow Girdle of rough stones and crags,' shifts to an autumn season and an autumnal tone; its place is named by the poet and two companions not for a person, but in 'self-reproach' for a thoughtless act – 'Point Rash-Judgment'. Here the 'happy idleness' of the walkers and the 'busy mirth' of the harvesters are sobered down by a recognition of the plight of an ailing fisherman struggling to 'gain/A pittance from the dead unfeeling lake'. Having initially misjudged the man as 'Improvident and reckless' to be fishing during harvest season, the three idle walkers wander into a myth, receive a lesson in charity, and memorialize their initial rash judgment in the place name.

Recognizing this fourth poem as a moral tale permits the further understanding of its kinship not simply with biblical etymological tales, but with a range of moral narratives, including fable, parable, allegory, and myth (*allegory*, as included in this list is akin to Wordsworth's use of the term in his motto). Discussing these narrative forms, Colin Murray Turbayne (1970) points out that each of them may be seen as 'extended or sustained metaphors', which present 'the facts which belong to one sort as if they belonged to another', and whose audience may or may not be told that metaphor is involved. Each of these forms is 'offered and meant to be understood in the spirit of serious make-believe': 'The vehicle for them all is usually a fictitious narrative which we make believe is true'. Each of these forms presents a story plus a moral lesson (pp. 19–20).

Wordsworth's tale of naming Point Rash-Judgment is an allegorical moral tale, or, to use his phrase, an 'endless allegory'. Like the others in the group it is not necessary or even very useful to take it literally, as personal history. Rather it should be read, in Turbayne's phrase, in the 'spirit of serious make-believe'. In Wordsworth's allegory, a delicate web of suggestion and allusion creates a narrative that wavers between seemingly factual and figurative accounts. One of the best kinds of evidence for its allegorical nature lies in the wealth of detail devoted to the journey and the landscape, which, along with the allusive language employed, creates a sense of a pilgrim's progress or a knight errant's journey toward the bit of moral enlightenment obtained at the end.

The three travelers begin their mythic journey one September morning by crossing a sort of Bridge Perilous, 'A narrow girdle of rough stones and crags,/A rude and natural causeway'. As is usual with the path of the pilgrim, it is a 'difficult way', which, once past the bridge, leads them into a 'privacy', an enchanted place by a dead lake (ll. 18, 65), ruled by the fairy presence of Queen Osmunda, royal moonwort, and associated in the poem with the Grecian Naiad and the Lady of the Lake, 'Sole-sitting by the shores of old romance', in whose realm the '*figure* of a Man' presents 'through a thin veil of glittering haze' an image of Man as fisher. Both the fisherman and the act of fishing are rich in associations. The Man is evocative of the Fisher King of Arthurian legend. Like the Fisher King, the Man is ill, wasted, and weak. He is engaging in the apparently hopeless enterprise of fishing a dead lake (a most surprising description of Grasmere Lake), which like the Fisher King's wasteland realm, reflects the moribund condition of the fisher. Fishing suggests a search of the depths – of the world or the soul – for treasure or wisdom. Alongside the Arthurian symbolism is that of the Christian tradition, wherein the fish is associated with Christ and the fisherman is suggestive of both Christ and his disciples, whom he made 'fishers of men' (Matt. 4:19).

Beyond the Arthurian and Christian implications, an even more interesting dimension of this 'figure of a Man' may be seen in his kinship with others of Wordsworth's solitaries – the hermit or the blind man of 'Tintern Abbey', the discharged soldier of *The Prelude*, or the leech-gatherer of 'Resolution and

Independence'. Like them, this figure is a shadow cast by the poet, a distorted and therefore unrecognized image of himself, who he is or what he may become. As a result of this 'meeting', the narrator says that he and his companions have given a 'memorial name' to the point from which the ailing man fishes – as uncouth a name as ever a mariner gave to site on 'a new-discovered coast'. 'Point Rash-Judgment' does indeed designate a place on a new-discovered coast, a bit of enchanted interior topography, where wisdom may be gained. It is named in a manner similar to Jacob's naming of Peniel, 'face of God', after a mysterious struggle with a night-caller who appears as the figure of a man, but whom Jacob recognizes as God (Gen. 34:22–30).

'To M.H.'

The last of the five 'Poems' was probably the first composed and like the first three tells of the naming of a place with a personal name. 'To M.H.' is a sort of prothalamion, naming for the bride-to-be, Mary Hutchison, a place called 'Mary's Nook', a garden spot with a mythical aura, a sort of revised Miltonic paradise. Wordsworth's paradise is located appropriately 'among the ancient trees', a phrase suggestive of that first garden and those most ancient trees of life and death. As with Milton's Paradise, there is 'no road, nor any wood-man's path' leading to this enclosure. In Milton's poem, the traveler can find no way through an overgrown thicket which guards Paradise, excluding 'All path of Man or Beast' (*Paradise Lost* IV, 177). Milton's Satan chooses to leap over the trees and walls, rather than try the gate on the far side of the garden. In the Wordsworthian revision, while road and path may be missing, the trees themselves have created a 'track, that [brings the travelers] to a slip of lawn,/And a small bed of water in the woods'.

The privileged speaker and companion are, like Milton's Adam and Eve, 'brought to' this place. The sense is that one cannot simply travel here and gain easy access, for it is not so much a place as a feminine space in which the speaker has a proprietary interest: it is, after all, 'Mary's Nook', and she, as the speaker says is '[his] sweet Mary'. In truth, Mary's Nook is a Wordsworthian spot of time. Getting there requires a sort of imaginative time travel: it is hidden, barred, unknown, a spot 'made by Nature for herself:/The travellers know it not, and 'twill remain/Unknown to them; but it is beautiful…' No rival traveler, no fallen and wayward angel, it is implied, will find his way here. The Nook, oddly enough, will remain 'unknown', despite the fact that the speaker knows it, tells about it, and names it. This business of *knowing* or *not knowing*, in conjunction with paradise imagery, in a poem dedicated to the bride-to-be, delicately raises the issue of conjugal love: Mary, the beloved, and this hidden garden are one: 'A garden inclosed is my sister, my spouse' (Song of Songs 4:12). She is beautiful; it is beautiful.

The speaker's knowledge may be a sort of forbidden knowledge. The poem's closing lines lapse into a subjunctive mode and remove the speaker a short distance from the garden. The lines sound an elegiac note in the foreknowledge of loss:

> And if a man should plant his cottage near,
> Should sleep beneath the shelter of its trees,

And blend its waters with his daily meal,
He would so love it, that in his death-hour
Its image would survive among his thoughts... .

The speaker, a mere mortal, a son of Adam,[4] lives like Adam near, but outside, the garden under sentence of death, lives with the inexpungeable image deep in his memory of a perfect garden and inviolable beauty once known, and, though closely guarded, inevitably to be lost. The image of the place survives in the thoughts of the man. Does the place have something like thoughts in which the image of the man and woman can survive? This possibility may be found here and there in Wordsworthian places. 'The Thorn' suggests in its details a spot transformed, shaped, and animated by something like human thought, memory, and feeling that inhere in the place and may be communicated to the perceptive visitor, as does the murderer's grave passage from the earliest version of *The Prelude* (cited above). Speaking of Sarnum Plain in *The Prelude*, the poet raises the possibility of reading such memories, of catching from such places 'a tone,/An image, and a character'; in this experience, the poet undergoes 'an ennobling interchange .../Both of the object seen, and eye that sees' ([1805], p. 456, Bk XII, ll. 363–79). A knowing place seems to be able to serve as a medium between the living and the dead. And yet, to receive that communication, the visitor must read in the place 'monumental hints' ([1850], p. 457, Bk XIII, l. 352). Such hints include, one supposes, a mound of turf in the shape of a grave, a child-sized and knotted thorn, a stone circle, a name chiseled in stone, a name, like 'Mary's Nook' recorded in a poem by William Wordsworth. In the case of 'To M. H.', the poet 'in his death hour' will know the place, and, one feels, the place, named and inscribed by the poet, will know him too, and will be subtly altered by that 'knowledge' an alteration noticeable to some, if only as monumental hints, a tone, image, and character which 'like a family of Ghosts' abide in the place.

Taken individually, each of the 'Poems' is an artifact whose subtle intricacy becomes apparent on close study. Like a Japanese paper flower dropped into water, each 'little incident', dropped into the medium of language, expands into an endless allegory. In the process the private, local, and trivial become universal and profound; the ephemeral becomes enduring. Taken as a group, the 'Poems' participate in the mythologizing of the poet's beloved landscape. Like Wallace, the poet has left names 'like wild flowers/All over his dear Country'; left his thoughts and visions inscribed in the land 'like a family of Ghosts/To people the steep rocks and river banks,/Her natural sanctuaries, with a local soul'. Unwilling to make one of a 'silent company' of the dead, to be without words, speech, language, the poet textualizes with names and poems the to him Edenic Grasmere, the place he calls 'my home' and 'my World' ('Home at Grasmere', 1987, p. 175, l. 42), his enduring possession assured through language. As a result, at Grasmere place and life have become one; the site has been transformed into a bit of Wordsworthian autobiography, identifiable now with its author who having achieved a material permanence and ultra-signification through and in this land, might with some justification declare, 'Grasmere – c'est moi!' How awesome is this place!

Notes

A version of this article appears as Chapter 4 in Westbrook, Deanne: *Wordworth's Biblical Ghosts*. New York: Palgravel from St. Martin's Press, 2001.

1. Wordsworth read Lowth's *Lectures* perhaps as early as March, 1798, and by September 30, 1800. He may have had access to Coleridge's notes on the *Lectures* by late in 1796 (Wu, 1993, p. 89). See especially Lowth's *Lectures* X and XI for his discussion of the forms of allegory.
2. All references to *The Prelude* are to the Norton edition (1979). The version of *The Prelude* cited will be indicated in square brackets.
3. The winged beings surrounding the divine throne in Ezekiel's vision and in Revelation appear to have captured Wordsworth's imagination, for they recur with some frequency in his poems, suitably disguised. For instance, in 'Home at Grasmere', Wordsworth has a vision reminiscent of that in 'It was an April morning', evocative of both Ezekiel and Revelation, wherein the poet looks about him at the sights of Grasmere and thinks 'Of Sunbeams, Shadows, Butterflies and Birds,/Angels and winged Creatures that are the Lords/Without restraint of all which they behold'. Here Wordsworth uses the word *Creatures* (the term used in Ezekiel and Revelation for the winged beings surrounding the throne), connects them with angels, and reacts to the thought of all these winged beings by 'stir[ring] in Spirit' (25-35). The winged beings appear to serve in all these texts not only as suggestive of the divine presence, but actually as metonyms for the divine. They recur in Book VI of *The Prelude* in the vision which succeeds Wordsworth's crossing of the Alps. During this visionary experience he perceives the divine in the voices and acts of nature perceived as a remarkable unity which is imagined as features of one face, and 'Characters of the great apocalypse' (a synonym for revelation), appearing in conjunction with Wordsworth's paraphrase (*Prelude* [1805], ll. 550-72) of Milton's description of God in *Paradise Lost* V 165. The biblical beings are singers of divine praise, as are the 'living things' in 'It was an April morning'. These winged creatures, these characters of the great apocalypse, repeat, 'Holy, holy, holy, is the Lord God Almighty,/who was and is and is to come' (Rev. 4:8), a refrain echoed in Wordsworth's 'Of first, and last, and midst, and without end'.
4. In 'Home at Grasmere', Wordsworth acknowledges himself as a type of Adam in Paradise, although actually more favored than Adam, asking,

> What Being, therefore, since the birth of Man
> Had ever more abundant cause to speak
> Thanks... .
> [S]urpassing grace
> To me hath been vouchsafed; among the bowers
> Of Blissful Eden this was neither given,
> Nor could be given, possession of the good
> Which had been sighed for ... . (117-26)

Chapter Nine

Reactionary and Romantic: Joseph de Maistre and Shelley

Arthur Bradley

In this discussion, I would like to explore the possible impact of the philosophy of Joseph de Maistre on the poetry of Percy Bysshe Shelley. Initially, no two writers seem to have less in common than the Catholic, anti-revolutionary philosopher and the atheist, revolutionary poet. Like many of his English Romantic contemporaries, Shelley blamed the form of reactionary ultramontane Catholicism which Maistre epitomized for the failure of the French Revolution. Indeed, something uncannily close to Maistre's sacrificial philosophy is caricatured in Shelley's poetry as fanaticism and even cannibalism. If Shelley brutally re-shaped Maistre for his own ideological ends, however, it is also clear that, in imaginative terms, he was re-shaped by him. In the epic revolutionary poem *Laon and Cythna*, Shelley's ideological contempt for Maistre's philosophy seems to be coupled with, and increasingly contradicted by, an aesthetic attraction to the philosopher's apocalyptic vision. The anti-revolutionary Catholic and the revolutionary poet have more in common than one would first think.

'... this monstrous power, drunk with blood ...'

When Joseph de Maistre's *Considerations on France* first appeared in 1797, it was an instant success with the French émigrés. Writing in what, for his conservative readers, were still troubling times, Maistre advanced an apocalyptic but ultimately reassuring vision of the future. Far from destroying the *ancien régime*, he suggests, the violence of the Revolution had purged the French people of their revolutionary fervour forever:

> All life, all wealth, all power was in the hands of the revolutionary authority, and this monstrous power, drunk with blood and success, the most frightful phenomenon that has ever been seen and the like of which will never be seen again, was both a horrible chastisement for the French and the sole means of saving France. (Lebrun, 1974, p. 41)

The reference to salvation is significant. For Maistre, the Revolution was a necessary fall without which future redemption would be impossible. He describes the Terror, too, in strikingly sacramental terms, comparing it to 'self-sacrifices, practiced by certain religious orders' (p. 62). Revealingly, *Considerations on*

France concludes by predicting the restoration of everything the Revolution had existed to overthrow: aristocracy, throne and above all altar. While Maistre's sacralization of revolutionary violence clearly reassured his French Catholic audience, it would only have confirmed the fears of an English Protestant one. In the 1790s, a growing number of English writers began to make uncannily similar connections between Catholic sacrament and Jacobin terror – albeit for very different reasons. As many scholars have argued (Paulson, 1983; Blakemore, 1988; Liu, 1989; Manquis, 1989), Romantic reactions to the Revolution were often characterized by implicit or explicit anti-Catholicism. For many English Romantics, the violence of the French Revolution was at least partially due to the residual Catholicism of the revolutionaries. To understand Shelley's response to French Catholicism – and by extension to Maistre – it must be seen in this context.

In an ironic inversion of de Maistre's attempts to sacralize 'this monstrous power drunk with blood', the English Romantics secularized Catholic sacraments like the Eucharist by seeing them as implicit justifications for revolutionary violence and even cannibalism. Indeed the Catholic cannibal – consuming the body and blood of a French aristocrat rather than Christ – quickly became one of the most popular English images of the Revolution. In one of the first newspaper pieces on the Revolution in 1789, a *Times* reporter mentions seeing a Jacobin 'tearing from the mangled body of another pieces of flesh, and dipping the same into a cup, which was eagerly drained by the executioners' (Paulson, 1983, pp. 42–3). In his *Reflections on the Revolution in France* (1790), Edmund Burke describes how a play about the St Batholomew's Day Massacre – in which the Cardinal of Lorraine is seen to order the slaughter – was currently stimulating the 'cannibal appetites' of Parisian audiences (O'Brien, 1969, p. 249). In his *Un Petit Souper à la Parisiènne* (1792), James Gillray draws a Parisian family relaxing 'after the fatigues of the day' with a plate of decapitated heads.

The Catholic-as-cannibal motif was not solely the prerogative of conservative opinion-formers like Gillray, Burke or *The Times* newspaper, however. In his *Conciones ad Populum* (1795), Samuel Taylor Coleridge gave it a more radical spin by turning the now famous images of French *sans-culottes* drinking blood and eating flesh back upon the reactionary British Government (Manquis, 1989, p. 376). By opposing the Revolution, Coleridge argues, William Pitt became responsible for the bloodshed it generated:

> Who, my Brethren! was the cause of this guilt, if not HE, who supplied the occasion and the motive? – Heaven hath bestowed on that man a portion of its ubiquity, and given him an actual presence in the Sacraments of Hell, wherever administered, in all the bread of bitterness, in all the cups of blood. (Patton and Mann, 1971, p. 74)

While Coleridge is supposedly attacking the violent opposition to the Revolution in Protestant England, it is interesting to note that he still describes the violence itself in Catholic terms: 'in all the bread of bitterness, in all the cups of blood'. Far from questioning the connection between Catholicism and violence, he extends it to cover non-Catholic violence too. By opposing the Revolution so savagely, the Protestant Pitt became an honorary Catholic.

Another radical who peddled this kind of anti-Catholic prejudice was William Hazlitt. For Hazlitt, the struggle for the Repeal of the Union was marred by the 'animal spirits' of the Irish people (Howe, 1930-4, IV, p. 104). This flaw was not restricted to the Irish national character, however. In his *Life of Napoleon* (1828-30), an uncannily similar instability in the French people is blamed for the collapse of the French Revolution. What connected the two peoples, and made their revolutionary aspirations so dangerous in Hazlitt's mind was Catholicism:

> Catholics may make good subjects, but bad rebels. They are so used to the trammels of authority, that they do not immediately know how to do without them; or, like manumitted slaves, only feel assured of their liberty in committing some Saturnalian licence. (XIII, p. 56)

Whereas Coleridge blamed the British for the descent of the French Revolution into anarchy, Hazlitt points the finger at the Catholicism of the revolutionaries (Manquis, 1989, p. 377). By their very nature Catholics could not rebel satisfactorily. The only way in which the Jacobins could have met his exacting standards for aspiring revolutionaries would, it seems, have been by converting to Protestantism: '[a] revolution, to give it stability and soundness, should first be conducted down to a Protestant ground' he concludes (Howe, 1930-4, XIII, p. 56).

By the late 1820s, the image of the Catholic cannibal was in danger of turning into a cliché. In *Childe Harold's Pilgrimage* (1812-17), Lord Byron did his best to summon up the spirit of the 1790s, but in the mid-1810s there was already something obligatory about lines like: 'France got drunk with blood to vomit crime/And fatal have her Saturnalia been/To Freedom's cause' (McGann, 1980-93, II, p. 156). Byron's second foray into anti-Catholic imagery was more successful (Manquis, 1989, p. 377). Describing the shipwreck scene in *Don Juan* (1818-23), and the imminent cannibalization of Juan's tutor, Pedrillo, he displays a lighter, more ironic touch:

> He died as born, a Catholic in faith,
> Like most in the belief in which they're bred,
> And first a little crucifix he kiss'd,
> And then held out his jugular and wrist. (McGann, 1980-93, V, p. 112)

Recognizing, perhaps, that the figure of the Catholic cannibal was finally losing his power to shock, Byron turns him into the butt of a characteristically black joke. The Catholic cannibal is himself cannibalized. Byron's point was no less polemical for the absence of overt polemic, however. The stoic manner in which Pedrillo accepts his cannibalization intimates that his religious faith has already acquainted him with, and prepared him for, such a savage death. By making this point, Byron comically reinvigorates the increasingly stale motif he had inherited from his Romantic predecessors. For a Catholic, it seems, cannibalism and being cannibalized are still the most natural things in the world.

This, then, is the context in which Shelley's response to French Catholicism (and Maistre) must be seen. To what extent did Shelley share the anti-Catholicism of his Romantic predecessors? Despite his radical beliefs, it is clear that his opinion of French Catholicism in this period was typical of the aristocratic, English Protestant background from which he came. Scratch beneath the glittering surface of Shelley's rationalism, and one quickly finds some recalcitrant prejudices. Not the least of these was his unquestioning adherence to one of the master tropes of Romantic anti-Catholicism: the Catholic cannibal.

While Shelley had a vegetarian's revulsion for carnivorousness of any kind, he always reserved a special disgust for the role of meat-eating in Christian ritual. In *The Vegetable System of Diets* (1814–15), he recounts how 'a certain horrible process of torture furnishes brawn for the gluttonous repasts with which Christians celebrate the anniversary of their Savior's birth' (Murray, 1993, I, p. 152). In *Queen Mab* (1813), he graphically contrasts the barbarity of Man's carnivorous Christian past with the tranquillity of his vegetarian, atheist future: 'no longer now/He slays the lamb that looks him in the face,/And horribly devours his mangled flesh' (Reiman and Powers, 1977, p. 62–63). If Shelley saw Christianity as carnivorous, however, it will be no surprise to find that he saw Catholicism, in particular, as cannibalistic. Belying his strident atheism, he explicitly writes the Preface to his play *The Cenci* (1819) from a Protestant perspective and obligingly complies with all the current Protestant clichés about the Catholic mentality:

> To a Protestant apprehension there will appear something unnatural in the earnest and perpetual sentiment of the relations between God and man which pervade the tragedy of the Cenci. It will especially be startled at the combination of an undoubting persuasion of the truth of the popular religion with a cool and determined perseverance in enormous guilt. (p. 240)

Revealingly, Shelley goes on to suggest that Catholicism is 'not a rule for moral conduct' indeed just the reverse: 'a passion, a persuasion, an excuse, a refuge; never a check' (p. 241). The play proper wastes no time in justifying this view. Filling up a bowl of wine, early in Act One, the treacherous Count Cenci exclaims:

> Oh, thou bright wine whose purple splendor [sic] leaps
> And bubbles gaily in this golden bowl
> Under the lamp light, as my spirits do,
> To hear the death of my accursed sons!
> Could I believe thou wert their mingled blood,
> Then would I taste thee like a sacrament ... (p. 250)

Drinking wine like blood, and blood like wine, Cenci is the Catholic cannibal *par excellence*. Like his Romantic predecessors, then, Shelley believed that Eucharist and cannibalism were all too easily confused in the Catholic mind. Moreover, he concurred with the general view that the apogee of this confusion was not the 16th century Rome of Count Cenci but the 18th century Paris of Robespierre:

> Who will assert that had the populace of Paris drunk at the pure source of the Seine and satisfied their hunger at the ever-furnished table of vegetable nature that they would have lent their brutal suffrage to the proscription-list of Robespierre? (Murray, 1993, I, p. 82)

The logical culmination of Catholicism, carnivorousness, and cannibalism – all closely bound together in Shelley's mind – was the Reign of Terror. Only by refraining from eating meat – which, in Shelley's logic, also meant refraining from being a Catholic – could the blood-bath have been prevented. For Shelley, evidently, a stable revolution needed to be conducted down to an atheist, vegetarian ground.

In summary, then, it is clear that many English Romantics believed Catholicism was an important factor in the descent of the French Revolution into anarchy. While philosophers like Maistre reassured French Catholics by comparing the Revolution to a religious sacrifice, they would only have confirmed the English suspicion that there was something reactionary, even regressive, in the Catholic faith. There is, admittedly, no evidence that the major English Romantics ever read Maistre – not many people did before the restoration of the French monarchy in 1815 – but his position as the principal exponent (and defender) of 'Throne and Altar' politics almost inevitably brings him into the line of fire whenever the subject of Catholicism comes up in their work. The most notable example of this is the cannibalism motif. In an ironic echo of Maistre's belief that the Jacobins were a 'monstrous power, drunk with blood', Coleridge created the figure of the Catholic cannibal, languishing 'in all the cups of blood'. In a still more ironic echo of Maistre's suggestion that this 'power' was 'the sole means of saving France', Byron intimated that the immediate effect of such visions of future salvation was to normalize, and implicitly justify, the violence they sought to redeem: '[a]nd first a little crucifix he kissed/And then held out his jugular and wrist'. Perhaps the most persistent English critic of Maistre's way of thinking, however, was Shelley. In a savage series of ripostes to the Maistrean suggestion that the Jacobins were unwitting agents of Catholic Providence, Shelley subscribed to the standard Romantic view that Providence was merely the pretext for their cannibalistic practices: 'a passion, a persuasion, an excuse a refuge; never a check'. So savage were Shelley's ripostes, however, that they begin to jeopardize his condemnations of Catholic savagery. Gratuitous images of 'mangled flesh' sit uneasily beside declarations of vegetarianism. While it is clear that Shelley was very critical of Maistre's philosophy, in other words, it is also apparent that his critique was partially compromised by the fact that his gory, apocalyptic imaginative vision in many ways resembled the philosopher's own. This contradiction – which is implicit in *Queen Mab* – became explicit in Shelley's own *Considerations on France*. In *Laon and Cythna* (1817), the epic poem which he later described as his 'beau ideal ... of the French Revolution' (Jones, I, p. 564), the anti-revolutionary tenor of Shelley's aesthetics became increasingly inimical to his pro-revolutionary ideology.

'... the Earth an altar, and the Heavens a fane ...'

In *Laon and Cythna*, Shelley describes a peaceful Greek revolution against a tyrannical Turkish Emperor. Despite the Emperor's attempts to imprison and torture them, Laon and his sister Cythna lead a successful uprising against him and a new state is founded upon democratic, and atheist, principles. But hardly has the new order been established than the Emperor recovers power in a bloody war and Islam is subject to a series of plagues and famines which threaten to engulf revolutionaries and counter-revolutionaries alike. Stricken with terror, the Emperor turns to a fanatical Christian Priest who convinces him that his predicament is a divine punishment which can only be expiated by the sacrifice of Laon and Cythna. In an act of martyrdom, the siblings surrender themselves, and are burnt together on the pyre, but they ultimately rise again to enter the

Temple of the Spirit – a visionary senate where the great minds of the past sit as an inspiration to future generations.

If *Laon and Cythna* was Shelley's attempt to understand what went wrong with the French Revolution – and what might be corrected next time round – what conclusions did he come to? One obvious difference between the real revolution and the ideal one he imagined here is that the latter is non-violent: [t]he panic which, like an epidemic transport, seized upon all classes of men during the excesses consequent upon the French Revolution, is gradually giving place to sanity' he wrote in the Preface to *Laon and Cythna* (Forman 1880, I, p. 87). A more subtle one is that the latter is not Catholic:

> It has ceased to be believed, that whole generations of mankind ought to consign themselves to a hopeless inheritance of ignorance and misery, because a nation of men who had been dupes and slaves for centuries, were incapable of conducting themselves with the wisdom and tranquillity of freemen so soon as some of their fetters were partially loosened. (p. 87)

Whereas the French Revolution failed because the Jacobins could not overcome their own reactionary Catholic instincts, which left them 'dupes and slaves for centuries', Laon and Cythna's revolution only seems to fail because they cannot overcome the reactionary instincts of the Emperor. Given Shelley's anti-Catholicism, perhaps the surest sign that one is supposed to blame the Emperor, rather than Laon and Cythna, for the failure of the revolution is the fact that it is he, not they, whom the poem depicts as Catholic.

In her revolutionary speeches, for example, Cythna is agnostic to the point of atheism: '"What then is God? ye mock yourselves, and give/A human heart to what ye cannot know:/As if the cause of life could think and live!"' (p. 234). The Emperor, on the other hand, is at least nominally Muslim and defers constantly to a Christian Priest who, in the revised version of the poem, is identified as Iberian: '"Were it not impious," said the King, "to break/Our holy oath?" – "Impious to keep it, say!"/Shrieked the exulting Priest' (p. 289). Perhaps the clinching evidence that the tyrants rather than the revolutionaries are Catholics, though, is the presence of the cannibalism motif. Like Coleridge before him, Shelley turns the favoured trope of reactionary anti-Catholics back upon the people who originally propagated it. The Emperor's greed for power is described in cannibalistic similes: he is 'the murderer/Who slaked his thirsting soul as from a well/Of blood and tears' (p. 184). The Christian priests who carry out the Emperor's sacrificial demands take his figurative tendencies all too literally: they are described as 'unholy men,/Feasting like fiends upon the infidel dead' (p. 274). In stark contrast to the cannibalistic tyrant and his priests, the revolutionaries are depicted as vegetarians: 'Never again may blood of bird or beast/Stain with its venomous [sic] stream a human feast' (p. 193).

By depicting the reactionaries, rather than the revolutionaries, as Catholic cannibals, Shelley reveals just how regressive an influence he believed Catholicism really was. Needless to say, an acquaintance with the philosophy of Maistre would hardly have dispelled this belief. While I should repeat that it remains very unlikely that Shelley ever read Maistre, his assaults on Christianity in *Laon and Cythna* do seem to spring from a familiarity with the 'Throne and Altar' brand of Catholicism that the philosopher did so much to popularize. In the famine sequence, for instance, Shelley puts this prayer into the mouth of one of the poem's cannibalistic priests:

> "O God Almighty! thou alone hast power!
> Who can resist thy will? who can restrain
> Thy wrath, when on the guilty thou dost shower
> The shafts of thy revenge, a blistering rain?
> Greatest and best, be merciful again!
> Have we not stabbed thine enemies, and made
> The Earth an altar, and the Heavens a fane,
> Where thou wert worshipped with their blood, and laid
> Those hearts in dust which would thy searchless works have weighed?" (p. 267)

Recalling – whether intentionally or not – the Maistrean suggestion that the violence of the French Revolution and its aftermath was a sacred expiation of past sins, Shelley argues that the concept of blood sacrifice was merely a sacralized justification for bloodshed: '[h]ave we not stabbed thine enemies/and made the Earth an altar, and the Heavens a fane,/Where thou wert worshipped with their blood...?'. The uncanny extent to which Shelley's poem coincides with specific aspects of Maistre's philosophy becomes even clearer if one compares this passage to one from Maistre's philosophical magnum opus, the *Soirées de Saint-Pétersbourg* (1809–21):

> Thus is worked out, from maggots up to man, the universal law of the violent destruction of living beings. The whole earth, continually steeped in blood, is nothing but an immense altar on which every living thing must be sacrificed without end, without restraint, without respite until the consummation of the world, the extinction of evil, the death of death. (Lively, 1965, p. 253)

By echoing Maistre so precisely here, whether by accident or design, Shelley's anti-Catholic satire acquires a specificity which was lacking in the satires of his predecessors. Whereas Coleridge, Hazlitt, et al refer to Catholicism as a broadly sacrificial phenomenon, it is perhaps significant that Shelley, alone, is able to re-ignite what Vigny (1926) called 'the incendiary spark of [Maistre's] fatal idea' (p. 250) (translation mine). Without wishing to suggest that there was anything specious in Shelley's satire on Maistre and his ilk, it is ironic that much of its power derives from the poet's ability to enter into and re-create, however subversively, the philosopher's aesthetic vision. Ideological dyspathy is the product of a certain imaginative sympathy. Once lit in Shelley's mind, however, it is clear that the 'incendiary spark' of anti-revolutionaries like Maistre proved increasingly difficult to extinguish with ideology.

The increasing tension between Shelley's latently reactionary imagination and his revolutionary ideology in *Laon and Cythna* has been noted by a number of critics, but very few have placed it in its political or historical context. Criticizing Shelley's poor grasp of 'the revolutionary process', for example, Richard Holmes (1974) argues that only in the extraordinarily violent war scenes 'did he find any adequate political image of his age: and it was an image of reaction, not of revolution' (p. 401). Criticizing Shelley's poor choice of 'the epic-romance form', Stuart Curran (1975) observes that these 'bloody battle scenes, designed to shock a doubting Thomas into political action, sit uncomfortably next to avowals of pacifism' (p. 29). The list of gratuitously violent scenes could go on: at one point in the poem, Cythna is graphically raped, at another, a hermit who helps Laon is vividly scalped and, of course, images of cannibalism abound. In scenes like these, the 'beau ideal' of the French Revolution is closer to something out of Géricault's *Raft of the Medusa* (1819). Whereas Holmes and Curran blame the presence of such images on Shelley's artistic or political naïveté, however, it should be recalled that they also belong to a tradition of anti-revolutionary writing which stretches back to Burke and, inevitably, Maistre.

One of the most compelling indices of Shelley's ideological horror of Maistrean philosophy is the cannibalism motif, and it is through this same motif that the poet's aesthetic fascination with that philosophy can also be traced. When considering cannibalism earlier, I argued that Shelley's decision to depict the reactionaries as Catholic cannibals was also a decision to reject Maistre's position on ideological grounds. If the suspicion remains that Shelley retained a certain aesthetic respect for that position, despite ideological differences, it is confirmed by the curious fact that the Emperor and his band of fanatical Christian followers are not actually the only cannibals in the poem. When held in captivity by the Emperor, the starving Laon begins to hallucinate and has this fantasy:

> A woman's shape, now lank and cold and blue,
> The dwelling of the many-coloured worm
> Hung there, the white and hollow cheek I drew
> To my dry lips – what radiance did inform
> Those horny eyes? whose was that withered form?
> Alas! alas! it seemed that Cythna's ghost
> Laughed in those looks, and that the flesh was warm
> Within my teeth! – a whirlwind keen as frost
> Then in its sinking gulphs [sic] my sickening spirits tost [sic].
> (Forman, 1880, I, p. 158)

Nor is Laon alone in having such fantasies. When she was imprisoned, Cythna tells her brother, she also dreamt about consuming him: '"[a]nd the sea eagle looked a fiend, who bore/Thy mangled limbs for food!"' (p. 222). The reason why Shelley should allow Laon and Cythna, who normally blanch at the prospect of eating meat of any kind, to succumb to the same cannibalistic desires as the Emperor and his priests has understandably evaded most critics of the poem, Holmes and Curran included. Perhaps the most ingenious suggestion has come from Richard Cronin (1981), who argues that such fantasies are a psychological defense-mechanism which prepare the revolutionary couple for their encounters with real cannibals like the reactionaries: '[t]he most disgusting barbarities ... are only human dreams'(p. 104). As clever as explanations like this are, they do not wholly reassure because, as W.B. Yeats (1961) noted, the customary subordination of dreams to reality simply did not operate in the poetry of 'one who believed "the thoughts which are called real or external objects" differed but in regularity of recurrence from "hallucinations, dreams, and the ideas of madness"' (pp. 76–7). Laon and Cythna's cannibalistic dreams are no less real than their revolutionary ones.

If Shelley's predilection for gratuitously violent imagery should not be dismissed as the naïve or harmless fantasies of an essentially revolutionary poet, it seems clear that they must be admitted as integral parts of his aesthetic vision, which contradict his revolutionary ideology. Like Laon and Cythna, who fantasize about eating each other but condemn the Emperor for being a cannibal, Shelley's imagination was unable to resist the reactionary mentality he hated so much. The sleep of reason breeds Catholic monsters. By showing that even ideal revolutionaries could be Catholic cannibals, moreover, Shelley was not re-instating the reactionary caricatures of bloodthirsty Jacobins that he had so cleverly inverted earlier in the poem, but rather casting doubt on his entire 'beau ideal' of non-religious and non-violent revolution. What remained certain was a poetic world in which revolutionaries and anti-revolutionaries, peacefulness and violence, good and evil, became increasingly difficult to tell apart – a world closer to Maistre than, say, Rousseau:

> There is nothing but violence in the universe; but we are spoiled by a modern philosophy that tells us all is good, whereas evil has tainted everything, and in a very real sense, all is evil, since nothing is in its place. (Lebrun 1974, p. 62)

Perhaps the most graphic example of Shelley's anti-revolutionary aesthetic is Laon and Cythna's sacrificial pyre, which provides a magnificent *mise en scène* to conclude the poem:.

> Our God may then lull Pestilence to sleep:-
> Pile high the pyre of expiation now!
> A forest's spoil of boughs, and on the heap
> Pour venomous gums, which sullenly and slow,
> When touched by flame, shall burn, and melt, and flow,
> A stream of clinging fire, – and fix on high
> A net of iron, and spread forth below
> A couch of snakes, and scorpions, and the fry
> Of centipedes and worms, earth's hellish progeny! (Forman, 1880, I, p. 271)

Many years after Shelley wrote these lines, in 1824, Mary Shelley wrote a letter to her friend Thomas Hogg about a visit to the German Opera: '[w]e liked the music, & the incantation scene would have made Shelley scream with delight flapping owls [sic]- ravens, hopping toads, queer reptiles – fiery serpents skeleton huntsmen [sic] …' (Bennett 1980, I, p. 450). One can almost detect the same 'screams of delight' in phrases like 'the *fry*/Of centipedes and worms' (stress mine) which, in the context of a sacrificial pyre, has a punningly sadistic playfulness. In a scene which is clearly intended to *condemn* Christian sadism, however, this playfulness is scarcely appropriate. Shelley savors the sacrificial pyre's grisly decorations almost as lovingly as the psychotic Christian priest who devised them. If Laon and Cythna's death scene represents Shelley's definitive ideological rejection of Maistrean philosophy, in other words, his aesthetic delight in the philosopher's sacrificial vision renders that rejection almost redundant. The 'incendiary spark' of Maistre lights an imaginative bonfire which consumes Shelley's 'beau ideal' of the French Revolution.

'... and there its haven found'

Of course, the poem does not quite end on the 'pyre of expiation'. In comparison to the graphic – almost pornographic – potency of Laon and Cythna's death scene, however, the scenes which depict their resurrection and admission into the Temple of the Spirit seem rather feeble and superfluous. By seeking to imagine, for almost the first time in the poem, the vindication of his revolutionary ideology, Shelley's aesthetic vision comes uncomfortably close to sterility. Hanging in a 'hollow sky', above a 'windless waveless lake' (Forman, 1880, I, p. 299–300), the spherical Temple has a certain geometrical beauty, perhaps, but in comparison to the Géricaultian vision of the sacrificial pyre, it is merely like an M.C. Escher illustration of Chaucer's *House of Fame*. Joseph de Maistre would not have found his 'haven' there, but neither, on this evidence, would Shelley:

> Motionless resting on the lake awhile,
> I saw its marge of snow-bright mountains rear
> Their peaks loft, I saw each radiant isle,
> And in the midst, afar, even like a sphere
> Hung in one hollow sky, did there appear
> The Temple of the Spirit; on the sound
> Which issued thence, drawn nearer and more near,
> Like the swift moon this glorious earth around,
> The charmèd boat approached, and there its haven found. (p. 300)

In this discussion, I have argued that Shelley was ideologically repulsed by, but aesthetically attracted to, the anti-revolutionary philosophy of Catholics like Maistre and the images which it authorized. This contradiction – which is always apparent in Shelley's poetry – became something of a crisis by the time of *Laon and Cythna*. Even Shelley's 'beau ideal' of the French Revolution depended upon images and ideas which elided and in some cases eclipsed his revolutionary ideology. 'Have we not stabbed thine enemies, and made/The Earth an altar, and the Heavens a fane…?'the Christian priests asked, and the poet's imagination, at least, answered with an emphatic affirmative. In *Laon and Cythna*, it is not too much to say that Shelley's revolutionary ideology was sacrificed on the altar of his anti-revolutionary aesthetics.

Acknowledgements

I would like to thank Bernard Beatty, Keith Hanley, Greg Kucich, Brian Nellist and Alan Rawes for their helpful comments on this paper at various stages in its development.

Chapter Ten

The Religion of Thomas Carlyle

Trevor Hogan

Introduction

Thomas Carlyle (1795–1881), the archetypal 'man of letters' and 'Victorian Sage', is central to an understanding of nineteenth century critical debates about religion and secularization within Britain (Abrams, 1971; Houghton, 1957; Landow, 1986; Morgan, 1990). His centrality, however, is variously understood as embodying either a counter-modern reassertion of Protestantism, a modern post-Christian pantheism, or post-religious secularism. Each of these interpretations is a plausible albeit partial account of Carlyle's ambiguous and complex religious stance as found in his experimental, *sui generis* text, *Sartor Resartus*, (hereafter *Sartor*). Trying to classify Carlyle's religious beliefs at the outset, however, misdirects our attention away from Carlyle's specific interest and achievement as a thinker of modernity and its origins writ large. Carlyle interpreted modernity as a revolutionary epoch that demands revolutions in our modes of being, knowledge and representation. For Carlyle, the revolutionary nature of the modern epoch could neither be apprehended by traditional modes of thought nor by the immanent logic of modern secular reason itself. Yet to understand modernity in its totality, was to Carlyle the most important spiritual task of the modern man of letters, especially one who was aspiring to participate in the new public spaces opened through and by literary markets. In particular, Carlyle was anxious to promote Goethe's ideal of *Weltliteratur*, a literature for all peoples and nations, secured via a continuous exchange and translation of ideas and literary traditions, genres and languages and thereby enlivening the latent cosmopolitan spirit of humankind.[1] In *Sartor*, Carlyle seeks a new religious negotiation of Christian and Classical traditions with modern European conditions and subjectivities. His complex example is appropriated and codified in various modern Anglo-American traditions that frequently invert and misread his originating ideas. So revolutionary is the form and the content of Carlyle's *Sartor*, that over one hundred and sixty years after its first publication, the book's meaning, genre, and arguments remain sources of controversy. These critical traditions are of interest as much for their differences as for what they reveal about *Sartor*. A reconsideration and a reconstruction of these critical receptions of *Sartor*, therefore, is an instructive exercise in itself. Yet, *Sartor* is more than the sum of the conflict of interpretations by its critics and readers. It is Carlyle's attempt at providing a revolutionary romance of modernity for would-be romantic revolutionaries of the new age. Like Goethe before him, and whose example Carlyle self-consciously endeavours to emulate, he tries to synthesise the antinomies of idealism and realism, romanticism and utilitarianism, politics and economics, reason and history, faith and reason, into a holistic representation of the modern revolution.

'Revolution', then, is Carlyle's central metaphor of modernity (Vanden Bossche, 1986, p. 77; Hogan, 1995). For Carlyle, modernity as epoch stretched back on the one hand at least five centuries to the rise of the Christian normative ideal of chivalry and the development of poetic civilizing processes in court society and language, and on the other, some three centuries to the sixteenth century with the simultaneous development of gunpowder and printing technologies, and the shift in European consciousness wrought by the Protestant Reformations across Europe (Carlyle, 1895; Shine, 1951).[2] To Carlyle, the specific incidences of revolutionary rupture in the social, political and economic ordering of modern society, most importantly as in the English Revolution of the seventeenth century and the French Revolution in the late eighteenth century, are part of a longer term macro-phenomenon of revolution which defines modernity as historical epoch. In both senses of the term 'revolution' (as 'event' and as 'epoch'), Carlyle reads revolution as having material, social and spiritual dimensions: as natural forces (frequently beyond human political and rational control and therefore having unforeseeable outcomes and consequences), as cultural events, and as containing spiritual meanings which have to be interpreted symbolically for their prophetic implications by historians and biographers alike. This is arguably why Carlyle was obsessed with interpreting the event of the French Revolution as both the 'Death-Birth' event which defines the modern epoch and yet simultaneously to be viewed as only a symptom of the larger social revolution called 'modernity' (Carlyle, 1989).

This essay, therefore, redresses *Sartor Resartus*, or 'the tailor re-tailored' in three ways: first by offering a revised outline of the book's threefold form; then, by reading across the grain of the main traditions of critical reception of the book; and, finally, by arguing for a revisionist sense of the book as nothing less than an attempt to write a modern Bible, a 'Book of Books' for revolutionary moderns who recognize that they themselves are as responsible for making the world afresh, as 'gods of the lower world' (Schiller) and 'benignant spiritual revolutionists' (Goethe).

Sartor's Clothing: The Form and Content of Three Books in One

Sartor is a work *sui generis*. It is without precedent or heirs in English literature, whether one studies Sartor's texture, style, genres, grammar, language, ideas, forms of reasoning, traditions, individual thinkers and influences. From the very first draft of the 'Thoughts on Clothes' essay written in 1830, Carlyle was seeking a poetic form to fuse his belief in thaumaturgy to that of science and criticism and the modern sense of complexity, specialization, pluralization, and fragmentation. The increasing complexity of the structure of each draft of his book, a drafting process which takes four years, suggests that he gradually realized that he could explore the consequences of the absent center of the modern revolution at the very edge of the abyss of nihilism, by using the form of the text to body forth the total content of the modern predicament. Rather than try to mirror the classicist and Protestant models which shared a common epistemological model of mimetic truth theories of coherence and correspondence, he tried to develop a de-centered mode of writing.

Carlyle stays close to the German Romantic sense of nihilism and seeks both an epistemological and an aesthetic depiction and response. The 'revolutionary times' were still without 'revolutionary thought' (*Sartor*, 1937, I:VI, p. 12),[3] and so Carlyle delivers Britain's first literary revolution of the epoch and does so with a vengeance: imbalance, excess, excitement; neologisms, Germanisms, and Latinisms; inversion, repetition, verbosity; the imperative, the interrogative, the present tense; genealogy, encyclopaedia, tradition; criticism, humour, thaumaturgic mysticism; Cervantes and Rabelais, Swift and Voltaire, Sterne and Jean Paul; Rabbinical and Kabbalistic Judaism, Pauline and Calvinist Christianity, Hellenism and Scandinavian and Teutonic mythologies all together. The carnivalesque bravado of Carlyle's bricolage, the sheer prodigality of his imagination and vocabulary, the perversity of his syntax and neologisms seem to suggest that he was trying to be a literary alchemist pouring the whole of western literature from antiquity to 1830 into one melting 'golden pot' (cf. Hoffman in Carlyle, 1896).

Sartor constitutes an 'epistemological revolution in form' (Rundle, 1992, p. 14). In the first place, *Sartor*'s subject matter is encyclopaedic in scope, it contains texts and commentaries on 'Things-in-General', with an aim to present a total view of the cosmos (Book One), of society (Book Three) and the self (Book Two) – a science of sciences as a 'philosophy of clothes' which integrates the science of knowledge (*Wissenschaftlehre*) with the science of consciousness (*Lebensphilosophie*). While it approximates the idea of 'totality', desired in the philosophical systems of Fichte and Schelling, it presents both the semiotic science as a poetic because symbolic mode of knowledge and the *Lebensphilosophie* as a philosophy of feeling – a mode of knowledge which must be experienced, believed, willed, enacted. These two aspects of 'Natural Supernaturalism' – the opinions of Teufelsdröckh (as the general Science of all things) and the life of Teufelsdröckh (as the archetypal philosophical-poetic biography) – are presented ironically so as to de-construct the book's – and therefore the author's – own pretensions to completion and to verisimilitude. *Sartor* not only encompasses everything that Carlyle knows about the world but everything he had learned to date in the art of writing, editing, reviewing and translating. As the reader proceeds through *Sartor* the optical frames for viewing the text continue to shift, dislocating, scattering and de-constructing the reader's commonsensical and empirical assumptions about the correspondence and coherence modes of truth, as well as about the common generic modes of representation themselves. This interpolation of texts, authorities, modes, languages, and discourses, forces the reader to follow the lead of the book's 'Editor' in actively trying to construct meaning out of the apparent chaos.

The first Book which purports to present 'the clothes philosophy' traces the genetic criticism (*werden*: origins) and encyclopaedic (*wirken*: influences) dimensions of 'clothes' and so re-contextualises the British reader's perception of science, philosophy, religion and their respective readings of nature and society. It casts a new light on the Enlightenment's 'Torch of Science', tracing humankind's progress from its 'artificial illumination' of critique to the transcendental illumination of the lamp of 'Pure Reason'. At first glance, then, the first Book would appear to offer an unambiguous path from British empiricism to German Transcendental Idealism, but this is to discount the radical epistemological skepticism of the Teufelsdröckhian discourse on clothes, designed to disorient the confidence of all

Truth-seekers, empiricist-materialist or idealist-metaphysical (*Sartor*, 1937, I:VIII, p. 54). Book Two picks up the question of Being by following the exemplary career of Teufelsdröckh in poetical and philosophical terms *à la* Schiller and Goethe. By offering a bricolage of Hebraic-Biblical narratives of liberation, Puritan narratives of individual conversion and a linear journey to salvation, and Romantic narratives of the circuitous journey to spiritual maturity, Book Two of *Sartor* presents Teufelsdröckh as an archetypal figure of modernity: in both its real conditions (as a representative type of the collective *Zeitgeist*) and revolutionary potentiality (as an emblematic figure of hope). Set in this wider revolutionary context of the modern epoch, however, the balance of *Sartor* shifts from Teufelsdröckh's biography in Book Two to the 'critique of civilization' in Book Three (McMaster, 1968). Book Three has quite a different structure to the first two books, for it is the completion of the dialectical movement from critical criticism (Book One) to critical affirmation (Book Two), and now to affirmative/believing criticism or prophecy of society (Book Three). Accordingly, the climax of affirmative *vision* is obtained in the middle of Book Three – not at its end as was the case in the previous two books with 'Pure Reason' (Book One) and 'The Everlasting Yea' (Book Two).

Such are the structure, key motifs and themes of *Sartor* when read from the point of view of the sub-title: 'The Life and Opinions of Herr Teufelsdröckh'. Yet Professor Teufelsdröckh only exists in the reader's imagination as a text within a text: 'if the Professor plays with the nature of the appearance of things, the Editor plays with the nature of the Professor's ironic appearance' (Baker, 1986, p. 230). 'The British Editor' is the most important character of *Sartor*. Without the Editor, there can be no introduction to the life or the opinions of Teufelsdröckh; the Editor is the 'reconstructor' of Diogenes Teufelsdröckh who is the emblematic universal man and the emblematic universal modern man. This text of 'the British Editor' is in turn dependent on the limited recourse of the editor to his own memory of one personal meeting with the Professor, and a series of fragments from two texts sent to him: 1) Volume One of a larger work on 'The Philosophy of Clothes', written in German; and 2) Teufelsdröckh's autobiographical writings (Franklin, 1977; Dibble, 1978). This second text in the editor's possession, from which he selectively quotes and paraphrases, is only made available to him as a chaotically arranged series of fragments, consisting of 'Six Paper Bags' each marked with a different Zodiacal Sign (1937, I:XI, p. 77–79).

To help and to retard the Editor in his endeavours to 'retailor the tailor' and his clothes philosophy, there is Teufelsdröckh's own amaneunsis, Herr Hofrath Heuschrecke (Councillor Grasshopper). Heuschrecke posts to the Editor the main texts by Teufelsdröckh with accompanying letters about the author, as well as some of Heuschrecke's own writings such as a Malthusian tract entitled 'Institute for Repression of Population' which in turn contains marginalia in Teufelsdröckh's own hand. In *Sartor*'s economy of literature, each author is the editor of the other. Heuschrecke, therefore, is the mediating figure between Teufelsdröckh and Editor, just as the Editor is the mediating figure between the Germans and the implied 'British Reader' who is the intended readership of the Editor's efforts. Each is trying to bring order out of chaos, and each in turn complicates the order for the other: mediation is both gain and loss, for a secondary interpretation brings both simplification and multiplication and every representation (because representation) defers revelation. Nor is this simply a rational, philosophical problem, for each interlocutor has a peculiar mix of motives, feelings, experiences and drives. Reason is not autonomous but mired in the chaos of nature which must be domesticated and given direction, in the life-world of its protagonists who must be tutored, and in their texts which must be deciphered.

Frequent reference to 'the British Reader' in the text, ensures that s/he emerges as the fourth main character of the book. 'The British Reader' emerges as another hermeneut, whose active participation is required if the meaning of the whole text of *Sartor*, which is some combination of its many constituent texts within texts, is to be discerned (Baker, 1986; Hruschka, 1992/93; Rundle, 1992). Hruschka likens the process to 'the intertexual pattern of scriptural commentary found in midrash' for both are 'obsessed with the connections between texts' (Hruschka, 1992/93, pp. 104–105).

It is a further curious 'fact' that the two British characters, 'the British Editor' and 'the British Reader' are without names and are only identified by their roles and activities. The paradox is that though the text we are reading is that composed by the Editor, it is only the Editor who speaks directly to the reader. Nevertheless, the attention of the reader is kept on the more sartorial Teutonic figures, which after all is the self-effacing function of any editor-reader. The implication is that the prosaic world of the editor is the real world of the modern and that as moderns we only learn the truth about ourselves and our world through editing and interpreting them via the poetic mode and across our parochial identities. Neither the German nor the British perspectives 'of things in general' can be absolutely authoritative: somewhere in the hermeneutic process of counterposing the ideal and the real, the poetic and the prosaic, the critical and the believing, the naive and the sentimental, and the transcendental and the immanent, is to be found the means by which the Editor-Reader in co-operative partnership are to re-make the modern world of perpetually conflicting authorities, texts and modes.

With and Against *Sartor*'s Interpreters: Modern Critical Traditions

If revolutions are measured by their immediate outcome, then Carlyle's sportive revolution on paper was a complete failure (Seigel, 1971, pp. 1–45; 101–38; Tennyson, 1965, p. 155). The initial hostility towards *Sartor* can be taken as an indicator of the book's revolutionary nature and novelty; it is a revolution without end for the critical debates still rage today. One hundred and sixty years of *Sartor* criticism appears to have spawned at least four characteristic critical postures on the relationship between the book's form and its content, each of which, I wish to argue, are in themselves inadequate readings. The intrepretations respectively hold that:

1) form (at least, in the last instance) is irrelevant to the argument and content of *Sartor*, for the latter is transparently obvious in any case;
2) form is an obstacle to the argument and content of *Sartor*, that is, on critical and aesthetic grounds alone, the book fails to achieve coherence. Sometimes this is turned into an accusation that Carlyle had chosen the wrong vehicle to achieve his ends;

3) form is intrinsic to the meaning and content of the book so that if one attends to a close reading of the form the meaning and content of the book will be revealed; and,
4) form is itself the content and meaning: the medium is the message.

The first interpretation views *Sartor* as a modern manifesto of personal idealism while the second interpretation sees a traditional spiritual message trapped in a barbaric style and obtuse structure – an ill-performed sermon. Here the assumption is made either that the book is a thinly disguised autobiography of Carlyle, or its meaning is to be equated with 'the Philosophy of Clothes', and the author's position is therefore equivalent to its propagator, 'Teufelsdröckh' (representatives of this view include Abrams, 1971, p. 68; Burke, 1969, p. 121f.; Holloway, 1965, p. 23; Muirhead, 1931, p. 141; Peterson, 1986).

The second critical perspective, that the form of *Sartor* is an obstacle to understanding its meaning, often assumes a similar stance as to *Sartor*'s meaning as the first critical position, but with a more antagonistic attitude to the book's form. Whereas the first critical perspective underestimates the radical nature of *Sartor*, the second position recognizes its formal radicalness and rejects it. While the view of *Sartor* as a personal idealist manifesto is mainly a twentieth century phenomenon, early nineteenth century critics, such as John Sterling, Ralph Waldo Emerson and John Stuart Mill, read the book more as an ill-performed sermon, with the philosophy of clothes reiterating the central and orthodox tenets of Calvinism but by means which poorly serve the author's ends. Carlyle responded to Sterling, for example, by suggesting that the classicist and puritan theories of rhetoric and homiletics have not only been made obsolete by changing conditions of reader reception, but the world-views which they presupposed had also been rendered uncouth (Carlyle to Sterling in Sanders, *et al.*, ed., 1970, 8, p. 135). The sacred-secular frame has been smashed once and for all, so that writing can be either secular or religious according to its historical, cultural and political frames and contexts. In a letter to Emerson, Carlyle suggests that the old sacred writings of the west no longer have purchase – so that God is literally displaced. Carlyle even implies that the sacred is a creation of humans alone; nevertheless, writing is most religious when it calls into question the 'secular' by reasserting the divine origin of all human action and speech (Bloom, 1986). Because 'the times were mad', Carlyle concedes to Emerson that *Sartor* was a wilful act of the individual believer which cannot hope to find a fair public hearing; nevertheless, he also counsels Emerson that it might be possible to hope for 'new times' when such speech-acts as *Sartor* might be find a 'friendly Space' (Carlyle to Emerson in Sanders, 1970, 7, p. 265).

Many twentieth century readers of *Sartor*, have been ignorant of the religious, linguistic, literary theories that informed the Carlyle-Sterling-Emerson conversations, so where the initial hostility to the book's form was one of religious offence, in the twentieth century hostility is directed towards the expressive questioning of the presumed canons of instrumental and logical rationality. And while late twentieth century readers might be attracted to the putatively nihilistic dimensions of the text, many will find *Sartor*'s immersion in the historic religious and literary traditions of Western civilization too formidable to approach let alone understand.

The third tradition of interpretation views *Sartor* as a comic, modern allegory in which form serves its pedagogic purpose. In one sense this critical position is a defensive apologetic against criticisms of *Sartor*'s imputed irrationalism. It endeavours to pay close attention to *Sartor*'s form in order to discern a clear and unambiguous final meaning. The best and most important example of this perspective, which – along with Holloway's *The Victorian Sage* (1953) – inaugurated a renaissance of interest in *Sartor* in the United States, is G.B. Tennyson's *Sartor called Resartus* (1965). Following the lead of earlier generations of scholars – most famously, Harrold and Wellek – Tennyson claims that Carlyle remained essentially a Puritan/Calvinist Christian in spite of his intense interest in German classical humanism, transcendental idealism, and romantic pantheism.

Tennyson suggests that the open question of *Sartor* is its apparent ambiguity about the metaphysical challenge of modernity, whereby the ontological center of the cosmos is deemed to have shifted from God to human consciousness, and in the process undermined the foundations of knowledge: does it advocate a specific solution to this problem or is it in fact carrying forth the essential undecidability of the question – as an '*agon* of scepticism'? (Helmling, 1988, p. 32). If the former reading is favoured, then Carlyle is either offering a counter-modern text (unlikely given the complexity of its forms) or a modern embodiment of liberalism, whether liberal Christian or liberal secularism. Many of the Victorians who turned to Sartor in the days of religious doubt treated the book as a way out of supernaturalist to naturalist modes of knowledge, with the attendant transposition of religious terminology to sacralize the profane activities of their own secular avocations. Matthew Arnold, especially in *Culture and Anarchy*, is the most paradigmatic embodiment of this interpretation and cultural strategy.

If the latter reading of *Sartor* as an 'agon of scepticism' is more plausible then there are a further two possible alternative ways to interpret *Sartor* on the question of modern spirituality: a choice between modernist humanist pessimism (Helmling, 1988; La Valley, 1968) and a post-modernist Gnosticism, a quasi-Nietzschian nihilism, in which nature is divinized and humankind is debased (Bloom, 1986, p. 14; Findlay, 1985; Miller, 1991). Tennyson addresses both these alternative readings of *Sartor* as an 'agon of scepticism' by focusing on the core chapters of Teufelsdröckh's crisis autobiography in Book Two: his pilgrimage from 'The Everlasting No', through 'The Centre of Indifference' to 'The Everlasting Yes'. He astutely identifies Teufelsdröckh's 'Everlasting No' experience as an interesting and dangerous theological experiment which directly confronts the problem of nihilism. Granting that Carlyle is no counter-modern thinker in *Sartor*, Tennyson interprets his theological experiment by advocating a middle path between the secular Carlyle of modernist, liberal secularists and the gnostic Carlyle of post-modernist sceptical relativists. Tennyson gently suggests that Carlyle remains a liberal, albeit heterodox Christian, implying a kind of Schleiermachian spirituality written from the side of human consciousness.

Tennyson's analysis of *Sartor* is very important as a clarification of its focus on consciousness and the centrality of religion to debates about the condition of modernity. His classicist premise, however – that there must be one answer to the question of the book's meaning – shapes his conclusion. Here, he appears to follow the Chicago school of literary criticism – most notably Wayne C. Booth – who recovered the Aristotelian emphasis on rhetoric and allegory (see Wellek, VI, 1986, pp. 63–7; Haney, 1978). *Sartor* is viewed as a metaphysical comedy which puts right those things which threaten to unravel into a dark chaos. In this view, the function of the irony in the text is merely rhetorical, polemical, and satirical, and not metaphysical or aesthetic. In this way, meaning, knowledge and wisdom can be reconstructed, and existential anxiety and metaphysical dualism are overcome with and through sincere faith in a monistic cosmic unity.

The fourth critical perspective interprets *Sartor* as oscillating between a modernist and a romantic irony – either way it is an example of inter-textuality whereby the medium becomes the message and the text becomes an ironic circle with an absent center. It picks up on the alternative reading that Tennyson wishes to argue against, that of Carlyle as a pantheistic gnostic who travels down the path toward sceptical relativism. This school of thought represents a fully-fledged rebellion against the previous generations of new criticism, structuralism and romantic critical theory which deemed *Sartor* to be an idealist manifesto, as well as against post-Tennyson critics who sought a unitary Christian meaning in and through the multifarious literary techniques. Instead, with the rediscovery of the importance of romantic irony and a linguistic turn in post-modern philosophy, there has been a new enthusiasm for *Sartor* as a proto-modernist or even a proto-post-modernist text. Some critics go so far as to argue that the form of *Sartor* becomes its only message, because its foregrounding of the problem of representation continually defers the possibility of meaning (Miller, 1991, pp. 315; 318). Instead of a rhetoric of eternity based on the allegory of mythic vision, common to many contemporary English romantic poets, this critical perspective emphasizes that Carlyle was, in de Man's terms, offering a 'rhetoric of temporality' without any ontology of spiritual essence behind or beyond the text (Findlay, 1985, p. 172).

According to this interpretation, however, *Sartor* is neither 'an eighteenth century polemic nor a modern de-construction; rather it is romantic irony'; it is essentially 'aesthetic and metaphysical, not rhetorical nor grammatical' (Haney, 1978, pp. 310; 311). *Sartor* asserts an ultimate metaphysical reality of the universe but as abundant chaos, which is given order in the process of humankind's *becoming*. The struggle of *poiesis*, of making meaning, is central to that which is represented. Romantic irony, therefore 'affirms multiplicity, growth, and change while recognizing the momentary need for unity, stability, system and illusory substance' (Haney, 1978, p. 314). This is what Schlegel meant by the necessity and the impossibility of having a philosophical system. For the romantic ironist, meaning is inherently contradictory and structure is dialectical. From Jean Paul, Carlyle learned how to combine the aesthetics and the metaphysics of romantic irony in the comic mode of the 'inverse sublime', whereby the infinite is found in the finite, the transcendental in the descendental, the supernatural in the natural:

> The humorist shares with the romanticist this longing for the infinite, this sense of the oppressiveness of finitude and all limiting forms. But he is a romanticist manqué. He lacks the ability to satisfy his needs by creating a positive vision of infinite beauty. All he can do is play with, disrupt, and ultimately 'annihilate' through laughter the forms that fail to satisfy or that oppress him. This is his inverse route to the Infinite. (Dale, 1981, p. 312)

Contrary to Tennyson's claim that *Sartor* is a revolutionary form serving a conservative end, Carlyle's 'esoteric comedy' of the 'inverse sublime' here becomes a revolutionary form and a revolutionary programme designed to 'initiate a readerly revolution' (Rundle, 1992, pp. 20; 14).

Sartor's Multiplying Revolutionary Scripts

The question of *Sartor*'s form and meaning then has continued to defy critics' best efforts. It is as though we are still catching up to the critical-aesthetic ideas of the eighteenth and early nineteenth century and Carlyle's own sense of what he was doing. As moderns or postmoderns we remain ensconced within traditions and *Sartor* remains notoriously difficult to classify. It is a dialectical philosophical treatise, a rhetorical essay, an editorial gloss, a book review, a philosophical-poetic fragment, a didactic novel, a fictionalized autobiography, a psycho-history of modern consciousness, a prophetic-rhapsodical manuscript, a comic-satirical extravaganza. It is all these things and more, but it is not one of these things alone.

In short, I wish to argue that *Sartor* is not so much a book as a 'Book of Books', a modern attempt to rewrite the Bible. The book's modernity lies in the author's hubris: this Book of Books – despite its editorial feints – is authored by one writer alone. It is Carlyle's self-conscious attempt to create the modern canonical text of texts made out of the 'organic filaments' of the whole canon of western literature which in turn is written out of the ancient scriptures of the Hebrews. As a modern Bible, it is written as a prophetic manuscript for those adept at hermeneutics, who recognize 'the open secret' of the cosmos and who are ready to be 'benignant spiritual revolutionists' and to live out of its manifold messages, replicating its media and purposes. Like the Bible, as a Book of Books, the messages and meanings are multiplied by and through each generation's appropriation of the texts, 'active readers' and 'editors' who 'consume the artefact' (Fish in Mellor, 1980) and 'perform its utterances' (Austin and Searle in Miller, 1991; Watson, 1988). *Sartor*, therefore, offers not one but manifold revolutionary scripts; here I note but five main revolutionary scripts by way of example.

Script One: Metaphysics for Moderns

The first revolutionary script is 'the natural supernaturalism' of the clothes philosophy, its non-foundational mystical version of transcendental idealism, and its theory of language as metaphorical hieroglyphics. With it, Carlyle becomes the 'first semiotician of Victorian Britain' (Watson, 1988, p. 162). The revolutionary vision of symbolic analysis advocated by *Sartor* is doubled: it requires both an x-ray vision to see through to the naked realities of the material universe and a seer-like vision to see through to the invisible realities of the sign-less inane of the two eternities which envelop and undergird our time-space world. These two types of optics, however, are but the dialectical pair of the descendental-transcendental, natural supernaturalism of the *Die Kleider*. Whereas Book One outlines the descendental-materialist dimension of the *Die Kleider*, the stripping of the layers of clothes to the naked, natural state of humankind and relates it to the cultural clothing of language, technology and labour, Book Three contains the transcendentalist dimension presenting Teufelsdröckh's general theory of symbols which in turn is the aggregated whole of his theory of language as metaphors, his anthropology that 'Man is a Tool-using animal' whose art is made out of subduing Nature, and his theory of culture as the visible emblems of the Divine Idea. Because symbols belong to the work of humankind and therefore to the realm of time and space, however, they must perennially be reinterpreted and remade by each generation and culture. Symbols do not in themselves participate in the Divine Idea which in Carlyle's view is – by definition – the eternal silence, unknowable, without content, a signless inane. This is where Carlyle's Teufelsdröckh parts company with Christian theologians, not least Coleridge, for whom the idea of the incarnation, and of the eternal *Logos* was central to his theory of symbols.

Script Two: The Modern Self

The second revolutionary script is the model of Professor Diogenes Teufelsdröckh as an allegory of modernity, as modern consciousness and its split, dis-eased state. Book II in its entirety is therefore a revolutionary script within itself, with the Chapters VII to IX as the famous dialectical triptych depicting the movement from negation to knowledge (*gnosis*) and from knowledge to faith or wisdom (*sophia*). The new mythus for the modern age is the revolution of individual consciousness which the biography of Teufelsdröckh narrates in philosophico-poetic form. The biography of Teufelsdröckh concentrates less on the Wisdom Teacher and more on the Wanderer who traverses Europe across the centuries and the nations, and who concerns himself with the great array of human activities, of building cities, fighting wars, tilling fields and writing books (1937, II:VIII, pp. 169–82; Cotsell, 1990, p. 84). Carlyle's picture of the cosmos as a chaos and the modern world as a labyrinth (prison, wilderness) presents Teufelsdröckh, as Prometheus, the 'Tool-using animal', the fire-deploying, hard working, pleasure-renouncing, productive force of perpetual creativity and growth, as the central cultural hero of modernity. This second revolutionary script of *Sartor* in its emphasis on the nature-culture dialectic is an early anticipation of Freud's *Civilization and its Discontents*, and shares an uncanny family resemblance to the young Marx's cultural anthropology as adumbrated in *The Paris Manuscripts* and *The Communist Manifesto*. Teufelsdröckh-Prometheus, however, does not have the final word in *Sartor*.

Script Three: The Idea of Totality and Modern Hermeneutics

When the biography of Teufelsdröckh and his clothes philosophy are read in tandem, *Sartor* offers a third revolutionary script – but only when it is accepted that both the new mythus and the new consciousness can only be represented via mediated texts, reconstructions by intermediary editors and offered to us as memory and hope rather than as 'real presence'. If, as readers we wish to join the British Editor in desiring to grasp the whole in the fragmentary and multiple dimensions of our lives and world, we are forced to become hermeneuts, editors, redactors, translators – in short, cosmopolitan readers, engaged in comparative, historical, encyclopaedic, genealogical, traditional, typological and symbolic hermeneutics.

We are obliged to enter the labyrinth and chaotic imbroglio of genres, modes, authorities, discourses, languages, epochs and texts if we are to grasp the limits of our own knowledge of the immeasurable and circumference-less cosmos:

> *Sartor Resartus* is, in many ways, a book about words, about meaning, about reading. In *Heroes, and Hero-Worship* (1841) Carlyle wrote "the true University of these days is a Collection of Books". By this definition *Sartor Resartus* may be viewed as a University. The great books of our culture are here in the pages of this book, woven together into a "new Mythus"... [In] *Sartor*... Carlyle wanted to be the prophet of the new Religion, a modern-day Mohammed writing the book that reveals the new Word. And the Word is that the true Religion of these days is a Collection of Books. (Hruschka, 1992/93, p. 107)

Script Four: Radical Social Theory

Out of these three revolutionary scripts, therefore, a fourth is begotten: *Sartor* as a prophetic manuscript for radical social theory, a modern form of social criticism which parallels the Hegelian dialectic of identity, negation and totality. Once the reader of *Sartor* is able to interpret the cosmos as a dynamic symbolism, s/he is enabled to read the social order accordingly: *Sartor* convinces the reader not so much 'to see different things, but to see things differently' (Baker, 1986, p. 222).

The third book of *Sartor* is the *Wissenschaftlehre* and the *Lebensphilosophie*, combined in his method of cultural semiosis, and applied to the task of historical and social criticism in the eschatological keys of memory and hope. The structure of Book Three clearly demonstrates this view of history and civilization: 'the present' is the broken middle of violent struggle; 'the past' is retrieved as a prophetic manuscript of utopian possibilities and proleptic acts of creativity; 'the future' continually breaks in on the present as radical openness, as pure possibility.

The cultural anthropology of *Sartor* is written in the comic and ironic modes, while the informing 'architectural ideas' consist of an eclectic mix of Scottish conjectural history and political economy, French sociology, German cultural criticism and poetics of the romantics and the dialectical method of the post-Kantian idealist philosophers. Consistent to the symbolic mode of interpretation of the Clothes Philosophy, society is not viewed as a thing-in-itself, but rather, following Novalis and Saint-Simon, a visible expression of the invisible bonds of religion: 'Religion is the Life-essence of Society' (1937, III:V, p. 232). But Society is now defunct in modern Britain, because the social idea which is religion has been destroyed and for communion there is instead a kind of sophisticated form of cannibalism practised on the poor (III:V, p. 232).

The Poor, 'like foundered Draught-Cattle' are perishing of 'Hunger and Overwork' while the Rich, 'still more wretchedly, of Idleness, Satiety, and Over-growth' (1937, III:V, pp. 232–233). The analysis is not one of moral denunciation alone, however, but rather contains the rudiments of a serious social theory which has three parts or steps: first, a theory of society as a religious idea of altruistic, organic community; second, a theory of society as material struggle with necessity: because of the struggle of necessity, humankind is engaged in a struggle over and against nature in order to produce its own cultural artefacts, which in turn generates a dialectic of struggle within society, of winners and losers, masters and slaves; and third, a theory of society which endeavours to keep the double focus of idealism and materialism as a universal and eternal struggle between necessity and freedom: the perpetual need and spiritual vocation of humankind is to turn the tendency towards sacrificial cannibalism of material fetish-worships back into the ideal of religion as a universal communion of saints, worshipping the transcendental idea of God, who is 'Father of Nature' (1937, II:X, p. 188).

According to the Teufelsdröckhian account, because in modern Britain, 'the Religious Principle' has been 'driven-out of most Churches' it expresses itself in superstition, fanaticism, and a whole 'class of 'Fetish-worships, or of Hero-worships or Polytheisms' and even 'Self-worship' (1937, III:X, pp. 274–5). All such expressions of modern worship have had ancient antecedents, but the novelty of the modern forms is that they are deemed as 'secular' by their participants. The two main 'Secular Sects' of modern Britain are characterized by Teufelsdröckh as 'The Dandiacal Sect' and 'The Drudge (or Poor-Slaves) Sect', and are classified according to their respective fetishes, rites, sacred sites, books, diet, clothing, housing, and forms of community association. The clothing puns and metaphors are stretched for their incipient comedy.

Sartor is the first satire of modern positivist sociology and anthropology, even before these sciences were given their ultimate codification in the mid-Victorian era by Comte, Spencer, Tylor, Fraser and company. But the overall purpose is entirely serious, for it is informed by a dialectical reading of the material and spiritual warfare of modern society between the two sects, or classes. The Dandiacal sect worships the self and money (which is considered to be a scarce object of desire), while the Drudges are 'earth-worshippers' whose scarce object of desire is bread but whose perennial experience is hunger and over-work. These two classes are not the only sects in society but are its most important groups. The whole organic form of society is called 'The Dandiacal Body' for it is the Dandies' form of worship and wants that determines the nature of their relationship to the 'Poor Slaves' who work for them, and the lot of the Drudges themselves. The needs of the Dandies (in other words, the do-nothing Aristocrats and the Millo-crat bourgeoisie) require the exploitation of the Poor-Slave Drudges (the Working Classes).

The secular public sphere of the government of things, the policing of people according to the basic value of utilitarianism and the market principle of *laissez-faire*, are but sophisticated forms of violent warfare, which have their metaphorical and ancient roots in ritual cannibalism, now called Malthusian population theory. Against this system, there stands the possibility of new religious communions – of non-exploitative social relations which would emerge from the ranks of the Drudges (1937, III:X, p. 285). Little wonder young Engels and Marx were impressed.

Script Five: Romantic Revolutions and Revolutionary Romance

Social prophecy in the modern revolutionary world, then, is no longer the task of lonely visionaries, rabbis and teachers, not even those called Diogenes Teufelsdröckh. According to *Sartor*, it is a double revolution: it has to become an inter-subjective, communitarian endeavour as well as a spiritual conversion of the individual self. This is the fifth and perhaps most important revolutionary script contained in *Sartor*. Again the revolution is a double one: of romantic revolutionaries and revolutionary romantics. As romantic revolutionaries, all readers have the potential to participate in the making of universal history as cosmopolitan citizens, travellers, and workers, as poetic constructors of cities, tilled fields and books: 'Produce! Produce!' (1937, II:IX, p. 197). As revolutionary romantics, all readers have the potential to participate in the making of world literature, of re-inscribing, re-interpreting and re-narrating our worlds of meaning as cosmopolitan editors, redactors, translators and readers: 'Close thy *Byron*; open thy *Goethe*!' (II:IX, p. 192). Readers can become authors who re-tailor the tailor when they become editors who edit the clothes volume. Moreover, while Carlyle is the author of this particular text, its authority is dependent upon what the reader brings to the reading process. The double meaning of revolution, as stasis and upheaval or rupture, is fully realised in *Sartor* as an ironic circle with an absent centre. The authorized word of this modern Bible deconstructs itself in a descent from author to text and finally to the reader as editor, interpreter and actor. The text has to be consumed by the reader in order for him or her to be converted to a new way of seeing and being: '*Sartor* is a text that ... elicits and transforms a poetics of authority into a poetics of devotion' (Rundle, 1992, p. 21).

Conclusion

Carlyle saw that the revolutionary nature of the modern epoch represented promise and threat, gain and loss alike. Modernity embodied the undermining of the metaphysical foundations of reason and imagination alike, the pluralization of society, the annihilation of time and space with technology, the fragmentation of pre-capitalist modes of production, and of pre-modern forms of spiritual authority and hierarchy. Wherever Carlyle looked, the divide between representation and material realities, between the ideal and the real, the noumenal and the phenomenal, belief and criticism, theory and action, and so forth, seemed to present intractable problems peculiar to moderns throughout Europe. When the economies of nature, of politics and society, of literature and of the self were read as a whole, the central predicament for Carlyle was a spiritual crisis wrought by a revolution in human consciousness. It was as though the cosmic circle with God as its centre had spiralled into an infinite regress and the dynamic cosmic struggle of good and evil had become secularized in an anthropomorphic direction so as to find a new site in the individual self.

This individual self, however, had lost all ontological foundations in a chaotic cosmos without meaning, direction or security and therefore could not be trusted to make good the lack identified. Romantic celebrations of the transcendental self were to Carlyle solipsistic inversions of a Cartesian view of nature. The emphasis on the inward vision of the individual artist-poet could not in itself provide a bridge across the abyss which separated subject and object, self and nature. To Carlyle, the romantic artist-poet's relation to society was more often than not an expression of an inward withdrawal, plaintive whingeing, or social alienation. Nevertheless, he recognized that this was a problem confronting one and all poets in the modern age, threatening the inner sanity of the poet him/herself and not just his/her relation to society.

The novelty of Carlyle's position in the first half of the nineteenth century was his refusal to give up the question of meaning on the one hand, and in his heightening the problem of finding it on the other. Such a combination offered no consolation to Protestants, closed off the illusory hopes of the Romantic poet as world legislator (Shelley), and yet damned the conceits of the self-proclaimed secularists and materialists. As such, *Sartor* both anticipates the Victorian debates about 'Culture' as the humanist overcoming of Christianity and contains their deconstruction *avant la lettre*. In its multifarious receptions and in the multiple texts within a text, *Sartor* remains one of the most significant European documents of the nineteenth century, especially for its grasp of the nature of the romanticism-enlightenment dialectic as it worked itself out across the revolutionary terrain of the social landscapes of modern Europe and the new world colonies. As such it is a remarkable anticipation of the nihilism endemic to the post-modernist discourses on reason and the sublime. Yet, Carlyle is not so much a nihilist as a modern mystic, a 'spiritual materialist' (Stockton, 1992), a writer of 'the word as text and the text as voice' (Watson, 1988). His mysticism is not a solitary or contemplative asceticism, however, but a collective exercise of believing editors as readers, and readers as editors and writers who together are perpetually remaking the material and imagined worlds through and in a 'poetics of devotion' (Rundle, 1992). Carlyle, at least in *Sartor*, is what today we might call a dialectical process theologian. To return to this source document of pre-Victorian post-romanticism, therefore, is to *uncover* the metaphysical presuppositions of modern secular reason, *re-cover* the still open question of postmodern religion and its future, and in the process *discover* afresh why the Victorians in particular were reluctant to embrace Carlyle's promethean and hybrid cross-dressing cultural criticism, preferring instead the image of the tailor himself to that of his re-tailoring of modernity.

Notes

1 Carlyle was an active promoter and practitioner of this concept, not least in his translations, editions and review essays of German and French literature and his industrious reading of European literature across six languages. Goethe himself, although the coiner of the term, *Weltliteratur*, never defines the concept in public, although his introduction to the German translation of Carlyle's *Life of Schiller* and his exchange of ideas in correspondence with Thomas Carlyle makes it evident what he means by it. See Norton, (ed.) 1887; Tarr, 1989.
2 Carlyle's genealogical histories of modernity are to be found in nearly all his historical writings as his whole writing career is directed at understanding modernity as revolution. Each of his major works depict the modern epoch in national and civilizational terms, exploring the British, French and German cases but also endeavouring to understand Ireland and North America too. For arguments on this line see Hogan, 1995; 1998. For specific incidences of the pre-*Sartor* Carlyle's reflections on the origins of modernity see his 'State of German Literature' (1827); 'Signs of the Times' (1829) which can be found in *Critical and Miscellaneous Essays* in any collection of Thomas Carlyle's Works. These collections contain the essays that Carlyle culled from his 'History of German Literature'. In turn, they were partially re-collected and edited by Hill Shine, *Carlyle's Unfinished History of German Literature* (1951).
3 Because of the great number and range of editions of *Sartor* I amend the Harvard citation conventions by citing the Book and Chapter number in addition to the specific page reference of my edition.

IV Christianity and Gender

Chapter Eleven

The Feminization of Piety in Nineteenth-Century Art

Jane Kristof

In view of the emphasis on, and evidence of, a drastic decline in Christian belief after the Enlightenment, it is rather surprising that there was still so much faith left to lose by 1900 and indeed into the third millennium. One explanation, of course, is that skepticism touched especially the sophisticated and the articulate, the urban and the male segments of the population – the kinds of people most likely to get into history books and anthologies – while the more tradition-bound elements of society, the provincial, the rural and the female, were relatively less affected. It is on the last category, the female, that this paper will focus.

Statistical data on the practice of religion, meager though it is, confirms that throughout the western world nineteenth-century women were more devout than men, and suggests that the dichotomy was particularly significant in France. The most reliable gauge of religious fidelity in Catholic areas is the reception of the Eucharist at Easter. In Paris and its environs during the middle decades of the nineteenth century observance of this obligation by men rarely exceeded 5% whereas it rarely fell below 20% among women. In Marseilles, in 1862, 57% of women but only 10% of men communicated at Easter (Lebrun, 1980, p. 323), while the corresponding figures for the diocese of Orléans in 1878 are 30% for women, and 5.5% for men (McLeod, 1974, p. 39).[1] Although the difference between male and female religious practice was much less pronounced in rural areas, it has been estimated that in the country as a whole three of every four practicing Catholics were women. Another index of the piety of French women is their increasing participation in religious orders; in 1790, nuns constituted about a third of the Church's work force, by 1830, 40%, and by 1878, 58% (Lebrun, 1980, p. 324).

Both anecdotal and statistical evidence suggests that across the Channel in Britain there was a real, but less drastic, gender difference in religious adherence. An ambitious survey of church attendance in inner London undertaken by *The Daily News* in 1902 showed that almost 66% of adult worshipers in the Church of England and about 64% in the Catholic Church were female, whereas women constituted about 54% of city's population. Nonconformist congregations were more evenly balanced, however (McLeod, 1974, pp. 30 and 308).

British women visiting the United States were struck by the religiosity of their American sisters. Wrote Mrs. Trollope (1949), 'I never saw, or read, of any country where religion had so strong a hold upon the women or a slighter hold upon the men' (p. 75), and that astute social commentator, Harriet Martineau (1966), thought that American women 'could not exist without religion' which seemed to her 'to superabound' (p. 147). Indeed, in nineteenth century America, there was always a strong correlation between the ratio of females to males in a state's population and the percentage of church membership in that state (Finke, 1992, p. 35), and the preponderance of women in church membership rosters, already evident in the seventeenth and eighteenth centuries, increased markedly in the nineteenth. There are indications, too, that the while the evangelical revival known as the Great Awakening of the mid-eighteenth century reduced this gender imbalance, the Second Great Awakening of the early nineteenth accentuated it (Shiels, 1981, pp. 45–62). Seldom, however, can the numbers have been so skewed as in Henry Ward Beecher's first congregation in Laurenceburg, Indiana, in the 1830s, which consisted of nineteen women and one lone man (Douglas, 1977, p. 98).

Artists of the nineteenth century clearly take note of these gender differences in religious commitment. Even a brief survey of period paintings indicates that the participants in religious devotions seem to be overwhelmingly, if not exclusively, female, whether they be listening to sermons, as in Gari Melcher's *The Sermon*, of 1886 (Smithsonian Institution), or Théodore Ribot's *At the Sermon*, of 1890 (Musée d'Orsay), receiving the Eucharist, as in Alphonse Legros' *The Communion*, of about 1876 (private collection), or Pascal Dagnan-Bouveret's *The Blessed Bread*, of 1885 (Musée d'Orsay), embarking on pilgrimages as in Giovanni Fattori's *Evening Pilgrimage*, of 1866 (Taragoni Collection, Genoa), or Jules Breton's *Young Women Going to a Procession*, of 1882 (Joslyn Art Museum, Omaha, NB), or kneeling in prayer as in Silvestro Lega's *Hour of the Ave Maria*, of about 1870 (Galleria d'Arte Moderna, Milan), or Maurice Denis' *Audi Filia*, of about 1890 (Musée des Beaux Arts, Lyon). And the pattern persists when, occasionally, believers are not idealized for their faith but ridiculed for their credulity: in Francisco Goya's *Capricho 52* (Figure 11.1), the worshipers who kneel before a dead tree decked out in a robe are also women.

There are, of course, exceptions, but they really are exceptions, and many of them fall into one of two categories: first, scenes like Goya's drawing, *The Mass*, of 1800–8 (Biblioteca Nacional, Madrid), or J. H. Lorimer's *The Ordination of Elders in a Scottish Kirk*, of 1891 (National Gallery of Scotland), that depict the exercise or distribution of official functions from which women were, by and large, systematically excluded, and, second, scenes like Danish painter Niels Bjerre's *The Prayer Meeting, Harboør (The Children of God)*, of 1897 (Kunstmuseum, Aarhus), based on the worship of small nonconformist sects, which actually do appear to have been relatively successful in engaging their male laity.[2]

When man and wife are shown together, their responses are often differentiated, subtly or not so subtly. An example is Hippolyte Bellangé's painting, *The Peddler of Plaster Figurines* (Figure 11.2), shown in the Salon of 1835 (Louvre). Here the wife admires an image of the Madonna and Child while her husband gazes at a statuette of Napoleon. *Forever Free*, an over life size marble group executed by the African-American sculptress Edmonia Lewis in 1867 (Howard University), commemorates the Emancipation Proclamation by depicting the reaction of a slave couple to the prospect of liberation. The man stands upright and brandishes aloft his broken shackle. The woman falls to her knees and clasps her hands in a prayer of gratitude.

Figure 11.1 Francisco Goya, *Capricho 52*, Art Resources.

Figure 11.2 Hippolyte Bellange, *The Peddler of Plaster Figurines* (Louvre), 1835 Art Resources.

Less clear cut is the gender distinction in Jean-François Millet's *The Angelus* (Figure 11.3), painted between 1855 and 1857 (Musée d'Orsay). Millet, himself, explained that the theme was inspired by his remembrance of how his grandmother made her family stop their work in the fields at the sound of the Angelus and repeat the prayer (quoted by Herbert, 1976, p. 87).[3] Art historian Robert Herbert (1976) notes that in the painting the woman is bathed in light while her husband is more shadowed and that the church spire is on her side of the composition. '...The real key to understanding the painting', he concludes, 'is to see the difference between the man and the praying woman. The man is not praying, but instead revolving his hat between his fingers while he waits for his wife to finish her prayers' (p. 87). But is this interpretation justified? The husband's head is bowed and his attitude is nearly as reverent as his wife's, so that the assertion that she is praying but he is not may simply prove that twentieth century historians are as predisposed as nineteenth century artists to assume the superior piety of women.

Some painters, like Alphonse Legros in *The Ex Voto* (Figure 11.4), of 1860 (Musée des Beaux-Arts, Dijon), François Bonvin in *The Poor's Bench: Remembrance of Brittany*, of 1864 (Musée Fabre, Montpellier), and Wilhelm Leibl,

Figure 11.3 Jean-Francois Millet, *The Angelus* (Musee d'Orsay), 1855–1857
Art Resources.

in *Three Women in Church* (Figure 11.5), of 1878–82 (Kunsthalle, Hamburg), juxtapose young and old female worshipers, thereby suggesting that faith is the habit of a lifetime, transcending age. Nevertheless, there is an attraction to both ends of the age spectrum, little girls and old women. Why should these phases of life seem particularly appropriate for the female worshiper? An obvious answer is that they represent the periods before and after a disturbing sensuality is seen as tainting her spirituality and making woman as much a temptation as a companion to man. Perhaps equally important, though, these two stages, childhood and second childhood, are characterized by a naiveté and simple trustfulness that can be associated with unquestioning religious belief.

Images of first communion were popular and naturally center on white clad children, as in Jules Bastien-Lepage's iconic portrait of his god-daughter, *The Communicant*, of 1875 (Musée des Beaux-Arts, Tournai), or Jules Breton's *The Communicants*, of 1884 (private collection, on loan to Perth Museum). Young girls are also featured in the works of two Hungarian realists: István Csók's *Do this in Memory of Me* (Figure 11.6), of 1890, and *Praying* (Figure 11.7) painted the following year by his close friend, Béla Iványi Grünwald (both in the Magyar

Figure 11.4 Alphonse Legros, *The Ex Voto* (Musee des Beaux-Arts, Dijon), 1860 Art Resources.

Nemzeti Galéria, Budapest).[4] Both artists seek to evoke an aura of spirituality through careful replication of natural phenomena. Csók's with a colored light that streams through the high windows to penetrate the shadows, Grünwald with the symbolic lilies that enframe the child. Another, less conventional image of prayer is Paul Gauguin's *Young Christian Girl* (Sterling and Francine Clark Institute), of 1894, where the bright, warm hues and bulky forms convey something of the intensity and awkwardness of adolescent religiosity. Needless to say, the theme of childish faith also lent itself to works that were facetious, arch or merely cute, exemplified by John Everett Millais' *My First Sermon* (Figure 11.8), painted in 1862–3 (Guildhall Gallery).

Appealing as they often are, devout little girls in the arts never attained a status comparable to that of their saintly sisters in literature, heroines like Dickens' Little Nell or Harriet Beecher Stow's Little Eva, nor even to that of their elderly grandmothers in painting. Moving scenes of old women pouring over their Bibles had, of course, an artistic pedigree that went back to Rembrandt's images of his mother, and they persist into the nineteenth century in such paintings as Hans Thoma's *The Artist's Mother in an Attic Room* (Private Collection), of 1871, again

Figure 11.5 Wilhelm Leibl, *Three Women in Church* (Kunsthalle, Hamburg), 1878–82 Art Resources.

Figure 11.6 Istvan Csok, *Do this in Memory of Me* (Magyar Nemzeti Galeria, Budapest), 1890.

accompanied by white lilies, or Adolf Hölzel's *Silent Prayer* (Figure 11.9), of about 1885 (Neue Pinakothek, Munich). In a Catholic equivalent, the old women sometimes hold a rosary in addition to, or instead of, a book. The Viennese Biedermeier master, Franz Eybl, produced a series of such works around the middle

The Feminization of Piety in Nineteenth-Century Art 173

Figure 11.7 Bela Ivanyi Grunwald, *Praying* (Magyar Nemzeti Galeria, Budapest), 1891.

of the century, of which *Leaving the Church*, of 1849 (Private Collection), is typical. Leibl's *The Old Parisian*, of 1869 (Wallraf-Richartz Museum, Cologne), and Cezanne's *Old Woman with a Rosary*, of about 1900 (National Gallery, London), both depict elderly women fingering their beads, their worn faces and gnarled hands perhaps a metaphor for the endurance of faith itself.

It is surely significant that almost all close-up studies of youthful or aged piety are drawn from the second half of the century and disproportionately from its last two decades. Richard and Caroline Bretell (1983) have pointed out that nineteenth century images of worship tend to shift focus from the external at the beginning of the period to the internal at its end, from the pageantry of religious ritual to the spirit of the individual believer (pp. 98–101).

Figure 11.8 John Everett Millais, *My First Sermon* (Guildhall Gallery), 1862–3 Art Resources.

The Feminization of Piety in Nineteenth-Century Art

Figure 11.9 Adolf Holzel, *Silent Prayer* (Neue Pinakothek, Munich), c. 1885 credit to Bayerische Staatsgemaldesammlungen, Munchen.

Figure 11.10 Thomas J. Barker, *The Secret of England's Greatness*, 1861, by courtesy of the National Portrait Gallery, London.

Female piety was seen as transcending class as well as age. It reaches to the highest levels of society: Jean Pierre Cortet's over life size marble statue of about 1825 shows Marie-Antoinette sustained in her anguish by an allegorical figure of religion (Chapelle Expiatoire, Paris); during the Second Empire the Empress Eugenie was sculpted, painted and photographed on her knees, while her consort, Napoleon III, typically remained standing; and a watercolor of 1839 by Peter Fende shows the Austrian Archduchess Sophie leading her children, including the future emperors Franz Joseph and Maximillian, in prayer (Albertina). In an appropriately Protestant version of monarchical piety, Queen Victoria, in 1861, is portrayed by Thomas J. Barker handing a Bible to an awestruck colonial (Figure 11.10) (National Portrait Gallery).

It is, nevertheless, the peasant woman who is most consistently associated with religious faith. Interest in, and admiration for, the peasantry, which was stimulated at mid-century by the pastoral novels of George Sand and the social commentary of Jules Michelet, culminated in later decades in the writings and teachings of Leo Tolstoy. An artistic parallel is seen in the monumental laborers of Millet and the idealized villagers of Jules Breton. Particularly picturesque and particularly devout were the peasants of Brittany whose regional costumes and traditional ceremonies attracted a number of painters including Breton himself, Eugène Boudin and

Figure 11.11 Paul Gaugin, *Vision After the Sermon* **(National Gallery of Scotland), 1988.**

Dagnan-Bouveret, and eventually inspired the devout female peasants of Gauguin, Emile Bernard, and their followers of the School of Pont-Aven.

The complex simplicity and sophisticated primitivism of such masterpieces as Gauguin's *Vision After the Sermon* (Figure 11.11), of 1888 (National Gallery of Scotland), or *The Yellow Christ* (Figure 11.12), of 1889 (Albright-Knox Art Gallery, Buffalo), reflect perhaps the paradoxical attitude of the artist, and implicitly the viewer, to the peasant women he represents. Robert Rosenblum wonders whether this attitude is 'one of charitable condescension toward people obviously less complicated than he, or one of awe and envy at the sight of a faith so difficult to come by in a world of science and machines' (p. 424). Presumably, in fact, both these reactions coexist, not only in Gauguin, but, in varying degrees and proportions, in most of his artistic forerunners and contemporaries. The selection of worshipers who differ from the artist in sex, age and class itself interposes a certain distance, and the taste for picturesque and traditional costume for female worshipers may hint that their faith is equally anachronistic.

The comments both of artists and critics also sometimes reinforce the assumption of condesending superiority. Gauguin wrote that in *The Vision After the Sermon* he

Figure 11.12 Paul Gaugin, *The Yellow Christ*, 1889, oil on canvas, 36 1/4 x 28 7/8, Albright-Knox Art Gallery, Buffalo, New York, General Purchase Funds, 1946.

had created 'a great rustic and *superstitious* simplicity' (quoted by Prather and Stuckey, 1987, p. 84; emphasis original), while his close friend, the Symbolist poet Charles Morice, referred to the women in *The Yellow Christ* as 'human brutes', and 'animals' (quoted in Prather and Stuckey, 1987, p. 221). Equally supercilious is the reference of the progressive critic Edmond Duranty to 'the rigid and machinelike stupidity' of the '*common* old women' of Legros' *Ex Voto* (quoted in Fried, 1996, pp. 186–7; emphasis original).

However, there seems to be a genuine ambivalence both in the culture as a whole and even in the individual painter toward peasant piety. Of course, many of the artists attracted to religious subject matter were themselves religious, for example Breton, Bernard and Denis, and their empathy is often reflected in their works. And even the unorthodox Gauguin included his own profile in the guise of the priest in *The Vision After the Sermon*, and tried to donate the painting to local churches, suggesting that at some level he identified with the 'rustic and *superstitious* simplicity' he had evoked. Moreover, an appreciation of peasant wisdom seems to have balanced contempt for peasant stupidity. Louis Pasteur is reported to have said: 'The more I know, the more nearly is my faith that of the Breton peasant. Could I but know all, I would have the faith of a Breton peasant woman' (quoted in *Catholic Encyclopedia*, Vol. XI, p. 537). The staunchly anticlerical historian, Michelet also eulogized peasant women and specifically older peasant women:

> I have seen some who toward the end of life – having preserved their best instincts through many hard trials, having cultivated their minds through reflection, and being elevated by the natural improvement of a pure and devoted life – no longer belonged at all to their own class, nor ... to any other, for they were truly superior to all.

And he concludes: 'Nowhere else have I ever met with such a union of two things generally believed to be distinct and even opposed – worldly wisdom and the spirit of God' (p. 114).

Not only the constancy, but also the quality of woman's faith is often noted. This is best seen in a comparison of the artistic images of male clergy on the one hand and of nuns on the other. Monks and priests are regularly presented as high living hypocrites.[5] One of Honoré Daumier's numerous anti-clerical cartoons, published in 1830, shows a conspicuously well fed priest turning his back on a starving beggar with the reflection, 'Blessed are they that hunger and thirst...'. The Russian realist V. G. Perov finds the same combination of callousness and self-indulgence in the Orthodox clergy. *The Refectory*, completed in 1876 (Russian Museum), depicts a lavish meal at a monastery to which a well dressed couple are made welcome, while a beggar family at one end of the hall and a Crucifix at the other are equally ignored. Clerical alcoholism seems to have been a particularly sensitive issue. Perov's *Easter Procession* (Figure 11.13), of 1861 (Tretyakov Gallery), which features a group of drunken priests stumbling out of a village tavern carrying their ceremonial paraphernalia, had to be withdrawn from exhibition at the behest of church authorities. Two years later, when Gustave Courbet depicted some inebriated clerics rolling home from an ecclesiastical assembly in *Return from the Conference*, the painting was excluded even from the Salon des Refuseés and was eventually bought and cut to pieces by an outraged Catholic. The flaws and foibles of the clergy remained, nonetheless, a staple of lighthearted popular genre. An example is

Figure 11.13 V.G. Perov, *Easter Procession* (Tretyakov Gallery, Moscow), 1861.

Georges Croegaert's *Pheasant for Dinner* (Christies) where three cardinals embark on a gourmet meal in a luxurious setting. The rococo pastoral that serves as their backdrop seems to echo their hedonistic lifestyle. Protestant clergymen fare better with artists: they tend to be neglected rather than disparaged.[6]

Nuns, however, are an entirely different story. They are almost always shown as not only charitable and spiritual but also beautiful. When, in 1898, M. V. Nesterov, a student of Perov, paints a cortege of female postulants in *Taking the Veil* (Figure 11.14) (Russian Museum), they have all the dignity and decorum that their male counterparts so notably lack in his mentor's *Easter Procession*. Nuns minister to the poor and sick and earn their respect and love. This is particularly seen in two paintings of Isidore Pils, *The Death of a Sister of Charity*, of 1850 (Musée des Augustins, Toulouse), and *The Prayer in the Hospice* (Figure 11.15), of 1853 (Musée de l'Assistance Publique, Paris). In both works the nuns are surrounded by the grateful recipients of their benevolence. Pils, himself, had been a patient at the hospital run by the Sisters of Charity and these works are his tributes to the Mother Superior and to Sister – later Saint – Isidora who had cared for him as a child. In fact the little boy kneeling beside Sister Isidora and looking out of the canvas is a

Figure 11.14 M.V. Nesterov, *Taking the Veil* (Russian Museum, St. Petersburg), 1898.

self portrait. The open primer on the floor in the foreground reflects the nun's concern to educate the children while they were hospitalized (see Weisberg, 1980, pp. 108–13). The role of the female religious orders in education is further highlighted in Bonvin's sketch for *The Girl's School*, of 1850 (Louvre). Again the work is based on personal experience: the artist's daughter attended such a school (Weisberg 1980, pp. 107–8).

Even in Protestant England nuns enjoyed special favor among artists, and particularly among Pre-Raphaelites (see Casteras, 1987, pp. 74–84). In *Convent Thoughts* (Figure 11.16), of 1851 (Ashmolean Museum), Charles Collins depicts an ethereally lovely young novice. She stands in a walled garden on an island, suggesting chastity, and beside her are white lilies symbolizing purity. Her fingers mark the pages of her prayer book as she contemplates a withered flower, presumably pondering the transience of earthly beauty. The literary tags that accompanied the painting's exhibition at the Royal Academy confirm the elevation of her thoughts and life. One is from Psalm 113:5: 'I meditate on all thy works; I

Figure 11.15 Isisdore Pils, *The Prayer in the Hospice* (Musee de l'Assistance Publique, Paris), 1853.

Figure 11.16 Charles Collins, *Convent Thoughts* (Ashmolean Museum, Oxford), 1851.

184 Reinventing Christianity

Figure 11.17 Peter Fendi, *The Visit to the Nun* (Collection of the Prince of Liechtenstein, Vuduz Castle), 1834.

muse on the work of thy hands'. The other is from *A Midsummer Night's Dream*: 'Thrice blessed they, that master so the blood, to undergo such a maiden pilgrimage'. Inevitably, such an image would divide the factions of the English religious scene, Catholic and Anglo-Catholic on the one hand and Evangelical on the other. Collins himself later converted to Catholicism while Ruskin wished that the young nun had opted for marriage and motherhood instead of the convent (Casteras, 1987, p. 82).

In *The Vale of Rest*, of 1859 (Tate Gallery), Millais represents a young sister digging a grave, with a vigor unexpected in a Victorian woman, under the supervision of an older nun. The work was praised by Edward Pusey, a leader of the Tracterian Movement, for illustrating that, 'death to the world is life to God...' (quoted by Casteras, 1987, p. 83). A final example of the British cult of the nun is Marie Spartali Stillman's *The Convent Lily*, of 1891 (Ashmolean Museum). Stillman follows Collins in introducing such emblems of religious commitment as the walled garden, the white lily, and the illuminated prayer book, but with a characteristically Pre-Raphaelite sensitivity to hair, she also gives her novice a natural halo of golden tresses.

The importance of the nun in transmitting faith to the young has already been noted in the paintings of Pils and Bonvin. It is further illustrated in the Austrian painter Peter Fendi's *The Visit to the Nun* (Figure 11.17), of 1834 (Collection of the Prince of Liechtenstein, Vuduz Castle), where a toddler solemnly reaches up to receive the sister's gift. But literally more central here is the role of the mother as, standing before an image of the Madonna and Child, she guides the little girl forward.

The significance of the mother as spiritual mentor is a common theme in nineteenth century genre. Fendi returns to it in 1842 in *Childish Devotion* (Figure 11.18) (Historical Museum of the State of Vienna), where again the Virgin and infant Jesus serve as a model, and almost a mirror image, of the contemporary mother and children. As the urban mother lifts her child to kiss the image, so the peasant mother raises hers to embrace a wayside wooden cross in Giovanni Segantini's *The Kiss at the Cross*, of 1881–82 (Kunstmuseum, St. Gallen). Her role as shepherdess, directing her flock toward its fold is undoubtedly intended to be seen metaphorically as well as literally.

In the Protestant version of this theme, not unexpectedly, the focus shifts from the image to the book. John Flaxman's *Monument to Lady Fitzharris*, of 1816–17 (Christchurch Priory, Hampshire), shows the young mother reading the Bible to her three sons. In Charles Cope's *Life Well Spent* (Figure 11.19), of 1862 (Christopher Wood Gallery), a paragon of domestic virtue knits as she drills her son on his lessons, possibly his catechism (see Casteras, 1987, p. 55). Prominently displayed on the table beside her is a large Bible, juxtaposed with a set of keys, and behind it the by now familiar white lily and a relief plaque of Jesus as Good Shepherd, with the inscription 'Feed my lambs'. In the foreground, a little girl combines rocking a cradle with reading a book, demonstrating thereby that she is profiting from her mother's example.

Reading is also at the heart of Winslow Homer's *Sunday Morning in Virginia* (Figure 11.20) (Cincinnati Art Museum), painted in 1877, during the Reconstruction, when literacy had only been permitted to former slaves for about a dozen years. Here, in a bare room, a black mother, or perhaps Sunday-school teacher, helps three children to decipher their Bible verses. Beside them an old woman turns aside, seeming to wonder both at the power of the words and at their accessibility to her grandchildren.

The scene of a mother encouraging her child in religious practices has such a built in potential for saccharine – a pitfall which few artists, in the foregoing sampling perhaps only Homer, entirely resisted – that it is easy to dismiss its popularity as merely a sentimental fiction. This would be a mistake, however. Although individually they may be unconvincing, cumulatively they point to an experience that seems to have been widespread, often deeply meaningful to the individual and socially significant for the transmission of religion. Verbal testimony supplements the visual in this respect: Samuel Taylor Coleridge remarks that Christianity 'is associated with your mother's chair and with the first remembered tones of her blessed voice' (Coleridge, 1853, Vol. 6, p. 264); and Immanuel Kant recalls how his mother, 'a sweet-tempered, affectionate, pious and upright woman ... who led her children to the fear of God by pious teaching and virtuous example' often took him into the countryside where 'she directed my attention to the works

Figure 11.18 Peter Fendi, *Childish Devotion* (Historical Museum of the State of Vienna), 1842.

Figure 11.19 Charles Cope, *Life Well Spent* (Christopher Wood Gallery, London), 1862.

of God, expressed herself with a pious rapture over His omnipotence, wisdom and goodness, and impressed on my heart a deep reverence for the Creator of all things' (Kant, 1960, p. xxvii).

The cloistered nun and the peasant wife, the young mother and the elderly widow, were all presumably isolated from the scientific and philosophical currents of their day so that their artistic association with Christian worship could suggest both their own naiveté and the anachronism of their faith. Indeed, nineteenth-

Figure 11.20 Winslow Homer, *Sunday Morning in Virginia* (Cincinnati Art Museum, John J. Emery Fund), 1877.

century commentators complained both of the intellectual complacency of women – Kant contended that 'the entire fair sex' had ignored the Enlightenment (Kant, 1986, p. 263) – and of their mental limitations. Schopenhauer's statement that 'women remain children their whole life long...taking appearance for reality, and preferring trifles to matters of first importance', is an extreme, but not an atypical, expression of this viewpoint (quoted in Bell, 1983, p. 270). However, the ambivalence already seen in attitudes to the peasantry is equally evident in regard to women. Several philosophers held that the mental processes of women were distinctly different, but not necessarily inferior, to those of men – the latter point made with varying degrees of conviction by its male spokesmen. This was the view of Kant: 'The fair sex has just as much understanding as the male, but it is a *beautiful understanding*, whereas ours should be a *deep understanding* ...' and of J.G. Fichte: 'It cannot be maintained that woman is inferior to man in regard to talents of mind: but it can certainly be maintained that the minds of man and woman have, by nature, a very different character' (quoted by Bell, 1983, pp. 242 and 263).

Generally the dichotomy was framed in terms of intuitive or experiential knowledge as opposed to rational analysis, and, as confidence in reason eroded over the course of the century, respect for feminine wisdom increased. American feminist Margaret Fuller described 'the especial genius of woman' as 'electrical in movement, intuitive in function, spiritual in tendency' (quoted in Rossi, 1973, p. 179), and her friend Ralph Waldo Emerson concurred, crediting woman with 'an oracular nature' and 'a certain power of divination' (Emerson, 1878, pp. 405 and 414). Tolstoy also acknowledges female insight in a moving passage of *Anna Karenina*. When dealing with a terminal illness in his family, Levin, in many ways a psychological self portrait of the author himself, discovers that he, and the learned philosophers he likes to read, 'knew not a hundredth part' of what his devout young wife and his devout old housekeeper, neither of them particularly educated or intelligent, understood about 'what sort of thing life was and what death was' (Tolstoy, 1965, p. 521).

The depiction of pious women, then, not only documents the actual state of religious practice in the nineteenth century. It also conveys both the intellectual vulnerability of traditional Christian faith but also its emotional – and demographic – resilience.

Acknowledgement

My thanks to my colleague, Prof. Sue Taylor, for her constructive suggestions and editorial advice.

Notes

1 Hugh McLeod cites Marcilhacy (1962, p. 556). McLeod also points out that a study of Mass attendance in France in the 1950s showed a much narrower gap between the sexes, the ratio being about two to one.
2 Other examples are Adolph Tidemand's *The Haugian Sect* (National Gallery Oslo), of 1852, and Ferdinand Hodler's early paintings of the rural sect with which he was then associated.
3 This explanation occurs in a letter from Millet to Siméon Luce wriiten in 1865.
4 On Csók and Grünwald see Weisberg (1992, pp. 172–5, 180–4).
5 A significant exception to this generalization is found in the work of Camille Corot who painted twelve images of monks, the earliest in the 1820s and the latest in 1874. All are sympathetic and depict their subjects reading, meditating or making music. Gary Tinterow (1996) speculates that Corot, who was himself unmarried and who always kept a copy of Thomas à Kempis' *Imitation of Christ* by his bedside, felt a personal identification with the monk (p. 380).
6 In Hook and Poltimore (1986, p. 98), the point is made that anticlerical images of the clergy are almost exclusively a Catholic phenomenon.

Chapter Twelve

Women's Theology and the British Periodical Press

Julie Melnyk

When in his essay 'Of Queens' Gardens', Ruskin (1865) identifies the 'one dangerous science for women' as theology, he complains,

> Strange, and miserably strange, that while they are modest enough to doubt their powers, and pause at the threshold of sciences where every step is demonstrable and sure, they will plunge headlong, and without one thought of incompetency, into that science in which the greatest men have trembled, and the wisest erred. (p. 73)

But where did women have any opportunity to 'plunge headlong' into theology? Where could they have exerted enough influence to worry the great Victorian sage? Barred from university and pulpit, they could publish neither learned treatises nor sermons, the traditional genres of theology. While some of their theological thought found its way into religious fiction or verse, or into devotional manuals,[1] much of their theological revisionism is to be found in the periodical press, especially in women's religious magazines. Two Evangelical publications edited by women, Charlotte Elizabeth Tonna's *The Christian Lady's Magazine* (1834–46) and Emma Jane Worboise's *The Christian World Magazine* (1866–86) demonstrate how their editors and contributors used biblical exegesis and commentary to emphasize liberatory aspects of Christianity, to feminize its patriarchal traditions, and to justify the expansion of women's public role.

The Periodical Press as Pulpit

Writing in *The Christian World Magazine*, the anonymous author of 'Literary Women' (1869) acknowledges the benefit to women of this increasingly influential medium: 'With the growth of the press has grown the direct influence of women on the world at large, and as periodicals have increased in number female authorship has waxed strong and become eminently creditable as well as profitable' (p. 535). Paradoxically, while much religious rhetoric was still openly hostile to women's participation in the public sphere, religious periodicals in particular offered significant opportunities for women writers and editors.[2] At the same time, some of the power and prestige of the pulpit was gradually being ceded to the press, as Emma Jane Worboise (1882), novelist and editor of *The*

Christian World Magazine, acknowledges in these editorial exhortations to potential contributors:

> And yet there is no profession more truly sacred than authorship; like the ministry, it ought to be a vocation rather than a profession ... Authorship is work, work of the most serious kind, and it must be done for God if it is to command his blessing; not for fame, not for emolument, though both are quite lawful, and even praiseworthy, as secondary aims ... 'Thank God for well-earned fame', wrote one of our best and noblest women-writers. Nor is money at all to be despised; in this life we cannot live respectably without it, and the laborer is worthy of his hire whether he till the soil, or preach the Gospel, or write books or magazine articles. True and worthy authors ... are dedicated to the noblest toil on earth! They rank with the ministers of God's Word, and in another way they do His work ... (p. 34)

Worboise claims for writers, including those writing for periodicals, equality with the clergy ('they rank with the ministers') and even superiority over them (their work is 'noblest'). Religious periodicals, then, could become a woman's pulpit, a powerful place to contribute to – and revise – theological thought.

While women authors and editors came from many different religious parties and denominations, they flourished in Evangelical and Dissenting circles for doctrinal and practical reasons. First, the doctrine of the priesthood of all believers, accepted by many Evangelical sects, de-emphasized the role of the clergy and the role of theological education as a source of religious authority, leaving women free to assume positions of greater authority in the chapels, as well as in the para-ecclesiastical world of Christian publishing. Moreover, since Dissenters tended to come from the lower-middle or working classes, Dissenting women were free from some of the restrictions of 'lady-like' behavior that confined middle-class women, including the prohibition against paid labor. (Note Worboise's attitude towards pay for writers in the above quotation.) Finally, as a marginalized religious minority, Dissenters maintained a crisis-mentality (like that of the early Methodists) which led them to call for the full mobilization of all workers, whatever their gender. Thus, while female editors in the Anglican High Church generally produced periodicals for children, such as Charlotte M. Yonge's *Monthly Packet*, or occasionally for other women, often under the direction of a paternalistic clergyman, evangelical Anglicans and Dissenters tended to give their female editors more authority. Both *The Christian Lady's Magazine* and *The Christian World Magazine* show the effects of such strong editorial leadership.

The Christian Lady's Magazine, which ran for twelve years in the first half of the century, was a decidedly intellectual periodical: in its first number, an article entitled 'From an Old Blue-Stocking' – unsigned but presumably by Tonna (1834) herself – advanced its fundamental proposition: 'the Christian lady ... may gently press on in the train of secure theology, and of metaphysics, and yet never lose sight of the place and office assigned to her by God' (p. 26). It included articles on controversial topics of the day (in the early numbers, for instance, on geology and Scripture and on *Tracts for the Times*); book reviews of both fiction and nonfiction; articles on Scripture, devotion, and theology; occasionally some serialized fiction (Tonna's *Helen Fleetwood* was serialized beginning in 1839); and even Hebrew lessons for intellectual women who wanted more direct access to Old Testament Scriptures.

The Christian World Magazine, in contrast, was intended to be a considerably more popular periodical. Its publisher, James Clarke, designed it to complement his weekly penny newspaper *The Christian World* and chose Worboise, his most popular novelist, as its editor. Reasonably priced at half a shilling, *The Christian World Magazine* aimed to supplant secular, middle-brow monthlies just as *The Christian World* meant to substitute for secular newspapers. (The periodical's full title reflects its ambitions: *The Christian World and General Intelligencer Containing the News of the Week: Combining a Companion for Leisure Hours, a Christian Treasury, and Readings for Sundays at Home: with a Record of Passing Events Forming a Religious, Literary, Educational, Philanthropic, Commercial, Agricultural, and Family Journal and Advertiser.*) In the first number's editorial address, Worboise (1866) envisions her magazine appealing 'to the old, and middle-aged, and young, to rich and poor, to workers in the bustling world and to dwellers in their quiet homes' (p. 2). Nevertheless, it is clearly a 'family' (read: women's) magazine: in addition to religious fiction, articles on science, and missionary records, the reader is promised a 'page or two monthly (devoted) to the consideration of housewifely duties', specifically 'dedicated to the Elder Daughters of my country' (p. 3). The first issues include stories to be read to children and even recipes.

Both editors, however, quickly move their periodicals toward more public topics and more controversial theology. Tonna acknowledges this explicitly in a Preface to Volume Thirteen (1840):

> It never was in the Editor's contemplation to make this little work a controversial one ... But events of stirring character have come to pass, a crisis of great moment has drawn nearer and nearer ... and even women that were at ease have been called upon to rise up, and to keep watch and ward with their brethren. It is for this cause that *The Christian Lady's Magazine* has perhaps appeared to lose somewhat of its feminine character (pp. ii–iii).

Although Worboise never acknowledged the change in her magazine in so many words, by Volume Three (1867) she has silently dropped the household hints; by Volume Ten (1874), the children's section has disappeared; and increasingly, articles on politics and on theology come to dominate the nonfiction offerings (Melnyk, 1996). Both editors clearly want to influence political and theological thought: they work to accomplish both partly through their inclusion of nonstandard interpretations of the Bible, particularly interpretations by women.

Scriptural Exegesis

Despite the more significant role granted to women in Evangelical denominations, women's right to interpret Scripture remained problematic for Evangelical sects. Evangelicals strongly affirmed, in the words of the resolution of the Christian Union Conference at Liverpool in 1845, 'The right and the duty of private judgment in the interpretation of holy Scripture' (p. 400). But the authority to make public those interpretations was not so easily won. Even John Wesley, who had firmly supported the preaching of Methodist women, in a letter to Sarah Crosby had singled out scriptural exegesis as the one rhetorical form forbidden them: 'In public you may properly enough intermix short exhortations with prayer; but keep as far from what is called preaching as you can: therefore never take a text' (quoted by Brown, 1981, p. 75). Nevertheless, though they often had to disguise their exegesis, female editors and authors seized the power of interpretation, the power to influence and alter the socially and politically potent Christian ideology, particularly as it affected women's roles in society.

Without claiming a woman's right to interpret scripture, editors could exert some influence by choosing carefully among available interpretations offered by men. But women writers for these magazines also found ways to incorporate biblical exegesis in less controversial forms. In their serialized religious fiction, a more acceptably feminine form, writers used homiletic exegesis openly, sometimes filtering their textual analysis through an admirable character, but often speaking in their own person to the 'congregation' of readers. Moreover, the novelistic device of epigraph allowed the author to print a biblical text at the head of each serialized chapter (in the same location on the page as in published sermons) and then indirectly explicate that text through the exemplum of that chapter's narrative.

Nonfiction writers seldom used the epigraph: perhaps in such a context its use would be too problematically reminiscent of the homiletic model. But they too often chose to reinterpret Scripture through narrative. Most often, the text appeared at the end of a article whose content altered the way it was perceived or interpreted. Thus, an article on the prison ministry and preaching of Sarah Martin ends 'Such a work was little regarded by men; yet, be assured, it was not unheeded by One who at the last will say, "Inasmuch as ye did it to one of these, ye did it unto Me"'! (Wagstaff, 1878, p. 479). The preceding narrative has already set the interpretive frame for the verse so that it legitimates some unusually public work for women. Signing herself as editor of *The Christian World Magazine*, Worboise (1873) ends an article on 'The Education of Girls' with 'Now they have only to knock, and it will be opened to them' (p. 515), again extending the scope of the text beyond its common interpretation. Stories of the lives of female preachers and theologians, such as Geraldine Dening and Dora Greenwell, also provide the opportunity for exegesis, sometimes in summaries of their teaching, other times as the narrative contains or suggests a biblical text. A witty remark made by Dening on her wedding day and included in Jessie Coombs's (1873) two-part biographical article neatly emasculates one of the most repressive of the Pauline injunctions against women's participation. After the toasts, when someone 'playfully proposed that the bride should return thanks', the female orator 'shook her head, saying merrily, "Oh no, no! Did you never read, 'Let your women keep silence'?"' (p. 348). Nevertheless, the narrative reveals that within two weeks of the wedding, she was back speaking from pulpits to earthly and heavenly acclaim.

Perhaps, as Carol Gilligan's (1982) work suggests, the choice of narrative interpretation reflects its significance to women's moral deliberation, its provision of 'a mode thinking that is contextual and narrative rather than formal and abstract' (p. 19). Thus, rather than beginning with a text and deducing correct behavior from it, as traditional sermons do, in women's periodical nonfiction the moral truths contained in the text arise out of concrete situations and moral dilemmas.

Biblical narratives, especially the stories of biblical women, also create opportunities for reinterpretation of texts directly relevant to women's social position. Both *The Christian Lady's Magazine* and *The Christian World Magazine* published long-running series of articles on female characters from the Bible: in the former 'Female Biography of Scripture' by 'Lydia', and in the latter, reprints of articles by Harriet Beecher Stowe, first published in America in the *Christian Union*, which Worboise called, improbably, 'Portraits of the Patriarchs'. Both series cite the examples of Deborah, Hannah, and Mary, as justifications of women's poetry and prophecy, quoting and analyzing their scriptural songs at some length; Deborah is also cited as a precedent for women's participation in political life ('Lydia' 1841; Stowe 1873a). 'Lydia' (1841) begins her analysis of Deborah with an unpromising biblical text – 'The head of the woman is the man, and the head of every man is Christ' – followed by an even less promising interpretation: 'silence, subjection, obedience; attention to household duties; to the care of the sick, to the education of children; ... these are the chief duties enjoined upon Christian women in the pages of the New Testament' (p. 337). As so often in nineteenth-century religious women's writing, however, the apparently conservative reaffirmation is followed by a liberatory 'But':

> But though, as a general rule, the sphere of woman leads her far from the strife and shew of life, and bids her rather to retire and submit, than to come forward and act; yet the voice of nature and revelation alike sanction those occasional instances, in which she has emerged from obscurity to enact the part of a ruler or a patriot; or to bow the hearts of all by strains of eloquence and passion ... when it has pleased the Holy Spirit to make the mind of woman, a channel for conveying to the whole intelligent universe some of the sublimest truths which man is capable of receiving, in strains as sweet as ever burst from mortal lips. (p. 339)

Just as 'Lydia' uses Deborah to justify women's public utterance and political authority, so Stowe (1873b) in her later series uses Miriam for similar purposes:

> The union of man and woman in this solemn public national act of worship was significant of the place which women held in the mind of the Jewish race, and that of their great leader. The prophetic gift was without respect of sex, and raised woman at once to the rank of a public teacher; and we shall find in subsequent Jewish history how this gift, in certain instances, exalted a woman to be for a time the head and leader of the State. (p. 373)

Through her reinterpretation of the relationship of Miriam with her brother Moses, Stowe argues for women's authority in public life: similarly, through her reinterpretation of Sarah's relationship with her husband, Stowe offers a liberatory moral for women in their private lives. An article published in *The Christian Lady's Magazine* and entitled 'Authority' (1841) discusses the text, 'Sarah obeyed Abraham, calling him Lord', which is used as part of the Anglican marriage service, and draws the obvious moral of wifely obedience (p. 13). The discussion in Stowe (1873c) is less reverent:

> The name Sarah means 'Princess'; and from the Bible story we infer, that ... Sarah was virtually empress and mistress of the man she called 'Lord'... and, while she called

Abraham 'Lord,' it is quite apparent from certain little dramatic incidents that she expected him to use his authority in the line of her wishes. (p. 295)

Thus, 'in setting Sarah before wives as a model of conjugal behaviour, no very alarming amount of subjection or submission is implied' (p. 295).

References to the story of Mary and Martha appear frequently in these religious periodicals; its interpretation becomes a focus for the controversy over women's proper roles. Some writers defend Martha's position, affirming the worth of 'women's work'; others use Jesus's endorsement of Mary's choice to vindicate women's intellectual ambition. One treatment of the story from *The Christian World Magazine*, the unsigned article 'Far Above Rubies' (1870), takes for its title a biblical allusion to the worth of women, an allusion which, I think, establishes this article as a reply to an earlier, more conservative article by E.R.A., 'Words About Women's Rights' (1867), which quotes the biblical passage at length. Rather than repeating the domestic virtues of a good wife from Proverbs, the article reinterprets the story of Mary and Martha as a new vision of womanhood which integrates the material and spiritual without privileging either: 'Practical yet intellectual, strong yet tender, broad yet devout, many-sided in apprehension of gifts and graces' (p. 305).

Lesser figures from Scripture are also called into service: the biography of the obscure 'Manoah's Wife' provides the opportunity for 'Lydia' (1842) to explicate Paul's bold statement: 'In Christ Jesus there is neither male nor female', emphasizing its liberatory and egalitarian aspects even as she argues for women's spiritual superiority as a result of their greater suffering: 'we may reasonably look for the most frequent exemplifications of Christian character in that sex which has to bear the largest burden of natural grief' (p. 503).

But the part of the Bible that women's magazines tried most urgently to reinterpret was the Genesis narrative, with its representation of Eve's role as 'helpmeet' and of women's subordination as just punishment for Eve's sin. In a series of articles in *The Christian Lady's Magazine* entitled 'Expository Remarks on Genesis' (1844), the anonymous author undertakes a modest rereading of the Fall. She or he affirms subordination as ordained by God, but emphasizes that female submission is essentially arbitrary, not based on any actual inferiority. The author also finds in the narrative an opportunity to attack not patriarchal power but the patriarchy's use of that power:

> she would not obey God's reasonable command, and so must be compelled to yield obedience to the (perchance) unreasonable mandates of a mortal man ... grievous ... are the woman's sorrows by reason of her subjection to that will of man which is now depraved by sin, and is consequently so often an unrighteous will. (p. 119)

Later in the century, religious women find it easier to launch more radical challenges. In 'Woman's Public Work: Its Scope and Limits', a female author A.B. (1877) challenges traditional interpretations of 'helpmeet':

> The Paradisaic arrangement and definition of the matter, summed up in the statement that woman should be the 'helpmeet' for man, though apparently clear and precise, has not been met with the comprehension and respect it deserves; ... Of course, there are not wanting dogmatic, masculine intellects capable of deciding the matter in five minutes

with a pompous relegation of womanly influence to the sphere of 'puddings and babies.' Even in the Imperial Parliament of England, and in the nineteenth century, we have heard loud, masterful voices proclaim the whole duty of woman with an imperative finality deliciously amusing to those who have studied the subject from other points of view than that which requires the concentration of all feminine energy and intellect on supplying the lordly half of creation with a sufficient number of shirt buttons. (pp. 626–7)

A.B. goes on to argue for her own definition of 'helpmeet', which expands to include any profession of service to humankind, including though not limited to economist, lawyer, doctor, minister, writer, scientific researcher, and Member of Parliament. This extraordinary expansion, however, is consistently represented as merely a correct interpretation of conservative biblical and cultural ideas of woman's work (see Melnyk, 1996).

The periodical press thus challenged the traditional power of the pulpit, providing a new forum for religious writing, one that women writers and editors could influence and exploit. They used this new forum to re-interpret the authoritative discourse of Christianity, a discourse which still retained public influence in Victorian Britain, thus empowering themselves ideologically and psychologically to claim a larger role in religious and social, and ultimately political and economic life.

Notes

1   For analyses of women's theology in these nontraditional genres, see Melnyk (1998).
2   That a woman should find the opportunity for a strong public voice within a patriarchal religious tradition generally resistant to the progress of women's rights seems paradoxical, but such paradoxes abounded. Religion was for nineteenth-century women a unique area of socially-acceptable participation and even predominance. A belief in the spiritual superiority of women took root during the eighteenth century, arising first from the religious revivals of Methodism and Evangelicalism, and gained currency in the nineteenth. This presumption of female superiority meant that women found opportunities in the religious realm generally denied to them elsewhere. For more detailed discussion of this ideological shift, see Davidoff and Hall (1987, pp. 73–148); Poovey (1984, chap. 1); Krueger (1992); Valenze (1985); Melnyk (1993, chap. 2).

Chapter Thirteen

The Feminist Theology of Florence Nightingale

Hilary Fraser and Victoria Burrows

Florence Nightingale's three-volume Suggestions for *Thought to the Searchers after Truth Among the Artizans of England*, written between 1850 and 1852, revised after her return in 1856 from the Crimea, and privately printed in 1860, makes a distinctively feminist intervention in the religious controversies of the 1850s.[1] In it, Nightingale offers a radical diagnosis of the fragmented contemporary spiritual and cultural condition, relating the fractures and fissures of modernity to the material conditions of women's lives. Fundamental to her argument is a recognition of layers of cultural difference: of the class difference that distinguishes the 'artizans' whom she addresses in the first volume of her work from the wealthy who are the subject of the subsequent volumes; and, crucially, of the gender difference that sets apart the life experiences of mothers and daughters and sisters from those of fathers and sons and brothers. She also acknowledges the imperatives of intellectual and sectarian difference, both within the Church, and between the faithful and those, including 'most of the educated among the operatives', who 'have turned their faces to atheism or at least to theism' (p. 8). Difference is, moreover, textually inscribed. *Suggestions for Thought* is nothing if not fragmentary. It is the site of competing discourses: of law and freedom, for instance, of obedience and resistance. Furthermore, in its very language and form, in the disjunct and multivocal urgency of its delivery, it exemplifies Nightingale's perception of the atomism of contemporary culture. But her passionate and erratic ruminations upon religion, society and the gender order are given coherence by a unifying discourse of the body that underwrites her thesis advocating a recovery of social cohesiveness through a recognition of diversity, and interestingly anticipates the intervention into medical history that, by the time of the book's private publication, will have come to define her popular reputation. Contemptuous of the domestic and patriarchal paradigm favoured by most writers on contemporary society and the Church, Nightingale proposes an alternative model for the nation and its religion that validates the individual, permits women to engage in work beyond the confines of the home, and radically redefines the ideal of 'the family of God'. 'We want to extend the family', she maintains, 'not annihilate it' (p. 179). This paper will investigate Nightingale's vision of a religion feminized and reconfigured in such a way as to legitimate and foreshadow her own transgressive incursion into the public sphere.

We want to begin by thinking about this female writer's strategies for entering a discourse from which women have traditionally been excluded. First of all, it is interesting to consider the ways in which the ideological categories of public and private, to which religious debate and women were, in the period, respectively consigned, are rhetorically collapsed in Nightingale's own discursive practices. She insists throughout *Suggestions for Thought* that '[t]hese two questions of religion and family are so intimately connected that to ask concerning the higher power or powers acknowledged in heaven and on earth is one' (p. 156). Such intimacies are textually enacted in writing that illustrates a theological point with a domestic example, that articulates a philosophical argument in an agonisingly personal voice, that moves between the dispassionate objective observation and the enraged subjective commentary with an ease that refuses the notion that either women and religion, or the personal and the political, occupy separate discursive categories.

Comparing the Church of England and the Roman Catholic Church in terms of the extent to which they exercise authority, for instance, Nightingale writes of those paradigmatically patriarchal institutions:

> The Church of England is expected to be an over-idle mother, who lets her children entirely alone, because those made her who had found the Church of Rome an over-busy mother. *She* imprisoned us; she read our letters; she penetrated our thoughts; she regulated what we were to do every hour; she asked us what we had been doing and thinking; she burnt us if we had been thinking wrong. We found her an over active mother, and we made the Church of England, which does not 'interfere' with her children at all. (p. 84)

Through the use of such figures, women are made to preside matriarchally and metaphorically over a domesticated Church which, when it comes to historical women, 'will not have them', because '[s]he does not know what to do with them' (p. 88). The sexual economy of 'separate spheres' is similarly unsettled by Nightingale's abrupt analogies between religious history and the contemporary social position of women. Rarely are such parallels explicitly signalled, nor are they tactfully ushered in; rather they take the form of a vigorous, dialectically structured critique. Typically a religious point is succeeded by an urgent questioning that troubles, rhetorically, the notion that the institutions and discourses of Christianity should or can be dissociated from women's lives, as in the following:

> Christ's temptation is the epitome of all life, as it was, no doubt, the epitome of his own, which he told to his disciples in that form. A sensitive, noble spirit could perhaps hardly bear to speak of it in any other form.
> Do we not live for 'forty days', often for as many years, in the wilderness, seeking bread and finding none? Have we not lived these many years trying to find bread in society, in the literary dawdling of a civilized life, in the charitable trifling of a benevolent life, in the selfish elegance of an artistic life? Have we not, in these deserts, these long, long weary years, tried to pick up food, and at last, craving and despairing of anything better, have we not eaten that which was not bread, applause and sympathy, for that which is not good, the vulgar distinction of social praise, the temporary forgetfulness of excitement? (p. 125)

We will return to Nightingale's extraordinarily powerful evocation of what she terms 'this life of starvation', but here we simply want to note how brilliantly she destabilizes the ideological binaries that traditionally exclude women from religious discourse through her subversive use of metaphorical language. Through an audacious reconfiguration of typology, *Christ* is represented as a type of the suffering modern *woman*.

'People are hardly aware', Nightingale writes, 'of the very great importance of the present phase of religious and domestic life, of the change going on, of the want of a Saviour, for this hour of peculiar trial' (p. 155), drawing attention at once to the interconnectedness of the religious and the domestic, and to the critical historical moment. Given the changes in women's position in society that have taken place over the past fifty years, she argues, '[I]t *is* the time for a few among the speculative and discontented to listen to more enlarged views of religion and to a life consistent with these' (p. 203). She identifies the age as one of fragmentation, one in which (using a characteristically domestic metaphor for spiritual crisis) 'atheism and indifference are man and wife' (p. 118). But it is a fragmentation that is felt on the pulse. She writes of women's sense of self-division ('there is no longer unity between the woman as inwardly developed, and as outwardly manifested' (p. 228)), as well as of how their motivation and energies are dissipated by the cultural constraints upon them: 'If I knew how, I ... would have a *single aim* of righteousness, and love, and benevolence, and beauty, and order; but I have a different aim every half-hour, without comprehensiveness, connexion, consistency' (p. 26). She is preoccupied with the way in which the fractured condition of modern civilization is mirrored in the disjointed nature of women's existence, and rails against 'the maxim of doing things at "odd moments"':

> When people give this advice, it sounds as if they said, 'Don't take any regular meals. But be very careful of your spare moments for eating. Be always ready to run into the kitchen and snatch a slice of bread and butter at odd times. But never sit down to your dinner, you can't, you know'. We know what can be done at odd times, a little worsted work, acquiring a language, copying something, putting the room to rights, mending a hole in your glove. What else is there? I don't know. Nothing requiring original thought: nothing, it is evident, which requires a form, a completeness, a beginning and an end, a whole, which cannot be left off 'at any time' without injury to it, which is not 'mere copying', in short. (pp. 71–2)

The submerged wordplay, which leads us from mending a hole in a glove to making a whole of a woman's life, suggests what is lost in the interstices of a woman's piecemeal day. And again there is that pervasive metaphor of hunger, here with disconcertingly modern overtones of (typically female) eating disorders. Nightingale demands answers of the institution that so conspicuously fails to provide for women who, forced to pass their lives under the regime of the odd moment, are cruelly deprived of a sense of personal integrity and fulfilment: 'For such women what does the Church of England do?' (p. 133). Her foregrounding of female subjectivity, and her poignant evocation of women's experiences of dislocation and alienation in this text make it clear that, in her view, the Church of England must address that particular 'woman question' before it can hope to overcome the disunities and fissures in its own fabric. 'The improvement of religion and society must go together', Nightingale contends, and specifically, she asks, '[t]he relation between parents and daughters, its nature, and how practically it should be worked out – how is this to be referred to the nature of God?' (pp. 174–5).

Elizabeth Barrett Browning's feminist heroine-poet Aurora Leigh similarly emphasises, at about the same date (1856), the connectedness of 'the natural' and the spiritual; she describes 'The great below clenched by the great above,/Shade here authenticating substance there,/The body proving spirit, as the effect/The cause' (*Aurora Leigh*, Bk 8, ll. 622–5). For Barrett Browning too, of course, the material conditions of women's lives provided a conduit to the spiritual. In ways that interestingly anticipate, by example, modern feminist critiques of the phallocentric mind/body duality by which woman is constituted as the negative 'other' of the valorised masculine mind, both writers insist upon the embodied subjectivity of women, and their claim to an intellectual and spiritual life.[2] Nightingale does not, like Barrett Browning in her construction of Marian Erle in *Aurora Leigh*, make an angel of her fallen woman, but she does unsettle the boundaries between 'good' and 'bad' women: 'The woman who has sold herself for an establishment, in what is she superior to those we may not name?', she asks (p. 266). Elsewhere she explicitly identifies the point of connection between the woman in the gutter and the woman in the drawing-room as the client of the one and the husband of the other:

> What has 'society' done for us?...What does it do for fallen women? ...What protection does she give those wretched women? What constraint does she put upon those men who make them what they are? Does she ever turn a shy look upon them? Not at all. On the contrary, she throws open her doors wide to them, vicious as they are, and ... says to the woman, 'Get out of my path'. While to him without whom the woman would not have been vicious, she offers her drawing-rooms and her high-bred daughters. (pp. 128–9)

Nightingale's text also troubles the boundaries, so stoutly defended by contemporary social commentators such as the egregious W.R. Greg,[3] between male and female desire, and between legitimacy and illegitimacy:

> Society takes pleasure in stimulating passion in every kind of way, by early excess in wine, late hours, schoolboy conversation and classical books, etc., etc., and then says, 'you must not gratify this in a legitimate way, under pain of exciting our censure – the illegitimate satisfaction is the only one we allow'. ...
> And we who are not 'fallen women', we talk about mankind creating mankind, – what has mankind done for us? It has created wants which not only it does not afford us the opportunity of satisfying, but which it compels us to disguise and deny. (p. 129)

At the close of this passage, Nightingale adverts to a trope, alluded to already, that is a recurring motif in this text, one that affords an intriguing instance of how she resists the conventional dualism of mind and body:

> [Society] says, if any one dies of hunger, 'you must not starve – so and so shall be punished if you do'; or 'you shall be provided for at the expense of society'. But it never says, 'you shall not starve spiritually – you must not want the bread of life – so and so shall be punished if you do, if you lack the satisfactions which are as necessary to the faculties and feelings as food is to the physical wants'. (p. 130)

By way of a constellation of images associated with food, appetite, hunger and starvation, Nightingale brings before the reader, in arrestingly graphic detail, the state of moral and intellectual malnutrition to which women have been systematically reduced.[4] Paradoxically, the physical body is summoned up in all its material actuality in support of an argument that women should not be valorised for their bodies:

> To have no food for our heads, no food for our hearts, no food for our activity, is that nothing? If we have no food for the body, how we do cry out, how all the world hears of it, how all the newspapers talk of it, with a paragraph headed in great capital letters, DEATH FROM STARVATION! But suppose one were to put a paragraph in the 'Times', *Death of Thought from Starvation*, or *Death of Moral Activity from Starvation*, how people would stare, how they would laugh and wonder! One would think we had no heads nor hearts, by the total indifference of the public towards them. Our bodies are the only things of any consequence. (p. 220)

Variations on the metaphor of starvation, a recurring trope in nineteenth-century women's writing, as Gilbert and Gubar have argued (1979), reinforce the image of woman as starving in that 'desert for the heart', her home. She sees mirages, that offer 'the *appearance* of food which disappears whenever you stretch out your hand to take it' (pp. 151–2). Another trope that is eloquent of the degrading denial of autonomy to women represents them as subjected to forced feeding. Not once, but twice in the text, being read aloud to is compared to a form of torture that brings to mind the treatment of hunger-striking suffragettes early in this century (see Showalter (1987, p. 130) and Gagnier (1988, p. 31)). 'Don't you feel', Nightingale asks, 'when you are being read to, as if a pailful of water were being poured down your throat, which, but that it comes up again just as it goes down, would suffocate you?' (p. 74). It is a horrific image of a woman gagging on her own enforced passivity and dependency:

> It is like lying on one's back, with one's hands tied and having liquid poured down one's throat. Worse than that, because suffocation would immediately ensue and put a stop to this operation. But no suffocation would stop the other. (p. 213)

Starvation and suffocation are, for Nightingale, apt metaphors for her society's denial and repression of female desire; appetite, or rather hunger, not for the 'Dinner' that, contemptuously echoing writers such as Isabella Beeton, she describes as 'the great sacred ceremony of this day, the great sacrament' (p. 210) in the well-regulated middle-class household, but for the truly great and the truly sacred that are travestied in the secular ritual. As in so much writing by nineteenth-century women, female desire is positively voracious in this text, embracing many passions, and taking many forms, its very ubiquitousness contesting the commonly-held notion, scornfully reiterated by Nightingale, that 'women have no passions' (p. 206). Vocational desire, in particular, is experienced with a libidinal intensity that sustains an extraordinary textual dynamic, drawing together the various elements of this diffuse and disjointed text, and propelling the argument with an irresistable logic. Critiquing Freudian and Lacanian models of desire as lack, Elizabeth Grosz has proposed a counter-theory of desire as 'not a lack but a positive force of production ... a force or energy which creates links between objects, which makes things, forges alliances, produces connections' (1989, p. xvi). *Suggestions for Thought* can be productively read against such a formulation, for it seems that it is through the textual articulation of desire that Nightingale 'produces connections', mends fractures, in a disarticulated world.

If the multiple discourses and fractured delivery of Nightingale's *Suggestions* are given coherence by a rhetoric of desire, bodily tropes may be said to perform a similar function. Nightingale criticises the 'learned men' who 'discuss together free will, necessity, the origin of evil, God's purpose, the most momentous questions of man's destiny ...[as] a mere matter of intellectual amusement', observing that '[i}t would not have been so had it been a search into man's muscles and arteries' (p. 195). Indeed, throughout the work, she draws parallels between 'theological science' and 'medical science' and 'sanitary science', to the disadvantage of the former (p. 193). It is perhaps because, as she points out, in this society '[w]e set the treatment of bodies so high above the treatment of souls' (p. 217) that Nightingale so often recurs to the body as a rhetorical strategy. Her language is strikingly corporeal, particularly in her representation of female suffering. Twice she refers to the practice of foot binding, which meant that 'the Chinese woman ... could not make use of her feet' (pp. 220–1): '"Suffering, sad" female "humanity"! What are these feelings which [women] are taught to consider disgraceful, to deny to themselves? What form do the Chinese feet assume when denied their proper development?' (p. 206). Elsewhere, a woman's crooked finger, the result of her refusal as a child to let her nurse change a dressing, is made to signify her disabled intellectual and social condition: 'And what is a deformed or crippled finger compared with a deformed or crippled *life*?' (p. 68). Nightingale deploys violent metaphors to shock:

> 'Robbed and murdered' we read in the newspapers. The crime is horrible. But there are people being robbed and murdered continually before our eyes, and no man sees it. 'Robbed' of their time, if robbing means taking away that which you do not wish to part with, slowly 'murdered' by their families. There is scarcely any one who cannot, in his own experience, remember some instance where some amiable person has been slowly put to death at home, aye, and at an estimable and virtuous home. (p. 70)

In variations on the theme, she describes how women are submitted to the torture of 'solitary confinement' (p. 149), and are turned into lunatics by their families ('[i]n fact, in almost every family, one sees a keeper, or two or three keepers, and a lunatic' (p. 137)).

As will be apparent, the body in this text is a site of pain and suffering, some of it imposed by the keepers and jailers of the family, some self-inflicted: '[w]e fast mentally, scourge ourselves morally, use the intellectual hair-shirt ... mortifying vanity ... ' (p. 207). Nightingale's strategy is, though, to turn pain to advantage, to apotheosise the figure of the suffering woman, to claim for her the status of martyr. In general terms, she demands the right to suffer, as preferable to the anaesthetism of feelings: 'Give us back our suffering, we cry to Heaven in our hearts – suffering rather than indifferentism; ... better have pain than paralysis!' (p. 208). More specifically, she writes her own script. Concluding a comparison of a bird, 'which builds its nest unerringly with a smaller range of faculties', with a man, 'wanting and suffering ... before his habitation was skilfully built', she expresses the hope that 'the bird, in another mode of existence, may rise to learn through suffering' (p. 19), like a man. Inevitably, in popular representations of her following her intervention at the hospital at Scutari, Nightingale was frequently figured as a bird, as we can see from a series of contemporary poems and images from *Punch*. In a poem entitled 'Scutari', for instance, the anonymous poet rhapsodises:

> Lady – thy very name so sweet,
> Speaks of full songs through darkness heard,
> And fancy findeth likeness meet
> Between thee and the bird,
>
> Whose music cheers the glooming wold,
> As thy low voice the anguish dim,
> That through these sad rooms lieth cold
> On brain and heart and limb.
> (*Punch*, or *The London Charivari*, 28, 1855, p. 61.)

In an illustration of 'The "Jug" of the Nightingale' (Figure 13.1; *Punch*, 27, 1854, p. 215), Nightingale is represented in the image of her ornithological namesake, flying to the rescue with her 'jug' (playing on the term for the distinctive note of the nightingale), full of fomentations, embrocations and gruel. And, picking up the theme, in the anonymous poem, 'The Nightingale's Song to the Sick Soldier', as again the elaboration on the nightingale as songbird suggests, she is depicted as bringing harmony to the chaos and disorder of war:

> Listen, soldier, to the tale of the tender NIGHTINGALE,
> 'Tis a charm that soon will ease your wounds so cruel,
> Singing medicine for your pain, in a sympathising strain,
> With a jug, jug, jug of lemonade or gruel…
>
> Singing pillow for you smoothed, smart and ache and anguish soothed,
> By the readiness of feminine invention;
> Singing fever's thirst allayed, and the bed you've tumbled, made,
> With a careful and considerate attention.
>
> Singing succour to the brave, and a rescue from the grave,
> Hear the NIGHTINGALE that's come to the Crimea,
> 'Tis a NIGHTINGALE as strong in her heart as in her song,
> To carry out so gallant an idea.
> (*Punch*, 27, 1854, p. 184)

Elsewhere, she becomes an 'immortal bird', as in portrayals of her presiding over her nurses' angelic ministrations to the sick and wounded (Figure 13.2; *Punch*, 27, 1854, p. 194). Here, the wings of the bird assume a distinctly other-worldly status, as the angel in the house becomes an angel at the front.

In *Suggestions for Thought*, Florence Nightingale writes herself into history, authorizing her desire to escape from '[t]he prison which is called a family' (p. 119) and take her place in public life, and carving out a place for herself as a modern-day Messiah. Throughout the text she reiterates her belief that the fragmented modern world is in need of 'saviours', of redemption through suffering, and at the same time compellingly describes the suffering of women, like herself, caught in 'the trammels of conventional life' (p. 170). George Landow has written very

Figure 13.1 The "Jug" of the Nightingale, *Punch*, 27, 1854, p. 125.

interestingly about Nightingale's subversion of biblical, as well as Greek, mythology in *Cassandra*, focusing particularly upon her rewriting of the passage from scripture in the epigraph 'The voice of one crying in the crowd, "Prepare ye the way of the Lord"', in order 'to claim for herself the position of a female John the Baptist preparing the way for a female Christ' (Landow, 1990, p. 42). Oddly, though, given his important study of typology in Victorian literature, art and thought, *Victorian Types, Victorian Shadows* (1980), he does not comment on the pervasive references elsewhere in *Suggestions for Thought* to the absence of a modern type of the saviour. People fritter away their lives 'because they have no type before them' (p. 68), Nightingale complains. 'How can nations improve ... if they have no type before them?' (p. 76), she demands. '[W]ithout a type before one of what human nature may become', she asks, 'how can any one work?' (p. 131). This emphasis on the type is a further manifestation of Nightingale's insistence

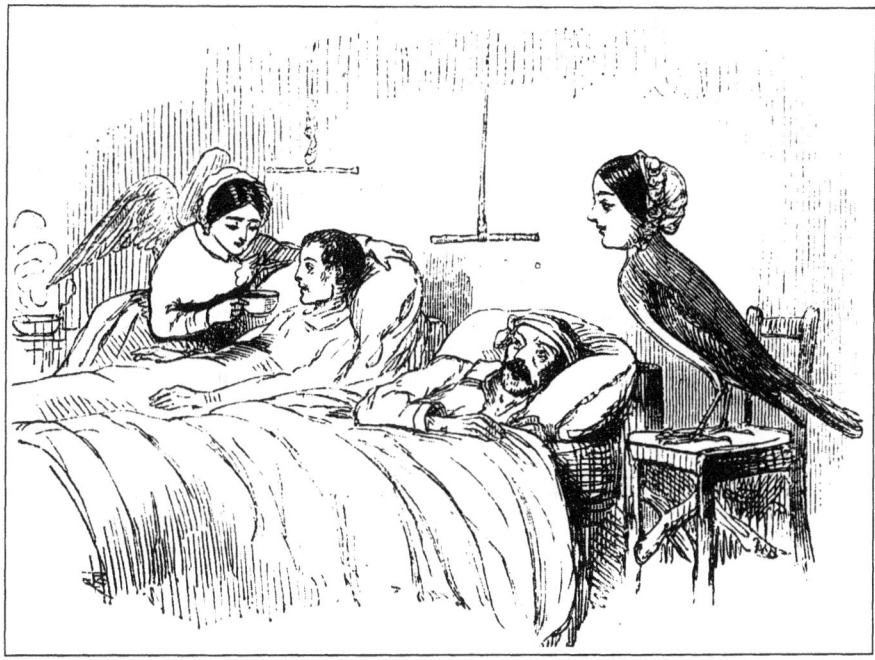

Figure 13.2 "Immortal Bird", *Punch*, 27, 1854, p. 194.

upon the connectedness of the physical and the spiritual, the signifier and the signified. The paradigmatic exemplum of spirit made flesh is, of course, Christ, described in *Aurora Leigh* as having 'come into our flesh,/As some wise hunter creeping on his knees/With a torch, into the blackness of a cave,/To face and quell the beast there – take the soul,/And so possess the whole man, body and soul' (*Aurora Leigh*, Bk 8, ll. 546–50). Increasingly outrageously, and inverting the fundamental principles of typology (whereby people and events are read as the material embodiment and divinely intended anticipation of Christ), Nightingale suggests that Christ's crucifixion was as nothing compared with the suffering of women: 'Suppose one says, How much worse not to strive to save thousands from a crucified *spirit* than to crucify one body, thereby transferring that lofty spirit to some other reign of God's universe!' (p. 202). Combining the idea of the biblical type with that of the biological type, the type of the evolving species, somewhat in the manner of Tennyson in his apotheosis of Arthur Hallam in *In Memoriam* (1850), Nightingale triumphantly proclaims:

> The more complete a woman's organization, the more she will feel it, till at last there shall arise a woman, who will resume, in her own soul, all the sufferings of her race, and that woman will be the Saviour of her race. (p. 227)

At the very time that William Holman Hunt was painting that icon of Protestantism *The Light of the World* (which was, interestingly, like *Suggestions for*

Thought, begun in 1851–53, and retouched in 1858), the woman who was herself to become iconised as 'the Lady with the Lamp' announces 'The next Christ will perhaps be a female Christ' (p. 230). In the poems referred to, she is represented in such a role, insofar as she rescues soldiers from the grave and is said to 'do' 'what Christ preached'. Other texts invoke her Christ-like qualities. Harriet Martineau, for instance, in the obituary she wrote when it was thought that Florence Nightingale was dying from a fever contracted in the Crimea, praises her as 'the nurse, and the dispenser of comfort and relief', and pictures her 'dressing wounds, bringing wine and food, carrying the lamp through miles of sick soldiers in the middle of the night, noting every face, and answering the appeal of every eye as she passed' – a picture confirmed by visual representations of the Barrack Hospital, Scutari. Martineau writes, 'We think to-day of the little Russian prisoner, the poor boy who could not speak or be spoken to till she had taken him in, and had taught him and made him useful; and how he answered when at length he could understand a question. When asked if he knew where he would go when he was dead, he confidently said: "I shall go to Miss Nightingale"' (Yates, 1985, pp. 196–7). Dispensing bread and wine and light from her lamp to Britain's Christian soldiers among the infidels, yet taking her place alongside the Almighty in heaven, Nightingale does indeed seem to have featured in the public imagination as a kind of female Christ.

A prominent theme that emerges from such representations of Florence Nightingale is of a woman who creates order and coherence out of chaos and fragmentation. Until she appeared in the Crimea, Britain's affairs were represented as being in the hands of a disorderly housewife (Figure 13.3),[5] who presides over a scene of disarray, and whose candle has gone out. By contrast, Nightingale brings a sense of calm and peace to the poorly-governed household of the nation, as is signified in the many contemporary portrayals of 'the Lady with the Lamp' at Scutari. But, significantly, her talent for organization is figured as practical, rather than abstract and intellectual, and womanly, an extension into the public sphere of qualities which are constructed as domestic and feminine. It might perhaps be useful at this point to turn to the views of the person who most famously debunked the saintly image of 'the Lady with the Lamp', Lytton Strachey. In his witty and influential brief biography of Nightingale in *Eminent Victorians* (1918), Strachey alternately monsters and ridicules his subject, saving his most disparaging remarks for her excursions into theological speculation in *Suggestions for Thought*. It is clear that he considered her to be ill-qualified to write on philosophical matters, and he lampoons her attempts to unravel, 'in the course of three portly volumes, the difficulties – hitherto, curiously enough, unsolved – connected with such matters as Belief in God, the Plan of Creation, the Origin of Evil, the Future Life, Necessity and Free Will, Law, and the Nature of Morality'. He renders ludicrous both her hubristic intellectual ambition and her unorthodox materialist perspective: 'She felt towards [God] as she might have felt towards a glorified sanitary engineer; and in some of her speculations she seems hardly to distinguish between the Deity and the Drains'. In short, he dismisses her as being 'simply an empiricist', concluding that '[h]er mind was, indeed, better qualified to dissect the concrete and distasteful fruits of actual life than to construct a coherent system of abstract philosophy' (Strachey, 1948, pp. 153–5). Such a division between 'concrete ... actual life' and a

Figure 13.3 The Disorderly Housewife, Marshall, 1992, p. 106.

'coherent system of abstract philosophy', like Strachey's mockery of the inappropriate and disruptive incursion of the personal into the theological argument, reinstates the very gendered categories that Nightingale's text is at pains to subvert. His criticisms, indeed, give the modern reader a lively sense of the gendered assumptions that a woman with aspirations to participate in public intellectual debate had to negotiate.

Mary Poovey has commented that '[o]ne of the most pressing theoretical issues facing feminists today is conceptualizing the complex relationship between "real" women – women as historical agents – and woman – the historically specific representation of the female that mediates the relationship of women and men to every individual, concrete woman' (1990, p. 29). That relationship is particularly complicated in the case of Florence Nightingale, whose self-representation was always so governed by strategy, and whose public construction by others was so imbricated in contemporary ideologies of gender, sexuality, domesticity, class and imperialism. Variously constructed as 'a housewifely woman' (Yates, p. 202), a ministering angel, and a saint, Nightingale was empowered to take a role in public affairs equalled, among women, only by the Queen. Poovey herself has persuasively analysed how Nightingale's own later writings on nursing authorized the persistent misrepresentations that characterized the mythology that grew up around her as soon as she entered the public space, and 'capitalized on the contradiction inherent in the domestic ideal in order to make even more radical claims for women than contemporary feminists did' (1988, p. 166). Always the opportunist, Nightingale, by this point elevated in hagiographical poems such as 'The Nightingale's Return' to the status of a saint ('our sweet Saint FLORENCE, modest, and still, and calm'),[6] invokes in her writings on nursing, as Poovey argues, 'the asexual, apparently classless image of woman by which her own exploits were publicly represented', the domestic ideal of 'the orderly, happy, middle-class home', and the institution of the family (1988, pp. 185, 190). It seems a far cry from the rage with which she exposed such ideological constructions in *Suggestions for Thought*. Whether it was a matter of strategy, or whether because the only language available to Nightingale to further her project of professionalizing nursing was so inescapably inflected by contemporary assumptions about the class and gender order that it was impossible to articulate her proposals in any other way, Nightingale's later writings both were considerably more conservative publications than *Suggestions for Thought* and reached a much wider audience. Such are the gains, and the costs, perhaps, of mending fractures. If *Suggestions for Thought* lacks coherence, it is because its first priority is to register fragmentation and difference. Benjamin Jowett criticised the book for being 'full of antagonisms', yet Nightingale did not take up his suggestions for how 'these could be softened' (Woodham-Smith, 1951, p. 350). Insofar as it does have coherence, it is a coherence conferred not by masculinist 'abstract philosophy' or by universalising ideology, but rather, as this paper has attempted to argue, by the desiring embodied female subject. Insofar as fractures are mended, they are the fractures that divide a woman from herself, and they are healed in the pursual, to quote Nightingale, of 'unity between the woman as inwardly developed and outwardly manifested' (p. 228).

Notes

1 All references in parenthesis, except where otherwise stated, are to *Florence Nightingale: Cassandra and other Selections from Suggestions for Thought*, ed. Mary Poovey. London: Pickering and Chatto, 1991.
2 See Cranny-Francis (1995, Introduction) for a useful critical overview of the literature. On the retheorization of the relation between the mind and the body see, in particular, Grosz (1994).
3 For an astute discussion of his article on 'the great social vice of Prostitution' in the *Westminster Review*, 53 (July, 1850): 238–68, see Poovey (1990).
4 Maud Ellmann (1993) notes that, 'Hegel, Feuerbach, Marx, and Freud, in spite of their divergences, agree that eating is the origin of subjectivity. For it is by ingesting the external world that the subject establishes his body as his own, distinguishing its inside from its outside' (p. 30). Note too Helena Michie's (1987) argument that female hunger 'figures unspeakable desires for sexuality and power' (p. 13).
5 Reproduced in Marshall (1992, p. 106).
6 *Punch*, or *The London Charivari*, 31, 1856, p. 73.

Chapter Fourteen

Elizabeth Gaskell, Gender and the Apocalypse

Robert M. Kachur

By the time Elizabeth Gaskell was writing *North and South* in 1854 and 1855, Revelation, the New Testament Apocalypse, had not only helped to shape public discourse about labor-management disputes, but had reinforced its highly polarized nature. On the one hand, middle-class writers associated with established, mainline churches tended to characterize discontented workers as agitators preparing the way for the antichrist; on the other, working-class writers associated with fringe religious movements tended to characterize unyielding capitalists as oppressors acting out antichrist-like tyranny.[1]

These established ways of using the Apocalypse to simplify and understand complex struggles between workers and manufacturers during the mid-Victorian period provide an important context for understanding Elizabeth Gaskell's use of the Apocalypse in *North and South*. Gaskell not only participates in this Apocalyptic mode of representing class struggle, but alters that mode significantly. Gaskell describes an imminent confrontation between workers and bourgeois factory owners in Apocalyptic terms – only to deconstruct the clear lines of good and evil that most Apocalyptic commentators were projecting onto battles between labor and management. In doing so, she critiques conventional associations between labor activity and Apocalyptic disruption on one hand, and the bourgeois order and God's Order on the other.

Even more significant, however, is how Gaskell's peculiar position as a Unitarian *woman* informs the way she draws on Apocalyptic discourse. Unlike Christina Rossetti and many lesser known women writers who used the Apocalypse to envision expanded roles for women within the church, Gaskell goes further, using the Apocalypse to envision expanded roles for women within society at large.[2] It is, in fact, Gaskell's desire to address two social issues simultaneously – women's roles and class conflict – which makes the Apocalypse a particularly compelling resource for her. Gaskell uses Apocalyptic allegory as what Bakhtin might call a mediating discourse through which class inequities and gender inequities can simultaneously be addressed (see Bakhtin, 1981, pp. 275–300).

Unions as Threat to God's 'Natural Order'

In order to understand Gaskell's use of Apocalyptic discourse in context, then, it is necessary to examine more closely its use by her middle-class contemporaries within the Anglican church and other orthodox Protestant churches. As Max Weber, E.P. Thompson and others have argued, mainline Anglican and Dissenting churches in late eighteenth- and nineteenth-century England – particularly the Methodist movement – helped shape and police what later became known as the industrial working class. Not surprisingly, the dynamics of this shaping and policing process were complex. What is of special interest here is the role that the idea of Apocalypse played in this policing function:

> The factory system demands a transformation of human nature, the "working paroxysms" of the artisan or outworker must be methodized until the man is adapted to the discipline of the machine. But how are these disciplinary virtues to be inculcated in those whose Godliness (unless they become overlookers) is unlikely to bring temporal gain? It can only be by inculcating "the first and great lesson ... that man must expect his chief happiness, not in the present, but in a future state". Work must be undertaken as a "pure act of virtue ... inspired by the love of a transcendent Being". (Thompson, 1968, pp. 397–8)

A strongly teleological worldview, then, far from merely fueling progressive political movements' efforts to establish a new order, undergirded attempts to preserve existing class structures. As Thompson documents, efforts to improve working and living conditions through union organization or government intervention were denounced by most mainline clergy (and the extensive network of lay leaders they helped organize) as being too worldly and temporally focused.

The Christian sect of particular interest here is the Wesleyan Methodist movement, which drew more working-class followers than any other religious group during the nineteenth century. Although there were individual Methodists, as well as split-off congregations from the Methodist church, who were advocates of labor reform, Wesley and his hand-picked clergymen generally supported industrial capitalism by encouraging workers to spiritualize and compartmentalize powerful emotional and sexual energies which threatened to undermine their productivity (Thompson, 1968, pp. 46–53; 420–40). Hence Methodists became known for their religious enthusiasm, manifest in passionate, visceral outbursts usually experienced in sanctioned church contexts, such as revival meetings. Often these outbursts were ignited by sermons and hymns focusing on the world to come, which Christ promised to prepare for the faithful. By equating 'faithfulness' with certain Christian virtues – self-discipline, patience, sobriety, and, most important of all, deference to authority – Wesley and the Methodist ministers who succeeded him helped workers reframe their machine-like work existence, as well as other experiences of class oppression, as a lifelong exercise in Christlike obedience preparing them for the eternal bliss promised in Revelation.

Similarly, Victorian commentators on the Apocalypse – and, most interestingly, women who otherwise use the Apocalypse to envision gender role reform – typically reinforce the class hierarchies inscribed in ecclesiastical organizations by vilifying those who challenge the status quo. Most often they do this within the context of characterizing the antichrist as one who will disrupt a 'natural' economic state of affairs. Anonymous female writer L.B.'s (1886) description of the antichrist as an unnatural usurper who only masquerades as a virtuous defender of the working class is particularly revealing:

> The miracles wrought, and especially the fire from heaven, would ... allude to the power possessed by [the antichrist] for a time to imitate closely the virtues of true religion ... The power even to kill will be claimed, and the power to interfere with the right to buy and sell will be exercised, – how possible this is has been seen in the conduct of some of the Trades-Unions. How far we may connect the Number of the Beast with this special interference with commerce is not clear, but at least in a money-getting age it may be noticed for consideration. (p. 47)

As his name implies, the antichrist's very essence is opposition to Christ; whatever he is for, Christ can be assumed to be against. Consequently, L.B.'s emphasis on the antichrist as one who will 'interfere with the right to buy and sell', as well as her further association of him with Trades-Unions, implies that Christ has sanctioned 'natural' laws of economy with which neither the government nor the workers themselves should interfere. Thus in her text and many other Apocalyptic texts Christ becomes the champion of a laissez-faire free market system; labor agitators and 'infidels' are lumped together as one spiritually and economically rebellious group.

The argument that class rebellion follows closely after spiritual rebellion was so often being made in interpretations of the Apocalypse by the time Gaskell wrote *North and South*, in fact, that one of the very few contemporary commentators to argue that laissez-faire acceptance of 'natural' laws of political economy is unchristian felt compelled to devote two chapters to the subject. The anonymous author of *Physical Science Compared with the Second Beast* (1865) argues that the wonder-working second beast or 'false prophet' described in Revelation is actually a personification of physical science, which during the Victorian era was resulting not only in new technological wonders, but also in the social science of Political Economy:

> Has Physical Science, the wonder-worker, given a mark, for the right hand or for the forehead, without which no man may buy or sell? It has given us Political Economy; a science which every year becomes more firmly established as true, which give laws to trade, which is hated and opposed by many as thoroughly antichristian, and which may be described simply as the science of getting rich. Now, when Science begins to give laws for the life of a man, it takes upon itself the office of a prophet or teacher; if the laws be wrong, it is a false prophet... . [T]he very fact of [laws] having been discovered to be natural makes it most probable that they will be true ... But to be *true* is not necessarily to be right in human matters ... For Political Economy teaches a man, that by working in obedience to certain general laws, and for his own interest solely, he will really in the end be doing more good to the whole community than he would be doing if he allowed present, and perhaps local, distress to turn him from following those principles, and to lead him to sacrifice himself for others. (pp. 68–71)

Just as interesting as the glimpse this writer gives into the class wars being fought through the Apocalypse is his acceptance of the idea that Utilitarian principles of Political Economy are 'natural'. Rather than challenging how Christians have naturalized the economic order, he equates what is natural with what is human and therefore fallen. According to him, following Utilitarian principles of Political Economy does result in the material prosperity that science promises; but it does not result in anything remotely resembling Christian service.

In addition to associating union activity with the antichrist's interference in buying and selling practices, Apocalyptic commentators writing during the mid-Victorian period typically characterize unions as parodies of the church, analogous to the antichrist being a parody of Christ. As the word 'union' suggests, the essence of any labor organization lies in its corporate nature; workers who are powerless to negotiate as individuals seek power as members of a large organization. Similarly, the Christian church is also supposed to operate as a body with each member's interest in mind: 'there should be no schism in the body; ... members should have the same care for one another' (1 Corinthians 12:25). For many Victorian Christians, the notion of a secular body composed of members so committed to each other seemed to challenge the church's purpose. The fact that grassroots labor groups imported many organizational strategies from the Methodist movement only reinforced the perception that they claimed church-like status, despite the presence of some devout Christians within their ranks. Hence another reason why Apocalyptic writings often discuss labor unions in the same breath as Roman Catholics and democratic infidels: they are all portrayed as providing a type of unity and brotherhood which challenges and parodies the true unity that the Protestant church provides. Mrs. Baxter's argument in *His Last Word* (1896) – that unions, political organizations and the Roman Catholic church will become vehicles for the antichrist to unify and thus rule the masses – is representative:

> The day in which we live is a day of confederations and unions. Answering to the union of nations in confederacies for mutual protection, we have the trades unions and the merchants' unions... . The Church of Rome makes no secret of her desire ... to bring about what she terms the union of Christendom, and few are aware how great is the progress she is making ... Outward religionism, without any conversion to God, is immensely on the increase, and is preparing for the time when the Antichrist ... shall make use of ... religionism which may allow of any personal opinion so long as those who profess it conform externally to the religion of the day. (p. 256)

Baxter's sinister portrayal of unionizers and Catholics is shared by the majority of middle-class Protestants writing about the Apocalypse during the mid-nineteenth century.

Adding the Woman Question to the Labor Problem

These writers provide an important context for reading *North and South*, in which Gaskell draws on the Apocalypse to do the unexpected. Although the novel ultimately justifies England's capitalist system, Gaskell uses Apocalyptic discourse to problematize the way middle-class writers project the Apocalypse onto conflicts between workers and bourgeois factory owners. Gaskell does frame the novel's climactic clash between labor and management in Apocalyptic terms, but only to deconstruct the clear lines of good and evil that Apocalyptic writers were projecting onto labor disputes. Spurred in part by the Unitarian tenet that education changes behavior, Gaskell attempts to humanize the working classes for middle-class readers, and thus move those readers to improve laborers' working and living conditions (see Fryckstedt, 1982, pp. 66–74).

It is not solely Gaskell's desire to enter labor debates that makes the Apocalypse such a compelling resource for her, however. Apocalyptic rhetoric, in fact, works against the kind of realism Gaskell strives for in depicting labor disputes; she must work against the totalizing effect of Apocalyptic binaries in order to achieve the more nuanced portrayal of the working classes that she seeks to create. Rather, it is Gaskell's desire to problematize class ideology *and* gender ideology at the same time that draws her to the Apocalypse. Like many of her female contemporaries who were writing devotional prose, Gaskell finds in Apocalyptic discourse a way to imagine greater agency for women in the public sphere. Unlike most of those other writers, however, Gaskell writes as a woman who is also a Unitarian, and thus an outsider to mainline Protestant circles.

In *North and South*, Gaskell suggests that the different forms of oppression experienced by middle-class women and the working class are also religious problems. More specifically, she argues that middle-class women and the working class have become social 'problems' because the largely Christian middle class has failed to recognize their essential humanity, and that this in turn results from the middle class's own problematic understanding of Christian faith and biblical discourse. Given that she is writing about religious problems, then, Gaskell faces a problem: How does a Unitarian – who would have been considered a type of infidel in most Protestant circles – go about trying to challenge the Christian faith and biblical understanding of more orthodox readers? What narrative strategies does she use to try to overcome her position as a religious outsider writing about 'religious' problems?

In order to make this argument to 'orthodox' Christians, Gaskell must overcome her position as a religious outsider, and does so through two narrative strategies. On one hand, she peoples her novel with an array of Christians from mainline Protestant denominations who must be re-educated to achieve a Unitarian understanding of their social obligations as followers of Christ. On the other hand, she draws on the Apocalypse, inscribing into her novel the Apocalyptic narrative's imagined means of eliminating social evils: through divinely inspired interventions from 'outside'. Within the narrative frame of North and South, outside intervention into the labor problem comes in the form of a woman, an outsider to the public sphere. It is no coincidence that Margaret Hale, Gaskell's outsider protagonist, is progressively defined in terms of Apocalyptic images of female strength. The Apocalypse provides, in Bakhtinian terms, a mediating discourse through which the labor problem and the woman problem can simultaneously be addressed.

In order to understand Margaret's transformation into an Apocalyptic 'angel in white' – a female agent in the public sphere who retains her upper-class sense of feminine propriety – we must first examine Bessy Higgins, the working-class visionary who projects that identity onto her. As we shall see, Gaskell's narrative of class wars fought by men is subsumed by a distinctly 'female' counter-narrative; in it, two women from different socio-religious backgrounds – Methodist, working-class Bessy and Anglican, upper-class Margaret – find in Apocalyptic discourse a way to overcome class conflict by identifying common ground as Christian women. Ultimately, it is when Margaret actualizes Bessy's vision of her as an Apocalyptic 'angel in white' that she, as a woman, is able to take on an important public role, intervening in an increasingly violent confrontation between labor and management.

Bessy Higgins: Gaskell's Working-Class Visionary

Although Gaskell draws on her extensive knowledge of the Bible to invoke a variety of allusions and quotations in *North and South*, the Apocalypse becomes her dominant biblical source once Bessy Higgins, the novel's female visionary, is introduced. Bessy, a young factory worker who is dying as a result of years of ingesting cotton fibers, has visions of the New World to come, and draws on passages from the Apocalypse to describe them. At first glance, the extremely devout Bessy seems to be a one-dimensional personification of Methodist repression: passive and uncomplaining, she frowns on her father's union activity, channeling her own frustrations and emotions into ecstatic meditations on the afterlife. Like Methodists described by Thompson and other historians, Bessy not only looks forward to the Apocalypse, but also to her own personal apocalypse – being united to Christ in death. She so strongly displays the Methodist preoccupation with and longing for death, in fact, that she tells Margaret she is not cheered by the prospect of recovering.

Although Bessy's incessant apocalypticism seems to make her wholly complicit in her own class and gender oppression, Gaskell makes it increasingly clear that the young woman embodies the contradictory impulses characteristic of Methodism itself. Unlike Calvinist sects, Methodism was characterized by a 'spiritual egalitarianism [which] had a tendency to break its banks and flow into temporal channels' (Thompson, 1968, p. 399). Unlike Calvinists who stressed the doctrine of election, Wesley and his followers emphasized the universality of man's sin and God's offer of grace. Although Wesley preached such egalitarianism within the context of separate spiritual and temporal economies, the 'constant sermonizing against Jacobinism' kept believers aware of the potential power of political subversion, and a number of Methodists became key strategists in unions and political organizations (Thompson, 1968, p. 430).

In Bessy's first exchanges with Margaret, she uses the Apocalypse – especially the seventh chapter's promise that believers who have suffered earthly tribulations will have every need met in heaven – to justify the privations she has endured as a working-class factory woman. But she cannot completely suppress her contradictory impulse to expose how the Apocalypse is used to justify the oppression of the working class. Just a few lines after the exchange quoted above, Bessy admits that the Methodist preoccupation with death and the New Earth helps her rationalize her sordid working and living conditions (Gaskell, 1982, p. 89). And as she and Margaret grow closer, Bessy more and more explicitly critiques Apocalyptic discourse as a tool used by ideological conservatives:

> "I think ... if all I've been born for is just to work my heart and my life away, and to sicken in this dree place, wi' them mill-noises in my ears for a little piece o' quiet – and wi' the fluff filling my lungs, until I thirst to death for one long deep breath ... I think if this life is

th' end, and there's no God to wipe away all tears from all eyes – yo' wench, yo'!" said she, sitting up, and clutching violently, almost fiercely, at Margaret's hand, "I could go mad, and kill yo', I could... . I've spoken very wickedly. Oh! don't be frightened by me and never come again... . I read the book o' Revelations until I know it off by heart, and I never doubt when I'm waking, and in my senses, of all the glory I'm to come to." (pp. 101-2)

In this passage, the intensity and swiftly changing tone of Bessy's expostulations reflect just how ideologically powerful, accessible and polarized Apocalyptic rhetoric had become by the mid-nineteenth century. The moment Bessy imagines rejecting bourgeois interpretations of the Apocalypse which justify her present misery, she lashes out in murderous rage at upper-class Margaret – the very kind of rage justified by revolutionary, working-class readers of the Apocalypse. This threatening emotional outburst is then quickly suppressed as Bessy reframes her anger through Methodism's spiritualizing vocabulary: She has momentarily succumbed to religious 'doubt' and consequently spoken 'wickedly.' Margaret reinforces Bessy's need to suppress her anger by reframing the outburst as a mere symptom of her illness, rather than the working conditions which caused the illness: 'Don't let us talk of what fancies come into your head when you are feverish' (p. 102).

Bessy's outburst occurs during the first of two candid conversations about suffering which are pivotal to a growing sense of intimacy and identification between Margaret and Bessy. The second conversation, rather than focusing on Bessy's lot as a member of the working class, focuses on Margaret's lot as an unmarried woman in her father's household. Angered by Bessy's comment that she has 'never known want or care or wickedness', Margaret suddenly insists that she, too, occupies a miserable position: she must take care of her ill mother, who would clearly more value the company of her exiled son, Margaret's brother; in addition, she must protect her emotionally fragile father – who has abdicated authority in family matters – from knowledge of her mother's physical condition. In effect, Margaret must take the burden of her entire family's well-being on herself.

(As if her unenviable position as an 'angel in the house' who must selflessly minister to everyone were not clear enough, Gaskell explicitly likens her to an angel in the title of chapter 19, 'Angel Visits.') Margaret's outburst furthers a process of identification between her and Bessy which begins after Bessy's outburst in the conversation before, when the two women realize that they are both 19 years old. Although Margaret can initially only see the class differences between them (reflecting sorrowfully on Bessy's ruined health and poor living conditions), her admission that 'none but [God] knows the bitterness of our souls' registers a growing awareness that they have both suffered as women – unmarried women who have been forced to assume the role of caretaker in functionally motherless households. Bound up in a small house in Milton without a defined set of public, charitable functions to perform as a cleric's daughter, Margaret feels choked by her increasingly narrow set of domestic duties; Gaskell positions Bessy, who is literally being choked as a result of performing her duties as a daughter, as her working-class double. By doing so, she suggests how the gender oppression Margaret experiences might be manifest under very different material circumstances.

Positioning Margaret and Bessy as differently classed 'doubles,' of course, is problematic. Their gendered identities, bound up as they are in their class identities, can neither be distilled nor easily compared, as critics such as Robin Colby (1995) have argued. Rather than attempting to minimize the issue of class in her critique of gender ideology, however, Gaskell calls attention to it. In the process of establishing similarities between Bessy and Margaret, Gaskell also foregrounds their overwhelming class difference: Margaret's transformation into an image of Apocalyptic female strength is clearly contingent on her position of social privilege as a member of the upper class. Turning now to the process of Margaret's transformation, I will show that although Gaskell uses the Apocalypse to envision a more progressive gender ideology, she also uses it to reaffirm prevailing class hierarchies. Her solution to the labor problem involves women, but not all women. It involves middle and upper-middle class women, whose bids for agency occur within existing class structures. Whereas Margaret becomes a female actor in an Apocalyptic vision – one articulated by Gaskell through the character of Bessy – Bessy only projects her desire for agency onto a differently classed woman. For Bessy even to try to gain agency in the public sphere, she would have to give way to her buried Apocalyptic rage and rebel against Milton's very class structure. Instead, she projects onto Margaret the identity of an Apocalyptic angel and then gains her 'reward'. She dies.

Margaret Hale: The Apocalyptic 'Angel in White'

Following Margaret's outburst, two events occur which signal the beginning of her transformation into an Apocalyptic female agent in the public sphere. The first is an exchange between Margaret and Bessy immediately afterwards: Bessy attempts to comfort Margaret with a passage from the Apocalypse. The second event, occurring a chapter later, is Margaret's decision to wear a white silk dress to the Thornton's dinner party. Because the choice seems insignificant to her (and, one may assume, to Gaskell's imagined reader), Margaret reflects on what a surprising stir it causes at her home and Bessy's: 'What had possessed the world (her world) to fidget so about her dress, she could not understand' (pp. 147-8). Considered apart, and apart from the context of contemporary appropriations of the Apocalypse, these events do not appear especially significant. Considered within the context of contemporary readings of the Apocalypse, however, they mark very important moments in Margaret's development as a different kind of 'angel' than an angel in the house. In the chapter appropriately entitled 'Angel Visits', Margaret becomes marked as the Apocalyptic angel of Bessy's vision – a vision of womanly competence being articulated by contemporary 'female' interpreters of the Apocalypse.

Bessy's attempt to comfort Margaret by quoting Revelation 8:11 meets with resistance:

> "Sometimes, when I've thought o' my life, and the little pleasure I've had in it, I've believed that, maybe, I was one of those doomed to die by the falling of a star from heaven; "And the name of the star is called Wormwood; and the third part of the waters became wormwood; and men died of the waters, because they were made bitter". One can bear pain and sorrow better if one thinks it has been prophesied long before for one: somehow, then it seems as if my pain was needed for the fulfillment; otherways it seems all sent for nothing."

"Nay, Bessy – think!" said Margaret. "God does not willingly afflict. Don't dwell so much on the prophecies, but read the clearer parts of the Bible." (p. 137)

Bessy fails to comfort Margaret with the Apocalypse here because her choice of Scripture is inappropriate. This verse about Wormwood predicts that vast numbers of people will die because of a toxic pollutant; Bessy, who is dying from years of ingesting industrial waste, sees herself reflected in it, while Margaret does not. An Apocalyptic prophecy of physical suffering which must simply be endured does not speak to her as an upper-class woman who would be an advocate for reform. As Gaskell's heroine, Margaret is also repelled by this passage for another reason. Clearly, it is the kind of Apocalyptic rhetoric being used by Christians such as Bessy to justify bourgeois oppression of the working classes; Margaret must shun such polarizing rhetoric in order to achieve her mission of helping factory owners and workers reach a compromise.

The passages of the Apocalypse which do speak to Margaret become clear in her next conversation with Bessy. After Margaret tells Bessy that she will wear a white silk gown during her formal introduction to Milton society at the Thorntons' dinner party, Bessy realizes that Margaret is the Apocalyptic woman she has seen in dream visions:

"But dun yo' know, I ha' dreamt of yo', long afore ever I seed yo'... . Yo'r very face, – looking wi' yo'r clear steadfast eyes out o' th' darkness, wi' yo'r hair blown off from yo'r brow, and going out like rays round yo'r forehead ... and yo' always came to give me strength, which I seemed to gather out o' yo'r deep comforting eyes, – and yo' were drest in shining raiment – just as yo'r going to be drest. So, yo' see, it was yo'!"

"Nay, Bessy," said Margaret, gently, "it was but a dream."

"And why might na I dream a dream in my affliction as well as others? Did not many a one i' the Bible? Ay, and see visions too!" ... Margaret was silent. At last she said, "Let us talk about it sometimes, if you think it true. But not now." (p. 149)

Bessy's vision of Margaret brings together two common Apocalyptic images of female strength: the twelfth chapter's Woman Clothed with the Sun, and the twenty-first chapter's Bride. Like the 'woman clothed with the sun, [who has] the moon under her feet, and upon her head a crown of twelve stars', Margaret is envisioned in sun imagery, with 'rays round [her] forehead' and 'shining raiment'; ten pages later, the narrator builds on Bessy's description by noting that Margaret's hair 'encircled her head like a crown' on the night of the dinner party (p. 159).[3] Like the Bride, of course, Margaret is clothed in a white gown which was bought for a wedding, and she is going to what Bessy calls a 'sumptuous feast', an allusion to Revelation's anticipated wedding feast between Christ and his people (p. 150). Even the Apocalyptic fascination with numbers enters the text at this juncture: the curious detail that the Thornton's party is on the twenty-first, which is repeated several times for no obvious reason, reinforces Margaret's identification with the Bride, who makes her appearance in the twenty-first chapter of Revelation.

Margaret's eventual willingness to discuss Bessy's vision further foreshadows her transformation into an 'Apocalyptic woman', which actually begins the night she clothes herself in white and goes to the Thorntons. It is at the Thorntons' party that she first consciously, if barely perceptibly, crosses gender boundaries, preferring to participate in the men's conversation about commerce than to converse about 'the petty interests which the ladies had been talking about' (p. 163). Given her previous indifference, even repulsion, to affairs of trade, Margaret's excitement about their talk is unexpected and significant:

> She liked the exultation in the sense of power which these Milton men had.... [T]hey seemed to defy the old limits of possibility, in a kind of fine intoxication, caused by the recollection of what had been achieved, and what yet should be.... [T]here was much to admire in their forgetfulness of themselves and the present, in their anticipated triumphs over all inanimate matter at some future time which none of them should live to see. (pp. 163–4)

It is the intoxicated tone of the men's conversation that impresses Margaret most. Significantly, the way Margaret describes their talk recalls the writings of female interpreters of the Apocalypse. Like those exegetes, these men generate an immediate sense 'of power,' of being able 'to defy the old limits of possibility' by focusing on anticipated 'triumphs ... at some future time.' Margaret admires their ability to derive a sense of power through teleological projection, going so far as to take a silent but 'very decided part' in their talk (p. 163).

The Thornton's dinner party is a fitting location for the onset of Margaret's 'Apocalyptic' transformation. It is at the dinner that she is introduced to the leading families of the new, industrial world of Milton; and it is among these people that she must forge a new public identity. As Coral Lansbury (1975) has observed, the awkwardness surrounding her initial offer to call on the Higgins family earlier in the narrative underscores her sense of cultural and vocational displacement (p. 104). Whereas Margaret's former position as the cleric's daughter secured her an acceptable and fulfilling public role as benefactress, she has no such recognized role in Milton. She must create one. At the Thornton's dinner party, Margaret not only gets her first inside view of Milton's more fluid socio-economic superstructure, but also of the imaginative process through which men such as Thornton redefine themselves as they try to work their way into public positions of power. In this process, men posit new possibilities for the present – new identities as masters over 'inanimate matter' – by positioning those possibilities as a partial fulfillment of an ultimate mastery they will achieve in a utopian world. Having left behind the pastoral, pre-industrialized society of her childhood, then, Margaret must learn to internalize such an imaginative process – one that posits an increased degree of agency in a changing world by appealing to an ideal future world in which agency, or mastery of one's material circumstances, is complete.

Margaret's growing resistance to gender restrictions, then, is presaged by her 'Apocalyptic' dress and stirred by listening to what she interprets as a kind of teleological projection also being engaged in by contemporary female interpreters of the Apocalypse. But these are not the only connections Gaskell makes between Margaret's emergent desire for agency in the public sphere and Apocalyptic discourse. At the party, John Thornton refers to John the author of the Apocalypse during his only sustained conversation with Margaret. This occurs as he attempts to clarify the difference between his phrase 'true man' and Margaret's use of the word 'gentleman':

"A man to me is a higher and completer being than a gentleman ...'[G]entleman' is a term that only describes a person in his relation to others; but when we speak of him as 'a man,' we consider him not merely with regard to his fellow-men, but in relation to himself, – to life – to time – to eternity... [E]ven a saint in Patmos [St. John] has his endurance, his strength, his faith, best described by being spoken of as 'a man.'" (p. 164)

As a stereotypical Calvinist, Thornton is a successful member of the bourgeois who embraces the Protestant work ethic and the sanctity of the free market system;[4] his mother has trained him to read these conservative ideologies, as well as a conservative gender ideology, into the Scriptures he knows so well. Here he articulates contemporary gender ideology by appealing to the Scriptures, defining one who has St. John's endurance, strength and faith – one, in other words, who acts – as a 'true man.' Thornton's appeal to the writer of the Apocalypse gives added significance to his engendering of agency as masculine. By choosing St. John to represent his ideal of a 'true man,' Thornton engenders the kind of agency that comes out of dwelling on Apocalyptic vision as inherently masculine and socially conservative. Like 'male' exegetes of the Apocalypse (Kachur, 1998), Thornton reads the Apocalypse as a document which speaks not so much to rectifying social injustices – to how Christians should relate to their fellow-men – but to a conservative, privatized notion of holiness which is just as easily practiced in utter isolation, and which is more likely to result in personal satisfaction and abstract reflections on time and eternity than to provoke action or reflection on the pressing social issues of the day. Like Jane Eyre, who learns in time to question St. John Rivers's uses of St. John's Apocalypse and other books of the Bible (Kachur, 1996), Margaret cannot at first 'speak her slow conviction' that Thornton's biblically based assertions about agency are misguided (p. 164). What she does, rather, is enact her conviction.

As the scene where Margaret first begins to resist limitations put on women's activity in the public sphere, the Thornton dinner party foreshadows her climactic act: putting herself between John Thornton and his workers when they threaten his life. Significantly, Margaret's heroic act of public service – an attempt to use her identity as a woman to prevent violence from breaking out – occurs at a scene dominated by men. Although the narrator acknowledges that women such as Bessy comprise part of the working class, individual women other than Margaret are absent from this public confrontation. Thus, Margaret's action straddles a purposely ambiguous middle ground in terms of challenging gender ideology. On one hand, she is able to defuse the conflict between Thornton and his workers precisely because she retains her identity as 'other' in terms of both gender and class; in her presence, both the less-than-genteel manufacturer and his workers feel that 'masculine' displays of physical aggression are inappropriate. On the other hand, however, Margaret foregrounds her classed and gendered identity as part of an attempt to redefine what kind of public role is appropriate for a lady:

"It was not fair," said [Margaret] vehemently, "that [the mill owner] should stand there – sheltered, awaiting the soldiers, who might catch those poor maddened [workers] as in a trap – without an effort on his part, to bring them to reason. And it was worse than unfair for them to set on him as they threatened. I would [intervene] again, let who will say what they like of me. If I saved one blow, one cruel, angry action that might otherwise have been committed, I did a woman's work." (pp. 190–1).

As Robin Colby (1995) has argued, Margaret thus redefines 'woman's work' to include interventionist activity in public spheres dominated by men. More specifically, I would add that Margaret suggests here that woman's work involves attempts to help groups of people achieve what Jurgen Habermas (1983) has called 'communicative action' in the public sphere, rather than merely surrendering to the impersonal directives of systemic forces such as the free market. Margaret implies that women can lead the way in bringing the subjectively felt reality of relationships to bear on impersonal consensus-building processes. Significantly, her highly individuated act of intervention in the conflict between Thornton and his workers is set against the failure of market forces to force them into consensus, and makes the involvement of another system, the legal system (in the form of government soldiers), unnecessary. Although Margaret's act in itself does not foster communicative action, it precipitates a chain of events which leads to Thornton and his workers forming relationships which help build a greater degree of consensus.

Margaret's pivotal act in the public sphere does not go unnoticed, of course. Her defiant remark, 'let who will say what they like of me' refers to her behavior being construed by religious and political conservatives (such as Mrs. Thornton) as a sign of romantic interest in John Thornton. Her attempt to assume the public role of peacekeeper as a woman is perceived by others in terms of a role typically associated with female agency – that of sexual and economic predator on the marriage market. The narrator, however, takes pains to show us that Margaret is not romantically interested in Thornton, and that she is, in fact, repulsed by him. Like the radical early nineteenth-century visionary Joanna Southcott (Taylor, 1983) and Anglo-Catholic nuns, Margaret becomes identified not as a bride *per se*, but as the Bride of Christ, who is represented in the Apocalypse; her transformation into a female agent in the public sphere depends on her sustaining an identity as a Bride who is, paradoxically, single, rather than subject to the headship of a husband.

Gaskell, of course, does ultimately satisfy the Victorian reader in search of narrative closure by betrothing Margaret to Thornton at the end of *North and South*. By that time, however, Margaret's public role as a landlord who has influenced working conditions in Milton is secure. Like Jane Eyre, who only marries Rochester after she has established a sense of agency and been given the inheritance to act on it, Margaret only becomes engaged to Thornton once she as heiress and landlord occupies a position of power over him in the public sphere of commerce. Only then can Gaskell allow the female character she has envisioned through Bride imagery become the kind of bride whose agency is legally compromised, an event kept out of our sight beyond the pages of her narrative.

Gaskell as Unitarian: Arguing for Outside Intervention

The biblical Apocalypse, like other Judeo-Christian apocalyptic narratives, envisions many important transformations taking place on earth. As Stephen O'Leary (1994) has observed, these transformations usually involve a temporal displacement of societal evils: unjust rulers and institutions are eliminated from the world at a future time. In evaluating why Gaskell draws on the Apocalypse to envision transformed gender relations in *North and South*, it is especially important to consider exactly how apocalyptic narratives posit that injustices will be eradicated. At the heart of apocalyptic narrative lies the promise that an outside agent will intervene on behalf of the oppressed – the 'outsiders' in terms of power structures – to bring order and justice. Fundamentally, then, the Apocalypse is a narrative in which people's positions relative to power structures are reversed. On one level, Christ's promise that 'the last shall be first' is fulfilled, in that God's downtrodden people are exalted into positions of power. On another level, God Himself intervenes from outside to eliminate evil once and for all, breaking from his typical New Testament mode of acting in earthly affairs through people such as prophets and apostles.

As a text which locates a transformative locus of power outside of contemporary power structures, the Apocalypse provides Gaskell with imagery and language which serves a dual purpose. Within *North and South*, it enables Gaskell to clothe her female protagonist in the kind of Apocalyptic raiment which reverses what Margaret's position as an outsider initially signifies. Alienated at first from Milton society and lacking a recognized public role, she later capitalizes on her position as an outsider to become an influential mediator in a pivotal labor dispute. In Gaskell's narrative of class wars erupting in a recently industrialized society, an outsider who can mediate between polarized camps is desperately needed. As one who by virtue of regional culture, class and gender remains outside of the fray between Milton workers and factory owners, Margaret is able to make allies in both the working-class Higgins household and the bourgeois Thornton household. Although Margaret's physical presence at the riot defuses that particular outbreak of violence, the more significant ramifications of her actions as an outside mediator are long-term: the impressions she makes on Nicholas Higgins and John Thornton enable those men to begin to engage in dialogue, which leads Thornton to institute reforms which make their working relationship more palatable to both.

On another level, this Apocalyptic positioning of redemptive power as coming from 'outside' the sphere it seeks to transform undergirds Gaskell's own effort to intervene in labor conflicts as an outsider. Gaskell's projection of an Apocalyptic identity onto her protagonist reflects not only her own preoccupation with overcoming restrictions placed on her as a woman in the public sphere, but also her preoccupation with overcoming restrictions placed on her as a Unitarian in a predominately Trinitarian society. Examining Gaskell's authorial stance toward Margaret and the other major characters in *North and South* helps illumine how she as an 'infidel' Unitarian attempts to reach Christians who considered themselves more orthodox. Rather than foregrounding a Unitarian approach to social problems by making one of her characters a Unitarian mouthpiece, Gaskell works through an implicitly Unitarian narrative voice and a cast of characters representing three key branches of orthodox Protestantism: Anglican Margaret, Methodist Bessy, and the Calvinist Thorntons. By foregrounding connections between religious identity and social identity, her narrator recasts social problems as religious problems and offers a religious solution: on both textual and metatextual levels, she attempts to re-educate Protestants whose inadequate understanding of their faith and their Bibles has resulted in two pressing social conflicts of the mid-century – the labor problem and the woman problem.

This desire to improve social conditions by educating individuals reflects Gaskell's own Unitarian training. As Monica Fryckstedt (1982, pp. 69–71) and others have documented, Gaskell herself played a pivotal role in the instruction of young women. As Thompson has pointed out, most Protestant sects during the early to mid-Victorian period sought first to proselytize and only secondarily to educate, primarily teaching doctrine and the reading skills necessary to access Scripture. By contrast, Unitarians sought first to educate people – not only to read, but to write and do arithmetic – believing in the innate human tendency to be drawn to truth and good works when properly equipped to make rational decisions. This optimistic belief in reason and innate goodness, of course, broke sharply with the traditional Protestant emphasis on human depravity, which lay behind the Anglican/Methodist belief in the necessity of strong ecclesiastical authority and the Calvinist notion of divine election for salvation. Not surprisingly, many Protestants denounced Unitarians for their emphasis on education, accusing them of 'putting the wrong ideas into the heads of the poor' (Fryckstedt, 1982, p. 69).

Gaskell's progressive Apocalyptic impulse in *North and South*, however, ultimately belies the conservative class bias of the Unitarian religious community as a whole. As Fryckstedt, Thompson and others have observed, mid-nineteenth century Unitarianism constituted an intellectual and cultural elite; although many Unitarians were advocates for the poor, the poor did not, by and large, mingle with them socially or join their churches. Methodism continued to claim the most working-class converts well into the latter half of the nineteenth century. Although the Apocalypse informs Gaskell's attempt to create a female Christian protagonist with agency, it also undergirds her attempt to preserve existing class hierarchies. Much as the Apocalypse's way of positioning a locus of power outside existing societal structures energizes Gaskell's critique of gender ideology, its way of positioning power as coming from 'above' to rescue the oppressed 'below' reinforces a hierarchical model of social action reminiscent of noblesse oblige. By clothing Margaret in Apocalyptic raiment, Gaskell reinforces her heroine's privileged class position; it is because she is superiorly placed that Margaret can bend down to help others and thus attempt to 'civilize' capitalism, as Lansbury (1975) has argued. Lest the reader miss the class subtext of Margaret's Apocalyptic identity, Bessy explicitly makes the connection. Again and again, Bessy explains Margaret's comforting effect on her by noting how she has come down to her from a better position, both as an upper-class lady and as the Apocalyptic angel of her vision.

As one of a small minority of Victorian women writers using Apocalyptic discourse to humanize, rather than vilify, workers agitating for reform, Gaskell does, nevertheless, stand out as an unusually progressive 'Apocalyptic' writer. She is one of the few mid-Victorian writers who try to deconstruct the Apocalyptic binaries being projected onto labor disputes. (Of the approximately 30 'Apocalyptic' texts by mid- to late-Victorian women which I have located in the British Library, only four explicitly resist the Apocalyptic binaries being projected onto labor disputes.) Like her contemporary, devotional writer Mrs. Charles (1892), she appeals to the Apocalypse to try to prevent, rather than fuel, an apocalyptic confrontation between rich and poor in England's industrial cities. Charles's warning that ignoring injustices has led to wars of classes: the volcanic outbreak of the French Revolution; fires of wrong and oppression smouldering underground through centuries bursting up through new outlets; again burning mountains falling into the sea, again stars falling to the earth, again earthquakes and pestilences, moral, social, religious, ending in the devastations of another World-Conqueror, striving in vain to weld the many kingdoms into an Universal Empire (p. 105)

recalls Gaskell's tale of a catastrophic riot narrowly averted. Although indignant about injustices and quick to validate working-class rage, both Charles and Gaskell write out of fear – fear of the consequences to existing class structures if people continue to ignore workers' complaints. Both writers try to avert such a premature Armageddon by writing not to the working class, but to their peers, and they do so through socially acceptable genres. The results of their efforts – Charles' devotional commentary on the Apocalypse, *The Book of the Unveiling* and Gaskell's Apocalyptic novel *North and South* – register the contradictory impulses inevitably expressed by Victorian women whose advocacy for social reform was qualified by their own investment in class privilege.[5]

Notes

1 For examples of working class appropriations of the Apocalypse, see Taylor (1983).
2 In Kachur (1998) I argue that 'orthodox' Victorian women spoke through the Apocalypse to make unorthodox bids for authority with special frequency between 1845 and 1900. Unlike earlier, more radical feminists who used the Apocalypse to break from established church systems, these women used it to try to create something new from within those systems: an authoritative female Christian voice. They, along with some men, wrote what I have called 'female' devotional exegesis of the Apocalypse; its allegorical and experientially-focused interpretive approach allowed them to project their specific and immediate desires for change into their readings of the Apocalypse. By contrast, 'male' exegesis (written largely by men but also by some conservative women), literalized the Apocalypse or explained its allegory in terms of unchangeable past events, thereby shutting down the book's allegorical instability and interpretive potential for reformers.
3 Compare the egalitarian vision of woman that Christina Rossetti (1892) conjures by meditating on the Woman Clothed with the Sun:

[As] instinctively we personify the sun and moon as he and she, I trust there is no harm in my considering that her sun-clothing indicates how in that heaven where St. John in vision beheld her, she will be made equal with men and angels; arrayed in all human virtues, and decked with communicable Divine graces: whilst the moon under her feet portends that her sometime infirmity of purpose and changeableness of mood have, by preventing, assisting, final grace, become immutable; she has done all and stands; from the lowest place she has gone up higher. (p. 310)

4 For more on the relationships between Dissenting traditions, the manufacturing class and the free market system, see Thompson (1968, pp. 385–406).
5 Describing the 'double-bind of nineteenth-century feminism', Terry Lovell (1987) writes: 'Feminism could not become revolutionary with respect to the prevailing gender-order without also challenging the class-order, because of the way that class-identity had become bound up with gender-differentiation. The majority of feminists were by no

means social revolutionaries. Few were fighting for the emancipation of the working class as well as of women... . What most wanted was the improvement of their own position without loss of caste' (pp. 104–5).

V Christianity and Science

Chapter Fifteen

Science and Secularization

John Hedley Brooke

In many of the master narratives concerning science and secularization, it is assumed that the two processes would be indissolubly linked. We are frequently reminded how the physical science of the French mathematician Laplace rendered the providentialist God of Newton obsolete; we are reminded of the cataclysmic effects of the earth sciences on a simple biblical faith; and we need no reminding of the sometimes dramatic shift in perceptions among those staggered to see the world as Charles Darwin saw it. Canonical utterances by Darwin himself conform to that easy flow from the sacred to the secular. Having once been charmed by William Paley's *Natural Theology*, Darwin eventually declared that arguments for design based on the perfection of organic structures were doomed by his theory of natural selection. In his *Autobiography* he would articulate the seductive formula that the more we know of the fixed laws of nature, the more incredible do miracles become (Darwin, 1958, pp. 86–7). Through the sciences – the natural as well as the historical – the supernatural was, it seems, progressively swallowed by the natural.

In this paper I suggest reasons why scientific progress and secular process should not be conflated. This requires some introductory remarks about the rather tired word 'secularization'. I shall then consider some paradoxes that arise in applying the term. Not least among them is that the term is used to describe two processes that pull in opposite directions – the separation of an academic discipline from theological concerns, and the reinterpretation of theological concepts as a result of fusion with that discipline. Finally, I shall focus on the discourse of natural theology which, depending on context, could be sacred, secular or both. The natural theology of Paley has been seen as a unifying discourse – one that functioned as a brake on the fragmentation of culture (Young, 1985, pp. 126–63). Yet the move from nature to nature's God and how it could best be made was itself a divisive issue well before the Darwinian impact was felt.

Some Preliminary Problems

It is possible to weld science and secularization together but if this is done through definition the result is hardly exciting. The *Shorter Oxford English Dictionary* gives as one definition of secularization: 'the conversion of an ecclesiastical or religious institution or its property to secular possession and use'. One does not have to be very bright to see a possible snag. Turning to the definition of 'secular', we find it means 'the world', especially as opposed to the Church. Because the natural sciences perforce explore this world, they almost become agents of secularity by definition.

But will this do? If we return to the founders of modern science, we encounter forms of spirituality in which conclusions about the natural world are suffused with religious meaning. Having discovered a mathematically elegant correlation between the orbital periods of the planets and their mean distances from the sun, Johannes Kepler confessed to being carried away by 'unutterable rapture at the divine spectacle of heavenly harmony' (Caspar, 1959, p. 267). Awestruck by the power of the Almighty to inject life into the minutest of mites, Robert Boyle presented himself as priest in the temple of nature (Fisch, 1953; Shanahan, 1994). The solar system described by Isaac Newton was a 'most beautiful system' that 'could only proceed from the counsel and dominion of an intelligent and powerful being' (Thayer, 1953, p. 42; Brooke and Cantor, 1998, pp. 1–7).

This leads us straight into a second problem because each of these examples (and many more) show how scientific enquiry may generate awe, not destroy it. Indeed, the assumption that the sciences automatically have an adverse effect on religious belief has been rightly challenged by Mary Douglas on the grounds that it represents an archaic survival of nineteenth-century positivism, that it mistakenly supposes religion to depend more on the physical environment than on the quality of social relations, and that it ignores those respects in which scientific knowledge may magnify rather than diminish a sense of awe and grandeur (Douglas, 1982).

An identification of scientific progress with secular process fails for a further and related reason. New scientific concepts are not merely susceptible of both theistic and naturalistic readings. Historically they have provided resources for both. Indeed one and the same concept has many times been manipulated to generate a sense of the sacred and of the profane. Crucial concepts in the development of western science – mechanical images of nature, the gravitational force of Newton, the principle of energy conservation, the unity of skeletal architecture in the vertebrate kingdom, even the 'big bang' in our own day – have been seized for a plethora of apologetic purposes, both sacred and profane (Brooke, 1991). The sciences have never simply led to secularization. At issue has always been the cultural meaning to be placed on new forms of science (Rudwick, 1986). The complication is obvious: the meaning we find in scientific innovation will depend very largely on our preconceptions. For Charles Darwin's American correspondent Asa Gray, the theory of evolution was not a threat to Christian theology but a positive contribution to the problem of theodicy. Through Gray's eyes it looked as if pain and suffering had a purpose after all. They were concomitants of a creative process in which a struggle for existence had been a *sine qua non* of the very possibility of our coming into being (Gray, 1963, pp. 310–13). A letter written from Africa in December 1860 by the explorer and missionary David Livingstone brings out beautifully the singularity of preconception that can make the master-narratives so vulnerable. 'By the way', Livingstone wrote to Richard Owen, 'Mr. Darwin's theory upsets my ideas somewhat. There does not seem to be any great struggle for existence going on in this wide continent. There is room enough and to spare for both men and beast. The latter seem to live quite jovially and often attain old age'. The 'somewhat' is delightfully ambiguous: it leaves us wondering about the extent to which he had been upset at all. It would, of course, be a serious error to pretend that the upset produced by Darwin was always so mild. Nor should we disregard the cumulative force of naturalistic theories in swaying those whose faith was contingent upon gaps in scientific knowledge. But there is clearly no simple trajectory from science to secularization. By focussing on the more reductionist of the nineteenth-century naturalists – Joseph Hooker and T.H. Huxley, John Tyndall and Francis Galton – we sometimes forget the continuing existence of the religiously more conservative scientists: William Thomson, for example, who wished to preserve the argument for design, or the Cambridge physicist George Stokes who cherished an evangelical faith (Wilson, 1984; Lightman, 1997, pp. 187–211).

The last of my preliminary problems again relates to the one-way flow implied by phrases such as the disenchantment or the desacralization of nature. What about the scientific thinkers who passed in their spiritual odyssey from the secular to the sacred? The nineteenth century's most prolific popularizer of geology, Hugh Miller, was one such. From humble beginnings as a stone-mason Miller was to become an expert on fossil fish, an accomplished essayist and tireless editor of *The Witness*, organ of the Free Church of Scotland. He had first come to geology when he still believed Christianity to be a 'cunningly devised fable', its doctrines 'absurd'. In an essay entitled 'Gropings of a Working Man in Geology', he recalled his first impressions of fossil forms: 'I was lost lost in admiration and astonishment, and found my very imagination paralysed by an assemblage of wonders that seemed to outrival, in the fantastic and the extravagant, even its wildest conceptions'. The language is suggestive perhaps of a surrogate religious experience. Following his conversion, his response to fossil forms was sacralised and formalised within a theology of redemption. Their beauty was celebrated as expressions of divine architecture. And because they presaged the work of human architects, Miller could argue that man and God shared the same aesthetic sensibilities (Brooke, 1996). In short, evidence from geology could shore up the biblical doctrine that man had been made in the image of God. We must not imagine that science and scepticism were identical twins. For Miller, the science of geology took on new meanings in the light of his evangelical faith. His science even supplied symbols of a degraded world, in the shape of 'repulsive reptiles' that bespoke a 'fallen spirit' (Miller, 1869, pp. 77–9).

Secularization and Paradox

Having raised some problems about the trajectory from sacred to secular, I now turn to a series of paradoxes that arise when the term secularization is used to describe the impact of scientific cultures. I shall refer to different *modes* of secularization in order to distinguish various ways in which the sciences have been seen as eroding religious belief. Not for a moment do I want to suggest that such erosion has not occurred. Those familiar with the correspondence between Darwin and his cousin Emma, before their pending marriage, will know how sensible Emma was of the danger to a biblical faith posed by Charles' questioning mentality – a mentality which she ascribed to the exigencies of a life in science (Burkhardt, 1986, pp. 171–2).

There is a deep paradox at the heart of discourse about the role of religious belief in the rise of modern science. In a searching study by Peter Harrison a contrast is drawn between two ways of reading the Bible, both of which, he argues, had implications for how God's other book, the book of nature, should be read. The older of the two conventions, characteristic of patristic and medieval theology, involved a quest for multiple and symbolic meanings of biblical texts, producing a rich tapestry of spiritual allegory. The correlate of this style of exegesis was the ascription of symbolic meanings to objects in the natural world on the understanding that the two books illumined each other. By contrast, the newer convention, which Harrison sees as a product of the Protestant Reformation, was characterised by the quest for literal, univocal interpretations of the sacred text. This shift in religious and literary sensibility is seen as profoundly important for the rise of science in Europe because it stripped natural objects of their emblematic accretions. In order to fill the ensuing vacuum, a new language was required for the analysis of nature's objects – one that permitted students of the second book to converge on similarly univocal interpretations (Harrison, 1998). The paradox here is that a literal reading of Scripture, so often seen as an impediment to the sciences, actually created the space for them. But it is doubly paradoxical in that where one has univocal meanings, the possibility of falsification arises. A literal reading of Scripture may have created space for the sciences but would soon be vulnerable to them.

The modes of secularization in which other paradoxes appear might be called the modes of refutation, of separation, of fusion, of silence, of displacement and of self-destruction. I shall briefly consider each in turn.

Refutation

The simplest connection between scientific advance and the erosion of belief is made when scientific conclusions are seen to contradict sacred texts. The mode of secularization might then be described as one of refutation. An extended age for the earth refuted the *Genesis* days of creation; a theory of evolution contradicted doctrines of *separate* creation. The problem here is that while such confrontational stances were adopted and still are by ultra-conservative religious groups and their scientistic critics, it was usually possible to reinterpret the sacred text without serious compromise to its authority. The *Genesis* days, for example, could be reconstituted, as they were by Hugh Miller, to refer to geological epochs; or, in an earlier harmonising device proposed by Thomas Chalmers and William Buckland, a convenient gap was found between 'in the beginning' and the first *Genesis* day – a gap in which oceans of geological time could be poured. The paradox is this: credibility was eventually lost not so much because the sciences had scored a direct hit as because religious harmonizers were often a victim of their own success. The more successful a scheme of harmonization the more problems it created when the sciences moved on. In this respect it has to be said that the Churches have sometimes got themselves into more trouble by espousing the latest science than by opposing or disregarding it. As historians of science have pointed out, it was the religious apologists not the scientific explorers who sank Noah's Ark: ever more inflatable vessels designed by biblical literalists became ever more unfloatable (Browne, 1983, pp. 1–31). Between 1810 and 1850 each new decade brought advances in geology that rendered the preceding harmonization schemes obsolete. As one of the contributors to *Essays and Reviews* observed, the damage had been done by dissonance between the harmonizers (Goodwin, 1860).

Separation

A second mode of secularization may also be less straightforward than it seems. The term has often been used to refer to the separation of academic disciplines from clerical control or theological bias. As Frank Turner (1978) among others has insisted, the demand for such autonomy was one of the rallying cries of a young generation of professionalising scientists coming into prominence in Britain in the 1850s and 1860s. It had been one of Charles Lyell's grievances that the teaching of geology in the older universities was in the hands of clerics who simply could not have the time to cultivate properly each of their split loyalties. Statistical evidence suggests that the clergy were indeed marginalized in scientific institutions during the second half of the nineteenth century (Turner, 1978). The word secularization might seem particularly apposite here. The right, or not, of the clergy to interfere in scientific debate was, after all, an issue in the celebrated encounter between Huxley and Samuel Wilberforce at Oxford in 1860. And yet, even leaving aside the mythical elements in that legend (Lucas, 1979; Gilley, 1981; Jensen, 1988), there are paradoxical consequences in equating the separation of science from religion with secularization. The reason is that such separation could have as one of its motives the protection of theology as much as the protection of science. The Oxford mathematician and philosopher Baden Powell provides a well-known example. From his perspective there was a radical solution to the territorial squabbles he had witnessed during his Oxford career. Allow the scientist freedom to document the laws of nature whatever they may be. But allow the theologians the province of morality as their special preserve (Powell, 1860; Corsi, 1988, pp. 209–24). In that way conflict could be avoided. We remember the Huxley/Wilberforce debate because of its anecdotal appeal, but we forget that the official sermon preached in Oxford during the 1860 British Association meeting was given not by Wilberforce but by Frederick Temple, a future Archbishop of Canterbury. Temple's rhetoric was directed against clerics who clung to their god-of-the-gaps. Scientific knowledge was to be welcomed because in expanding our knowledge of natural laws it created a stronger presumption that the world was also governed by moral laws (Temple, 1860; Moore, 1979, p. 89).

Fusion

The paradoxes can be etched more clearly when we recognise a third mode of secularization. Here the emphasis falls not on the separation of science from theology, or theology from science, but on their fusion. In older texts it used to be said that by the end of the seventeenth century science had achieved a revolutionary break from theological constraint. The austere world of Newton's *Principia* seemed detachable from theological concerns even if it was not quite so detached in Newton's own mind. But that is precisely the problem. Revisionist accounts of Newton's achievement have stressed how much his world was shaped by alchemical and biblical motifs (Dobbs, 1991; Mandelbrote, 1993; Iliffe, 1998). Indeed much of seventeenth-century natural philosophy was characterised not by a separation of science from theology but by an unprecedented fusion (Funkenstein, 1986). Attributes of the deity such as omnipresence and providential care were translated into scientific terms, superficially strengthening them, but in reality transposing them into more precisely defined targets for their detractors.

Similarly the sciences of the nineteenth century were sometimes invoked to authenticate traditional doctrines. It was easy enough to correlate original sin with the beast within; easy enough to see in the fossil record a succession of creative acts. The Cambridge geologist Adam Sedgwick rejoiced that those who had grounded their atheism in the eternity of organic forms could be so easily confounded. It was easy enough to entertain visions of evolutionary progress that had a religious aura (Brooke, 1991, pp. 303–17). In retrospect we can see that some of these fusions would be destructive of faith; but are we happy to accept the label of secularization for efforts conceived to defend and re-define one's faith in contemporary terms? The paradox is that the word should be used to describe the two quite different, indeed contrary, processes of separation and fusion.

Silence

There is a fourth mode of secularization that need involve neither separation nor fusion. It is the mode of silence. Darwin once remarked that the most effective way of combatting religious prejudice was not to attack its dogmas head on. It was wiser to do so indirectly by affirming contrary positions, from which readers could draw their own conclusions. The sciences could endanger a simple faith because of what they declined to say. Promoting his cyclical view of earth history late in the eighteenth century, James Hutton had notoriously observed that geology was silent on the beginning and end of the world (Gould, 1988, pp. 61–97). Unlike his mentor Buckland, Lyell was effectively silent on the place of Noah's flood in the earth's physical history. In the privacy of his metaphysical notebook Darwin calculated that 'to avoid stating how far, I believe, in Materialism, say only that emotions, instincts degrees of talent, which are hereditary are so because brain of child resembles parent stock'. Referring to this passage, David Kohn has astutely observed that 'if one basic process of secularization is the translation of theologically grounded concepts, then another process of secularization is silence' (Kohn, 1989, p. 224). The silence was most deafening in the *Origin* itself where humankind was so conspicuous by its absence. The refusal to say what the religious believer wants to hear can be a potent challenge. But might there not again be an element of paradox in the use of the word secularization in such contexts? Silences may also create infinite spaces. As Hutton's defenders pointed out, to say that geology furnished no vestige of a beginning nor prospect of an end was not the same as saying that there had been no beginning and would be no end. Lyell may have wished to rid his science of Moses, but he still saw evidence of what he called a Presiding Mind in the fact that new species appeared to have been introduced whenever and wherever a receptive environment had materialised (Bailey, 1962, p. 93; Yeo, 1986). And in Darwin's silences there are deep ambiguities. His public utterances concealed a complex amalgam of theistic and agnostic beliefs, which fluctuated from the conviction that the universe as a whole could not be the product of chance to the seriously agnostic view that he had no grounds on which to trust such convictions (Brooke, 1985; Burch Brown, 1986; Kohn, 1989). The latter position was deeply secular but a conviction that the world could not have arisen through chance did not have to be.

Displacement

A fifth mode might be called secularization through the displacement of religious belief rather than through its erosion. It is frequently assumed in historical writing and is attractive as a model because it may capture critical shifts in the lives of individuals. Think of Darwin spell-bound in the rain forests of South America, already losing his intention to become a clergyman. The aesthetic sensibilities that had been associated with his nominal Christianity were translated into a response to the sublime. His language was assuredly that of a surrogate religion: 'Twiners entwining twiners, tresses like hair – beautiful lepidoptera – Silence – hosannah' (Desmond and Moore, 1991, p. 122). But we are, I think, still left with a paradox when using the term secularization in such a manner. If by secularization we mean the displacement of one form of spirituality, or one form of religion, by another, can the alternative religion ever not be a religion? And when is an anti-religion not a religion? Do we have the criteria to answer such questions? Another problem is that the word secularization, if used in this way, can conceal the extent to which the alternative spirituality may still be dependent on that which it ostensibly displaces. As his aesthetic sensibilities atrophied later in life, Darwin made the striking admission that his former perception of beauty in nature had undoubtedly been connected with a belief in God (Darwin, 1958, p. 92).

Self-destruction

For my last mode of secularization I turn to that respect in which religions may self-destruct or at least lose their credibility through internecine wrangling. In his famous essay on atheism, Francis Bacon warned that the greatest danger to religion came not from the sciences but from religion itself. Later in the seventeenth century Robert Boyle was disturbed by a proliferation of competing puritan sects: 'Let a man come to London', he wrote, 'and he shall come near to losing his faith' (Rattansi, 1972, p. 21). For Boyle the study of nature was an invincible way of restoring belief in a Christian God. And it is precisely because so much faith was placed in the ability of the sciences to fulfil that role that there was later so much heartache when they could no longer oblige. In histories of religious thought it is not at all unusual to find natural theology presented as a vehicle of secularization. In the work of Michael Buckley it is even made responsible for the origins of modern atheism as it invited its own refutation (Buckley, 1987). There certainly were many respects in which it dug its own grave. One of these concerns the fragmentation that took place in nineteenth England before Darwin. If, however, the word secularization is used to describe the self-destructive aspect of natural theologies, it is difficult to avoid a sense of paradox, and perhaps for two reasons. It seems paradoxical that strategies designed to *defend* the rationality of faith should be seen as intrinsically secular. And it could also be argued that religious concerns retain a higher profile when internecine debates continue to sustain them. In his study of *Religion and Society in Industrial England* Alan Gilbert concluded that the long association of political issues with Church-Chapel confrontation had the effect of 'delaying for more than half a century the most obvious manifestations of secularization' (Gilbert, 1976, p. 205). From this perspective the continuation of religious controversy, rather than the attainment of consensus, can be seen as militating against rather than contributing to a secular society.

This last paradox leads me to my final question: how fragmented was natural theology in the decades before Darwin? Did the world-view of Paley constitute a common context until Darwin showed how nature could counterfeit design? I have argued elsewhere that we must take seriously the diversification and resilience of natural theology in the period both before and after Darwin (Brooke, 1991 and 1994). This complicates the picture yet again, because in the process of diversification it is possible to see both the sacred in the secular and the secular in the sacred.

The Fragmentation of Natural Theology

My argument here is that during the first half of the nineteenth century there was already sufficient fragmentation within the discourse of natural theology to prevent it from fulfilling the cohesive religious functions which its advocates tacitly claimed for it. In this last section, I shall rehearse some considerations that support such a conclusion.

The critical response to works of natural theology was often deeply divided. A prime example would be the response to the anonymous *Vestiges of the Natural History of Creation* (1844) authored by the Edinburgh publisher Robert Chambers. Chambers' account of a law of development in the organic kingdom was dressed in the rhetoric of natural theology, but this did not prevent its denunciation as a work of base materialism. It was so described by that doughty champion of natural theology Adam Sedgwick. In his private correspondence, Chambers more or less admitted that his theistic vocabulary had been used to sugar the pill: 'I am happy to say that I have been able at the end to introduce some views about religion which will help greatly, I think, to keep the book on tolerable terms with the public, without compromising any important doctrine' (Secord, 1989, pp. 171–2). The problem was that, by the 1840s, it was possible to detect such a ruse. In his review of Vestiges for *The Guardian*, R.W. Church issued a warning: 'The *Vestiges* warns us, if proof were required, of the vanity of those boasts which great men used to make, that science naturally led on to religion' (Yule, 1976, pp. 266–8). There had been many such boasts by men of science without dissimulation, but Church's High Church admonition highlights a deep ambiguity in much of the natural theology literature. That which at first sight looks like a defence of religious orthodoxy can also be read as an apologia for science. The most recent research on the *Bridgewater Treatises*, written in the 1830s, suggests they were generally valued more as works of scientific popularization than as a unified set of theological essays (Topham, 1992 and 1998).

Another respect in which arguments for design in nature were too weak to provide a consensus arises from the fact they could be associated both with the defence of Christian orthodoxies and the defence of deistic alternatives. This may help to explain why they survived for so long, in that one could make the right noises without having to commit oneself to too much doctrinally (Brooke, 1997). But the design argument had been used by Voltaire as well as Newton, by Paine as well as Paley, by Joseph Priestley as well as the orthodox priesthood. In his brilliant work on the politics of evolution, Adrian Desmond has associated natural theology with the custodians of Oxbridge privilege (Desmond, 1989). Certainly it was attacked by medical reformers and other radicals whom he identifies. But, as Jonathan Topham has recently observed, it was perfectly possible for political agitators to subscribe to a natural theology of their own. The trick was simply to contend that the *status quo* in the structure of society was a distortion of the natural. Natural theologies could be used to legitimate reform as well as defend conservative social structures. Depending on their formulation they could still be politically divisive (Topham, 1993, pp. 205–46).

For another sense of fragmentation we might look to the remarkable diversification of natural theology in the middle decades of the nineteenth century. There was such a rich repertoire of arguments to sustain the move from nature to nature's God that they could be developed in different and competing directions. Paley's argument had been premised on analogies between anatomical and mechanical structures; but he had allowed for a different kind of argument in which the *laws* of nature were instruments of the deity. In the *Bridgewater Treatise* of William Whewell, it was the felicitous combinations of these laws that were indicative of a Creator. As Jonathan Smith shows us in the previous chapter, there was a third genre of natural theology in which typological readings of nature were associated with redemptive themes. For Philip Gosse, the beauty and harmony of the rock pool were symbols of that 'new earth' that would accompany Christ's triumphal return. Yet another form of natural theology was developed in the English speaking world to remedy one of the defects of Paley's argument. The key to understanding anatomical structures, according to Paley, was their function, for which they had been purposefully designed. The elaborate structure of the human eye was the perfect exemplar. But it soon transpired that an alternative key was necessary – one that could take care of the fact that not every structure had a function and that there were structural resemblances between the vertebrates. Indeed, the idea of a unity of skeletal structure was advanced in France as a direct alternative to the teleology of Georges Cuvier. To remove the sting from this subversive anatomy, Richard Owen constructed a quite different argument for design based on the notion of an archetypal structure – an idea in the mind of a deity who had subsequently supervised its various instantiations (Desmond, 1989, pp. 335–72; Rupke, 1994). Yet another form of natural theology was that developed by Hugh Miller, whose vision of earth history was far removed from that of Paley. Not only did Miller champion the idea of progressive creation, he also developed arguments grounded in aesthetics to present the human being as a co-worker with the deity in the improvement of nature (Miller, 1869). Given this range of resources for the construction of a natural theology, it should not be surprising that internecine competition and fragmentation would occur.

The competition is clearly visible in a debate that occurred in the mid-1850s, still some years before Darwin published. The antagonists were eminent men of science who had crossed swords before. One was William Whewell, now Master of Trinity College Cambridge; the other David Brewster, student of optics, biographer of Newton, and a pugnacious Scot. They had fallen out in the 1830s over the aims of the newly founded British Association for the Advancement of Science. Brewster looked to government for the sponsorship of scientific research; Whewell could think of nothing worse than being tied to government patronage. One would finish up advising on fisheries instead of analysing the tides. They had fallen out again when Whewell had published his *Bridgewater Treatise* (1833). Indeed Brewster's review already shows a splitting of the seams in the articulation of natural theology. Whewell was happy to invoke theoretical terms such as the aether to celebrate the foresight of the Creator. But this was anathema to Brewster, who did not even accept a wave theory of light. The Scotsman did have a point: to erect a natural theology on the shifting sands of scientific theory might prove a short-sighted strategy. They had fallen out again when Whewell published his *History of the Inductive Sciences* (1837). It was a history in which Brewster could not find his name. In his review he had accused Whewell of neglecting Scotsmen altogether. 'He even says I hate Scotch women', Whewell observed in exasperation (Brooke, 1977, p. 244).

Now in the 1850s they were falling out on that aetherial but perennial subject of extra-terrestrial life. Brewster was for it; Whewell against. It was a tricky topic because there could be theological arguments on both sides. Whewell appears to have been worried that the doctrine of Incarnation would be compromised if there were intelligent life elsewhere in the universe (Crowe, 1986, 265–99). Brewster, in contrast, could not tolerate the wastage in nature if the countless myriads of stars did not shine on other worlds. Both were vehement defenders of natural theology but their debate shows how easily it could disintegrate as a house divided against itself. Whereas Brewster admitted no waste in the economy of creation, Whewell displayed many features of creation destitute of purpose. For Whewell the very notion of a plurality of worlds glossed over the strongest argument for the craftsmanship of a deity – the well-nigh perfect adaptation of terrestrial life to terrestrial conditions. Brewster looked to the resourcefulness of a Creator who might match intelligent life to any conditions. For Whewell a plurality of worlds was dangerous to Christianity, not only because of the issues of Incarnation and Atonement, but also because the idea could nurture a subversive belief (discernible in Chambers's *Vestiges*) that life might naturally evolve where propitious conditions existed. From Brewster's angle, to maintain our solitude in the universe was tantamount to admitting that the appearance of life on earth was a lucky fluke.

In the 1850s both Brewster and Whewell still required a divine initiative to account for the appearance of intelligent life, but it is striking how desolate Whewell's universe had become. Emptying the heavens of life, he left his readers with the image of an abortive nature. He would refer to the asteroids as the remains of a planet that had failed in the making. Scattered through the universe were many *sketches* of design. The universe itself was 'so full of such rudiments of things, that they far outnumber the things which outgrow their rudiments' (Whewell, 1854, p. 331). This desolate view of things was published six years before Darwin's *Origin* and by an Anglican clergyman. It might be said that from Whewell's perspective, Brewster had secularized Christianity; and from Brewster's that Whewell had secularized the universe. But how paradoxical it would be to use such language when both believed they were defending the same true faith.

Chapter Sixteen

Contextualising the 'War' between Science and Religion

Gowan Dawson

In the preface to the published version of his Presidential Address to the British Association at Belfast, brought out with unusual haste by a publisher with an eye to the main chance in September 1874, John Tyndall (1874) observes 'I have been, and continue to be, the object' of 'numberless strictures and accusations, some of them exceeding fierce'. His radical assertion that the potential for life is inherent in matter and does not require a distinct creative act, he concedes, 'has provoked an unexpected amount of criticism' (p. v).[1] Tyndall's materialism, as Ruth Barton (1987) and Stephen S. Kim (1996) have both pointed out, was carefully qualified by his insistence that all phenomena have their roots in a vaguely understood cosmic life. The concession that materialism is a limited philosophy, however, took up only a small portion of the Address, and was virtually ignored by Tyndall's clerical antagonists. A torrent of devout indignation erupted in August and continued throughout the latter part of 1874. Tyndall, as Frank M. Turner (1981) has noted, 'had succeeded in sparking perhaps the most intense debate of the Victorian conflict of science and religion. It aroused far more controversy than the Huxley-Wilberforce encounter' (p. 170). In the following years, moreover, Tyndall's position continued to be assailed by orthodox critics. Throughout the 1870s his 'materialist' manifesto provided a convenient focus for religious opposition to the more radical conclusions of modern science.

The virulent censure of the Belfast Address engendered a febrile atmosphere of conservative outrage which engulfed other 'advanced' and secular writers. In February 1873 the publication of Walter Pater's *Studies in the History of the Renaissance* had elicited the disapprobation of both reactionary critics and Anglican theologians. It is significant to note, however, that much of the most explicitly hostile criticism of Pater's book was made between 1874 and 1877 rather than immediately after its publication.[2] While the clamour over the book's perceived hedonism was at first largely confined to the academic enclaves of Oxford, the eruption of a rhetoric of clerical indignation in the following year produced a context in which the aesthetic philosophy advocated by Pater became a matter of much wider concern. Much recent scholarly work on the reception of *Studies* (Dellamora, 1990; Dowling, 1994) has construed the orthodox opprobrium which it provoked as part of a primarily homosexual scandal. The critical response to *Studies*, as well as Pater's subsequent institutional marginalisation, have been attributed to the entrenched homophobia of the Oxford establishment. I will propose, however, that the crisis of scientific materialism in the summer of 1874 underwrites much of the overtly hostile response which Pater's volume received both from the pulpit and in the periodical press.

Science and aestheticism might seem an odd pairing considering the latter's assertion of art's autonomy from extra-aesthetic concerns. The early 1870s, however, mark a particular point of crisis in the social shift from a largely clerical to a secular and scientific cultural elite mapped out in the work of historians such as T.W. Heyck (1982) and A.J. Engel (1983). Factors such as the extension of the franchise to rate-payers in the large industrial cities in 1867 and the removal of religious tests for university degrees in 1871, as well an economic downturn and the shift in the European balance of power from France to Germany, undermined the relative stability which had prevailed at mid-century. In this transitional period divergent discourses collided and interpenetrated as 'advanced' attitudes in both science and art were contested by an increasingly imperilled orthodoxy.

My argument is that theological hostility to the re-emergence of a pre-Christian understanding of the natural world conjoined the conventionally disparate discourses of science and aestheticism. Many of the advances made by science in the nineteenth century had been underwritten by the ancient doctrine of atomism, which implicitly disavowed the idea of Providence operating in nature. Religious antagonists indicted the exponents of this godless Classical *physics* with at the same time reviving an immoral pagan *ethics*. Over the previous two millennia Christian doctrines had provided a metaphysical criterion for morality. Without this, it was now warned, civic society would collapse under the burden of man's unfettered natural selfishness. This pessimistic understanding of morality, furthermore, had definite ideological implications. As L.S. Jacyna (1981) has pointed out,

> dualism and the insistence upon the control of spirit over matter sustained both a philosophy of social relations and a more specific political message. The former comprised an insistence upon the necessity of authority in society. Men could not order themselves; they needed a higher power to do so. Secondly, an *ecclesiastical* authority was seen as an indispensable part of that power. Both these propositions were, in a sense, 'conservative'. (p. 123)

In the absence of this conservative ecclesiastical authority, humanity would cast off all restraint and descend once more into the debauched sensualism of the pagan world. Tyndall's belligerently anti-clerical Address was censured for advocating the disreputable atheistic hedonism of the Greek philosopher Epicurus. Significantly, Pater was at the same time similarly rebuked for urging that maximising the intensity of experience was the only valid aspiration of this brief existence. While Pater's affinity with Epicurean hedonism has been widely recognised, the insinuations of pagan sensualism levelled at Tyndall's Address are less well-known. The ostensibly separate discourses of science and aestheticism nevertheless overlap in the theological censure of the revival of pagan belief systems.

In the first part of the Belfast Address, Tyndall maps out a highly tendentious version of intellectual history from Democritus to contemporary thinkers such as Herbert Spencer. Commencing in fifth-century BC Athens, he asserts 'The principles enunciated by Democritus reveal his uncompromising antagonism to those who deduced the phenomena of nature from the caprices of the gods' (p. 4). In Ancient

Greece, Tyndall maintains, 'free-thinking and courageous men' (p. 2) who had encountered Eastern thought became dissatisfied with the 'anthropomorphic form' (p. 1) of current ideas concerning the universe, and began 'to place natural phenomena on a basis more congruent with themselves' (p. 2). In 'the depths of history' (p. 2) Tyndall discerns the beginnings of a rigorously materialist explanation of the natural world which eschews any form of supernatural intervention.

Democritus, as well as Epicurus and the Roman poet Lucretius, are identified as the chief exponents of this materialist epistemology in the Classical world. They developed an 'atomic philosophy' (p. 4) which asserts that atoms in empty space, combining in accordance with mechanical laws, are the materials from which all things are constructed. Both organic and inorganic bodies are compounds of these everlasting atoms which continually disperse and enter into new combinations. Epicurus considered that this philosophy, which teaches that 'Nature pursues her course in accordance with everlasting laws, the gods never interfering', could 'free the world from superstition and the fear of death' (p. 6). These three thinkers established a scientific agenda which expunged the primitive idea of capricious divinities operating in the natural world for several centuries.

Tyndall explicitly connects these ancient doctrines with the most advanced conclusions of nineteenth-century science. Democritus's propositions, he writes, 'are a fair general statement of the atomic philosophy, as *now held*' (p. 4; my emphasis). Likewise, Tyndall equates Empedocles's suggestion that combinations of atoms which are suited to their environment adhere for longer than unsuited compounds with Spencer's philosophy of evolution: 'more than 2,000 years ago the doctrine of the "survival of the fittest", which in our day, not on the basis of vague conjecture, but of positive knowledge, has been raised to such extraordinary significance, had received at all events partial enunciation' (p. 5). In his Address Tyndall uses this historical connection to identify Victorian scientists not as radical innovators but rather as part of a lengthy tradition of materialist thought which pre-dates the Christian beliefs of his orthodox antagonists.

In the second part of his Address, Tyndall switches his attention to modern science. It is Pierre Gassendi's restoration of the atomic philosophy in the seventeenth century, he maintains, which has underwritten the nineteenth-century regeneration of scientific materialism. He asserts 'In our day there are secessions from the theory, but it still stands firm ... In fact, it may be doubted whether, wanting this fundamental conception, a theory of the material universe is capable of scientific statement' (pp. 26–7). What Tyndall styles the 'grand generalizations' of 'our day' (p. 45) are really experimentally verified developments of the old atomic philosophy. The immense advances of modern science which Tyndall imperiously maps out have their origin in a philosophy of matter which is over two thousand years old.

The general periodical press afforded a textual site for much of the devout censure of Tyndall's advocacy of the pagan exponents of atomism. While the response of liberal publications was at best equivocal, the conservative press instigated a furious denunciation of Tyndall and his scientific conclusions. Scientific materialism was assailed for heralding the failed theories of an archaic past as the very latest manifestations of intellectual progress. Atomism had been discarded amidst the decay of the Roman Empire, and would not now satisfy the vastly more complex intellectual requirements of the late nineteenth century. For religious commentators, the resemblance between aspects of Classical and modern philosophy merely undermined the intellectual pretensions of contemporary thought. As Turner (1973) has pointed out, orthodox censure of the scientific revival of an ancient understanding of the natural world had several polemical advantages. He writes

> The scientific publicists would lose the benefit of novelty. Their modernity would stand discredited. Liberal Christians might conceivably appear more intellectually advanced than men of science ... the defenders of religion would achieve a new, much needed self-assurance and self-confidence from knowledge that they opposed a philosophy that Christianity had overcome in the past and by implication could overcome again. (p. 333)

Many contributors to the periodical press made use of Tyndall's insistence on the pagan origins of present-day materialism to denigrate the intellectual authority of modern science.

The devout censure of the scientific revival of Classical materialism also had a further polemical advantage which Turner's account overlooks. The Victorian exponents of this ancient understanding of the natural world could be portrayed as implicitly advocating the immoral sensualism which had precipitated the downfall of pagan antiquity. Tyndall's advocacy of Epicurean *physics* could be equated with the disreputable hedonist *ethics* long ascribed to that school. Henry Reeve (1875), editor of the *Edinburgh Review*, dismisses contemporary thought as merely a return to the conjectures of 'the pre-Socratic age' (p. 4); Tyndall's recent valorisation of Classical materialism represents merely a highly visible instance of this peculiar intellectual anachronism. At the same time, Reeve also conjoins this apotheosis of the ancient doctrine of atomism with the notorious hedonist ethics of the Epicurean school. He writes 'Are we to return to Paganism or something behind Paganism – to the flux of Heraclitus, the *noûs* of Anaxagoras, or the atoms of Democritus – are we to take our morals from Epicurus and our gods from Lucretius?' (p. 3). What Reeve terms the 'Lucretian doctrines of Professor Tyndall' (p. 2) can lead only to a bestial emphasis on earthly pleasure. Scientific materialism will uproot the true morality which Christianity has bestowed upon the world, and cast humanity once more into the sordid pit of pagan depravity.

Tyndall's antagonistic Address had been delivered in a hotbed of Calvinist orthodoxy. The pulpits of downtown Belfast now reverberated with sermons imprecating his materialist conclusions. Many made the same damaging connection between the Epicurean atomism heralded as the basis of modern science and the infamous doctrine of sensualism long ascribed to that school. Whereas Tyndall extols the rejection of the primitive notion of an anthropomorphic deity operating in the natural world as evidence of human progress, Calvinist theologians, with their emphasis on the Fallen condition of man, contended that it would leave him bereft of any sense of morality. Without a metaphysical criterion for morality, it was warned, civic society would soon collapse under the intolerable burden of man's unconstrained sinfulness.

Robert Watts, Professor of systematic theology at Belfast Presbyterian College, makes an explicit connection between Tyndall and Epicurus. In a sermon preached to a huge congregation at Fisherwick Place Church, he contends 'Epicureanism, as interpreted and expounded by the poet Lucretius, constitutes the warp and the woof of Professor Tyndall's philosophy. His mission, like that of Epicurus, is to rid the world of the gods. Epicurus aimed at the extirpation of the gods of Greece; Dr. Tyndall aims at the extirpation of the Jehovah of the Bible' (Watts, 1874, p. 20). Watts goes on, furthermore, to argue that Tyndall's apotheosis of a pre-Christian conception of the universe must inevitably entail the revival of the debauched ethics of the pagan world. He declares

> The very name of Epicure has become a synonym for sensualist. The system has wrought the ruin of the communities and individuals who have acted out its principles in the past; and if the people of Belfast substitute it for the holy religion of the Son of God, and practice its degrading dogmas, the moral destiny of the metropolis of Ulster may be easily forecast. (p. 21)

Watts emerged as Belfast's principal defender of orthodox Calvinism. He challenged both Tyndall and T.H. Huxley to confront him in a local public debate, and took their subsequent refusals as a tacit admission of defeat.

Expatriate members of the Irish Presbyterian Church were similarly implicated in the controversy. James McCosh (1875), who had left Ulster in 1868 to become President of Princeton College, penned a response to Tyndall's materialist manifesto after having 'procured a copy' when 'about to set sail from Great Britain last autumn, on my return to America' (p. iii). Akin to Watts, he likewise identifies nineteenth-century materialism with the disreputable ethics of the pagan world. McCosh implies that the irreligious hedonism which precipitated the decline of the Roman Empire, may re-emerge to similar effect in the nineteenth century under the guise of modern science. He writes

> We can believe with Montesquieu that the Epicurean philosophy exercised an influence in deteriorating the character of the Romans, in hastening their ripeness into rottenness, and determining their fall; we can understand this when we look into these fragments of obscene Epicurean verses which have come out of the fires of Pompeii to testify against the inhabitants. We confess that we have fears of the results when the new physics come to crystallize into the creed of the rising generation, and to lead the literature and inspire the prevailing sentiment of the age. (p. 12)

McCosh's rebuttal of the Belfast Address aligns the earnest professionalising science propounded by Tyndall and Huxley with the obscene poetry and illustrations of Classical antiquity. The moral corruption of first-century Rome, according to this analysis, provides a cautionary warning of the inevitable consequences of the unbelief predicated by present-day materialism.

These denunciations of Tyndall's scientific creed can be located in a long tradition of Christian hostility towards Epicureanism, which dates back as far as the last centuries of the Roman Empire. In the closing years of the pagan world the Epicurean conception of an empirically explainable natural world unaffected by impassive gods had been a rival epistemology to the emergent Christian doctrine of a divinely ordained universe. In particular, the Epicurean repudiation of any form of resurrection was wholly antagonistic to the emphasis of the early Church on the promise of an eternal hereafter. Paradoxically, the Victorian conflict between science and religion, which, as Turner (1978) has argued, was largely a contest between theological and scientific publicists over which group of intellectuals should steer the increasingly urbanised and industrial nation through the vicissitudes of modernity, was fought out in precisely the same terms as this archaic conflict.

Several religious commentators invoked a specifically Pauline rhetoric in their rebuttal of Tyndall's implicit Epicureanism. In his first epistle to the Corinthians, Saint Paul avows, that lacking firm belief in the Resurrection, men will inevitably revert to the licentious pagan axiom: 'let us eat and drink; for to morrow we die' (I Corinthians xv:32; the expression is also found in Isaiah xxii:13). Many religious writers specifically ascribed this hedonist slogan to Victorian scientific materialism. In a sermon preached in the parish church of Wellington in Somerset, Edwin Marriner appropriates this Pauline rhetoric to refute Tyndall's negation of the doctrine of personal immortality. He exhorts his auditors to eschew such insidious unbelief

> if there is no Hereafter, no reunion of soul and body at the Resurrection Day, then, of what use are gifts, attainments, memories, studies, if they are all to be, as if they had never been, in a few short years? Why, then, we had better enjoy ourselves as mere animals, to the fullest possible extent, saying with the worn-out voluptuary, "Vanity of Vanities!" .... "Let us eat and drink, for to morrow we die!". (Marriner, 1874, p. 16)

Like the fractious Corinthians in the first century, the parishioners of Wellington are admonished against embracing a debauched pagan belief system which denies the promise of an eternal hereafter.

It was not merely in Anglican sermons that this Pauline rhetoric was ascribed to Tyndall's materialist creed. The pessimistic conjecture that without a metaphysical criterion for morality civic society would inevitably collapse under the burden of man's unfettered natural selfishness was propounded in a variety of textual sites. An unsigned 'Epistle in Verse' by James Casey also imputes pagan depravity to modern science. Casey's (1875) doggerel asserts

> *...the folly and pride of those arrogant men*
> *Would fain make the world turn pagan again;*
> *Would unchain every vice, every passion release,*
> *And drive from the world all order and peace ...* (p. 6)

The poem goes on, moreover, to invoke precisely the same Pauline rhetoric as Marriner's sermon. It maintains

> *If you preach to mankind there's no heaven nor hell,*
> *Will they cease to do evil or care to do well?*
> *And will they not rather repeat the old cry,*
> *"Eat, drink, and be merry, to-morrow we die"?*
> *Does not reason then tell us how sad is the fate*
> *Of those who seek wisdom from Tyndall the great?* (pp. 13–14)

Casey's barbed couplets lampoon Tyndall's scientific creed from an eminently orthodox theological perspective endorsed in several Anglican sermons. Many of the varied criticisms of scientific materialism similarly equated Tyndall's valorisation of Classical *physics* in the first part of the Belfast Address – in particular his advocacy of the Greek philosopher Epicurus – with the depraved hedonist *ethics* long ascribed by religious commentators to the pagan world. This alignment of Tyndall with an infamous doctrine of atheistic sensualism, I want to argue, directly connects the scandal of scientific materialism in the early 1870s with the contemporaneous outcry over the perceived hedonism of Pater's first book.

Studies in the History of the Renaissance, a collection of eight essays, five of which had previously been printed in the *Westminster Review* and the *Fortnightly Review*, was published in February 1873 by Macmillan & Co. Much of the material in Pater's book was significantly informed by the intellectual context of the radical/liberal periodicals where it had initially appeared alongside the work of conspicuous agnostics and evolutionary naturalists such as John Stuart Mill, Herbert Spencer, George Henry Lewes, Huxley and Tyndall. Most significantly, the 'Conclusion' to the book, which had first been published in the *Westminster* as the concluding section of an unsigned review of William Morris's poetry, apotheosised aesthetic hedonism as the most astute response to the version of human existence predicated by recent scientific discoveries. In it Pater (1873) famously asserts

> A counted number of pulses only is given to us of a variegated, dramatic life. How may we see in them all that is to be seen in them by the finest senses? How can we pass most swiftly from point to point, and be present always at the focus where the greatest number of vital forces unite in their purest energy? To burn always with this hard gem-like flame, to maintain this ecstasy, is success in life. Failure is to form habits ... (pp. 210–1)[3]

He goes on

> ... we are all condamnés, as Victor Hugo says: les hommes sont tous condamnés a morte avec des sursis indéfinis: we have an interval, and then our place knows us no more. Some spend this interval in listlessness, some in high passions, the wisest in art and song. For our one chance is in expanding that interval, in getting as many pulsations as possible into the given time. (p. 212)

While this had been admissible within the pages of the radical and anonymous *Westminster*, when it appeared in a book which both named Pater and identified him as a 'Fellow of Brasenose College, Oxford', the 'Conclusion' at once transgressed the borders of late-Victorian respectability.

In both ancient universities *Studies* was widely connected with the discourses of materialism and pagan hedonism. On successive Sundays between 27 April and 11 May 1873, the University Preacher at Cambridge, Frederick William Farrar, delivered three sermons to undergraduates at St. Mary's Church, in which he lamented the advent of modern secularism, and alluded more than once to Pater's recently published book. In the first sermon, Farrar (1874) warns that 'the icy wind of atheism, stealing through our literature with almost inarticulate whisper, is chilling the hearts of many' (p. 10), and making young men oblivious to the divine ordinances of God. It is primarily the recent advances in materialist science which he sees at the root of 'the ever-widening scepticism of this generation' (p. 23). Science, Farrar maintains, cannot affirm the idealist *Truth* which underwrites morality in the Christian tradition. He observes if life be but a semblance and death but an extinction, and if, amid an infinitude of Time peopled by myriads of existences, and an infinitude of Space teeming with innumerable worlds, man be an atom tossed out of nothingness and destined to become but dust 'blown about the desert or sealed within the iron hills'; – if this be so, – oh, dreary dreary gospel of a darkness taking itself for exceptional enlightenment! – if God be nothing, and Man be nothing, what then is Virtue, and what is Truth? (pp. 11–12)

This modern negation of Christian morality, moreover, closely parallels the insidious pagan ethics advanced by Epicurus. Farrar declaims

If we sin, what does it matter to blind infinite Forces which may crush us, but cannot love? If we repent, what will the Æons and the Spaces care for our repentance? Are we any better than what the Greek atheist said we were, 'dumb animals, driven through the midnight upon a rudderless vessel, over a stormy sea'? 'Let us eat and drink, for to-morrow we die'. (p. 12)

Farrar's Pauline rhetoric imputes an Epicurean hedonism to scientific mappings of the material universe and the forsaken position of man within its infinite expanse.

Significantly, Farrar's next paragraph implicitly connects Pater with scientific materialism as well as the corrupt pagan ethics ascribed to Epicurus. He admonishes his undergraduate auditors

And though these opinions, and such as these, have for the young all the *'fascination of corruption'*, – though they have all that destroying and agonising beauty which the great painter infused into the horror of the Gorgon's countenance, on which men must gaze though it turned them into stone, – yet God forbid that there should be many of you, my younger hearers, who should have subtly slidden into such treacherous unbeliefs. (p. 13; my emphasis)

This passage, in which Farrar exhorts his youthful audience to eschew the siren voices of modern unbelief, contains an unattributed quotation from Pater's November 1869 essay now reprinted as 'Lionardo Da Vinci'. Apropos of Leonardo's painting *Medusa* (now attributed to an unknown painter of the Flemish School), Pater (1873) remarks 'What may be called the *fascination of corruption* penetrates in every touch its exquisitely finished beauty' (p. 98; my emphasis). In Farrar's sermon this Paterian trope figures as an image of the insidious allure which unbelief and atheistic hedonism hold for the young. Likewise, the picture which Pater is discussing provides Farrar with an apposite metaphor for the moral petrifaction of undergraduates seduced by the scepticism of contemporary science. This implicit allusion to a passage recently reprinted in *Studies* connects the book at once with the dubious discourses of scientific materialism and Epicurean hedonism. Akin to Tyndall's materialism, furthermore, Pater's progressive aestheticism is tainted by its association with the disreputable Epicurean shibboleth 'Let us eat and drink, for to-morrow we die'.[4]

After August 1874, however, the controversy in the ancient universities over Pater's godless advocacy of aesthetic hedonism became part of a wider cultural scandal in which scientific materialism was vehemently denounced for further undermining the moral foundations of a society already fissured by the shift from a largely clerical culture to a socially nebulous urban industrialism. As Brian Wynne

(1979) observes, 'A sense of general social crisis was expressed which was attributed to the debilitating consequences of industrialism and its materialist credo ... society ... was seen as falling apart under the atomistic nihilism of the scientific naturalists' (p. 174). From the beginning, orthodox critics had located elements of scientific materialism and atheistic hedonism in Pater's book, but in the indignant outcry over Tyndall's Address which erupted in the following year these issues took on a new importance which persisted throughout the rest of the decade. In this febrile atmosphere of clerical outrage, Pater's aestheticism was transformed from a primarily pedagogical concern of the ancient universities, to a matter of urgent public solicitude. Mrs. Humphry Ward (1885), soon herself to become the subject of ecclesiastical censure, recalls that at this time *Studies* was 'the object of many denunciations, and, like some heretical treatise of the second or third century, received definite episcopal reprimand' (p. 132). Significantly, this reprimand was made only a few months after Tyndall's highly visible assertion of the antagonism of modern science towards the clerical establishment.

In his Episcopal Charge to the clergy of the diocese in April 1875, John Fielder Mackarness, the Bishop of Oxford, berated Pater's 'Conclusion' as the primary manifestation of an insidious unbelief then sweeping through the university. Mackarness (1875) concedes that 'unbelief has gained for the time a victory, by which Church and Chapel alike are sufferers, and souls are lost to Christ' (p. 13). The materialist creed preached with such proselytising vehemence in London and the large industrial cities has provoked unrest among the agricultural population and gained adherents even among Fellows of the university. The ethical consequences implicit in contemporary unbelief, Mackarness alleges, are foregrounded in the Paterian imperative to maximise the intensity of our brief existence. He asserts

> Learners in the school of unbelief have been taught that it is folly to disturb themselves for the sake of others: they have lost all motive for serious action: self-restraint and self-sacrifice are discovered to be 'mere moral babble'; it is, at the best, an amiable weakness to do good. Human life is but the interval, longer or shorter, which condemned mortals have to pass before they die. 'Our one chance', it is said, 'is in expanding that interval, in getting as many pulsations as possible into the given time ... Not the fruit of experience, but experience itself is the end ...' (pp. 15–16)

Mackarness does not name the author of this hedonist injunction, but he makes it clear that Pater's audacious avowal of his unbelief will undermine the already frail morality of weak-minded undergraduates, as well as damaging the religious reputation of the university. While his Charge does not make the prevalent connection between nineteenth-century sceptical unbelief and licentious pagan ethics, Mackarness nonetheless discerns the same 'correspondence between our modern infidelity and modern degeneracy of character' (p. 17) which had alarmed Tyndall's initial antagonists. Aesthetic hedonism, like scientific materialism, will undermine the moral foundations of civic society.

This connection between aestheticism and science was made even more explicit in the general periodical press. For example, in an article on 'Hellenic and Christian Views of Beauty', published in the March 1880 number of the *Contemporary Review*, the Reverend Richard St. John Tyrwhitt laments the prevalence of unbelief in the nineteenth century, which has corrupted the spiritual source of true beauty. The decadent immorality of recent literature and art, he contends, merely reflects the intellectual dominance of irreligious modern scientific thought. Aestheticism, moreover, has become fatally intertwined with the doctrines of science. Tyrwhitt (1880) proclaims 'Science, culture, and æsthetics, or their best advertised professors, are at present united by a joint cupidity, founded on a common atheism; or, let us say, agnosticism; or use any other unmeaning term which the Decadence may demand' (p. 481). The materialist epistemology of modern science sanctions the immorality of aestheticism, but without a moral dimension there can be no true beauty. Tyrwhitt asserts

> The appeal so eagerly made by artistic immoralists to science, begging her, on the ground of a common atheism, to *come down and deliver them from virtue*, can never lead to a stable alliance. Science may be godless if men will have it so, and scientific men may be immoral, though we do not know any who are at all that way; but mere denial and plain wickedness will not produce any beauty, or disprove the fact that the traditions of art were preserved by religious persons. (p. 482; my emphasis)

Significantly, this passage implicitly invokes the lascivious debauchery of the pagan world. In it Tyrwhitt paraphrases a line from Algernon Charles Swinburne's notorious poem 'Dolores'. In this sexually explicit hymn to a sadomasochistic pagan goddess of lust and cruelty, an inhabitant of early Christian Rome implores 'Come down and redeem us from virtue,/Our Lady of Pain' (Swinburne, 1904, p. 163). In Tyrwhitt's rendering of the line irreligious science assumes the role of Swinburne's libidinous pagan deity. It underwrites the 'highly undesirable insurrection against decency' (p. 480) which Tyrwhitt perceives in recent art. The disparate discourses of science and aestheticism can be seen to continue to intersect in this orthodox hostility towards paganism which persisted in the periodical press throughout the 1870s and beyond.

Tyndall and Pater published remarkably similar responses to the imputations of pagan hedonism made against them in the 1870s. In his Presidential Address to the Birmingham and Midland Institute in October 1877, Tyndall insists that many secular thinkers uphold a strong sense of personal morality. He declares 'there are amongst us many whom the gladiators of the pulpit would call "atheists" and "materialists", whose lives, nevertheless, as tested by any accessible standard of morality, would contrast more than favourably with the lives of those who seek to stamp them with this offensive brand' (Tyndall, 1877, p. 614) Tyndall also responds *directly* to the imputations of hedonism: '"Let us eat and drink, for to-morrow we die" is by no means the ethical consequence of a rejection of dogma' (p. 613).

Pater likewise disputes the aptness of Saint Paul's exhortation against licentious hedonism for nineteenth-century unbelief. In his 1885 novel *Marius the Epicurean* he contends

> *Let us eat and drink, for to-morrow we die!* – is a proposal, the real import of which differs immensely, according to the natural taste, and the acquired judgement, of the guests who sit at the table. It may express nothing better than the instinct of Dante's Ciacco, the accomplished glutton in the mud of the *Inferno*; or, since on no hypothesis does man 'live by bread alone', may come to be identical with – 'My meat is to do what

is just and kind'; while the soul which can make no sincere claim to have apprehended anything beyond the veil of immediate experience, yet never loses a sense of happiness in conforming to the highest moral idea it can clearly define for itself; and actually, though but with so faint hope, does the 'Father's business'. (p. 83)

Pater endeavours to demonstrate that the refined aesthetic hedonism eulogised in his first book might in some perspectives be interchangeable with more orthodox ethical positions. The Epicurean creed, he affirms, might even become synonymous with Christian doctrine.[5] In response to the devout outcry of the early 1870s, Tyndall and Pater similarly contest the pessimistic theological assumption that without a metaphysical criterion for morality civic society will ultimately give way under the unrestrained selfishness which is man's original condition.

Although there has been a trend in the historiography of Victorian science to emphasise accommodation between science and religion rather than conflict (Moore, 1979), more recent scholarly work which recognises the ideological and professional aspects of scientific thought has begun to eschew this exclusively harmonious view. In his recent biography of T.H. Huxley, for example, Adrian Desmond (1994) contends 'Not only is the "warfare" image hackneyed; so is the reaction to it – the demilitarized history born in the 1970s which smoothes over the Victorian conflict. The point is not to deny the struggle, any more than to refight the good fight' (p. xv).[6] Desmond proposes that historians should instead endeavour to 'understand the social currents' (p. xv) which underwrite the conflict. My interdisciplinary study of the connection between aesthetic writing and contemporary science, I want to suggest, can contribute significantly to this essentially historiographical project. While the nineteenth-century conflict between religion and science has traditionally been conceived within a relatively narrow disciplinary framework, it can be mapped onto wider areas of late-Victorian culture, revealing the outlines of a more general discord than has previously been recognised. In this broader, interdisciplinary framework, what have previously seemed to be purely literary disputes, such as the clerical indignation provoked by aestheticism in the 1870s, can be viewed as part of a wider antagonism between science and religion in this period. It is important to recognise, however, that in this paper I delineate merely one of the many contexts of the broad material culture in which the ideological and professional conflict of science *contra* faith needs to be embedded by scholars working across a broad variety of disciplines.

Acknowledgements

This paper has benefited greatly from suggestions and comments made by those who heard previous versions at the conference on Nineteenth-Century Religion at the University of Lancaster in July 1997, and at a research seminar in the History and Philosophy of Science Division at the University of Leeds in November 1997. I am particularly grateful for the assistance given to me by Sally Shuttleworth and Geoffrey Cantor.

Notes

1. The controversy compelled Tyndall to retract some of his more incendiary rhetoric. In the published version of the Address he excised many controversial sections, and the language of his claim for the potency of life in matter, as well as the concluding sentences which refute the doctrine of personal immortality, was considerably toned down.
2. Ian Small also makes this point. In his Introduction to *Marius the Epicurean*, he writes of Pater's earlier volume 'The reaction to the book in the mid-1870s was in fact stronger than at the moment of its publication', but he attributes this to 'personal ... disagreements being disguised as academic ones' (Pater, 1986, p. xiii).
3. The 'Conclusion' was dropped from the second edition in May 1877, and altered when it was restored to the January 1888 third edition.
4. This was not, however, the first time that Pater's position had been associated with this hedonist slogan. S. R. Brooke, an undergraduate at Corpus Christi College, Oxford, and a member of the 'Old Mortality' Society, recorded in his diary for 20 February 1864 that Pater's paper to the Society on 'Self-Culture' presented a view of life even more debased than that of the Epicurean school. He asserts 'To sit in one's study all [day] and contemplate the beautiful is not a useful even if it is an agreeable occupation; but if it were both useful and agreeable, it would hardly be worth while to spend so much trouble upon what may at any rate be wrested from you. If a future existence is to be disbelieved the motto "Let us eat and drink for tomorrow we die" is infinitely preferable' (Seiler, 1987, p. 12).
5. Pater here perhaps takes his lead from John Stuart Mill. In his 1861 book *Utilitarianism* Mill defends the nobility of Epicureanism, which he views as a precursor of the ethics of utility. He writes 'there is no known Epicurean theory of life which does not assign to the pleasures of the intellect, of the feelings and imagination, and of the moral sentiments, a much higher value as pleasures than to those of mere sensation' (Mill, 1985, p. 258). Like Pater, Mill goes on to equate utilitarianism with Christian doctrine: 'In the golden rule of Jesus of Nazareth, we read the complete spirit of the ethics of utility. To do as you would be done by, and to love your neighbour as yourself, constitutes the ideal perfection of utilitarian morality' (p. 268). Mill's influence on Pater has been discussed by Timothy Weiss (1987).
6. Kim (1996) likewise observes 'in Tyndall's theater, the war was real. In the thick of the war between the orthodox clergymen and the enterprising young scientists in late Victorian England, the life and work of John Tyndall stands out as a witness to the reality, and indeed the seriousness, of the war ... Tyndall's war was indeed not against faith, but rather against religious dogmatism of some ecclesiastics and inveigled scientists who wished to repress the rise of scientific naturalism' (pp. 24–5).

Chapter Seventeen

Philip Gosse and the Varieties of Natural Theology

Jonathan Smith

With the publication of *Father and Son* in 1907, Edmund Gosse made his father, Philip Henry Gosse, an exemplar of the wrong-headed Victorian Protestant fundamentalism that futilely resisted the advancing tide of scientific naturalism epitomized by Darwin's theory of natural selection. The book's opening sentence declared it to be the record of a struggle between 'two epochs' (Gosse, 1965, p. 5); the 'great moment in the history of thought' (p. 75) that divided them was the two-year period culminating in the publication of the *Origin of Species* in 1859. Although 'every instinct' in his father's intelligence 'went out at first to greet the new light', Edmund lamented that 'a recollection of the opening chapter of Genesis checked it at the outset' (pp. 76–7).

While this reading of Gosse's intellectual life contains elements of truth, it seriously oversimplifies, as Frederic Ross (1977) has shown, both Gosse's science and his reaction to Darwin.[1] Nonetheless, Edmund's account, as evidenced by its longstanding inclusion in a section on evolution in the second volume of *The Norton Anthology of English Literature*, remains influential within nineteenth-century literary studies and continues to provide a convenient example of the hostility between Darwinism and religion. The work of historians of science and religion on nineteenth-century natural theology, however, enables us to characterize Gosse's scientific publications more precisely. Gosse's natural theology differed in important respects from that contained in the works, both specialist and popular, of his contemporaries. Acutely aware of the limitations and even dangers of the most common versions of natural theology, Gosse turned more insistently to typological readings of nature. In keeping with his insistence on revealed religion and his fascination with Biblical prophecy, Gosse found in the marine life of England's southwestern coast glimpses of the 'new earth' of Christ's triumphal reign. By examining Gosse's incorporation of Darwin into his books of the 1850s, 1860s, and 1870s, we can chart both Gosse's changing attitude to Darwin and his attempts to appropriate Darwin's work into his own distinctive natural theology.

As an accomplished draftsman and lithographer, Gosse depended as much on his detailed and vibrantly colored illustrations as on his texts to communicate his views. These colorful illustrations, which helped fuel a vogue for seashore excursions and drawing-room aquariums, served as visual representations of both traditional natural theological readings of nature and his own typological ones. Yet if we look not simply for what Martin Rudwick (1992) calls the 'symbiosis' of pictorial representation and textual explanation (p. 231), but for the fractures and gaps between them, we can also see exposed some of the tensions and contradictions – personal, professional, and cultural – embedded in Gosse's work and especially in his efforts to combat Darwinism.

Gosse was already a respected naturalist who had published in both the popular and scientific presses when he joined the Plymouth Brethren in 1847. This group, which stood aloof from both the Anglican Establishment and Dissenting churches, believed in the inerrancy of Scripture, rejected ritual and hierarchy, encouraged public testimonials of faith as a tool for proselytization, and scrutinized Biblical prophecy for guidance on the conduct of believers in what they believed were the rapidly-approaching final days of divine judgment and the subsequent return of Christ (Callahan, 1996; Coad, 1968). While living in London, Gosse preached extempore sermons to a congregation at Hackney; moving to Marychurch, just outside of Torquay, in 1857, he quickly became the main preacher and administrator of the small community of Brethren there.

Even before his move to Devonshire, Gosse had made the study of the marine life of England's southwestern coast his specialty. More important, he was among the independent developers and most prominent popularizers of the salt-water aquarium. During the 1850s and 1860s a flood of books, many of them beautifully illustrated, issued from his pen. These books extolled both the aesthetic pleasure and the scientific and religious knowledge to be gained from the observation of coastal marine life. But they also served as practical manuals on how to collect specimens, how to construct an aquarium, and how to conduct observations, including microscopical ones. *A Naturalist's Rambles on the Devonshire Coast* (1853), *The Aquarium* (1856a), *Tenby: A Sea-Side Holiday* (1856b), *Evenings at the Microscope* (1859) and *A Year at the Shore* (1873) all combined personal narrative with scientific description and practical advice. *A Manual of Marine Zoology* (1855–6) and Gosse's scientific magnum opus, *Actinologia Britannica: A History of the British Sea-Anemones and Corals* (1860a), were designed as reference works for both beginners and advanced zoologists.

The popularity of Gosse's books spurred holiday travel to Devonshire, fueled an aquarium craze that in turn created a network of related businesses, and made marine biology a 'rational recreation' for middle-class visitors to the shore (Allen, 1994; Bailey, 1978; Rehbock, 1980; Travis, 1993). Indeed, Gosse's works must be seen within this social context of seaside life, for it is there that his science and religious views merge. In his history of the Devon resorts, John Travis notes that in the first half of the nineteenth century such resorts had become associated with the idleness and frivolous pleasure-seeking of the watering-places like Bath after which they were modeled. As the development of the railroads made the Devon resorts more accessible to middle-class visitors, the demand for rational recreations in this culturally underdeveloped region increased. Gosse's books were thus an effort to 'testify', to provide idle hands with something intellectually and morally uplifting to do. 'Few, very few', wrote Gosse in *A Naturalist's Rambles*, 'are at all aware of the many stirring, beautiful, or wondrous objects that are to be found by searching on those shores that every season are crowded by idle pleasure-seekers' (1853, p. v). Yet Gosse believed that such searching would lead the pleasure-seeker to God, for the careful study of the habits and anatomy of 'even the lowest forms of animal being' brings us 'to say with the Psalmist, "I will praise Thee; for all is fearfully and wonderfully made"' (p. 54). And as Gosse contends in *The Aquarium*, such careful study, whether in the field, in the aquarium, or through a microscope, 'will not fail to reward us with increased knowledge of His works and ways' (1856b, p. 38).

In their studies of popular Victorian natural history writing, Lynn Merrill (1989) and Lynn Barber (1980) have presented Gosse as an important but typical exponent of British natural theology. Certainly Gosse is not reluctant to echo Paley's emphasis on the skillfully designed anatomical 'contrivances' of his specimens, and like the authors of the Bridgewater Treatises he frequently praises the evidence of Divine power, wisdom, and goodness.[2] '[T]he contrivances of [marine creatures'] organization', he writes in *A Naturalist's Rambles*, 'are the fruit of his infinite Wisdom' and thus elicit 'adoring wonder and praise' (1853, p. 20). *Evenings at the Microscope* is especially fulsome in its praise of Paley's watchmaker-God, whose 'wondrous skill' and 'Divine mechanics' are evident in the 'perfect adaptation of organ to function, of structure to habit' that marks all His works (1859, pp. 46, 248). This is equally true of the gorgeous coloration of these marine creatures, whose beauty, Gosse believed, has been provided by the Creator for our pleasure and delight. Their 'exquisite tints' are 'the pencillings of his almighty Hand' (1853, p. 20); to admire them represents not prurient ogling but 'the gratification of our sense of beauty', which has been 'implanted in our nature by the beneficent Creator, expressly for our satisfaction' (p. 354).

But the natural theology in Gosse's books was nonetheless rather different from that in most works of popular natural history. Despite the popularity of Paley's arguments, the fear existed, as Fyfe (1997) has shown, that natural theology could lead unwittingly to deism or provide fodder for materialists. While both Paley and the Bridgewater authors were careful to stress natural theology's limitations and its inferiority to revealed religion, such qualifications could be obscured in works that did not repeatedly connect the evidence of nature to that of Scripture.[3] As a result, Gosse often offered frank and forceful critiques of natural theology. In a chapter on 'The Right Use of Natural History' in *The Aquarium*, he acknowledges that 'some of the attributes of the Creator ... may be deduced from his works', but he goes on to insist that 'a man may be a most learned and complete expounder of natural theology, and yet be pitiably blind on the all-important subject of a sinner's justification with God' (1856a, pp. 199–200). In a fallen universe, nature is not divine, and natural theology cannot possibly teach us the path to salvation. After Darwin's publication of the *Origin*, Gosse was even more emphatic. He closed *A Year at the Shore*, which he announced was 'the last occasion of my coming in literary guise before the public' (1873, p. 327), with an attack on the natural theology of popular scientific writing. While decrying the open assaults on religion in many scientific works, Gosse argued that most popular natural theology was 'equally dangerous and more insidious' for ignoring 'the awful truths of God's revelation' (p. 325). Natural theology, he wrote, is valuable to someone who is already a Christian, but 'to attempt to scale heaven with the ladder of natural history, is nothing else than Cain's religion; it is the presentation of the fruit of the earth, instead of the blood of the Lamb' (p. 326). To avoid this pitfall, Gosse articulated a natural theology in which nature, if read correctly, pointed beyond a kindly Creator to the promises and prophecies of the Christian revelation.

In carrying out this program, Gosse confirmed what John Brooke (1977, 1979, 1991) has emphasized, that natural theology is better understood in terms of natural theologies, with different versions reflecting various religious cultures. In Gosse's case, his natural theology was shaped by the beliefs and exegetical practices of evangelicalism and of the Plymouth Brethren in particular. Central to Gosse's approach was his application of typological interpretation to the natural world (on typology in Victorian culture, see Landow (1980)). Since the Scriptures frequently employ natural objects as symbols or types of truths that might be rejected if articulated directly, we are free, Gosse argues, to utilize the same process with the actual objects of nature (1956a, p. 206). If we do so, 'the world of created things around us may become a mirror continually reflecting heavenly things' – not merely the attributes of the Creator, but 'the God of revelation, the God of Grace, the God and Father of our Lord Jesus Christ' (p. 208). According to Gosse, we must study nature and the Bible with great care and in great detail, for both teach salvation through faith, and both speak to what will occur in the final days.

Examples of such readings of nature appear throughout Gosse's books but are most prominent, prior to *A Year at the Shore*, in *A Naturalist's Rambles* and *The Aquarium*. A seaweed that is dull when removed from the water but brilliant when re-submerged 'may be compared to some Christians, who are dull and profitless in prosperity, but whose graces shine out gloriously when they are plunged into the deep floods of affliction' (1956a, p. 93). The mode of eating of the broad-claw crab, whose hairy claws sweep food to its mouth, reminds Gosse of 'the Gospel net, mentioned by our Lord', which is itself used as an image both of the church and of the subsequent separation of nominal from true believers (p. 43). But the most common and most extensively developed typological interpretations of nature emerge from Gosse's discussions of coastal rock pools.

The extraordinary concentration of marine life in these pools made them the focus of Gosse's field observations and the textual and visual centerpieces of his books. His narratives frequently move from one pool to another, his illustrations frequently attempt to represent species in this natural environment, and his descriptions frequently end with a typological reading of their significance. Gosse recurrently figures the pools as gardens that can either be 'harvested' of their specimens or metaphorically strolled through for the pleasure they afford. Edenic allusions abound, but the pools are a prelapsarian Eden. In *Tenby*, anemones hang from the walls of one pool 'like some ripe pulpy fruit, tempting the eye and the mouth' (1956b, p. 23). In *A Naturalist's Rambles*, Gosse drops to his knees at the side of a rock pool at Oddicombe, bringing his face close to the surface of the water in a position that recalls Milton's Eve. But instead of gazing at his own reflection, or even of seeing through a glass, darkly, Gosse asserts that when the naturalist who worships God peers through the surface, 'the whole interior' of the pool becomes 'distinctly visible' (1853, p. 55).

Indeed, Gosse is himself a sort of Adam rather than an Eve, for the glories of the future are revealed to him in these unfallen nooks of Creation. The pools look forward as well as backward in time, providing a glimpse of the coming reign of Christ on earth and of the heavenly Jerusalem. In *A Naturalist's Rambles*, Gosse describes the amount and variety of marine life contained on a small piece of stone chiseled from the side of a rock pool. What strikes him most, however, is the 'vast amount of happiness we here get ... a glimpse of!' (1853, p. 207). Not one of these tiny creatures, Gosse claims, is lacking in health or food, and hence each is experiencing, relative to its capacities, full and continuous pleasure. Although Adam's sin is borne by the whole creation, 'yet we may suppose that at least the invertebrate portions of the animal creation suffer their share of the fall rather corporately than individually, rather nominally, in dignity, than consciously, in pain or want' (p. 208). This fairly typical Paleyan optimism regarding the distribution of pleasure and pain in nature is couched in characteristically Gossean terms. The rock pools are as close as we can come to a vision of the utter profusion and perfect happiness in nature prior to the fall. As a result, they also suggest what nature will be like when Christ returns and establishes, with his saints, his reign on earth, when 'creation shall be more than reinstated in primal honour' and 'even these low-born atoms ... shall ... get an augmentation of happiness, and thus take their humble share in the blessing of the redeemed inheritance' (p. 355). The Christian naturalist thus has a right and a responsibility to study the rock pools and their inhabitants as 'a part of his own inheritance', as the 'estate' that will 'in due time be his own possession' (p. 355). The pleasure we take in the rock pools, which seem to be almost immune from the consequences of the fall, is a type of the pleasure we shall some day take in all of nature.

In *The Aquarium*, Gosse extended this view in a precise typological reading of corralines as the heavenly Jerusalem. 'It is not too much to presume', he suggests, 'that the order and fashion of material things' were 'expressly planned' to reflect 'ideas of heavenly and unseen things'. Coral, Gosse argues, as 'a City ... of myriad individuals' sharing 'a common life', reflects that heavenly City where 'happy spirits in resurrection bodies' collectively form 'an individual being': 'the Church of the living God, the Bride of Christ' (1956a, pp. 117–19). Such an extraordinary reading, fully in keeping with Gosse's eschatologically-concerned evangelical theology, is very different from the natural theology commonly deployed in similar books, where 'the order and fashion of material things' would have been taken merely as a sign of the wisdom and beneficence of the Almighty Architect.

It is in this light that we must approach Gosse's illustrations. Gosse's books were insistently visual, copiously illustrated from *A Naturalist's Rambles* on. To insure the accuracy of colors, Gosse, starting with *The Aquarium*, produced not only the original drawings but also the lithographic 'pattern' plates. In his biography of his father, Edmund Gosse recalled that the plates of sea anemones in *A Naturalist's Rambles* were such a 'revelation' that 'several of the reviewers refused altogether to believe in them', and that the even more spectacular illustrations in *The Aquarium* 'made a positive sensation, and marked an epoch in the annals of English book illustration' (1890, p. 340; see Figure 17.1). Moreover, the illustrations were intimately connected to the visuality of the text, the culmination of a series of scopic acts. First, the collecting narratives invited the reader to see vicariously the contents of each rock pool, jetty crevice, or marine cavern. Then these specimens were brought home for observation in one of Gosse's aquariums and/or through a microscope. Finally, Gosse's illustrations generally attempted to represent the specimen as it appeared in its natural environment.

The mediating function of the aquarium in this process cannot be underestimated. As Martin Rudwick (1992) has noted in his study of nineteenth-century pictorial

Figure 17.1   Philip Henry Gosse, Plate V from *The Aquarium*, 2nd edition (London: Van Voorst, 1856). Courtesy of University of Michigan Libraries.

representations of the prehistoric world, until the development of the aquarium made the aquarium-view part of Victorian culture's iconography, scientists were reluctant to depict underwater scenes for fear of being labeled fanciful or speculative (pp. 98, 179–80, 233). By describing his specimens as seen both in nature and in the aquarium, Gosse made the latter a stand-in for the former. His illustrations, although based on aquarium and even microscopical observations, thus could be used to represent 'natural' scenes. And by providing his readers with extensive instructions on building and maintaining an aquarium, obtaining specimens, and conducting experiments and observations, Gosse made it possible for them to replicate these visual acts and to connect this artificial, domesticated environment with its wild counterpart.

The representations of coastal marine life in Gosse's books were thus designed to illustrate both the Paleyan vision of organisms designed for their environments and Gosse's own typological readings. The first step in this process was to stress that his drawings illustrated *living* creatures. As Edmund later noted, his father had long complained that natural history had become 'a science of dead things', a study not of living organisms in their natural environments but of dried, stuffed, preserved – and consequently deformed and distorted – specimens (1890, p. 228). Clearly the existence of a living God, actively caring for his creation and leaving signs of its fate, could be better seen in living creatures, and the aquarium made that possible. But the interests of Paleyan natural theology were served in Gosse's illustrations primarily by aesthetic beauty. To see creatures 'in their proper haunts' was to see them 'with their beauty of form and brilliance of colour' (1856a, p. vii) – and to know how beneficent God had been in providing us with such pleasure even among the lowest creatures in the most unlikely places. The emphasis on the Creator's wisdom and goodness in designing species with anatomical contrivances relevant to their particular environmental niches, on the other hand – something frequently demonstrated through dissection – tended to be confined by Gosse to his textual descriptions of microscopical investigations. Although Gosse's depiction of representatives of a variety of species in some 'proper haunt' implicitly reinforced the connection between species and environment, this was not his focus – and could not be, given his view of the limitations of most forms of natural theology.

As with his texts, Gosse's illustrations ultimately elevate his own typological readings of nature over Paleyan ones. As Frank Turner (1993) has emphasized, British natural theology in both the eighteenth and nineteenth centuries was closely tied to utilitarian readings of nature, the existence of suffering and death in the natural economy minimized or justified by an appeal to some larger (and often unknown) Divine purpose. This 'commercial social vision' implicit in natural theology, Turner argues, contributed to the very secularization of nature that so offended its supporters. Gosse, whose son later characterized the Plymouth Brethren as pursuing a 'Utopian dream of a Christian socialism' (1890, p. 213), seems to have sensed this. As we have seen, Gosse, too, saw nature as full of joy and happiness, but a happiness almost unlimited and universal, untainted by competition or suffering. In Gosse's typological readings of the rock pools, the focus is not on the relationship between individual and environment but on the relationship among individuals in an environment. His illustrations captured this by presenting a sort of aquatic peaceable kingdom, with different species coexisting in a benign setting, each with adequate resources. The rock pools are pictured as having the same qualities as the unfallen Garden of Eden and the redeemed nature that Gosse's texts claim they represent. It is the visual glimpse of the 'inheritance', the 'estate', that awaits the true believer and will be shared in common with all other believers.

Gosse's millennial vision faced a special challenge after Darwin published the *Origin*, however, for Gosse had played an important role in disseminating Darwin's research on barnacles to a popular audience. Darwin's work was published by the Ray Society in a specialized two-part monograph in 1851 and 1854, and Gosse moved quickly to incorporate it into his own books. In the first part of his *Manual of Marine Zoology* (1855–6), Gosse calls Darwin the 'paramount authority' (p. 170) on barnacles. In *Tenby*, Darwin's monograph is a 'monument of research and acumen' whose most startling discovery – that the water flea and acorn barnacle are not separate species but two stages in the life of the same species – Gosse has 'the pleasure of confirming' (1856b, p. 118). He even provides a Paleyan gloss on the phenomenon, declaring that this 'wonderful process' of metamorphosis is obviously 'ordained' by 'the wisdom of God' (p. 120).

With the appearance of the *Origin*, Gosse apparently realized that in putting Darwin's barnacles to work in support of the argument from design, he had made himself as vulnerable as the popular expositions of natural theology he despised.[4] Barnacle metamorphosis could be just as easily ascribed to natural selection as to the wisdom of God, so Gosse sought to neutralize the danger. In *A Year at the Shore*, Gosse damns Darwin with the faintly praising epithet of 'a perfectly dependable naturalist' (1873, p. 145) and is content merely to describe his researches – celebrations of Darwin's achievement and the Creator's wisdom vanish. At the same time, Gosse turned increasingly to Darwin's *Beagle* narrative for evidence that he either incorporated into anti-evolutionary arguments or employed in his own typological readings of nature. The Darwin of the South American rain forests or South Pacific islands is used to demonstrate that the rock pools of the English coast are not the only sites that testify to the Christian's inheritance. In *The Romance of Natural History*, Gosse quotes one of Darwin's descriptions of Tahiti but then follows it with a vision of the earth after Christ's return:

> I have delighted to believe, that, ... when, in the millennial kingdom of Jesus, and, still more, in the remoter future, ... the earth – the 'new earth', – shall be endowed with a more than paradisiacal glory, there will be given to redeemed man a greatly increased power and capacity for drinking in and enjoying the augmented loveliness. (1861, p. 343)

Tahiti may seem a paradise to Darwin, but for Gosse it, too, is best interpreted typologically as a sign of the 'more than paradisiacal glory' of the redeemed earth.

Gosse's drawings show him making a similar visual move, but the comparison of drawings and text often exposes the tenuousness of his representations. Despite his insistence that the aquarium permits us 'to bring a portion of the sea ... to the side of our study-table' (1873, pp. 62–3), Gosse drew individual organisms in isolation, often under a microscope, and almost invariably without the slightest hint of surroundings. He did not, in other words, draw aquarium scenes. Rather, as Edmund pointed out in his father's *Life*, he constructed them:

in late years he was accustomed to make a kind of patchwork quilt of each full-page illustration, collecting as many individual forms as he wished to present, each separately coloured and cut out, and then gummed into its place on the general plate, upon which a background ... was then washed in. (1890, p. 341)

An examination of Gosse's (1839–61) drawings at the Horniman Museum in London not only confirms this, but also suggests that this method was used as early as *A Naturalist's Rambles* and began to become common in *Actinologia Britannica*, which originally appeared in parts in 1858–9 and thus bracketed the announcement of Darwin's theory.

The timing of this shift in Gosse's illustrative methods is surely not completely accidental. In her study of nineteenth-century American zoological illustration, Ann Shelby Blum (1993) has argued that financial considerations encouraged the use of composite plates full of different species, which in turn codified comparative methods in zoology to such an extent that the evolutionary debates had virtually no effect on illustration conventions (pp. 122, 142, 236–7). Her account, however, tends to treat taxonomic methods as atheoretical and to underestimate the degree to which existing conventions could be modified or exploited for theoretical purposes. Certainly Gosse's 'patchwork' approach had technical advantages and was governed in part by material constraints, but it also fitted nicely with his parallel shift in textual emphasis to a natural theology heavily informed by typological readings of nature. He could remove specimens from their various natural settings, mix them together in his aquarium, draw them in isolation, and then re-assemble the individual drawings into a scene presented as a single location in nature where these various specimens lived in harmonious profusion in the peaceable kingdom that prefigured the world of the second coming.

As Christopher Hamlin (1986) has noted in his study of the aquarian Robert Warington, however, this harmonious profusion was in practice notoriously difficult to establish and maintain. An imbalance of plants and animals, the mixing of predators and prey, fluctuations in light or temperature – any of these could turn an aquarium into a site of death and destruction. As a result, most aquarium writers initially reflected a tension between what Hamlin calls 'the harmonious aquarium' and 'the evangelical aquarium', with the former increasingly de-emphasized in favor of the latter. From replicating in miniature 'the Creator's wisdom and goodness in establishing a beautiful, bountiful, healthful, and self-sustaining world' (pp. 134–5), the aquarium became 'a stage for endless moral dramas' (p. 147) involving individual creatures, a place for observing moral conditions, drawing moral lessons, and imposing moral improvements on the inhabitants. Gosse, while exemplifying this tension in his earliest books, resolved it in a somewhat different way. He retained a vision of the 'harmonious aquarium', but it symbolized the Creation's past and future states as much as mirroring its present one. And that vision was most easily depicted in his illustrations.

Gosse's visual natural theology, and the problems associated with it, can be exemplified by two plates from *A Year at the Shore*. In the first, Gosse's plate (1873, plate III; see Figure 17.2) contains a species of sea cucumber with a dotted siponocle. Although the original drawing of the sea cucumber at the Horniman (1839–61, 69+; see Figure 17.3) contains no background, the later plate conveys a sense of the

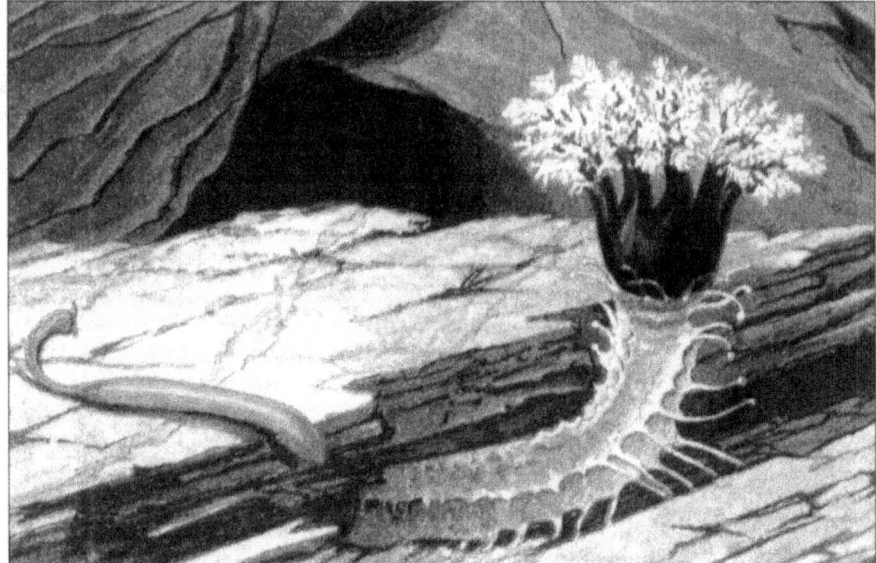

Figure 17.2 Philip Henry Gosse, Plate II from *A Year at the Shore* (London: Isbister, 1873).

location from which Gosse's text says he obtained it. The dotted siponocle, however, is very different in appearance from the sea cucumber and is not mentioned as having been present in the same environment. Its presence in the plate can nonetheless be accounted for by Gosse's explanation that siponocles are the species that connect sea cucumbers with worms, despite their very different appearance from both. The plate is thus the visual rendering of what he calls in *Actinologia Britannica* 'radiations of relation' (1860a, p. 39), the matrix of complex affinities within and among species. It provides the visual depiction of the fecundity of the Creator's world, of the related but distinct forms that fill every niche of the natural economy. But it does so only by creating an illusion: the juxtaposition, though presented as existing in nature, is not confirmed by Gosse's narrative. And in its attempt to stand as a silent alternative to Darwinian accounts of species relation, it seems almost to invite the Darwinian explanation that these 'radiations of relation' are the result of natural selection operating over time on a common ancestor.

In the second plate, Gosse (1873, plate IX) depicts the green opelet and the orange-disk anemone in a scene suggestive of the isolated 'rocky channels' that his text gushes over for the beauty and profusion of their inhabitants (1873, p. 78). Yet Gosse's narrative reveals that he obtained the green opelet not in the rocky channels but in a heap of seaweed dredged up in open water a half-hour's row away. As with the first plate, Gosse's cut-and-paste patchwork is used to support his reading of nature, but Gosse's text also potentially undermines the visual statement of his plates – and thus of the typological readings based on them – by revealing that they are not 'natural', and in some senses not even accurate, at all. And with the Darwinian view of nature making the peaceable kingdom look increasingly violent

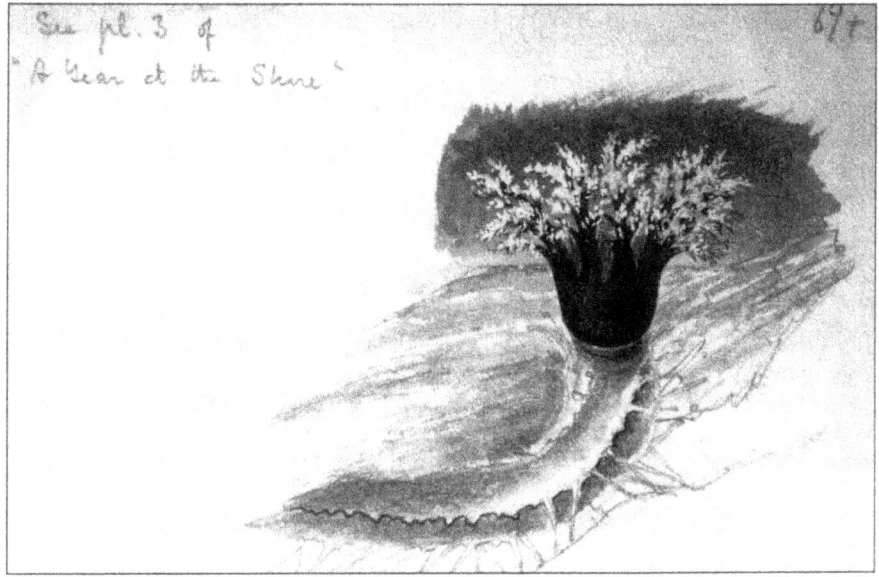

Figure 17.3 Philip Henry Gosse, *British Sea-Anemones and Corals: Original Sketches and Drawings*, item 69+. Courtesy of the Horniman Museum, London.

and competitive, Gosse's 'patchwork' plates came to seem increasingly forced both to the public and to Gosse himself. Edmund asserts that the plates of *A Year at the Shore* 'were a source of acute disappointment' to his father, that while the 'individual forms' were produced with 'extreme accuracy', the overall 'effect' was less harmonious and provided less pleasure (1890, p. 341).

After Philip Gosse's death, his son recalled a childhood collecting expedition during which he and his father came upon a group of women similarly engaged and 'cackling joyously over a rarity they had secured'. Overcome with curiosity, Philip asked to examine their specimen and, after doing so, pronounced it a far more common species. The women, however, refused to believe him: they 'drew themselves up with dignity, and sarcastically remarked that ... it *was* the rarity, and that "Gosse is our authority"' (1890, p. 288; original emphasis). This anecdote captures the dilemma in which Philip Gosse frequently found himself, the way in which his work was used against him or led to unexpected and unwelcome consequences. He wished to defend his science on religious grounds, but to rely on natural theology was to 'ignore the awful truths of God's revelation' (1873, p. 325). Reading those truths in nature, however, put him increasingly at the margins of a modern science associated more and more with 'infidelity'. Moreover, it did not prevent, as Edmund put it, the 'perversion of his work' by others 'to support a theory inconsistent with the record of creation' (1890, p. 337), a theory that in turn exposed the constructedness of his own textual and visual images of nature. The 'rational recreation' that would teach the middle classes spiritual truths instead became a fad whose focus was merely aesthetic and whose result was the creation of a very worldly network of dealers and suppliers. In testifying to the beauty of the Devonshire rock pools, Gosse had unwittingly contributed, as he himself lamented, to the wholesale destruction of the very natural sites that stood as types of the redeemed Garden of Eden and the Heavenly Jerusalem. But if Gosse was part of an intellectual epoch whose cultural influence was receding, he nonetheless remained an authority for thousands of readers, his readings of the testimony of the rock pools widely diffused in Victorian culture.

Acknowledgments

My thanks to John Brooke for his comments and suggestions. Research for this paper was supported in part by the National Endowment for the Humanities, the Office of the Vice President for Research at the University of Michigan-Ann Arbor, and the Office of Research and Sponsored Programs at the University of Michigan-Dearborn.

Notes

1. Ann Thwaite's (1984) biography of Edmund Gosse also provides a fuller and more accurate account of Gosse's childhood relationship with his father than that offered in *Father and Son*.
2. On Paley and the influence of his natural theology in nineteenth-century Britain, see Fyfe (1997), Gillespie (1990), and LeMahieu (1976). On the natural theology of the Bridgewater Treatises, the eight books 'On the Power, Wisdom, and Goodness of God, as Manifested in the Creation' published in the 1830s as a result of a bequest by the eighth Earl of Bridgewater, see Gillispie (1959), Robson (1990), Topham (1998), and Young (1985). Formerly viewed in the aggregate as an updated version of Paley and a final assertion of the design argument before its demolition by Darwin, the Bridgewater Treatises are now regarded as providing different versions of natural theology that went beyond merely extending Paley and that continued to be influential even after 1859.
3. Gillespie (1990), LeMahieu (1976), and Robson (1990) show that neither Paley nor the Bridgewater authors elevated natural over revealed religion. Gillespie (1984) and Yeo (1986) demonstrate that fears of the misuse of natural theology were justified, arguing that natural theological positions were often easily appropriated by evolutionists; Topham (1998) charts the range of political and theological uses to which the Bridgewater Treatises were put.
4. In their discussions of Darwin and natural theology, Bowler (1977) and Ospovat (1981) argue that by the 1850s leading scientists like Richard Owen had successfully shifted attention away from the 'contrivances' arguments of Paley and the Bridgewater authors to a focus on natural laws as evidence of a superintending Divine mind. That Gosse's books do not follow this shift is no doubt attributable to both the anti-evolutionary implications of the Paleyan view and the susceptibility of natural laws to materialist rather than idealist interpretations, this latter point demonstrated by Gillespie's (1984) study of conchology before and after the *Origin*. Gosse's articulation of his own version of natural theology, rather than simply falling back on Paley and the Bridgewater Treatises, is particularly striking in this context.

Conclusion

Linda Woodhead

This volume provokes a reassessment of the familiar account of Victorian Christianity as a religion 'in crisis'. Certainly the century brought unprecedented social, political, economic and cultural change, and certainly – as many chapters highlight – Christianity was profoundly affected by such change. Yet it was not merely a passive victim of such forces, nor was its fate simply decline or decay. As many chapters in this volume show, Christianity was actively and centrally involved in many of the most important cultural shifts and debates of the nineteenth century, and was transformed and reinvented in the process.

An important aspect of the reinvention of Christianity in the Victorian era was the growth of diversity. As Christianity responded to change in different ways – provoking, resisting, embracing or selectively appropriating – so existing differences were accentuated and new ones developed. This volume highlights the three main varieties of Christianity which resulted.

First, transcendent forms of Christianity which reasserted themselves with new force during the course of the century. Fortress Catholicism furnishes the Roman Catholic example. Though it stood in some continuity with earlier forms of Catholicism, it also represented a radical departure which enabled it to survive in an era of nation-states. Its system of centralized and rationalized control enabled it to develop extremely powerful forms of socialization which embraced and held the faithful within 'mother church' from cradle to grave. Revitalized Evangelicalism also falls into this category of transcendent Christianity. Again, its roots lay in the previous century in the transformation of Protestant piety witnessed (for example) in the Methodist revival. But it was in the nineteenth-century that Evangelicalism came into its own and developed its characteristic emphases on the inner conviction born of the experience of salvation through Christ, the saving power of the cross, the authority of the Bible, and the urgency of evangelization. The vitality of transcendent forms of Protestant and Catholic religion would be demonstrated very clearly in the later nineteenth century not only 'at home' but also on the mission field.

Second, vitality was also evident in a liberal Christianity which grew in influence through the course of the century, coming to particular prominence in its closing decades. After mid-century liberal forms of Catholicism were suppressed by the highly effective tactics of a virulently anti-modernist Roman Catholic church, leaving liberal Protestantism to hold the field. Its influence was consequently greatest in countries where Protestantism was dominant, as in North America. Various chapters in the volume discuss some of the key features of such liberalism, including its shift of spiritual focus from transcendence to humanity, its optimism and its activism. They show how these values meshed with broader modern cultural trajectories and supported the interests of an increasingly confident middle class.

And they reveal how, despite intensification of labour unrest and 'the woman problem' at the end of the century, liberals continued to view themselves as the guarantors of modern civilization and progress.

Finally, the volume draws attention to the way in which alternative spiritualities were beginning to gain a hearing in the later part of the nineteenth century, not only from small numbers of committed and counter-cultural adherents, but from more mainstream culture. Spiritualism, for example, gained significant numbers of followers in the second part of the century, whilst preachers of a 'New Spirituality' like those who appeared at the World's Parliament of Religions in 1893 were also beginning to have an impact (hard though it is to measure its extent). Far from being a development wholly independent of Christianity, the volume shows how some forms of alternative spirituality developed within a Christian milieu (Swedenborgianism, Transcendentalism and literary-Romantic forms of Christian imagination, for example), whilst others – even those brought from 'the East' by men like Vivekananda, or those most hostile to Christianity (like Theosophy) – had much in common with some of the most central tenents of liberal Christianity. It is also clear that both liberal Christianity and alternative spirituality were stimulated in part by reaction against crusading forms of transcendent Christianity – and vice versa.

To highlight the vitality of these varieties of Christian and quasi-Christian religion is not to deny that they were often on the defensive. As several chapters reveal, they could be defensive about one another, and they could be defensive about many of the changes bracketed under the heading of 'modernization'. Liberals accused conservatives of being dangerously reactionary, whilst conservatives accused liberals of diluting the faith. Both attacked alternative spiritualities, which they saw as beyond the pale of true Christian belief altogether, whilst more radical advocates of a 'new reformation' criticised both liberals and conservatives for failure to meet the spiritual needs of the day. More general threats included the rise of the secular state and the appropriation of many of the churches' social, political, and economic functions; the development of an urban working class which in many places eluded the churches' control; the gradual democratization of society; calls for women's emancipation; the undermining of the authority of the Bible by historical criticism and new scientific discoveries; and the rise of a discourse of scientific materialism. Yet defensiveness led not only to crisis and decline, but also to renewed efforts of self-definition, consolidation and outreach.

In many ways this picture of a plural and often conflictual religious and cultural landscape brings the nineteenth century into closer connection with the twentieth. But there are important discontinuities as well as continuities. Perhaps the most interesting continuity concerns the dominant varieties of Christian and alternative religion, for these appear to have remained central in the religious landscape of the twentieth century. But there have also been significant changes. Liberal Christianity, for example, is no longer as confident, even in its Protestant strongholds. One reason is that its status as something of a 'civil religion' in places like North America left it vulnerable to challenges to the social and political orders which it had helped legitimate (such challenges included such diverse phenomena as the rise of fundamentalism and the counter-cultural movements of the 1960s). Similarly, reaction against some of the central elements of Victorian culture – including reliance on concepts such as progress and a universal humanity – necessarily involved a reaction to the liberalism which helped sustain them. Yet despite its defensiveness and the many criticisms it faces, one recent survey suggests that liberal Christianity remains the dominant variety of Christianity in the USA today (Ammerman, 1997a; 1997b), despite the continuing decline of mainline churches.

The process whereby those disillusioned with liberal Christianity migrated to alternative forms of spirituality in the nineteenth century appears to have continued into the twentieth and twenty-first centuries. Yet hard evidence for the growth of alternative spirituality remains hard to come by – given the non-institutional nature of such religiosity it is inevitably difficult to measure the number of those practising it. What appears to have been the case, however, is that many patterns established by the end of the nineteenth century continued into the twenty-first – including a turn to Eastern wisdom and the reception of Eastern gurus in the West, and an openness to women and the feminine. Furthermore, many of the core affirmations of alternative spirituality as these have been outlined in this volume appear to have remained steady, even whilst there have been some significant shifts away from other nineteenth-century themes. The connections between Christianity and alternative Christianity, for example, seem to have loosened somewhat. Emphasis on the importance of unifying 'East and West' has also declined (presumably in step with decolonization), whilst a growing emphasis on self-development and the techniques for accomplishing it have come to characterise much alternative spirituality, as has a more 'holistic' view of the individual as body, mind and spirit. Hand in hand with the latter development has gone a shift from concern with other worlds and cosmologies to a focus upon this world and this life – part of the 'turn to life' which is described below.

Finally, despite the predictions of secularisation theory, transcendent forms of Christianity have continued to show considerable vitality in the twentieth century. Evangelicalism in particular has grown in strength across the globe. Two more recent developments, however, are new. Both the rise of Charismatic Evangelicalism and of Protestant fundamentalism have roots in developments within late nineteenth-century Evangelicalism (such as the development of pre-millenial dispensationalism), but are distinctive of the twentieth and twenty-first centuries. Whilst Charismatic Christianity can claim to be the most rapidly growing form of Christianity since the late twentieth century, Roman Catholicism has continued to be the most numerically powerful throughout the modern period. Remarkably, the system of Fortress Catholicism was only seriously challenged in the post-war period, and its demise can be dated to the reforms of Vatican II (1962–5). Under the leadership of Pope John Paul II, however, clear attempts have been made to revive or protect aspects of the earlier fortress period – including a renewed concentration of papal power, emphasis on the importance of the family, and Marian devotions.

As well as highlighting diversity, this volume suggests a number of quite general trends in nineteenth-century Christianity. Again, some of these have appear to have a continuing influence into the twentieth century and beyond. A number seem worthy of special note:

First, privatization, domestication, feminization. Several chapters have drawn attention to the way in which social differentiation led to a focus of religious energies on the sphere of personal and intimate life. The consequence, as we have also seen, was not only that much religion increasingly became a 'private' as much as a 'public' matter, but that it was localised in the domestic sphere and in many ways became the prerogative of women. In most churches, however, institutional power continued to be in the hands of men throughout the nineteenth century – a situation which the twentieth century did little to reverse. The twentieth century also saw the more conservative or transcendent wings of both Protestant and Roman Catholic churches place a very heavy stress on the importance of 'family values'.

Second, a turn to the heart. An increasing emphasis on the importance of emotion and deeply-felt experience appears to have been a characteristic of nineteenth-century religion of all varieties – from Fortress Catholicism (in which devotion to 'the sacred heart' of Jesus intensified, for example), to Evangelical and alternative religion. The Romantic influence on this process has been noted; its relation to the domestication and feminization of religion must also be taken into account. Again, this turn appears to remain characteristic of twentieth- and twenty-first-century Christianity.

Third, detraditionalisation. Not only in liberal Christianity and alternative forms of religion, but also to some extent in Evangelicalism, a dissatisfaction with 'traditional religion' and the 'externals' of religion (institutional structures, clerical authority, dogmas and rituals) is apparent right through to the present day. The 'inner' essentials of religion, including experience, emotion and individual action gain correspondingly greater importance, whilst the 'self' becomes a key source of authority.

Fourth, a turn to 'life'. A trend which gathered pace during the twentieth century is already apparent in the nineteenth – a turn away from 'dualistic' religiosity which stresses the greater reality and importance of the 'other world' towards an understanding of religion as an enhancement of *this* world. We have seen an early appearance of this trend in the work of Romantics like Emerson; it appears to have become more widespread throughout the course of the nineteenth century and is most evident in many forms of liberal Christianity and alternative religion. Even more conservative forms of Christianity like the Catholicism of Pope John Paul II, however, demonstrate an increasing concern with matters of 'life' in the here and now – including human rights and the life of the unborn child.

Fifth, universalisation. Whilst transcendent forms of Christianity generally remain exclusivistic, it is possible to see the development of a new stress on the ultimate unity of *all* religions in many other forms of Christianity. The most tolerant forms of such universalism view all religions as equally valid paths to truth. In this they contrast with even the most extreme forms of such universalism in the nineteenth century which generally held that one particular religion (Christianity) best captures the truth. What we do not find in nineteenth-century religion then is a stress on the value of difference *per se*. The latter appears to be more distinctive of the late twentieth and twenty-first centuries – or, some would say, of 'postmodernity'.

Finally, secularisation. The influence of secularisation theory on the study of nineteenth-century religion has already been noted. The picture of Christian variety which emerges from this volume may cast doubt on more simplistic assertions about universal and inevitable secularisation in the nineteenth century, but it does not necessarily involve a total denial of the reality of secularisation. The contributions to this volume suggest not that all the hypotheses which cluster around the heading of secularisation theory should be abandoned, but that they should be articulated and investigated in a more differentiated and nuanced fashion. Monolithic theories of unilinear religious decline mask the patchiness of secularisation and obscure its many different causes. To give just one example: several chapters have shown that generalisations about the universally corrosive effects of science and 'rationalisation' are grossly misleading. On the other hand, the reality of the process of social differentiation, and its profound and often corrosive effects on Christianity has been amply illustrated.

Neither secularisation nor the other trends enumerated above should be understood as monolithic, unilinear or inexorable. Rarely do they apply to all varieties of nineteenth- century (or later) Christianity. All are decisively affected by different social, economic and political contexts. And different trends may coexist, even when they are incompatible – as do secularisation and sacralisation. The Christianity which is revealed once the veil of unilinear theorising is drawn aside appears at once more various, complex, fragmented, and interesting than has sometimes been imagined.

Notes

For analyses of women's theology in these nontraditional genres, see Melnyk (1998).

That a woman should find the opportunity for a strong public voice within a patriarchal religious tradition generally resistant to the progress of women's rights seems paradoxical, but such paradoxes abounded. Religion was for nineteenth-century women a unique area of socially-acceptable participation and even predominance. A belief in the spiritual superiority of women took root during the eighteenth century, arising first from the religious revivals of Methodism and Evangelicalism, and gained currency in the nineteenth. This presumption of female superiority meant that women found opportunities in the religious realm generally denied to them elsewhere. For more detailed discussion of this ideological shift, see Davidoff and Hall (1987, pp. 73-148); Poovey (1984, chap. 1); Krueger (1992); Valenze (1985); Melnyk (1993, chap. 2).

References

A.B. 1877: Woman's Public Work: Its Scope and Limits. *The Christian World Magazine*, 13, pp. 626–34.
Abrams, M.H. 1971: *Natural Supernaturalism: Tradition and Revolution in 'Romantic Literature'*. London: Oxford University Press.
Ahlstrom, Sydney E. 1972: *A Religious History of the American People*. New Haven and London: Yale University Press.
Albanese, C.L. 1977: *Corresponding Motion, Transcendental Religion and the New America*. Philadelphia: Temple University Press.
Allen, David Elliston 1994: *The Naturalist in Britain: A Social History*. 2d ed. Princeton: Princeton University Press.
Allen, Gay Wilson 1981: *Ralph Waldo Emerson: A Biography*. New York: Viking.
Allwood, John 1977: *The Great Exhibitions*. London: Studio Vista.
Ammerman, Nancy 1997a: *Congregation and Community*. New Brunswick, New Jersey: Rutgers University Press.
Ammerman, Nancy 1997b: Golden Rule Christianity. Lived Religion in the American Mainstream. In Donald G. Hall (ed.), *Lived Religion in America: Toward a Theory of Practice*. Princeton, NJ: Princeton University Press, pp. 196–216.
Authority 1841. *The Christian Lady's Magazine*, 16, pp. 13, 16.
Badger, Reid 1979: *The Great American Fair: The World's Colombian Exposition and American Culture*. Chicago: Nelson Hall.
Bailey, Edward 1962: *Charles Lyell*. London: Nelson.
Bailey, Peter 1978: *Leisure and Class in Victorian England: Rational Recreation and the Contest for Control*. London: Routledge.
Baker, Lee C.R. 1986: The Open Secret of *Sartor Resartus*: Carlyle's Method of Converting his Reader. *Studies in Philology* 83, pp. 281–335.
Bakhtin, Mikhail M. 1981: *The Dialogic Imagination: Four Essays*. Michael Holquist (ed.) Austin, TX: University of Texas Press.
Barber, Lynn 1980: *The Heyday of Natural History, 1820–1870*. Garden City, NY: Doubleday.
Barker, Eileen 1985: New Religions Movements: Yet Another Great Awakening? In Phillip E. Hammond (ed.): *The Sacred in a Secular Age: Towards Revision in the Scientific Study of Religion*. Berkeley: University of California Press, pp. 36–57.
Barrows, John Henry (ed.): *The World's Parliament of Religions: An Illustrated and Popular Story of the World's First Parliament of Religions, Held in Chicago in Connection with The Columbian Exposition of 1893*. 2 Vols. London: The Review of Reviews Office, 1894. 2 Vols.
Bartholomeusz, Tessa 1993: Dharmapala at Chicago: Mahayana Buddhist or Sinhala Chauvinist? In Eric J. Ziolkowski (ed.) 1993: *A Museum of Faiths. Histories and Legacies of the 1893 World's Parliament of Religions*. Atlanta, Georgia: Scholars Press, pp. 235–50.
Barton, Ruth 1987: John Tyndall, Pantheist: A Rereading of the Belfast Address. *Osiris*, 2nd Series, 3, pp. 111–34.
Baxter, Mrs. M. 1896: *His Last Word: Bible Readings in Revelation*. Second edn. London: Christian Herald.
Bell, Linda (ed.) 1983: *Visions of Women*. Clifton, NJ: Humana Press.

Bellah, Robert 1967: Civil Religion in America. *Daedalus*, Vol 96, No 1, Winter 1967, pp. 1–21.
Bellah, Robert, Madsen, Richard, Sullivan, William M., Swidler, Ann and Tipton, Steven 1985: *Habits of the Heart. Individualism and Commitment in American Life*. Berkeley, Los Angeles and London: University of California Press.
Bennett, Betty T. 1980 (ed.): *The Letters of Mary Wollstonecraft Shelley*. 2 vols. Baltimore and London: The Johns Hopkins University Press.
Bentley, James 1978: *Ritualism and Politics in Victorian Britain: The Attempt to Legislate for Belief*. Oxford: Oxford University Press.
Blakemore, Stephen 1988: *Burke and the Fall of Language: The French Revolution as Linguistic Event*. Hanover, NH: University Press of New England.
Blavatsky, H.P. 1970a: *Isis Unveiled*, 2 vols., Pasadena, California: Theosophical University Press.
Blavatsky, H.P. 1970b: *The Secret Doctrine*, 2 vols, Pasadena, California: Theosophical University Press.
Bloom, Harold. 1986: 'Introduction'. In *Thomas Carlyle*. Harold Bloom (ed.) New York: Chelsea House.
Bloomfield, Morton W. 1952: *The Seven Deadly Sins*. East Lansing: Michigan State Press.
Blum, Ann Shelby 1993: *Picturing Nature: American Nineteenth-Century Zoological Illustration*. Princeton: Princeton University Press.
Bowler, Peter J. 1977: Darwinism and the Argument from Design: Suggestions for a Reevaluation, *Journal of the History of Biology*, 10, pp. 29–43.
Braude, Ann 1989: *Radical Spirits. Spiritualism and women's rights in nineteenth-century America*. Boston: Beacon Press.
Brettell, Richard R. and Brettell, Caroline B. 1983: *Painters and Peasants in the Nineteenth Century*. Geneva: Skira.
Brooke, John 1977: Natural Theology and the Plurality of Worlds: Observations on the Brewster-Whewell Debate. *Annals of Science*, 34, pp. 221–86.
Brooke, John 1979: The Natural Theology of the Geologists: Some Theological Strata. In L. J. Jordanova and Roy S. Porter (eds) *Images of the Earth: Essays in the History of the Environmental Sciences*. Chalfont St. Giles: British Society for the History of Science, pp. 39–64.
Brooke, John 1985: The Relations between Darwin's Science and his Religion. In John Durant (ed.) *Darwinism and Divinity*. Oxford: Blackwell, pp. 40–75.
Brooke, John 1991: *Science and Religion: Some Historical Perspectives*. Cambridge: Cambridge University Press.
Brooke, John Hedley 1991a: The Fortunes and Functions of Natural Theology. In *Science and Religion: Some Historical Perspectives*. Cambridge: Cambridge University Press, pp. 192–225.
Brooke, John 1994: Between Science and Theology: The Defence of Teleology in the Interpretation of Nature, 1820–1876. *Journal for the History of Modern Theology*, 1, pp. 47–65.
Brooke, John 1996: Like Minds: The God of Hugh Miller. In Michael Shortland (ed.) *Hugh Miller and the Controversies of Victorian Science*. Oxford: Oxford University Press, pp. 171–86.
Brooke, John 1997: The Natural Theology of the Geologists: Some Theological Strata. In Ludmilla Jordanova and Roy Porter (eds.) *Images of the Earth*. Second edition, Stanford in the Vale: The British Society for the History of Science, pp. 53–74.
Brooke, John and Cantor, Geoffrey 1998: *Reconstructing Nature: The Engagement of Science and Religion*. Edinburgh: T. and T. Clark.
Brown, Earl Kent 1981: Women of the Word: Selected Leadership Roles of Women in Mr. Wesley's Methodism. In Hilah F. Thomas and Rosemary Skinner Keller (eds) *Women in New Worlds*. Nashville: Abingdon, pp. 69–87.

Brown, W. Martin 1877: *The Pathway to Rome* or, *Ritualism and its Remedy.* London.
Browne, Janet 1983: *The Secular Ark: Studies in the History of Biogeography.* New Haven: Yale University Press.
Browning, Robert 1971 [1868]: *The Ring and the Book.* Ed. Richard D. Altick. London: Penguin Books.
Buckley, Michael 1987: *At the Origins of Modern Atheism.* New Haven: Yale University Press.
Budd, Susan 1977: *Varieties of Unbelief: Atheists and Agnostics in English Society 1850–1960.* London: Heinemann.
Burch Brown, Frank 1986: The Evolution of Darwin's Theism. *Journal of the History of Biology,* 19, pp. 1–45.
Burg, David 1976: *Chicago's White City of 1893.* Lexington: University Press of Kentucky.
Burke, Kenneth. 1969: 'Carlyle on "Mystery"'. In *A Rhetoric of Motives.* Berkeley: University of California Press.
Burke, Marie Louise 1983–87: *Swami Vivekananda in America: New Discoveries.* 3rd ed. 6 volumes. Calcutta: Advaita Ashrama.
Burkhardt, Frederick *et al.* (eds) 1986: *The Correspondence of Charles Darwin,* Vol. 2. Cambridge: Cambridge University Press.
Burton, Katherine 1942: *In No Strange Land.* New York: Longmans, Green & Co.
Cahier, Charles 1874: *Nouveaux Mélanges d'Archéologie,* t. 1. Paris: Didot frères.
Callahan, James Patrick 1996: *Primitivist Piety: The Ecclesiology of the Early Plymouth Brethren.* Lanham, MD: Scarecrow.
Campbell, Bruce F. 1980: *Ancient Wisdom Revived: A History of the Theosophical Movement,* Berkeley and Los Angeles: University of California Press.
Carlyle, Thomas 1889: *The Works of Thomas Carlyle.* 30 vols. London: Chapman, Hall.
Carlyle, Thomas 1895: *Critical and Miscellaneous Essays* Volumes I-VII, London: Chapman & Hall.
Carlyle, Thomas 1896–1899: *German Romance* Vols. 21 and 22 *The Works of Thomas Carlyle* (ed.). H.D. Traill. London: Chapman & Hall.
Carlyle, Thomas 1937: *Sartor Resartus: The Life and Opinions of Herr Teufelsdröckh* (ed.) Charles Frederick Harrold. New York: The Odyssey Press.
Carlyle, Thomas 1989: *The French Revolution: A History* (eds) K.J. Fielding and David Sorensen. Oxford: Oxford University Press.
Carpenter, J. Estlin 1905: *James Martineau, Theologian and Teacher. A Study of his Life and Thought.* London: Philip Green.
Casanova, José 1994: *Public Religions in the Modern World.* Chicago and London: The University of Chicago Press.
Casey, James 1875: *Tyndall and Materialism and Gladstone and the Vatican Decrees. Two Epistles in Verse.* Dublin: James Duffy and Sons.
Caspar, Max 1959: *Kepler,* London: Abelard-Schuman.
Casteras, Susan P. 1987: *Images of Victorian Womanhood in English Art.* Cranbury, NJ: Associated University Presses.
The Catholic Encyclopedia, 11, 1911: New York: Encyclopedia Press.
Chadwick, Owen 1960: *The Mind of the Oxford Movement.* London: Adam and Charles Black.
Chadwick, Owen 1970: *The Victorian Church,* 2 Vols (Part I, 1829–1859, Part II, 1860–1901). London: Adam and Charles Black.
Chadwick, Owen 1975: *The Secularisation of the European Mind.* Cambridge: Cambridge University Press.
Charles, Mrs. [Elizabeth] Rundle 1892: *The Book of the Unveiling: Studies in the Revelation of St. John the Divine.* London: Society for Promoting Christian Knowledge.
Charlesworth, James H. (ed.) 1983: *The Old Testament Pseudepigrapha,* 2 vols, Garden City, New York: Doubleday.

Chew, Samuel 1954: Spenser's Pageant of the Seven Deadly Sins. In *Studies in Art and Literature for Bella da Costa Greene*. Princeton: Princeton University Press.
Christian Union Conference at Liverpool 1845. *The Christian Lady's Magazine*, 24, p. 400.
Clarke, Peter B. 1992: New Religious Movements. In I. Harris, S. Mews, P. Morris and J. Shepherd (eds): *Contemporary Religions. A World Guide*. Harlow: Longman.
Clarke, Peter B. 1997: Introduction: Change and Variety in New Religious Movements in Western Europe c. 1960 to the Present. In E. Arweck and P. B. Clarke (eds): *New Religious Movements in Western Europe. An Annotated Bibliography*. Westport, CT.: Greenwood Press, pp. xvii-xliii.
Coad, F. Roy 1968: *A History of the Brethren Movement*. Exeter: Paternoster.
Cobbe, Frances Power 1898 (1850): *The Practice of Confession in the Church of England*. 4th Ed. London: T. Fisher Unwin.
Colby, Robin B. 1995: *'Some Appointed Work To Do': Women and Vocation in the Fiction of Elizabeth Gaskell*. Westport, CT: Greenwood Press.
Coleridge, J.T. 1869: *A Memoir of John Keble*. 2nd ed. London.
Coleridge, S.T. 1853: Table Talk. In Prof. Shed (ed.) *The Complete Works of Samuel Taylor Coleridge*. New York: Harper.
Coombs, Jessie 1873: A Sketch of the Life and Character of Geraldine Dening. *The Christian World Magazine*, 9, pp. 283–295; 347–62.
Corsi, Pietro 1988: *Science and Religion: Baden Powell and the Anglican Debate, 1800–1860*. Cambridge: Cambridge University Press.
Cook, E. T. and Wedderburn, Alexander (eds) 1903–12: Library Edition *The Works of John Ruskin*. 39 vols. London: George Allen.
Cotsell, Michael. 1990: 'Carlyle, Travel and the Enlargements of History'. In M. Cotsell (ed.) *Creditable Warriors, Vol. 3: 1830–1876, English Literature and the Wider World*. London: The Ashfield Press.
Cranny-Francis, Anne 1995: *The Body in the Text*. Melbourne: Melbourne University Press.
Cronin, Richard 1981: *Shelley's Poetic Thoughts*. London: Macmillan.
Crowe, Charles 1967: *George Ripley: Transcendentalist and Utopian Socialist*. Athens, GA: University of Georgia Press.
Crowe, Michael 1986: *The Extra-Terrestrial Life Debate, 1750–1900*. Cambridge: Cambridge University Press.
Curran, Stuart 1975: *Shelley's Annus Mirabilis: The Maturing of an Epic Vision*. San Marino, CA: Huntington Library.
Curry, Clifford 1988: *Beyond the Rainbow: Reflections on the Spiritual Significance of Colours*. London: Seminar Books.
Curtis, Georgianna Pell (ed.) 1909: *Some Roads to Rome in America*. St. Louis: B. Herder.
Dale, Peter Allan. 1981: 'Sartor Resartus and the Inverse Sublime: The Art of Humorous Deconstruction'. In Morton W. Bloomfield (ed.) *Allegory, Myth, and Symbol*. Cambridge: Harvard University Press.
Darwin, Charles 1958: Nora Barlow (ed.) *The Autobiography of Charles Darwin*. London: Collins.
Davidoff, Leonore and Hall, Catherine 1987: *Family Fortunes: Men and Women of the English Middle Class, 1780–1850*. Chicago: University of Chicago Press.
Davies, G.C.B. 1954: *Henry Phillpotts: Bishop of Exeter, 1778–1869*. London: SPCK.
Debidour, Victor H. 1961: *Le Bestiaire sculpté du Moyen Age en France*. Paris: Arthaud.
Delavenay, Emile 1971: *D. H. Lawrence and Edward Carpenter*, London: Heinemann.
Dellamora, Richard 1990: *Masculine Desire: The Sexual Politics of Victorian Aestheticism*. Chapel Hill: University of North Carolina Press.
Delumeau, Jean 1977: *Catholicism between Luther and Voltaire: A New View of the Counter-Reformation*. London: Burns and Oates.

de Maistre, Joseph Marie 1993. *Les Soirées de Saint-Petersbourg*. 11e entretien. Jean-Louis Darcel ed. Geneva: Editions Slatkine.
Denison, Keith 1983: Dr Pusey as Confessor and Spiritiual Director. *Pusey Rediscovered*. Ed. Perry Butler. London: SPCK.
Desmond, Adrian 1989: *The Politics of Evolution*. Chicago: University of Chicago Press.
Desmond, Adrian and Moore, James 1991: *Darwin*. London: Michael Joseph.
Desmond, Adrian 1994: *Huxley: The Devil's Disciple*. London: Michael Joseph.
de Tocqueville, Alexis 1965: *Democracy in America*. London: Oxford University Press.
Dibble, Jerry A. 1978: *The Pythia's Drunken Song: Thomas Carlyle's 'Sartor Resartus' and the Style Problem in German Idealist Philosophy*. The Hague: Martinus Nijhoff.
Dobbs, Betty Jo 1991: *The Janus Faces of Genius*. Cambridge: Cambridge University Press.
Dora Greenwell 1872: *The Christian World Magazine*, 8, pp. 447–64.
Douglas, Ann 1977: *The Feminization of American Culture*. New York: Alfred A. Knopf.
Douglas, Mary 1982: The Effects of Modernization on Religious Change. *Daedalus*, issued as *Proceedings of the American Academy of Arts and Sciences*, 111 (1), pp. 1–19.
Dowling, Linda 1994: *Hellenism and Homosexuality in Victorian Oxford*. Ithaca: Cornell University Press.
Druce, G.C. 1923: An account of the Myrmeleontoidea or Ant-Lion. *The Antiquaries Journal*, III. London.
Edwards, Frederick 1829: *Inez, A Spanish Story Founded on Facts, Illustrating One of the Many Evils of Auricular Confession*. Lyme.
Eliade, Mircea et al (eds) 1987: *The Encyclopedia of Religion*. 16 vols. New York: Macmillan.
Eliot, T.S. 1934: *After Strange Gods: A Primer of Modern Heresy*, London: Faber.
Ellmann, Maud 1993: *The Hunger Artists: Starving, Writing & Imprisonment*. London: Virago.
Ellwood, Robert S. Jr 1979: *Alternative Altars: Unconventional and Esoteric Spirituality in America*. Chicago: University of Chicago Press.
Ellwood, Robert S. Jr 1994: *The Sixties Spiritual Awakening: American Religion Moving from Modern to Postmodern*. New Brunswick, New Jersey: Rutgers University Press.
Ellwood, Robert S. Jr 1997: *The Fifties Spiritual Marketplace: American Religion in a Decade of Conflict*. New Brunswick, New Jersey: Rutgers University Press.
Emerson, Ralph Waldo 1878: Woman. In *The Complete Works of Ralph Waldo Emerson*. Boston: Houghton Mifflin.
Emerson, Ralph Waldo 1975: *The Journals and Miscellaneous Notebooks of Ralph Waldo Emerson*. Cambridge, Mass; London: Belknap Press.
Emerson, Ralph Waldo 1983: *Essays and Lectures*. New York: Library of America.
Engel, A.J. 1983: *From Clergyman to Don: The Rise of the Academic Profession in Nineteenth-Century Oxford*. Oxford: Clarendon Press.
E.R.A. 1867: Words About Women's Rights. Part III. *The Christian World Magazine*, 3, pp. 149–51.
Expository Remarks on Genesis 1844. *The Christian Lady's Magazine*, 21, pp. 118–121.
Faber, Geoffrey 1933: *Oxford Apostles*. London: Faber and Faber.
Far Above Rubies 1870. *The Christian World Magazine*, 6, pp. 298–306.
Farrar, Frederick William 1874: *The Silence and the Voices of God, with Other Sermons*. London: Macmillan & Co.
Fields, Rick 1992: *How the Swans Came to the Lake. A Narrative History of Buddhism in America*. 3rd edition. Boston, Mass.: Shambahla Publications.
Findlay, L.M. 1985: 'Paul de Man, Thomas Carlyle and The Rhetoric of Temporality'. *Dalhousie Review* 65, pp. 159–81.
Findling, John E. 1994: *Chicago's Great World Fairs*. Manchester and New York: Manchester University Press.

Finke, Roger 1992: *The Churching of America, 1776–1990: Winners and Losers in our Religious Economy*. New Brunswick, NJ: Rutgers University Press.
Finley, C. Stephen 1989: Bunyan among the Victorians: Macaulay, Froude, Ruskin. *Literature and Theology*, 3, pp. 77–94.
Fisch, Harold 1953: The Scientist as Priest: A Note on Robert Boyle's Natural Theology. *Isis*, 44, pp. 252–65.
Forman, Harry Buxton 1880 (ed.): *The Works of Percy Bysshe Shelley in Verse and Prose*. 8 vols. London: Reeves and Turner.
Forrester, David 1989: *The Young Doctor Pusey: A Study in Development*. London: Mowbray.
Fortescue, R.H. 1854: *A Correspondence between E.B. Pusey ... Plymouth*. London.
Franklin, Stephen C. 1977: 'The Editor as Reconstructor: Carlyle's Historical View as a Shaping Force in the Fiction of *Sartor Resartus*'. *Ball State University Forum* 18/iii, pp. 32–39.
Fried, Michael 1996: *Manet's Modernism or, The Face of Painting in the 1860s*. Chicago: University of Chicago Press.
Fryckstedt, Monica Correa 1982: *Elizabeth Gaskell's Mary Barton and Ruth: A Challenge to Christian England*. Stockholm: Almqvist & Wiksell International.
Funkenstein, Amos 1986: *Theology and the Scientific Imagination from the Middle Ages to the Seventeenth Century*. Princeton: Princeton University Press.
Fyfe, Aileen 1997: The Reception of William Paley's *Natural Theology* in the University of Cambridge. *British Journal for the History of Science*, 30, pp. 321–35.
Gagnier, Regenia 1988: Mediums and the Media: A Response to Judith Walkowitz. In *Representations* 22, Spring 1988.
Garbett, James 1849: *Modern Philosophical Infidelity; or the Personality of God: A Sermon Preached before the University of Oxford on Sunday January 28th 1848*. London: Hatchard.
Garnett, C. 1984: Swedenborg and Mystical Enlightenment in England. In *Journal of the History of Ideas*, 45.
Gaskell, Elizabeth [1855] 1982: *North and South*. The World's Classics ed. Oxford: Oxford University Press.
Gero, Stephen 1977: *Byzantine Iconoclasm during the Reign of Constantine V*. Louvain: Corpussco.
Gilbert, Alan 1976: *Religion and Society in Industrial England*. London: Longman.
Gilbert, Sandra and Gubar, Susan 1979: *The Madwoman in the Attic: The Woman Writer and the Nineteenth-Century Literary Imagination*. New Haven and London: Yale University Press.
Gill, Stephen (ed.) 1987: *The Oxford Authors: William Wordsworth*. Oxford and New York: Oxford University Press.
Gill, Stephen 1989: *William Wordsworth, A Life*. Oxford: Clarendon Press.
Gillespie, Neil C. 1984: Preparing for Darwin: Conchology and Natural Theology in Anglo-American Natural History. *Studies in the History of Biology*, 7, pp. 93–145.
Gillespie, Neil C. 1990: Divine Design and the Industrial Revolution: William Paley's Abortive Reform of Natural Theology. *Isis*, 81, pp. 214–29.
Gilley, Sheridan 1981: The Huxley-Wilberforce Debate: A Reconstruction. In Keith Robbins (ed.) *Religion and Humanism*. Oxford: Blackwell, pp. 325–40.
Gilligan, Carol 1982: *In A Different Voice: Psychological Theory and Women's Development*. Cambridge, Mass.: Harvard.
Gillispie, Charles Coulton 1959: *Genesis and Geology: A Study in the Relations of Scientific Thought, Natural Theology, and Social Opinion in Great Britain, 1790–1850*. New York: Harper & Row.
Godwin, Joscelyn 1994: *The Theosophical Enlightenment*. Albany: State University of New York Press.

Goodrick-Clarke, Nicholas 1985: *The Occult Roots of Nazism*, New York: New York University Press.
Goodwin, C. W. 1860: On the Mosaic Cosmogony. In Benjamin Jowett, Frederick Temple, *et al. Essays and Reviews*. Fifth edition, 1861, London: Longman, pp. 207–53.
Gosse, Edmund 1890: *The Life of Philip Henry Gosse*. London: Kegan Paul.
Gosse, Edmund 1965: *Father and Son*. Boston: Houghton Mifflin.
Gosse, Philip Henry 1839–1861: British Sea-Anemones and Corals: Original Sketches and Drawings in Colour by Philip Henry Gosse and His Correspondents, 1839–1861. Horniman Museum Library, London.
Gosse, Philip Henry 1853: *A Naturalist's Rambles on the Devonshire Coast*. London: Van Voorst.
Gosse, Philip Henry 1855–56: *A Manual of Marine Zoology for the British Isles*. London: Van Voorst.
Gosse, Philip Henry 1856a: *The Aquarium*. 2d ed. London: Van Voorst.
Gosse, Philip Henry 1856b: *Tenby: A Sea-Side Holiday*. London: Van Voorst.
Gosse, Philip Henry 1859: *Evenings at the Microscope*. London: SPCK.
Gosse, Philip Henry 1860a: *Actinologia Britannica: A History of the British Sea-Anemones and Corals*. London: Van Voorst.
Gosse, Philip Henry 1860b: *The Romance of Natural History*. First series. London: Nisbet.
Gosse, Philip Henry 1861: *The Romance of Natural History*. Second series. London: Nisbet.
Gosse, Philip Henry 1873: *A Year at the Shore*. London: Isbister.
Gossner, Johannes Evangelist 1822: *The Heart of Man, either a Temple of God or a Habitation of Satan*. Reading, PA: Henry B. Sage.
Gould, Stephen 1988: *Time's Arrow, Time's Cycle*. Harmondsworth: Penguin.
Gray, Asa 1963: *Darwiniana*. Cambridge, MA: Harvard University Press.
Greenhalgh, Paul 1988: *Ephemeral Vistas. The Expositions Universelles, Great Exhibitions and World's Fairs, 1851–1939*.
Grosz, Elizabeth 1989: *Sexual Subversions: Three French Feminists*. Sydney: Allen and Unwin.
Grosz, Elizabeth, 1994: *Volatile Bodies: Towards a Corporeal Feminism*. Sydney: Allen and Unwin.
Grundmann, Herbert 1927: Der Typus des Ketzers in Mittelalterlicher Anchauung, Kultur und Universalgeschicte. *Walter Goetz zu seinen 60 Geburtstate*, Leipzig: B. G. Teubner.
Habermas, Jürgen 1983: *The Theory of Communicative Action*. Thomas McCarthy trans. Boston, MA: Beacon Press.
Halbfass, Wilhelm 1988: *India and Europe: An Essay in Understanding*. Albany: State University of New York Press.
Hamlin, Christopher 1986: Robert Warington and the Moral Economy of the Aquarium, *Journal of the History of Biology*, 19, pp. 131–53.
Hanegraaff, Wouter 1997: *New Age Religion and Western Culture: Esotericism in the Mirror of Secular Thought*. State University of New York University Press.
Haney, Janice. 1978: "Shadow-Hunting": Romantic Irony, *Sartor Resartus*, and Victorian Romanticism. *Studies in Romanticism* 17:2, pp. 307–33.
Hardouin-Fugier, Elisabeth 1982: Qui a renversé léléphant? constructeurs et détracteurs de la nouvelle église de Fourvière (1870–1896), *Cahiers d'Histoire* II.
Hardouin-Fugier, Elisabeth 1988: *Voir, revoir Fourvière*. Hauteville-Lompnes: Gabriel Lardant.
Hardouin-Fugier, Elisabeth 1990: *La Gloire de Lyon, la peinture de l'école lyonnaise du XIXe siècle*. Gifu: Nippon Printing Co.
Hardouin-Fugier, Elisabeth 1993: *Miniguide de Fourvière*. Lyon: SME.
Harman, Barbara Leah 1988: In Promiscuous Company: Female Public Appearance in Elizabeth Gaskell's *North and South*. *Victorian Studies* (30) 3, pp. 351–73.

Harris, Joseph 1852: *Auricular Confession: Not the Rule of the Church of England ... Plymouth*. London.
Harrison, P. 1990: *'Religion' and the Religions in the English Enlightenment*. Cambridge: Cambridge University Press.
Harrison, Peter 1998: *The Bible, Protestantism, and the Rise of Natural Science*. Cambridge: Cambridge University Press.
Harvey, Van A. 1964: *A Handbook of Theological Terms*. New York: Macmillan.
Hatchard, John 1852: *A Statement by some of the clergy ... Plymouth*. London.
Hay, Stephen 1970: *Asian Ideas of East and West: Tagore and his Critics in Japan, China and India*. Cambridge, Mass.: Harvard University Press.
Heelas, Paul 1996: *The New Age Movement. The Celebration of the Self and the Sacralization of Modernity*. Oxford, UK and Cambridge, Mass. USA: Blackwell.
Helmling, Steven. 1988: 'The "Thaumaturgic Art of Thought": Carlyle's *Sartor Resartus'. The Esoteric Comedies of Carlyle, Newman, and Yeats*. Cambridge: Cambridge University Press.
Helmstadter, Richard and Lightman, Bernard (1990), *Victorian Faith in Crisis: essays on continuity and change in nineteenth-century religious belief*. London, MacMillan.
Hepworth, Mike and Bryan S. Turner 1982: *Confession: studies in deviance and religion*. London: Routledge.
Herberg, Will 1955: *Protestant-Catholic-Jew: An Essay in American Religious Sociology*. Garden City, N.Y.: Doubleday.
Herbert, Robert 1976: *Jean François Millet*. London: Arts Council of Great Britain.
Heyck, T. W. 1982: *The Transformation of Intellectual Life in Victorian England*. London: Croom Helm.
Hogan, Trevor. 1995: *Modernity as Revolution: Thomas Carlyle and the Absent Centre of British Social Theory*, La Trobe University, Bundoora, Victoria, Australia.
Hogan, Trevor. 1998: Carlyle and Sismondi: Reading European Modernity from the Margins. *Carlyle Studies Annual* 18, pp. 123–44.
Hogan, William 1846: *Auricular Confession and Popish Nunneries*. London.
Holloway, John. 1965: 'Carlyle' and 'Carlyle as Prophet-Historian'. *The Victorian Sage: Studies in Argument*. 1953. New York: W. W. Norton.
Holmes, Richard 1974: *Shelley: The Pursuit*. London: Weidenfield and Nicolson.
Hook, Philip and Plotimore, Mark 1986: *Popular 19th Century Painting: A Dictionary of European Genre Painters*. Woodbridge, Suffock: Antique Collectors' Club.
Hook, Walter F. 1848: *Auricular Confession: A Sermon*. London.
Hooker, Richard 1901 (1600): *Confession and Absolution*. Ed. Rev. John Harding. London: Charles Murray.
Houghton, Walter E. 1957: *The Victorian Frame of Mind, 1830–1870*. New Haven: Yale University Press.
Houghton, Walter R. (ed.) 1894: *Neely's History of the Parliamen of Religions and Religious Congresses at the World's Columbian Exposition*. Chicago: Rand McNally.
Howe, P.P. 1930–4 (ed.): *The Complete Works of William Hazlitt*. 21 vols. London: J.M. Dent.
Hruschka, John. 1992/93: Carlyle's Rabbinical Hero: Teufelsdröckh and the Midrashic Tradition. *Carlyle Annual* 13, pp. 101–108.
Hyde, Virginia 1992: *The Risen Adam: D.H. Lawrence's Revisionist Typology*, University Park, Pennsylvania: Pennsylvania State University Press.
Iliffe, Robert 1998: A 'Connected System'? The Snare of a Beautiful Hand and the Unity of Newton's Archive. In Michael Hunter (ed.) *The Formation and Exchange of Ideas in Seventeenth-Century Europe*. Suffolk: Boydell, pp. 137–57.
Irénée de Lyon 1984: *Contre les Hérésies*. Adelin Rousseau trans. livre III, 2. 3. Paris: Cerf.
Jack, Ian, Smith, Margaret, Fowler, Rowena and Inglesfield, Robert (eds.) 1983–95: *The Poetical Works of Robert Browning*. 5 vols. Oxford: Clarendon.

Jacyna, L.S. 1981: The Physiology of Mind, the Unity of Nature, and the Moral Order in Victorian Thought. *British Journal for the History of Science*, 14, pp. 109–132.

Jensen, Vernon 1988: Return to the Wilberforce-Huxley Debate. *British Journal for the History of Science*, 21, pp. 161–79.

Johnson, Glen M. 1993: Ralph Waldo Emerson on Isaac Hecker: A Manuscript with Commentary. *The Catholic Historical Review.* 79, pp. 54 - 64.

Jones, Frederick L. 1964 (ed.): *The Letters of Percy Bysshe Shelley.* 2 vols. Oxford: Clarendon Press.

Jones, R.K. 1974: The Swedenborgians, an Interactional Analysis'. *A Sociological Year Book of Religion*, 7.

Kachur, Robert M. 1998: Envisioning Equality, Asserting Authority: Women's Devotional Writings on the Apocalypse, 1845–1900. In Julie Melnyk (ed.) *Women's Theology in Nineteenth-Century Britain: Transfiguring the Faith of Their Fathers.* New York: Garland, pp. 3–36.

Kachur, Robert M. 1996: The Apocalyptic Ventriloquist: Re-examining Charlotte Bronte's Famous Last Words in *Jane Eyre* and *Villette.* In *Getting the Last Word:British Women and the Authoritative Apocalyptic Voice (1845–1900).* Unpublished dissertation.

Kallenberg, Brad J. 1995: Conversion Converted: A Postmodern Formulation of the Doctrine of Conversion. *Evangelical Quarterly*, 67(4), pp. 335–64.

Kant, Immanuel 1960: *Religion within the Limits of Reason Alone.* Theodore M. Greene and Hoyt H. Hudson trans. New York: Harper Torchbooks.

Kant, Immanuel 1986: *Philosophical Writings.* Ernst Behler and Volkmar Sander (eds) New York: Continuum.

Kent, John. 1978: *Holding the Fort: Studies in Victorian Revivalism.* London: Epworth Press.

Ker, Ian 1988: *John Henry Newman.* Oxford: Oxford University Press.

Kinkead-Weekes, Mark 1996: *D.H. Lawrence: Triumph to Exile, 1912–1922.* Cambridge: Cambridge University Press.

Kim, Stephen S. 1996: *John Tyndall's Transcendental Materialism and the Conflict Between Religion and Science in Victorian England.* New York: Edwin Mellen Press.

Kohn, David 1989: Darwin's Ambiguity: The Secularization of Biological Meaning. *British Journal for the History of Science*, 22, pp. 215–39.

Kopf, David 1979: *The Brahmo Samaj and the Shaping of the Modern Indian Mind.* Princeton: Princeton University Press.

Krueger, Christine L. 1992: *The Reader's Repentance: Women Preachers, Women Writers, and Nineteenth-Century Social Discourse.* Chicago: Univ. of Chicago Press.

Landow, George P. 1980: *Victorian Types, Victorian Shadows: Biblical Typology in Victorian Literature, Art, and Thought.* Boston: Routledge.

Landow, George 1986: *Elegant Jeremiahs: The Sage from Carlyle to Mailer.* Ithaca, New York: Cornell University Press.

Landow, George P. 1990: Aggressive (Re)interpretations of the Female Sage: Florence Nightingale's *Cassandra.* In Thaïs E. Morgan (ed.) *Victorian Sages and Cultural Discourse: Renegotiating Gender and Power.* New Brunswick and London: Rutgers University Press, pp. 32–45.

Lansbury, Coral 1975: *Elizabeth Gaskell: The Novel of Social Crisis.* London: Paul Elek.

L. B. 1886: *Short Notes on the Revelation.* London: J. Masters & Co.

La Valley, Albert J. 1968: *Carlyle and the Idea of the Modern.* New Haven: Yale University Press.

Lawrence, D.H. 1936: *Phoenix, The Posthumous Papers of D.H. Lawrence*, ed. Edward McDonald, London: Heinemann, 1936.

Lawrence, D.H. 1968: *Phoenix II: Uncollected, Unpublished and Other Prose Works*, ed. Warren Roberts and Harry T. Moore, London: Heinemann, 1968.

Lawrence, D.H. 1979–93: *The Letters of D.H. Lawrence*, ed. James Boulton and others, 7 vols, Cambridge: Cambridge University Press.

Lawrence, D.H. 1980: *Apocalypse and the Writings on Revelation*, ed. Mara Kalnins, Cambridge: Cambridge University Press.
Lawrence, D.H. 1985: *Study of Thomas Hardy and Other Essays*, ed. Bruce Steele. Cambridge: Cambridge University Press.
Lawrence, D.H. 1988: *Reflections on the Death of a Porcupine and Other Essays*, ed. Michael Herbert, Cambridge: Cambridge University Press: 1988.
Leary, Stephen D. 1994: *Arguing the Apocalypse: A Theory of Millennial Rhetoric*. New York: Oxford University Press.
Lebrun, Richard A. 1974 (trans.): *Considerations on France* by Joseph de Maistre. Montreal and London: McGill-Queen's University Press.
Lebrun, François (ed.) 1980: *Histoire des Catholiques en France du XVe Siècle à nos Jours*. Toulous: Privat Liddon, Henry Parry 1894: *Life of Edward Bouverie Pusey*, 4 vols. London.
LeMahieu, D.L. 1976: *The Mind of William Paley: A Philosopher and His Age*. Lincoln, NE: University of Nebraska Press.
Liddon, Henry Parry 1899: *Life of Edward Bouverie Pusey*, 4 vols. London.
Life of Swami Vivekananda by his Eastern and Western Disciples:1979. Calcutta: Advaita Ashrama.
Lightman, Bernard 1987: *The Origins of Agnosticism: Victorian Unbelief and the Limits of Knowledge*. Baltimore and London: Johns Hopkins University Press.
Lightman, Bernard 1997: 'The Voices of Nature': Popularizing Victorian Science. In Bernard Lightman (ed.) *Victorian Science in Context*. Chicago: University of Chicago Press, pp. 187–211.
Lineham, P.J. 1978: The English Swedenborgians. University of Sussex, D. Phil thesis.
Lineham, P.J. 1988: The Origins of the New Jerusalem Church. *Bulletin of the John Rylands Library*, 70.
Literary Women 1869. *The Christian World Magazine*, 5, pp. 531–38.
Liu, Alan 1989: *Wordsworth: The Sense of History*. Stanford: Stanford University Press.
Lively, Jack 1965 (ed. and trans.): *The Works of Joseph de Maistre*. London: George Allen and Unwin.
Lovell, Terry 1987: *Consuming Fiction*. London: Verso.
Lowe, Thomas 1852: *Confession and Absolution: A Reply*. London.
Lowth, Robert 1787: *Lectures on the Sacred Poetry of the Hebrews*. 2 vols. Tr. G. Gregory. London: J. Johnson. Repr. 1969: Hildesheim: Georg Olms Verlag.
Lucas, John 1979: Wilberforce and Huxley: A Legendary Encounter. *The Historical Journal*, 22, pp. 313–30.
'Lydia' 1841: Female Biography of Scripture: Deborah. *The Christian Lady's Magazine*, 16, pp. 337–49.
'Lydia' 1842: Female Biography of Scripture: Manoah's Wife. *The Christian Lady's Magazine*, 17, pp. 503–12.
McClintock 1995: *Imperial Leather. Race, Gender and Sexuality in the Colonial Context*. London and New York: Routledge.
McCosh, James 1875: *Ideas in Nature Overlooked by Dr. Tyndall. Being an Examination of Dr. Tyndall's Belfast Address*. New York: Robert Carter & Brothers.
McDannell, Colleen 1986: *The Christian Home in Victorian America, 1840–1900*. Bloomington: Indiana University Press.
McDannell, Colleen and Lang, Bernhard 1988: *Heaven: A History*. New Haven; London: Yale University Press.
McDannell, Colleen 1989: Catholic Domesticity, 1860–1960. In Karen Kennelly, C. S. J. (ed.): *American Catholic Women: A Historical Exploration*. New York: MacMillan Publishing/London: Collier MacMillan Publishers, pp. 48–80).
McGann, Jerome J. 1980–93 (ed.): *Lord Byron: The Complete Poetical Works*. 7 vols. Oxford: Clarendon Press.

McGrath, Alister 1994: *Christian Theology*. Oxford: Blackwells.
McLeod, Hugh 1974: *Class and Religion in the Late Victorian City*. Hamdon, CT: Archon Books.
McLeod, Hugh 1981: *Religion and the People of Western Europe 1789–1970*. Oxford: Oxford University Press/Opus.
McLeod, Hugh 1984: *Religion and the Working Class in Nineteenth-Century Britain*. London: MacMillan.
McMaster, Rowland D. 1968: 'Criticism of Civilization in the Structure of *Sartor Resartus*'. *University of Toronto Quarterley*, 37, pp. 268–80.
Machin, G. I. T. 1987: *Politics and the Churches in Great Britain 1869–1921*. Oxford: Clarendon Press.
Mackarness, John Fielder, Bishop of Oxford 1875: *A Charge Delivered to the Clergy of the Diocese of Oxford, at His Second Visitation, in the Cathedral Church of Christ, April 20 1875*. Oxford: James Parker.
MacKenzie, John M.: 1985: *Propaganda and Empire: The Manipulation of British Opinion 1880–1960*. Manchester: Manchester University Press.
Mâle, Emile 1924: *L'art religieux du xiie siècle en France*. Paris: A. Colin.
Mâle, Emile 1972: *The Gothic Image*. Dora Nussey trans. NY: Harper & Row.
Mandelbrote, Scott 1993: 'A Duty of the Greatest Moment': Isaac Newton and the Writing of Biblical Criticism. *British Journal for the History of Science*, 26, pp. 281–302.
Manquis, Robert M. 1989: English Romanticism and the Terror. *Studies in Romanticism*, 28, pp. 365–77.
Marcilhacy, C. *Le Diocèse d'Orléans sous l'Episcopat de Mgr. Dupanloup*. Paris: Plon, 1962)
Marshall, Dorothy 1992: *The Life and Times of Victoria*. London: Weidenfeld and Nicolson.
Martin, David 1969: Towards Eliminating the Concept of Secularisation. In *The Religious and the Secular*. New York: Schocken Books.
Martin, David 1978: *A General Theory of Secularisation*. New York: Harper and Row.
Martin, David 1967: *A Sociology of English Religion*. London: SCM Press.
Martineau, Harriet 1966: *Society in America,* vol. 3. New York: AMS Press.
Marriner, Edwin T.J. 1874: *'The Raising of the Widow's Son at Nain': A Sermon in Reply to Professor Tyndall's Address at Belfast*. London: Simpkin, Marshall & Co.
Mellor, Anne K. 1980: 'Carlyle's *Sartor Resartus*: A Self-Consuming Artifact'. *English Romantic Irony*. Cambridge, Massachusetts: Harvard University Press.
Melnyk, Julie 1993: *Faith of Our Mothers: Women's Religious Utterance in Nineteenth-Century Britain*. Unpublished Ph.D. Dissertation, University of Virginia.
Melnyk, Julie 1996: Emma Jane Worboise and *The Christian World Magazine*: Christian Publishing and Women's Empowerment.
Melnyk, Julie 1998: *Women's Theology in Nineteenth-Century Britain: Transfiguring the Faith of Their Fathers*. New York: Garland.
Merrill, Lynn L. 1989: *The Romance of Victorian Natural History*. Oxford: Oxford University Press.
Meyers, Jeffrey (ed.) 1985: *D.H. Lawrence and Tradition*, Amherst: University of Massachusetts Press.
Michelet, Jules 1973: *The People*. John P. McKay, trans. Urbana, IL: University of Illinois Press
Michie, Helena 1987: *The Flesh Made Word*. New York: Oxford University Press.
Miegge, Giovanni 1955: *The Virgin Mary, the Roman Catholic Marian Doctrine*. Waldo Smith trans. Philadelphia: Westminster Press.
Mill, John Stuart 1985: *Utilitarianism*. Ed. Mary Warnock, London: Fontana Press.
Miller, Hillis J. 1991: '"Hieroglyphical Truth" in *Sartor Resartus:* Carlyle and the Language of Parable'. *Victorian Subjects*. Durham, North Carolina: Duke University Press.

Miller, Hugh 1869 [1857]: *The Testimony of the Rocks*. Edinburgh: Nimmo.
Miller, Perry 1950: *The Transcendentalists: An Anthology*. Cambridge: Harvard University Press.
Miller, Perry 1963: *Margaret Fuller: American Romantic*. Ithaca, N.Y.: Cornell University Press.
Milton, Colin 1987: *Lawrence and Nietzsche*, Aberdeen: Aberdeen University Press.
Montgomery, Robert E. 1994: *The Visionary Lawrence: Beyond Philosophy and Art*, Cambridge: Cambridge University Press.
Moore, James R. 1979: *The Post-Darwinian Controversies: A Study of the Protestant Struggle to Come to Terms with Darwin in Great Britain and America 1870–1900*. Cambridge: Cambridge University Press.
Morgan, Thaïs E. (ed.) 1990: *Victorian Sages and Cultural Discourse: Renegotiating Gender and Power*. New Brunswick: Rutgers University Press.
Muirhead, John H. 1931: Carlyle's Transcendental Symbolism. In *The Platonic Tradition in Anglo-Saxon Philosophy: Studies in the History of Idealism in England and America*. London: Allen and Unwin.
Murray, E. B. 1993 (ed.): *The Prose Works of Percy Bysshe Shelley*. 2 vols. Oxford: Clarendon Press.
Murphet, Howard 1972: *Hammer on the Mountain. The Life of Henry Steel Olcott*. Wheaton, Illinois: The Theosophical Publishing House.
Newsome, David 1993: *The Convert Cardinals: John Henry Newman and Henry Edward Manning*. London: John Murray.
Nietzsche, Friedrich 1961: *Thus Spoke Zarathustra*, trans. R.J. Hollingdale, Harmondsworth: Penguin.
Nietzsche, Friedrich 1990: *Twilight of the Gods/The Anti-Christ*, trans. R.J. Hollingdale, Harmondsworth: Penguin.
Nockles, Peter 1994: *The Oxford Movement in Context*. Cambridge: Cambridge University Press.
Norton, Charles Eliot (ed.) 1887: *Correspondence Between Goethe and Carlyle*. London: Macmillan.
Obeyesekere, Gananath 1995: Buddhism, Nationhood, and Cultural Identity: A Question of Fundamentals. In Martin E. Marty and R. Scott Appleby (eds): *Fundamentalisms Comprehended* (Volume V, The Fundamentalisms Project). Chicago: University of Chicago Press.
O'Brien, Conor Cruise 1969 (ed.): *Reflections on the Revolution in France* by Edmund Burke. Harmondsworth: Penguin.
Oecumenical Documents of the Faith 1950: Thomas H. Brindley and Frederick W. Green (eds) London: Methuen.
Ollard, S.L. 1915: *A Short History of the Oxford Movement*. London: A. R. Mowbray and Co.
Ospovat, Dov 1981: *The Development of Darwin's Theory: Natural History, Natural Theology, and Natural Selection, 1838–1859*. Cambridge: Cambridge University Press.
Pater, Walter 1873: *Studies in the History of the Renaissance*. London: Macmillan & Co.
Pater, Walter 1986: *Marius the Epicurean*. Ed. Ian Small, Oxford: Oxford University Press.
Patrologia Latina 1844–64: Jacques Paul Migne (ed.) Paris: J.P. Migne.
Patton, Lewis and Mann, Peter 1971 (eds.): *Conciones ad Populum. Or Addresses to the People in Lectures 1795 on Politics and Religion* by Samuel Taylor Coleridge. Princeton: Princeton University Press.
Paulson, Ronald 1983: *Representations of Revolution (1789–1820)*. New Haven and London: Yale University Press.
Peckham, Morse 1961: *Beyond the Tragic Vision: The Quest for Identity in the Nineteenth Century*. New York: George Braziller.

Perrin, Sainte-Marie 1896: *La basilique de Notre-Dame de Fourvière, son origine, son esthétique, son symbolisme.* Lyon: Vitte.
Peterson, Linda H. 1986: 'Carlyle's *Sartor Resartus:* The Necessity of Reconstruction'. *Victorian Autobiography: The Tradition of Self Interpretation.* New Haven: Yale University Press.
Phillpotts, Henry 1825: *Letters to Charles Butler.* London.
Phillpotts, Henry 1852: *Confession and Absolution*; A Letter to the Dean of Exeter. London.
Physical Science Compared with the Second Beast or The False Prophet of Revelation 1865. London: Rivingtons.
Pinkney, Tony 1990: *D.H. Lawrence and Modernism,* Iowa City: University of Iowa Press.
Pitra, Dom Jean-Battiste 1884: Clavis Codex Claremontanus. *Analecta Sacra Spicilegio Solesmensi,* II, Solesme.
Poovey, Mary 1984: *The Proper Lady and the Woman Writer.* Chicago: Univ. of Chicago Press.
Poovey, Mary 1988: *Uneven Developments: The Ideological Work of Gender in Mid-Victorian England.* Chicago: University of Chicago Press.
Poovey, Mary 1990: Speaking of the Body: Mid-Victorian Constructions of Female Desire. In Mary Jacobus, Evelyn Fox Keller and Sally Shuttleworth (eds) *Body/Politics: Women and the Discourses of Science.* New York and London: Routledge, pp. 29–46.
Poovey, Mary (ed.) 1991: *Florence Nightingale: Cassandra and other Selections from Suggestions for Thought.* London: Pickering and Chatto.
Powell, Baden 1860: On the Study of the Evidences of Christianity. In Benjamin Jowett, Frederick Temple, et al. *Essays and Reviews.* Fifth edition, 1861, London: Longman, pp. 94–144.
Powell, Geoffrey 1990: The Anglican Tradition: from the Reformation to the Oxford Movement. In Geoffrey Powell, Martin Dudley and Geoffrey Rowell (eds) *Confession and Absolution.* London: SPCK, pp. 91–119.
Prather, Marla and Stuckey, Charles F. 1987: *Gauguin, a Retrospective.* New York: Park Lane
Presbyter, Anglicanus [Joseph H. Harris] 1852: *Auricular Confession: Not the Rule of the Church of England,* A Letter to the Bishop of Exeter. London.
Prickett, Stephen (1986): *Words and* The Word*: Language, Poetics and Biblical Interpretation.* Cambridge: Cambridge University Press.
Prothero, Stephen 1996: *The White Buddhist. The Asian Odyssey of Henry Steel Olcott.* Bloomington and Indianapolis: Indiana University Press.
Punch, or *The London Charivari* 27 (1854) and 28 (1855).
Pusey, E.B. 1839: *Letter to Lord Bishop of Oxford on the Tendency to Romanism imputed to Doctrines Held of Old, as Now, in the English Church.* Oxford.
Pusey, E.B. 1846: *Entire Absolution of the Penitent.* London.
Pusey, E.B. 1851: *A Letter to the Lord Bishop of London in Explanation of Some Statements Contained in a Letter by Rev. W. Dodsworth.* London.
Pusey, E.B. 1854: *A Correspondence between the Rev EB Pusey and the Rev R.H. Fortescue.* London.
Pusey, E.B. 1878: *Advice for Those Who Exercise the Ministry of Reconciliation through Confession and Absolution.* Oxford.
Rambo, Lewis R. 1993: *Understanding Religious Conversion.* New Haven: Yale University Press.
Rattansi, Piyo 1972: The Social Interpretation of Science in the Seventeenth Century. In Peter Mathias (ed.) *Science and Society, 1600–1900.* Cambridge: Cambridge University Press, pp. 1–32.
Raychaudhuri, Tapan 1988: *Europe Reconsidered. Perceptions of the West in Nineteenth Century Bengal.* Delhi: Oxford University Press.

Reed, John Shelton 1996: *Glorious Battle. The Cultural Politics of Victorian Anglo-Catholicism*. Nashville and London: Vanderbilt University Press.
Reeve, Henry 1875: Mill's *Essays on Theism. Edinburgh Review*, 141, pp. 1–31.
Rehbock, Philip F. 1980: The Victorian Aquarium in Ecological and Social Perspective. In Mary Sears and Daniel Merriman (eds.) *Oceanography: The Past*. New York: Springer-Verlag, pp. 522–39.
Reiman, Donald H. and Powers, Sharon B. 1977 (eds.): *Shelley's Poetry and Prose*. New York and London: W. W. Norton.
Renan, Ernest 1927: *The Life of Jesus*, London: Dent.
Robson, John M. 1990: The Fiat and Finger of God: The Bridgewater Treatises. In Richard J. Helmstadter and Bernard Lightman (eds) *Victorian Faith in Crisis: Essays on Continuity and Change in Nineteenth-Century Religious Belief*. Stanford: Stanford University Press, pp. 71–125.
Rosenberg, Joel 1987: 'Jeremiah and Ezekiel'. In Robert Alter and Frank Kermode (eds). *The Literary Guide to the Bible*. Cambridge: The Belknap Press of Harvard University Press, pp. 184–206.
Rosenblum, Robert and Janso, H. W. 1984: *Nineteenth Century Art*. Englewood Cliffs, NJ: Prentice Hall
Rosomer, William S. and Stoffolano John G. jr 1994: *The Science of Entomology*. Iowa: Univ. of Iowa Press.
Ross, Frederic R. 1977: Philip Gosse's *Omphalos*, Edmund Gosse's *Father and Son*, and Darwin's Theory of Natural Selection. *Isis*, 68, pp. 85–96.
Rossetti, Christina G. 1892: *The Face of the Deep*. London: Society for Promoting Christian Knowledge.
Rossi, Alice S. (ed.) 1973: *The Feminist Papers from Adams to de Beavoir*. New York: Columbia University Press.
Rowell, Geoffrey 1983: *The Vision Glorious*. Oxford: Oxford University Press.
Rudwick, Martin 1986: The Shape and Meaning of Earth History. In David Lindberg and Ronald Numbers (eds.) *God and Nature: Historical Essays on the Encounter between Christianity and Science*. Berkeley: University of California Press, pp. 296–321.
Rudwick, Martin 1992: *Scenes from Deep Time: Early Pictorial Representations of the Prehistoric World*. Chicago: University of Chicago Press.
Rundle, Vivienne. 1992: '"Devising New Means": *Sartor Resartus* and the Devoted Reader'. *Victorian Newsletter* 82, Fall, pp. 13–22.
Rupke, Nicolaas 1994: *Richard Owen: Victorian Naturalist*. New Haven: Yale University Press.
Rusk, Ralph (ed.) 1939: *The Letters of Ralph Waldo Emerson*. New York.
Ruskin, John 1865: Of Queens' Gardens. *Sesame and Lilies*. Philadelphia: Henry Altemus, 1899.
Rydell, Robert W. 1984: *All the World's A Fair. Visions of Empire at American International Expositions, 1876–1916*. Chicago and London: University of Chicago Press.
Said, Edward 1978: *Orientalism*. London: Routledge.
Sams, Henry W. (ed.) 1958: *Autobiography of Brook Farm: A Book of Primary Source Materials*. Englewood Cliffs, New Jersey: Prentice Hall.
Sanders, Charles Richard, Kenneth J. Fielding, Clyde de L. Ryals, *et al.* (eds) 1970: *The Collected Letters of Thomas and Jane Welsh Carlyle*. Durham, North Carolina: Duke University Press.
Schneider, Daniel J. 1986: *The Consciousness of D.H. Lawrence: An Intellectual Biography*, Lawrence, Kansas: University Press of Kansas.
Schwab, Raymond 1984: *The Oriental Renaissance: Europe's Rediscovery of India and the East 1680–1880*. Columbia: Columbia University Press.

Seager, Richard Hughes, ed. 1993: *The Dawn of Relgious Pluralism. Voices from the World's Parliament of Religions, 1893*. La Salle, Ill.: Open Court.
Seager, Richard Hughes 1995: *The World's Parliament of Religions: The East/West Encounter, Chicago, 1893*. Bloomington and Indianapolis: Indiana University Press.
Secord, James 1989: Behind the Veil: Robert Chambers and *Vestiges*. In James Moore (ed.) *History, Humanity and Evolution*. Cambridge: Cambridge University Press, pp. 165–94.
Seigel, Jules P. (ed.) 1971: *Thomas Carlyle: The Critical Heritage*. London: Routledge and Kegan Paul.
Seiler, R. M. (ed.) 1987: *Walter Pater: A Life Remembered*. Calgary: Calgary University Press.
Selincourt, Ernest de (ed.) 1952: *The Poetical Works of William Wordsworth*. 5 vols. Oxford: The Clarendon Press.
Shanahan, Timothy 1994: *Teleological Reasoning in Boyle's Disquisition About Final Causes*. In Michael Hunter (ed.) *Robert Boyle Reconsidered*. Cambridge: Cambridge University Press, pp. 177–92.
Shiels, Richard D. 1981: The Feminization of American Congregationalism, 1730–1835. *American Quarterly*, 33, pp. 45–62.
Shine, Hill. (ed.) 1951: *Carlyle's Unfinished History of German Literature*. Lexington: University of Kentucky Press.
Showalter, Elaine 1987: *The Female Malady: Women, Madness and English Culture, 1830–1980*. London: Virago.
Sigman, Joseph. 1972: "Diabolico-Angelical Indifference": The Imagery of Polarity in *Sartor Resartus*. *Southern Review* (Australia) 5, pp. 207–24.
Sigman, Joseph. 1974: Adam Kadmon, Nifl, Muspel and the Biblical Symbolism of *Sartor Resartus*. *English Literary History*, 41, pp. 233–56.
Smith, L. 1994: God and Man and Man in God. Swedenborg Summer School Papers,1994.
Spurgeon, Charles Haddon 1856–61: *The New Park Street Pulpit containing Sermons preached and Revised by the Rev. C.H. Spurgeon*. 6 vols. London: Passmore, Alabaster.
Spurgeon, Charles Haddon 1897–1900: *C.H. Spurgeon's Autobiography*. 4 vols. London: Passmore, Alabaster.
Stockton, Kathryn Bond. 1992: 'Bodies and God: Post Structuralist Feminists Return to the Fold of Spiritual Materialism'. *Boundary* 2 19:2, pp. 113–49.
Stowe, Harriet Beecher 1873a: Portraits of the Patriarchs: Deborah, Poet and Prophetess. *The Christian World Magazine*, 9, pp. 412–18.
Stowe, Harriet Beecher 1873b: Portraits of the Patriarchs: Miriam and Moses. *The Christian World Magazine*, 9, pp. 368–73.
Stowe, Harriet Beecher 1873c: Portraits of the Patriarchs: Sarah the Princess. *The Christian World Magazine*, 9, pp. 295–301.
Strachey, Lytton 1948 (1st pub. 1918): *Eminent Victorians*. Harmondsworth, Middlesex: Penguin.
Stromberg, Peter G. 1993: *Language and Self-transformation: a Study of the Christian Conversion Narrative*. Cambridge: Cambridge University Press.
Swatos, William H. Jr. (ed.) 1994: *Gender and Religion*. New Brunswick (USA) and London (UK): Transaction Publishers.
Swinburne, Algernon Charles 1904: Dolores. In *Poems and Ballads (First Series): The Poems of Algernon Charles Swinburne*. 6 vols., London: Chatto and Windus, I, 163.
Symondson, Anthony, ed. (1970), *The Victorian Crisis of Faith*. London: SPCK.
Tarr, Rodger L. 1989: *Thomas Carlyle: A Descriptive Bibliography*. Pittsburgh: University of Pittsburgh.
Taylor, Barbara 1983: *Eve and the New Jerusalem*. New York: Pantheon Books.
Temple, Frederick 1860: *The Present Relations between Science and Religion: A Sermon Preached on July 1, 1860 before the University of Oxford*. Oxford: Parker.

Tennyson, G.B. 1965: *'Sartor' Called 'Resartus': The Genesis, Structure, and Style of Thomas Carlyle's First Major Work*. Princeton, N. J.: Princeton University Press.
Thayer, H.S. (ed.) 1953: *Newton's Philosophy of Nature: Selections from his Writings*. New York: Hafner.
Theobaldus Episcopus 1972: *Theobaldi 'Physiologus'*. P.T. Eden (ed.). Cologne: Brill.
Thiollier, Félix 1891: *L'oeuvre de Pierre Bossan, architecte*. Montbrison: Brassard.
Thompson, E.P. 1968: *The Making of the English Working Class*. Middlesex, England: Pelican Books.
Thwaite, Ann 1984: *Edmund Gosse: A Literary Landscape, 1849-1928*. London: Secker and Warburg.
Tindall, William 1972: *D.H. Lawrence and Susan His Cow*, New York: Cooper Square Publishers.
Tinterow, Gary, Pantazzi, Michael and Pomarède, Vincent 1996: *Corot*. New York: The Metropolitan Museum distributed by Harry N. Abrams.
Tipton, Steven 1984: *Getting Saved from the Sixties. Moral Meaning in Conversion and Cultural Change*. Berkeley, Los Angeles and London: University of California Press.
Tolstoy, Leo 1965: *Anna Karenina*. Constance Garnett trans. New York: Modern Library.
Tonna, Charlotte Elizabeth 1834: From an Old Blue-Stocking. *The Christian Lady's Magazine*, 1, p. 26.
Tonna, Charlotte Elizabeth 1840: Preface. *The Christian Lady's Magazine*, 13, pp. i-iii.
Topham, Jonathan 1992: Science and Popular Education in the 1830s: The role of the *Bridgewater Treatises*. *British Journal for the History of Science*, 25, pp. 397–430.
Topham, Jonathan 1993: 'An Infinite Variety of Arguments': The *Bridgewater Treatises* and British Natural Theology in the 1830s. Lancaster University Ph.D. Dissertation.
Topham, Jonathan 1998: Beyond the 'Common Context': the Production and Reading of the Bridgewater Treatises. *Isis*, 89, pp. 233–62.
Topsell, Edward 1658: *The History of the Four-Footed Beasts and Serpents and Insects*. London: E. Cotes.
Toulmin, Stephen 1992: *Cosmopolis. The Hidden Agenda of Modernity*. Chicago: The University of Chicago Press.
Travis, John F. 1993: *The Rise of the Devon Seaside Resorts, 1750-1900*. Exeter: Exeter University Press.
Troeltsch, Ernst 1931: *The Social Teaching of the Christian Churches*. 2 volumes. London: George Allen and Unwin; New York: MacMillan.
Trollope, Frances 1949: *Domestic Manners of the Americans*. Donald Smalley ed. New York: Alfred A. Knopf.
Turbayne, Colin Murray 1970: *The Myth of Metaphor*. Rev. ed. Columbia: University of South Carolina Press.
Turner, Frank M. 1973: Lucretius Among the Victorians. *Victorian Studies*, 16, pp. 329–348.
Turner, Frank M. 1978: The Victorian Conflict between Science and Religion: A Professional Dimension. *Isis*, 69, pp. 356–76.
Turner, Frank M. 1981: John Tyndall and Victorian Scientific Naturalism. In W. H. Brock, N. D. McMillan, and R. C. Mollan (eds.) *John Tyndall: Essays on a Natural Philosopher*. Dublin: Dublin Royal Society, pp. 169–80.
Turner, Frank M. 1990: The Victorian Crisis of Faith and the Faith that was Lost. In Helmstadter, R. and Lightman, B. (1990), pp. 9–38.
Turner, Frank M. 1993: The Secularization of the Social Vision in British Natural Theology. In *Contesting Cultural Authority: Essays in Victorian Intellectual Life*. Cambridge: Cambridge University Press, pp. 101–27.
Tweed, Thomas A. 1992: *The American Encounter with Buddhism 1844-1912. Victorian Culture and the Limits of Dissent*. Bloomington and Indianapolis: Indiana University Press.

Tyndall, John 1874: *Address Delivered Before the British Association Assembled at Belfast, With Additions.* London: Longmans, Green, and Co.
Tyndall, John 1877: Science and Man. *Fortnightly Review*, 22 n. s., pp. 593–617.
Tyrwhitt, Richard St. John 1880: Hellenic and Christian Views of Beauty. *Contemporary Review*, 36, pp. 474–91.
Valenze, Deborah M. 1985: *Prophetic Sons and Daughters: Female Preaching and Popular Religion in Industrial England.* Princeton: Princeton University Press.
Vanden Bossche, Chris R. 1986: 'Desire and Deferral of Closure in Carlyle's *Sartor Resartus* and *The French Revolution'. Journal of Narrative Technique* 16, pp. 72–8.
Vigny, Alfred de 1926: *Stello.* Paris: Libraire Alphonse Lemerre.
Wagstaff, F. 1878: Mrs. Fry's Rival. *The Christian World Magazine*, 14, pp. 476–9.
Walker, Williston 1985: *A History of the Christian Church.* New York: Charles Scribner's Sons.
Wallace, Ruth A. 1991: Feminism: Expanding the Horizons of the Sociology of Religion. In David G. Bromley (ed.) *Religion and the Social Order*, Vol. 1, *New Developments in Theory and Research*, pp. 253–262. Greenwich, CT: JAI Press.
Ward, W.R. 1972: Swedenborgianism. *Studies in Church History*, 9.
Ward, Mrs. Humphry 1885: Marius the Epicurean. *Macmillan's Magazine*, 52, pp. 132–139.
Warhol, Robyn R. 1989: *Gendered Interventions: Narrative Discourse in the Victorian Novel.* New Brunswick, NJ: Rutgers University Press.
Washington, Peter 1993: *Madame Blavatsky's Baboon.* New York: Schocken Books.
Watson, Roderick. 1988: Carlyle: The World as Text and the Text as Voice. In *The History of Scottish Literature: Volume 3: The Nineteenth Century.* Edited by Douglas Gifford. Aberdeen: Aberdeen University Press.
Watts, Robert 1874: *Atomism: Dr. Tyndall's Atomic Theory of the Universe Examined and Refuted.* Belfast: William Mullan.
Webb, Timothy 1977: *Shelley: A Voice not Understood.* Manchester: Manchester University Press.
Wellek, René. *A History of Modern Criticism: 1750–1950.* New Haven: Yale University Press, Volumes I and II, 1955; Volumes III and IV, 1965; Volumes V and VI, 1986.
Wenzel, Siegfried 1967: *The Sin of Sloth: Acedia in Medieval Thought and Literature.* Chapel Hill: University of North Carolina Press.
Weisberg, Gabriel P. 1992: *Beyond Impressionism: The Naturalist Impulse.* New York: Harry N. Abrams.
Weisberg, Gabriel P. 1980: *The Realist Tradition: French Painting and Drawing, 1830–1900.* Cleveland: Cleveland Museum of Art.
Weiss, Timothy 1987: Walter Pater, Aesthetic Utilitarian. *Victorians Institute Journal*, 15, pp. 105–22.
Whewell, William 1854: *Of the Plurality of Worlds: An Essay. Also a Dialogue on the Same Subject.* London: Parker.
White, Theodore H. 1984. *The Book of Beasts, being a translation from a Latin Bestiary of the twelfth century* Theodire H. White (ed.) NY: Dover.
Wilberforce, R. G. 1881: *Life of the Right Reverend Samuel Wilberforce, D.D. with selections from his diaries and correspondence,* vol. 2. London.
Wilson, Daniel 1851: *A Revival of Spiritual Religion the Only Effectual Remedy for the Dangers which now Threaten the Church of England.* London: Hatchard.
Wilson, David 1984: A Physicist's Alternative to Materialism: The Religious Thought of George Gabriel Stokes. *Victorian Studies*, 28, pp. 69–96.
Woodham-Smith, Cecil 1951: *Florence Nightingale 1820–1910.* New York: McGraw-Hill Book Co.
Woodhead, Linda and Heelas, Paul 2000: *Religion in Modern Times. An Interpretative Anthology.* Malden, USA and Oxford, UK: Blackwell.

Woodhead, Linda 2001: The Impact of Feminism on the Sociology of Religion. In Richard Fenn (ed.) *Companion to the Sociology of Religion*. Oxford: Blackwell.
Woodruff, Helen 1930: The Physiologus of Bern, A Survival of Alexandrian Style in a Ninth Century Manuscript. *Art Bulletin*, XII.
Woofenden, W.R. 1981: *Swedenborg and Twentieth Century Thought*. Pamphlet. Sydney, Australia.
Worboise, Emma Jane 1866: Editorial Address. *The Christian World Magazine*, 1, pp. 1–3.
Worboise, Emma Jane 1873: The Education of Girls. *The Christian World Magazine*, 9, pp. 507–15.
Worboise, Emma Jane 1882: Inkshed and Authorship. *The Christian World Magazine*, 18, pp. 33–4.
Wordsworth, William 1952: *Poetical Works*. Ernest de Selincourt (ed.). 5 Vols. Oxford: The Clarendon Press.
Wordsworth, William 1987: *The Oxford Authors*. Stephen Gill (ed.). Oxford and New York, Oxford University Press.
Wordsworth, William 1979: *The Prelude: 1799, 1805, 1850*. Jonathan Wordsworth, M.H. Abrams, and Stephen Gill (eds.). New York and London: W. W. Norton & Company.
Worthen, John 1991: *D.H. Lawrence: The Early Years, 1885–1912*, Cambridge: Cambridge University Press.
Wu, Duncan 1993. *Wordsworth's Reading, 1770–1799*. Cambridge: Cambridge University Press.
Wuthnow, Robert 1988: *The Restructuring of American Religion*. Princeton, NJ: Princeton University Press.
Wynne, Brian 1979: Physics and Psychics: Science, Symbolic Action, and Social Control in Late Victorian England. In Barry Barnes and Steven Shapin (eds) *Natural Order: Historical Studies of Scientific Culture*. London: Sage, pp. 167–186.
Yates, Gayle Graham (ed.) 1985: *Harriet Martineau on Women*. New Brunswick, NJ: Rutgers University Press.
Yates, Nigel 1983: *The Oxford Movement and Anglican Ritualism*. London: The Historical Association.
Yates, Nigel 1988: 'Jesuits in Disguise?' Ritualist Confessors and Their Critics in the 1870s. *Journal of Ecclesiastical History*, 39 (2), pp. 202–16.
Yeats, W.B. 1961: The Philosophy of Shelley's Poetry. In *Essays and Introductions*. London: Macmillan.
Yeo, Richard 1986: The Principle of Plenitude and Natural Theology in Nineteenth-Century Britain. *British Journal for the History of Science*, 19, pp. 263–82.
Young, Robert M. 1970: The Impact of Darwin on Conventional Thought. In Symondson 1970, pp. 13–35.
Young, Robert M. 1985: *Darwin's Metaphor: nature's place in Victorian culture*. Cambridge: Cambridge University Press.
Young, Robert 1985: *Darwin's Metaphor: Nature's Place in Victorian Culture*. Cambridge: Cambridge University Press.
Young, Robert M. 1989: Natural Theology, Victorian Periodicals and the Fragmentation of a Common Context. In *Darwin's Metaphor: Nature's Place in Victorian Culture*. Cambridge: Cambridge University Press, pp. 126–63.
Yule, John-David 1976: The Impact of Science on British Religious Thought in the Second Quarter of the Nineteenth Century. Cambridge University Ph.D. Dissertation.
Ziolkowski, Eric J. (ed.) 1993: *A Museum of Faiths. Histories and Legacies of the 1893 World's Parliament of Religions*. Atlanta, Georgia: Scholars Press.

Index

A.B. (female author) 196–7
absolution of sins 69–70, 72, 74
aestheticism 240, 246–9
Agnew, Sir William 104
Agréda, Marie-Jesus de 47
Ahlstrom, Sydney 87
Aitken, Robert 98
Alcott, Bronson 109
alternative religious movements 10, 264–6
Anaxagoras 242
Andrews Snell, Minnie 91
animal imagery (at Fourvière basilica) 45–65
animal rights 101
ant-lion image 51–4
anti-Catholicism 140–47
Anti-Mourning Association 103
Apocalyptic writing 17, 211–25
aquaria, use of 255–6, 259
Arian heresy 61
Arnauld, Antoine 63
Arnett, Bishop 85
Arnold, Matthew 28
  Culture and Anarchy 155
Arthurian symbolism 135
asceticism 69–70
atheism 6, 13, 201, 234–5, 245–8
atomism 240–42
Augustine, Saint 28

Bacon, Francis 235
Bakhtin, Mikhail M. 211, 215
Banks, E.W. 97
baptism 68, 70
Barber, Lynn 253
Barker, Thomas J. 176
barnacles 258
Barrett Browning, Elizabeth 202
Barrows, John Henry 84–90
Barton, Ruth 239
Bastien-Lepage, Jules 169
Baxter, Mrs M.: *His Last Word* 214
Baxter, Richard 29, 34
Beecher, Henry Ward 166

Beeton, Isabella 203
Bellah, Robert 81, 87
Bellange, Hippolyte 14, 166
Bentley, James 68, 76
Bernard, Emile 177, 179
Besant, Annie 93
Bible, the
  and the concept of God 122
  critical study of 7, 264
  interpretation of 10–11, 119–23, 193–6, 231–2
  literal reading of 232
  narratives from 16–17, 195–6
  origins of 123–6
  prophecy in 251–2
  as the Word of God 30
Bjerre, Niels 166
Blake, William 100–101, 103, 119
Blanchon, Joannès 40
Blavatsky, Madame H.P. 11, 92, 121–5
  The Secret Doctrine 124–6
Blomfield, Charles James, Bishop 72
Bloom, Harold 121
Blum, Ann Shelby 259
Boehme, Jakob 98
Boethius: *Consolatione Philosophiae* 64–5
Boissieu, A. de 47
Bonney, Charles 84–9, 102
Bonvin, François 168–9, 181, 185
Booth, Wayne C. 155–6
Bossan, Pierre 37–49 *passim*, 55, 63–5
Boudin, Eugène 177
Boyle, Robert 230, 235
Brahmo Samaj sect 91
Bretell, Richard and Caroline 173–6
Breton, Jules 166, 169, 177, 179
Brewster, David 237–8
Bridgewater Treatises 236–8, 253
British Association for the Advancement of Science 237
British Empire Exhibition (1924) 83–4
Brook Farm community 105, 108–110
Brooke, John 254
Brotherton, Joseph 101, 103–104

Browne Goode, G. 83
Browning, Robert
    Christmas Eve and Easter Day 29, 31–2
    The Ring and the Book 75
Brownson, Orestes 10, 105, 110, 112
Buckland, William 232, 234
Buckley, Michael 235
Buddhism 92
Bunyan, John 28–9, 33–5
    Pilgrim's Progress 32
Burke, Edmund 146
    Reflections of the Revolution in France 140
Burton, Katherine 105–108, 112–113
Butler, Charles 72
Butler, W.J. 71
Byron, Lord 143
    Childe Harold's Pilgrimage 141

Calvinism 107, 111, 154, 216, 224, 242–3
cannibalism 139–47 *passim*, 159–60
Cardinal Sins, representation of 49–54
Carlyle, Thomas 119, 125
    Sartor Resartus 13–14, 29, 149–62
Carpenter, Edward 11, 121–2
    Civilization, Its Cause and Cure 123
    Love's Coming of Age 123
Carpenter, Estlin 101
Casey, James 244
Cassian, John 49
Catherine of Genoa 108
Cezanne, Paul 173
Chadwick, Owen 7–8, 67–8
Chalmers, Thomas 232
Chambers, J.C. 76
Chambers, Robert: *Vestiges of the Natural History of Creation* 236, 238
Chambord, Duke of 64
Charismatic Christianity 265
Charles, Mrs [Elizabeth] Rundle 224–5
Chaucer, Geoffrey: *House of Fame* 148
childhood 100–101, 170
The Christian Lady's Magazine 15, 191–2, 195–6
Christian Union 193
The Christian World (newspaper) 193
The Christian World Magazine 15, 191–3, 195–6
Christianity, diversity within 263–4
Church, R.W. 236
Church of England, criticisms of 27
Church Socialist Society 104

Clark, Francis Edward 88
Clarke, James 193
class divisions 199, 211–18 *passim*, 265, 267
    see also middle classes; working classes
Clavis of Melito 59–62
Clement XI, Pope 63–4
clergy, the
    artists' depictions of 179–80
    involvement in science 233
    role of 192
Clowes, William 98
Cobbe, Frances Power 76–7
Colby, Robin 218, 222
Coleridge, Samuel Taylor 140–45 *passim*, 158, 185
    Conciones ad Populum 140
Collins, Charles 181–5
Columbian Exposition (1893) 8, 83–4, 88
confession
    general or private 69
    see also private confession
conversion narratives 28–35
conversions to Roman Catholicism 10, 105–113
Coombs, Jessie 194
Cope, Charles 185
Cortet, Jean Pierre 176
Council of Chalcedon 61–2
Council of Ephesus 61
Council of Trent 63
Council of Nicaea 61–2
Courbet, Gustave 180
Cowherd, William 101
Croegaert, Georges 180
Cronin, Richard 146
Crosby, Sarah 193
Csók, István 169–70
cults 98
Curran, Stuart 145–6
Curtis, Georgianna Pell 105
Cuvier, Georges 237
Cyril of Alexandria 61

Dagnan-Bouveret, Pascal 166, 177
The Daily News (of London) 165
Darwin, Charles 230–31, 235–6
    Autobiography 229
    Origin of Species 20, 35, 123, 234, 251–3, 258
Daumier, Honoré 179
Davies, G.C.B. 68

Dechelette, M. 57–8
Décôte, Charles 44
Deism 87, 90
Delavenay, Emile 122–3
Delumeau, Jean 3
Democritus 240–42
Dening, Geraldine 194
Denis, Maurice 166, 179
Descartes, René 9, 103
design, arguments from 236, 258
Desmond, Adrian 19–20, 237, 249
Detroisier, Rowland 101
Devonshire, holidaying in 252
Dhamma 92
Dharmapala, Anagarika 85, 92–5
The Dial (journal) 105
Dickens, Charles 30, 100, 170
Didelot, Chanoine 47
Doddridge, Philip: *Rise and Progress of Religion in the Soul* 29
domesticity 5–6, 15–16, 67, 75, 94, 201, 208–209, 266
Douglas, Ann 15
Douglas, Mary 230
Doyle, Arthur Conan 100
Druce, G.C. 54
Dufraine, Charles 47
Duranty, Edmond 179

Eder, David 123
Eliot, George 103, 119, 124
  After Strange Gods 119
Emerson, Ralph Waldo 97, 105–106, 112–113, 154, 189, 266
  'The Transcendentalist' 106–111
Empedocles 241
Engel, A.J. 240
Engels, Friedrich 160
Enlightenment, the 11–12, 86–7, 101, 151, 165, 188
Epicurus and Epicureanism 240–46, 249
epigraphs 194, 206
Escher, M.C. 148
Eugenie, Empress 176
Eutyches of Constantinople (and Eutychian heresy) 61
Evagrius of Pontus 49
Evangelicalism 2–3, 5, 27–34, 68, 70, 74–5, 103, 192–3, 263–6
evolution, theory of 8, 20
  see also Darwin, Charles: *Origin of Species*

Eybl, Franz 173

Faber, Geoffrey 68, 71
family values 266
Farrar, Frederick William 245–6
Fattori, Giovanni 166
feminism 199, 202, 209
Fende, Peter 176, 185
Fichte, J.G. 189
Flaxman, John 185
foot binding 204
Forrester, David 68
Fortescue, R.H. 73–4
Fortress Catholicism 4–6, 263, 265–6
Foucault, Michel 5, 76, 78, 120–21
Frank, Waldo 123
Franklin, Benjamin 87
French Revolution 13, 139–48 *passim*, 150
Freud, Sigmund 74, 203
  Civilization and its Discontents 158
Froude, J.A. 97
Fruitlands 109–110
Fryckstedt, Monica Correa 224
Fuller, Margaret 111, 189
fundamentalism, Protestant 265
Fyfe, Aileen 253

Galton, Francis 231
Garbett, James 30
Gaskell, Elizabeth: *North and South* 17, 211–25
Gassendi, Pierre 241
Gauguin, Paul 170, 177, 179
gender differences in religious commitment 165–6
gender relations 14–17, 67, 75, 77, 90–91, 196–7, 199, 208, 215, 223, 266
geology 231–4
Gibbons, Cardinal 85
Gilbert, Alan 235
Gilbert, Sandra 203
Gill, Stephen 128
Gilligan, Carol 194
Gillray, James: *Un Petit Souper à la Parisiènne* 140
Gladstone, William Ewart 28
Gnosticism 155–6
God
  Biblical concept of 122
  personal and personalised 13
  transcendence of 2
  Word of 30

Goethe, Johann Wolfgang von 149, 152
good works 103, 107–109
Gosse, Edmund 261
  Father and Son 20, 251
Gosse, Philip Henry 20, 237, 251
  books on marine biology 252–62
  illustrations by 255–61
Gossner, Johann 51
Goya, Francisco 166
Grasmere 137
Gray, Asa 230
Great Awakening 166
Great Exhibition (1851) 83
Greenwell, Dora 194
Greg, W.R. 202
Gregory the Great, Pope and Saint 49, 51
Grosz, Elizabeth 203
Grünwald, Béla Iványi 169–70
The Guardian 236
Gubar, Susan 203

Habermas, Jurgen 222
Hamlin, Christopher 259
Harbutt, William 97
Hardouin-Fugier, Elisabeth 43, 45
Hardy, Thomas 119
Harris, Joseph 75
Harrison, Peter 231–2
Hazlitt, William 140, 145
  Life of Napoleon 141
heaven, views of 102–103
Hecker, Isaac 10, 105, 108–112
hedonism 240–48
Hegel, G.W.F. 125
Henry of Susa 49
Heraclitus 242
Herberg, Will 4, 86–7
Herbert, Robert 168
heresy 37, 61, 119
heresy mosaics (at Fourvière
  basilica) 55–63
Heyck, T.W. 240
Hindmarsh, James and Robert 98
Hinduism 9, 89–91
Hogg, Thomas 147
Holloway, John: *The Victorian Sage* 155
Holmes, Richard 145–6
Hölzel, Adolf 170
Homer, Winslow 185
Honorius of Autun 49–50
Hook, Walter F. 77
Hooker, Joseph 231

Hooker, Richard 69
Houghton, Walter E. 9
Hruschka, John 153, 159
Hugo, Victor 245
Hunt, William Holman 207
Hutchison, Mary 136
Hutton, James 234
Huxley, T.H. 19, 231, 233, 239, 243, 245, 249
Hyde, Virginia 119
hyperculpabalization 3

Iconoclasm 62
idealism 106
immanence 12, 82
imperialism 83–4
Incarnation, doctrine of 6, 238
Irenaeus 37, 60
Irish nation 141
Isidora, Sister (later Saint) 181

Jacyna, L.S. 240
Jansen, Cornelius Otto 63
Jansenism 9, 60, 63–4, 103
Jefferson, Thomas 87
Jesus Christ
  historical 7, 11
  human and divine natures of 61–2
  images of 62
John Paul II, Pope 265–6
Johnson, Glen M. 112
Jones, R.K. 98
Jowett, Benjamin 210
Judaism 125
Judge, William Q. 93

Kabbala, the 124–5
Kallenberg, Brad 33
Kant, Immanuel 14, 17, 97, 187–9
Keble, John 68, 70
Kent, John 68, 74–5
Kepler, Johannes 230
Kim, Stephen S. 239
Kinkead-Weekes, Mark 123
Kohn, David 234

labour disputes 224
Landow, George 205–206
Lang, Bernhard 102
Lansbury, Coral 220, 224
Laplace, Pierre Simon 220
Lateran Councils 62–3, 69

Law, William 98
Lawrence, D.H. 10–11, 119–26
  Apocalypse 120–21
  'Hymns in a Man's Life' 120
L.B. (female writer) 213
Lega, Silvestro 166
Legros, Alphonse 166–9
Leibl, Wilhelm 168–9, 173
Leonardo da Vinci 246
Lewes, George Henry 245
Lewis, Edmonia 166
liberal Christianity 5–9, 34, 84–90 *passim*,
  94, 99, 155, 242, 263–6
Liddon, Henry 68
Liguori, Alphonsus 63
Lineham, P.J. 104
Livingstone, David 230
Lodge, Oliver 100
Lorimer, J.H. 166
Louis XIV, King 64
Lovejoy, Arthur 101
Lowth, Robert 127
Lucretius 241–3
Luther, Martin 63, 112
Lutheranism 58, 63
Lyell, Charles 233–4
Lyon
  Cathedral 43, 55
  see also Notre Dame de Fourvière

McCosh, James 243
McDannell, Colleen 102
Machin, G.I.T. 76
Mackarness, John Fielder 247
Madedonian heresy 61
magazines, women's 15–16, 191–7
Magee, Rev. 75
Maistre, Joseph de 13, 44, 139–48 *passim*
  Considerations on France 139–40
  Soirées de Saint-Pétersbourg 145
Majumdar, Protap Chandra 91
Mâle, Emile 45–50, 54–5, 59–60
Malthusian theory 160
Manichaeism 62–3
Marie-Antoinette 176
Marriner, Edwin 244
Martin, Sarah 194
Martineau, Harriet 165–6, 208
Martineau, James 6
Marx, Karl 158, 160
Maskell, William 72–3
materialism 106, 239–42

  see also scientific materialism
Mather, Ralph 98
Melcher, Gari 166
Merrill, Lynn 253
Mesmerism 9
Methodism 31–3, 98, 212–17 *passim*, 224,
  263
Meyers, Jeffrey 119
Michelet, Jules 176–9
middle classes 8, 90, 112, 215, 218, 261,
  263
Mill, John Stuart 8, 154, 245
Millais, John Everett 170, 184
Miller, Hugh 232, 237
  'Gropings of a Working Man in
    Geology' 231
Millet, Jean-François 168, 177
Milton, John 100
  Paradise Lost 136
Missions to London 74
modernity 149–50, 161, 199
monism 9, 82, 89, 91, 94–5, 156
Montesquieu, Baron 243
Montgomery, Robert 119
Morice, Charles 179
Morris, William 245
motherhood 185
Müller, Max 101
Myers, W.H. 100
mysticism 162

Nagarkar, B.B. 85
Napoleon III, Emperor 176
narratives *see* Bible, the; conversion
  narratives
natural theology 18, 20, 229, 235–8, 251–9
Naturalism (secular thinking) 64
Neale, John Mason 72
neo-platonism 99
Nesterov, M.V. 180
Nestorian heresy 61
new religious movements 81
New Spirituality 81–2, 85, 91–5, 264
Newman, John Henry 67–8, 71
Newton, Isaac 229–30, 233, 236
Nicholas of Cusa 99
Nietzsche, Friedrich 11, 119, 121
  The Anti-Christ 122
Nightingale, Florence: *Suggestions for
  Thought* 16–17, 199–210
nihilism 155, 162, 247
Nockles, Peter 67, 72

non-conformism 20
Notre Dame de Fourvière, Lyon 3, 37–65
nuns 14–15, 165, 179–88 *passim*, 222

occultism 123, 125
Olcott, Colonel 92–3
O'Leary, Stephen 223
Ollard, S.L. 68
Otis, Harrison Grey 1
Owen, Richard 230, 237
Owen, Vale 100
Oxford Movement 67–71

Paine, Thomas 236
Paley, William 229, 236–7, 253, 255, 257
Papacy, the, power and authority of 13, 62–3, 265
Pascal, Blaise 9, 63, 103
Pasteur, Louis 179
Pater, Walter
   Marius the Epicurean 248–9
   Studies in the History of the Renaissance 19, 239–40, 245–7
Paul, Jean 156, 196, 200
Paul, Saint 28, 35, 244, 248
Paulist Fathers 108–9, 112
peasants, artists' depictions of 176–9, 185, 188
Perov, V.G. 179
Perrin, Sainte-Marie 37, 42–7, 51–65 *passim*
Personalism 103
Pestalozzi education 100
Phillpotts, Henry, Bishop 72–3
Physiologus 49
piety
   Evangelical form of 28
   female 14–15, 165–77 *passim*, 188–9
Pils, Isidore 180–1, 185
Pitman, Sir Isaac 97
Pitra, J.B. 59–60
Pitt, William 140
Pius IX, Pope 4
Plymouth Brethren 252, 254, 257
Poeschl, Philipp Friedrich 51
political economy, principles of 213–14
polytheism 89–90
Poole, Alfred 74
Poovey, Mary 209–210
Porcupine magazine 97
Powell, Baden 233
Prickett, Stephen 133

priesthood of all believers, doctrine of 192
Priestley, Joseph 236
private confession 5, 67–78 *passim*
private life, intrusion into 5–6, 67, 77–8, 265–6
Prynne, George 73
Pryse, James 123
public testimony 34–5
Public Worship Regulation Act (1874) 76
Punch 204
Pusey, Edward 68–73 *passim*, 76, 184

Quesnel, Pasquier 63

Rambo, Lewis 32, 35
Redesdale, Earl of 76
Reeve, Henry 242
Renan, Ernest 11, 125
   Life of Jesus 121
revolution, dual meaning of 150, 161
Ribot, Théodore 166
Ripley, George 108–112
Ripley, Sophia 10, 105, 108–112
ritual practices 68
Ritualist movement 72, 74–6
rock pools 254–5, 257–8, 262
Romanticism 11–12, 68, 140, 266
Rosenblum, Robert 177
Ross, Frederic 251
Rossetti, Christina 211
Rousseau, Jean-Jacques 147
Rudwick, Martin 252, 255–6
Rundle, Vivienne 151
Ruskin, John 15, 28, 119, 184
   Fors Clavigera 29
   'Of Queens' Gardens' 191
Russell, Bertrand 122

Said, Edward 88
St Bartholomew's Day Massacre 140
Salisbury, Lord 5, 75
Salmon, Joseph 98
salvation 3–4, 28, 31, 34–5, 103, 139
Sand, George 176
Schiller, Johann Christoph Friedrich von 152
Schneider, Daniel 119
Schopenhauer, Arthur 188–9
science
   and aestheticism 240, 247
   and religion 11, 17–21, 229–33, 239, 243–4, 248–9, 267

Index

scientific materialism 19, 241–7, 264
secularization 165, 266–7
　definition of 229–30
　and paradox 231–6
Sedgwick, Adam 234, 236
Segantini, Giovanni 185
semiotics 157
Sen, Keshub Chandra 91
sermons 29, 32–5, 77, 244–5
sexuality 15, 67, 73–7, 100, 123, 126
Shaftesbury, Lord 76
Shelley, Mary 147
Shelley, Percy Bysshe 12–13, 139–48
　passim, 162
　The Cenci 142
　Considerations on France 143
　'Laon and Cythna' 13, 139, 143–8
　Queen Mab 142
　The Vegetable System of Diets 142
sinfulness, human 2–4, 70, 90
Sisters of the Good Shepherd 110
Skinner, Henrietta Channing
　Dana 106–107
social reform 17, 225
social theory 159–60
Society of the Holy Cross 76
Society for Psychical Research 100
Sophie, Archduchess of Austria 176
Southcott, Joanna 222
Spencer, Herbert 84, 240–41, 245
Spiritualism 9, 100, 264
Spurgeon, Charles 2–3, 27–35
starvation, metaphor of 202–203
Sterling, John 154
Stillman, Marie Spartali 184–5
Stokes, George 231
Stowe, Harriet Beecher 170, 195–6
Strachey, Lytton 17
　Eminent Victorians 208–209
Stromberg, Peter 30
Swedenborg, Emmanuel 9
　Conjugial Love 100
Swedenborg Society 97, 99
Swedenborgianism 86, 88, 97–104, 264
Swinburne, Algernon Charles:
　'Dolores' 248
The Syllabus of Errors 4–5

Tait, Archibald Campbell, Archbishop 74, 76
Tayler, J.J. 97
Temple, Frederick 233

Tennyson, Alfred 207
Tennyson, G.B. 155–7
Theosophical Society 9, 92–3
theosophy 82, 93, 123, 264
Thiollier, Felix 43, 45
Thoma, Hans 170
Thompson, E.P. 212, 224
Thomson, William 231
Thoreau, Henry David 109
The Times 74, 76, 140
Tipton, Steven 81
Tocqueville, Alexis de 87
Tolstoy, Leo 177, 189
Tonna, Charlotte Elizabeth 191–3
Topham, Jonathan 237
Topsell, E. 50
Tractarianism 68–72
trade unions 212–214
Transcendentalism 2–10, 105–12, 263–5
　reaction against 6, 264
transubstantiation 107
Travis, John 252
Troeltsch, Ernst 81
Trollope, Frances 165
Tulk, C.A. 103–104
Turbayne, Colin Murray 135
Turner, Frank 233, 239, 242–4, 257
Tweed, Thomas 10, 92
Tyndall, John 231, 248–9
　Belfast Address (1874) 19, 239–47
Tyrwhitt, Richard St John 247–8

Ultramontanism 3, 5, 44, 61–2, 65, 139
Unitarianism 91, 215, 223–4
United States 4–5, 8, 165–6, 264–5
universal religion 87–94, 266

Vatican II Council 265
Vedanta Society 90
vegetarianism 101, 142–4
veneration of images 62
Victoria, Queen 75–6, 176, 209
Vigny, Alfred de 145
Vincent of Beauvais 55
Virgin Mary 61–3, 185
Vivekananda 9, 81, 85, 88–95, 264
Voltaire 236
voyeurism 73–4

Waldo, Peter 57
Wale, Augusta 73
Ward, Mrs Humphry 1, 7, 247

Ward, W.R. 98
Washington, Peter 123–4
Watts, Robert 242–3
Weber, Max 212
Wesley, John 27–9, 193–4, 212, 216
West, Richard 74
Whewell, William 237–8
  History of the Inductive Sciences 238
Whitefield, George 27
Whitman, Walt 119
Widenfeldt, Adam 63
Wilberforce, Samuel, Bishop 19, 71, 233, 239
Wilson, Daniel 27
Winderspin, Samuel 100
The Witness (journal) 231
women's intellect 188–9
women's piety 14–15, 165–77 *passim*, 188–9
Worboise, Emma Jane 191–5
Wordsworth, Dorothy 132

Wordsworth, William 127–37
  advertisement by 127–9
  'Home at Grasmere' 131–2
  'Poems on the Naming of Places' 12, 127–9, 132–7
  The Prelude 129–31, 135–7
  'The Ruined Cottage' 129–30
working classes 212, 215–16, 219, 225, 264
world fairs 83
World Parliament of Religions (Chicago, 1893) 8–9, 82–95, 102, 264
Worthen, John 120
Wuthnow, Robert 4–5
Wynne, Brian 246–7

Yates, Nigel 68, 72–4
Yeats, W.B. 146
Yonge, Charlotte M. 192

Zeitgeist 152

For Product Safety Concerns and Information please contact our EU
representative GPSR@taylorandfrancis.com
Taylor & Francis Verlag GmbH, Kaufingerstraße 24, 80331 München, Germany

www.ingramcontent.com/pod-product-compliance
Lightning Source LLC
Chambersburg PA
CBHW071346290426
44108CB00014B/1454